Real Estate Finance

Fourth Edition

Real Estate Finance

Fourth Edition

John P. Wiedemer

University of Houston

Reston Publishing Company, Inc.
A Prentice-Hall Company
Reston, Virginia

Library of Congress Cataloging in Publication Data

Wiedemer, John P.
    Real estate finance.

    Includes index.
    1. Real estate business—United States.   2. Mortgages
—United States.   3. Housing—United States—Finance.
I. Title.
HD1375.W53 1983   332.7′2′0973   83–2899
ISBN 0–8359–6559–7

Editorial/production supervision and
interior design by Camelia Townsend

©1983 by Reston Publishing Company, Inc.
A Prentice-Hall Company
Reston, Virginia 22090

10   9   8   7   6   5

PRINTED IN THE UNITED STATES OF AMERICA

Contents

Foreword

Land is a scarce and limited resource. Its availability and use are so basic to human life that they form the foundation upon which societies are organized and function. Inherent in the structure of every society is a system designed to deal with the multitude of relationships concerning land.

In this society, private ownership of real property is an established and guarded right. Here too, systems have been developed that recognize this right and facilitate the individual's exercise of this right.

The economic importance of real estate transactions is obvious. So obvious, in fact, that most people are only vaguely aware of the tremendous impact of real estate transactions on the financial market. The potential size and number of these transactions give the appearance of something too complicated to understand. This appearance is both deceiving and dangerous.

An individual purchasing a home is obligating a large portion of his personal income. The real estate salesperson is concerned with the economic well-being of his or her client. Complications notwithstanding, buyers, sellers, brokers, and others are faced with an urgent need to know.

Admittedly, the field of real estate finance is in a state of continuous change; change in practices, methods, clientele, and sources. This circumstance should not be viewed with alarm, for change is inherent in progress. Professionals in real estate, like professionals in every field, must stay abreast of these changes if they are to remain professionals.

Newcomers to the field must gain a solid foundation in the basic principles and terminology of real estate finance. The real estate profession's clientele need at least a working knowledge of these same principles and terms.

In order to fulfill these needs, accesss to accurate, current information is necessary. The information required is available from many sources. Unfortunately, information of this type is normally presented in an obscure and unimaginative form that makes learning a labor and is of limited educational value to all but the specialist.

In this sense, Wiedemer's book is unique. Not only is the information current and technically accurate, it is presented as an information discussion. His discussion of methods and elements of real estate finance are objective and complete.

His book contains the information necessary to fulfill the needs of the beginner and is thorough enough to be a valuable resource for the established professional. The book has been written in such a way that the novice can understand the language of the professional.

Mr. Wiedemer has been a lecturer in real estate at the University of Houston since 1970. He has brought to his classroom the knowledge and enthusiasm of a leader in his field. He approaches his teaching duties with a sincere desire for his students to learn. This approach is immediately evident in his book.

A true professional, Wiedemer wants to give back something to the profession that has been good to him. This book and his continuing work in education are overt expressions of this willingness and desire.

James C. Taylor, J.D.
Dean Emeritus, Continuing Education
University of Houston

Acknowledgments

The author gratefully acknowledges the expert advice, assistance, and encouragement of the following persons who made possible the preparation and writing of this book.

Richard L. Chumbley, *Richland College, Dallas, Texas*

R. L. Cobb *Loan Guaranty Officer, Veterans Administration, Houston*

Joseph P. Conte *President, Conte Investments, Inc., Houston*

Jack Daniels *Chairman of the Board, First City Financial Corp. Albuquerque, New Mexico*

James E. Howze *President, Jones Real Estate Colleges, Inc. (Texas)*

Floyd Kowalski *Former Chief Mortgage Credit Examiner, Federal Housing Administration, Houston*

Patricia McAuliffe *McAuliffe & Associates, Houston*

Arthur Morales *President, SanPao Industries, Houston*

William A. Painter *Former Director, Houston Office, HUD, Federal Housing Administration*

Donald McGregor, Jr. *Real Estate Investments, Houston*

Wallace Perry *Vice President, Coldwell Banker, Houston*

William Robertson, Jr., *Assistant to the Supervisor, HUD/FHA Houston*

Russell Sanders *Chief, Mortage Credit Branch, HUD/FHA Houston*

James C. Taylor, J. D. *Dean Emeritus, Continuing Education, University of Houston*

Mary Anne Templin *Vice President, Marketing, Capital Title Company, Inc. Houston*

Beth Van Houten, *Corporate Relations, Federal National Mortage Association, Washington, D.C.*

Joe P. Wallace *Wallace and Associates, Realtors, Houston*

Verlyne Wallace *Wallace and Associates, Realtors, Houston*

George Young *In memoriam and grateful remembrance, University of Houston*

And a Special Acknowledgment to my wife, Margaret Ivy Wiedemer, for organization and editing assistance plus her kind patience.

Introduction

The financing of real estate, which includes homes, shopping centers, office buildings, farms, and factories, is the largest demand on credit markets in this country. By 1983, the mortgage debt outstanding had topped 1,700 billion while the federal debt was passing 1,100 billion.

The variety of procedures that make the mortgage loan system function is the result of long experience in meeting constantly changing requirements. Many of the basic controls and patterns for lending developed from the depression years of the 1930's. They reflect the efforts of a number of men and women working through private industry and government agencies to achieve more and better buildings, particularly houses providing better living conditions. One might say it is this system that attempts to match dreams with reality and make them come true.

The goal of this book is to acquaint the reader with the sources of mortgage money; where it comes from and the normal requirements for disbursement. Also, an emphasis is placed on terminology as used in the financial community, and especially in real estate markets. There are, of course, some differences in the methods and terminology as used in different regions of the country, but the focus is on common practices. Today, mortgage money moves freely across state lines and regional differences are diminishing in importance.

In the past decade, inflation and steadily rising interest costs have dramatically altered the mortgage loan industry. No longer is the home buyer offered a simple choice of mortgage loans with very limited alternatives. The need for lenders to achieve greater flexibility of income from their mortgage loan investments has resulted in an explosion of adjustable rate mortgage plans; those that allow periodic adjustments in the rate of interest on a long term loan. Further, to help delay the impact of higher housing costs, particularly as faced by first home buyers, a variety of graduated payment mortgage plans have been developed. These plans offer an arbitrary reduction in the amount of initial monthly payments which is used to qualify buyers with a lesser income. To make an intelligent comparison of the mortgage options available, the home buyer and real estate agent must have adequate knowledge of how the different repayment plans function.

One of the significant changes in lending patterns since 1979 has been the entry of home-sellers into the business of helping to finance the sale of their property. Increasing home values has brought substantial increase in the amount of a home owners equity. To make a sale possible, sellers have engaged in many imaginative plans to handle monthly payments that are initially very favorable for the buyer. Payment of the principal amount is delayed for a few years anticipating a more favorable mortgage market when other financing could be obtained. These plans, generally called "creative financing," have resulted in serious problems when refinancing has not been available at reasonable costs. To help offset these problems, the mortgage industry in 1982 offered home sellers default mortage insurance plus an opportunity to sell their loans (meaning convert them into cash) on about the same basis as the regular lenders do. The industry tries to accomodate the changing needs. It is important that we know what benefits derive for each of us.

John P. Wiedemer

Real Estate Finance

Fourth Edition

History and Background

The history of real estate financing presents a fascinating record of man's learning to live with, and enjoy the benefits of, the land he lives on. While private ownership of land can be traced back to civilizations existing over 2500 years ago, only in the last several hundred years has it become possible for the average person to own property.

Early Financing Methods

In ancient Rome men of means were most often the hereditary large landlords whose land in the provinces had gained them admission to the Curia. This membership required their residence in the city, allowing them to extend their political, religious, and economic influence throughout Rome. Other members included administrators and shareholders of the tax-gathering societies whose treasuries were assured of capital funds. Of course, these societies were open only to the privileged few, unlike our modern investment institutions.

In medieval times, under the feudal system, land was owned primarily by the king, the nobility, or the church. Thus landownership was restricted to the very few, and those who did possess rights to land could pledge their property rights as security for a loan. In these earlier

1

times there were no savings banks or other institutions capable of accumulating investment capital, and only a few individuals of great wealth were capable of making loans. Besides the severe limitations on investment activity imposed by there being very few property owners, an equally severe limitation was caused by the lack of money—a problem that still exists with many of us today! Historically the growth of widespread landownership parallels the increase in pools of money available for long-term loans.

With the advent of the Industrial Revolution in the eighteenth century, more individuals became capable of producing wealth with their ideas and their machinery. People began to find that they had another option opened to them; the life of a serf grubbing an existence from land owned by the nobility was no longer the only way to make a living. With the more widespread wealth came the demand for ways to make better use of accumulated money, and the seeds of our publicly owned savings institutions started to grow.

Colonial America

Prior to the Industrial Revolution, colonial America felt the need for capital to build its new homes and businesses. Many groups began to join together for mutual protection and mutual help. Savings were pooled in informal clubs or fraternal groups in order to provide lendable funds for members wishing to build a house, make an addition to their building, or to construct a barn. Organizations were created to provide fire protection for their members. And some groups arranged for periodic payments into the club treasury, which provided for a lump sum payment to the member's family at his death. The only problem here was that without regulation and accurate reserves based on mortality rates, the groups grew older, failed to attract younger members, and often went broke.

In spite of these setbacks, the desire for economic security and the need for the protection of capital helped spawn the banks, savings associations, and life insurance companies of the nineteenth century which have become great assets to our nation today. These older institutions, along with many younger ones, plus some exciting new pools of money such as pension funds and trust funds, are now providing us with the funds needed to own and develop our land. Table 1-1 gives a chronological outline of when the major institutions were formed in this country.

TABLE 1-1

Chronology of Key Agencies and Institutions Associated with Real Estate Finance in the United States

1759	Charter date of the oldest life insurance company in the United States. The Presbyterian Ministers Fund issued its first policy in 1761. The name was changed to Presbyterian Annuity and Life Insurance Company in 1889, thereafter insuring Protestant ministers, their wives, and theological students.
1781	Bank of North America, the oldest commercial bank in this country, opened in Philadelphia. It was chartered by the Pennsylvania legislature and incorporated by the Continental Congress for the purpose of providing money to wage the Revolutionary War against England through pooling of private and public resources.
1791	First Bank of the United States was the original effort to establish a national bank. This institution was promoted by Alexander Hamilton and chartered by the Congressional Federalists. The initial capitalization was $10 million, of which 20 percent was owned by the national government. The bank terminated in 1811 due to considerable opposition in Congress.
1812	The first public life insurance company was formed under the name of Pennsylvania Company for Insurance on Lives and Granting Annuities.
1816	The second Bank of the United States was established to exert some controls over private banks and to regulate the U.S. monetary system. This second attempt to establish a national banking system was successfully opposed by President Andrew Jackson and closed down in 1836.
1816	The first mutual savings bank was established and still operates under its original name—Philadelphia Savings Fund Society. The bank was organized to operate for the interests of its shareholders (its depositors), and it encouraged savings by persons of modest means.
1831	The first savings association chartered for the purpose of accumulating capital for building houses was founded by Samuel Pilling and Jeremiah Horrocks under the name of Oxford Provident Building Association in Philadelphia. The first mortgage loan for the purpose of buying a home was made to Comly Rich of Philadelphia in the amount of $375.00. Monthly payments were $4.90.
1835	New England Mutual was chartered as the first of the modern forms of life insurance companies.
1863	The federal government resumed responsibility for the regulation of currency. After the closing of the second Bank of the United States in 1836, state-chartered banks had issued their own bank notes which circulated as currency.
1913	The Federal Reserve Bank was established by the federal government as a national bank to administer currency and to regulate federally chartered commercial banks and any state-chartered banks that met membership requirements.
1916	The government created the Federal Land Bank as a system to raise money through the sale of bonds for the purpose of making loans to farmers.

(continued)

TABLE 1-1 (continued)

1932	Under the administration of Herbert Hoover, the Reconstruction Finance Corporation was established to provide direct government loans to private business.
1932	The Federal Home Loan Bank was created as a regulatory agency to charter federal savings and loan associations and to supervise their operations.
1933	On March 6, 1933, President Franklin D. Roosevelt closed all banks in the country to halt disastrous runs. Thereafter, those deemed in satisfactory condition could reopen. Within one year, the number of operating banks in this country was reduced from 30,000 to 16,000.
1933	Home Owners Loan Corporation (HOLC) was created to sell bonds and use proceeds to refinance existing homeowner indebtedness. It was liquidated in 1951.
1934	Securities and Exchange Commission (SEC) was established to regulate the issuance and sale of all types of securities to the general public.
1934	Federal Housing Administration (FHA) was created to utilize the credit of the federal government to insure home loans and thus encourage lending from private sources.
1934	Federal Deposit Insurance Corporation (FDIC) provided a means to insure deposits in commercial banks against losses due to bank failure.
1934	Federal Savings and Loan Insurance Corporation (FSLIC) provided a corporate body similar to the FDIC that insures deposits in savings associations.
1937	Local Housing Authority (LHA) allowed for the creation of quasi-government agencies for the purpose of developing low-cost housing for lower income families.
1938	Federal National Mortgage Association (FNMA) was the government agency established to provide funds for the purchase of FHA-insured loans.
1944	Veterans Administration (VA), created in 1930, established a home loan guaranty program for veterans during World War II.
1946	Farmers Home Administration (FmHA) was established to make and insure loans to farmers and ranchers.
1965	Department of Housing and Urban Development (HUD) resulted from the reorganization of various government operations intended to coordinate and expand housing programs.
1968	Government National Mortgage Association (GNMA) was created from the partitioning of the Federal National Mortgage Association as an agency under HUD to handle housing assistance programs and loan management functions.
1969	Truth-in-Lending Act became effective as a part of the Consumer Credit Protection Act. Its purpose is to require lenders to give meaningful information on the cost of consumer credit.

TABLE 1-1 (continued)

1970	Federal Home Loan Mortgage Corporation (FHLMC) established by the Federal Home Loan Bank Board to sell bonds and use the proceeds to purchase mortgages from member savings associations and other lenders.
1970	Environmental Protection Agency (EPA) created to develop rules and procedures for the improvement of our natural heritage and to enforce requirements for proper land development.
1974	Housing and Community Development Act passed by Congress consolidated a number of federal programs such as Urban Renewal, Model Cities, Neighborhood Facilities, Open Space, Water and Sewer Facilities plus some lending authority into a single program. Federal funds are made available to local communities which follow national guidelines and determine how the money is to be spent.
1974	Real Estate Settlement Procedures Act (RESPA), as amended in 1976, was directed toward providing better information on the settlement process to help home buyers make informed decisions.
1974	Equal Credit Opportunity Act (ECOA) prohibits discrimination in consumer credit transactions.
1977	Federally chartered credit unions were authorized to make long-term (up to 30 years) real estate loans.
1978	Community Reinvestment Act (CRA) expands the concept that regulated financial institutions must serve the needs of their community.
1979	Federal Home Loan Bank first approved alternative mortgage plans for writing by federally chartered savings associations.
1980	Congress passed the Depository Institutions Deregulation and Monetary Control Act. It brings a fundamental change in the operations of depository financial institutions. Greater flexibility is given in the types of loans that can be made, and all covered institutions may offer interest-bearing checking accounts. (Interest rate ceilings on deposits are to be phased out by 1986.) Reserve requirements are established at uniform levels by the Federal Reserve Bank.

Development of Mortgage Banking

In a growing country like the United States, the pools of lendable money were not always readily available where needed or were not always known to a potential borrower. To help bridge the gap, a new industry gradually developed that is now known as *mortgage banking*. The precise date of its origin would be difficult to state because the mortgage banking business has developed from a small service or brokerage facility in the late 1800s into a major banking industry today. Initially, a lawyer, or perhaps a real estate broker with contacts in the investment world, would arrange a loan for a client and charge a service fee; and as some individuals became quite adept at this business, the placement of loans became their principal occupation. Even today, a large number of mortgage bankers come from first- or second-generation family-owned businesses.

Lending Reforms from the Great Depression

In the early 1900s, potential borrowers had four main sources from which to seek a loan—a bank, a savings association, an insurance company, or a wealthy individual. Or they could minimize their search by turning their problem over to a loan broker, who usually had several potential sources of funds available for a small fee. But the rules were quite different then. A house loan might be 50 percent of the lender's estimate of value, to be repaid in full in five years—no amortization, no escrow account—a system that could cause an instant collapse—and did. Also, without proper regulation, an individual or company could sell mortgage bonds up to the appraised value of a projected development, say a Florida resort hotel. And the "appraisal" could be made by no less an authority than the person trying to sell the bonds! In the 1920s these were the "gold bonds," which pretty much disappeared from circulation during the Depression.

The collapse of the real estate loan market in the early 1930s brought a flood of foreclosures with farms, houses, and businesses swept away. It is the now-passing generation who determined that there must be a better way.

Many historic changes were wrought in our economy under the administration of Franklin Delano Roosevelt to prevent future economic disasters. The demand by some economists in those days to "control the economy" or to "eliminate depressions" was the source of many jokes and was not taken too seriously by most people, including much of the business community. But controls were established nonetheless.

The Securities and Exchange Commission was brought into existence to regulate the sale of all types of securities to the general public. The bankruptcy laws were revised to deter one or two creditors from destroying a cash-short business at the expense of all the other creditors.

But the area of change bearing on our special interests encompasses the sweeping reforms made in real estate finance beginning with the closing of all banks in 1933. To start patching up the economy, the

Home Owners Loan Corporation was formed that same year to issue government-guaranteed bonds and to use the proceeds to refinance homeowners' indebtedness. Over one million houses were refinanced through this agency, and with the new liquidity in our financial institutions, stability was gradually restored.

A year later, in 1934, the Federal Housing Administration was created to provide home loan insurance. It did not then, and does not today, make loans. It provides a loan insurance policy, insuring the lender against loss through default, if the FHA qualifications are met. However, many bankers and other lenders, inherently opposed to any government intrusion, especially in an area where character judgment was considered all important, simply refused to recognize a government-insured commitment.

Hence, a few years later, in 1938, the Federal National Mortgage Association, FNMA or "Fannie Mae," was established to buy FHA-insured mortgage loans and then to resell them as markets could be found. This agency provided the real beginnings of the so-called secondary market for mortgage loans, which may be broadly defined as any purchaser of a mortgage loan who does not participate in its origination. Money to finance FNMA purchases was derived from the sale of bonds.

By 1940, the pressures of a war economy brought an expansion of FHA activities to encourage housing in defense-designated areas and to permit financing of large apartment or multifamily projects. In 1944, Congress passed legislation permitting the Veterans Administration to guarantee mortgage loans made by private lenders to veterans.

Post–World War II Expansion

The post–World War II growth of government-assisted financing has paralleled and supported the growth of the mortgage banking industry. Were it not for the lubrication provided by multiservice mortgage bankers, the government would be much less efficient in spreading its insured programs to those needing loan assistance. Both the FHA and the VA lean heavily on mortgage bankers approved by these agencies as having met their standards, and who are therefore qualified (1) to disseminate correct requirements and data to the public; (2) to secure the necessary information on a loan applicant's qualifications; and (3) to arrange prompt funding for the loan upon issuance of a government commitment.

The growth of government programs has not diminished the continuing expansion of savings associations and insurance companies in providing mortgage loans, either direct to clients or through correspondents, for houses, apartments, and commercial buildings.

In addition, the recent years have seen a new pool of money entering the real estate field in pension and trust funds. Since most of these funds have little contact with the general public, such moneys move primarily through the mortgage banking industry.

The Changing Mortgage Market

The decade of the seventies brought some welcome innovations to the field of mortgage financing. Early in the decade, the big secondary market, made up of purchasers of mortgage loans, established procedures to trade in conventional mortgages in addition to the well-established FHA/VA-type of loans. Then the FHA began experimental work on a graduated payment mortgage form as a possible means of assistance for first home buyers. By the end of the seventies, these and other efforts culminated in the approval of several new mortgage instruments that allow lower monthly payments in the early years. As the decade closed, institutional lenders were beginning to raise mortgage money through a procedure that had been successfully developed by the Government National Mortgage Association—the sale of mortgage-backed securities to other institutional investors and to the general public as well.

No other major industry is as dependent on borrowed money as is housing. And few industries are as important to the general economy. Because of this, the government has long sought to stabilize the flow of mortgage money. But it is difficult to give assistance to one segment of the demand for borrowed money while trying to place restraints on another. The precise effects of a restrictive monetary policy in a free economy are hard to control without legislating credit priorities. Instead of following so drastic a course, the government has encouraged increased savings in the basic sources of mortgage money and has introduced greater flexibility into mortgage procedures.

Early in the decade, the Federal Home Loan Mortgage Corporation was set up to buy residential loans, primarily from savings associations. Then, private mortgage insurance was encouraged, broadening the market substantially for conventional mortgage loans. But the "money crunch" of 1974–75 dealt a hard blow to housing and the construction industry in general as people withdrew savings from the major mortgage lending institutions to seek higher returns from other investments. Not the least of these attractive "other investments" was the federal government's sale of Treasury bills, at ever-increasing yields, to finance its own spending plans.

The lesson learned from this experience produced a fairly obvious solution: allow savings associations as a major source of mortgage money to pay higher interest rates so as to remain competitive with other investments. Thus, a series of longer term savings certificates was introduced that allowed for higher interest rates. This was topped off by a six-month money market certificate that allowed payment of an interest rate equal to the Treasury bill yield as determined each week through their auctions. The minimum deposit was initially set at $10,000, the same as required for a Treasury bill. (Savings associations may pay ¼ percent over the T-bill rate.) In addition, large certificates of deposit ($100,000 and over) were unrestricted as to interest rate paid.

By the end of the decade, the score on this particular solution to mortgage lenders' money problems was beginning to tally: money remained generally available for mortgage loans, but the interest cost rose to unprecedented levels.

In the meantime, other developments were having an effect on mortgage lending that created a surprising amount of elasticity in the demand for housing and substantially offset the effects of higher and higher mortgage interest rates. Keep in mind that in years past, and as recently as 1975, a fractional increase in the mortgage interest rate was enough to disqualify a number of prospective home buyers; their incomes would simply fall a little short of meeting the increase in monthly payment. Of course, this still occurs, but there remain many buyers able to qualify. The reasons for this changing market bear recapping.

First, the Equal Credit Opportunity Act of 1974 made the wife's, or coborrower's, income of equal weight to that of the husband. No longer could a wife's income be downgraded or simply ignored. Suddenly there was a tremendous increase in the gross amount of income that could justify a mortgage loan. Families learned to take full advantage of this increased mortgage power and often bought larger and more expensive homes. There is little question that this one-time jump in borrowing power contributed to the escalating cost of housing during the last half of the decade.

Second, one of the lasting effects of the efforts to prohibit discrimination has been a substantial increase in the number of two-income families. So great has been the change that now roughly one-half of the homes purchased are bought by two-income families. The larger incomes thus represented are better able to absorb the cost of higher monthly payments. This development is certain to continue, increasing the demand for housing.

Third, the age group of 25 to 34 years provides the largest market for housing. During the 1970s, the post–World War II baby boom reached this age level and will continue to add strength to the demand curve well into the 1980s.

Fourth, ongoing inflation added its own insidious pressure to housing demand and the escalation of housing prices. In some areas of the country, speculative buying of houses became quite common. What other tangible asset had shown a better increase in value in the past five years? Many families found the equity value of their home to be their largest single asset—and growing at rates that exceeded annual inflation. While peacetime inflation has been a rarity in the history of this country, it was becoming more and more an accepted way of life. By 1982, inflation was beginning to subside; housing prices in a number of areas began to decline. The 1980s portend a return to basic home values without the speculative pressures of the past.

A Review of Corporate Finance

About half of the money flowing into mortgage loans is coming from the sale of various kinds of securities rather than from savings deposits. The sale of securities is the business of the financial markets. It is the way corporations raise equity money and one way they can borrow money. The student of real estate finance needs to know what kinds of securities are offered for sale and what each represents. Hence, a review of basic corporate finance follows.

Corporations are financed through the sale of securities, paper certificates that represent some kind of an investment in the corporate structure. There are two major classes: (1) stock certificates representing an ownership, or equity, interest in the corporation and (2) bonds representing a loan to the corporation. Stock evidences ownership; bonds evidence indebtedness.

Stock Certificates

The ownership interest in a corporation is represented in the shares of stock outstanding. *Common stock* is the basic ownership share and entitles its owner to a portion of the corporate profit which is distributed in the form of a *dividend*. The amount of the dividend is determined periodically by the board of directors of the corporation. There is another class of stock, called *preferred*, which holds a prior claim over common stock to a share of the corporate profit but usually at a not-to-exceed fixed rate of return.

Authorized shares are the number of shares approved by the state charter to the corporation. *Issued* shares are those that have been sold. *Treasury* shares are those acquired and held by the corporation itself.

Stock of the large, publicly held corporations is traded on various exchanges in major cities throughout this country and some foreign countries. The market value of publicly traded stock is only indirectly related to its actual earnings which is its share of corporate profit. Corporations seldom pay out the full amount of their profit in dividends as some of the profit is usually retained to finance company growth. So the price for which a share of stock may be sold depends in part on its earnings record but also on future expectations of the company's profitability; that is, the speculative component of the stock's value.

Bonds

A corporation can borrow money through the sale of bonds to investors. Thus, the corporation has an additional source of funds not generally available to an individual or even to small, less well-known corporations. Bonds are offered in several categories:

Debenture bonds   An unsecured promise to repay, in effect a corporate IOU. The sale of debenture bonds is widely used by the Federal National Mortgage Association to raise part of the money it uses to buy mortgages.

Mortgage bonds   Secured by a pledge of real estate.

Equipment bonds   Secured by a pledge of equipment such as railroad cars or airplanes.

Utility bonds   May be secured by a pledge of certain assets of a regulated utility company.

Government bonds   Federal government promises to pay (no specific assets pledged) with maturity over ten years.

Municipal bonds   Can be state or municipal issue, may or may not pledge tax or improvement revenue, and offers interest that is exempt from federal income tax.

Mortgage-backed bonds   Secured by the pledge of a block of mortgage loans which are held by a trustee.

To qualify for sale in the public markets, all such securities must have prior approval by the Securities and Exchange Commission. Approved securities are bought and sold daily on the open exchanges which deal in securities that trade in fairly large volume and offer near continuous price quotes. Securities with lesser trading activity may be bought and sold on the "over-the-counter" market which works in occasional trades on a quoted "bid and ask" range of prices. There is a third market that deals in large blocks of securities sold directly to major investors, such as insurance companies and pension funds, bypassing a portion of the trading commissions earned by investment bankers and stock brokerage firms.

Bonds trade freely at fluctuating prices, as do shares of stock. However, most bonds offer a fixed interest rate of return, rather than the uncertain dividend that may be paid to the stockholder. The fixed interest rate of the bond (the face rate or nominal rate) controls the price for the bond. If market interest rates go up, the bond price falls, which increases the return for the investor based on the fixed interest rate. Thus, there is an inverse movement in the bond market; if bond prices rise, it means that interest rates are falling and if bond prices fall, it means that interest rates are rising. Bonds are offered in $1,000 denominations or multiples of $1,000, and the price can be quoted in a dollar amount or a percentage figure.

Example   A $1,000 bond offers an interest rate of 15 percent which pays $150 each year to the holder of the bond. The bond is sold for $925. The party paying $925 still receives an interest payment of $150 each year which amounts to a return of 16.22 percent on the $925 invested. At maturity, the holder of the bond would pick up an additional $75, which is the difference between the $925 paid and the face amount of $1,000 at which the bond is redeemed by the issuer. Thus, the total return, or yield, on the investment includes both the annual interest and the price differential when the bond is redeemed at maturity.

One other type of corporate borrowing should be mentioned as it is being used to finance construction by a few large builders. This is the sale of *commercial paper*. Commercial paper is a simple promise to pay that is unsecured; that is, a corporate IOU. The term is generally short, like 30 days to 270 days. The largest issuer of commercial paper is General Motors Acceptance Corporation. Yields offered on commercial paper are generally competitive with the short-term money market rates, running about 2 percent higher than 91-day Treasury bill yields.

Financing Real Estate in the Future

As the decade of the seventies closed, the emphasis for new solutions to the old problem of finding sufficient mortgage money at a marketable cost began to turn towards new sources of money once again. Probably the largest contributor of increased funds during the 1970s was the rapid expansion of the secondary market. Many loan originators who would never sell a loan in the past learned that additional funding could be obtained through selling loans to big secondary market purchasers. The purchasers' funds came from several new sources, such as pension funds, which had not previously participated in the mortgage market.

The increased use of mortgage-backed securities as a method of raising funds has become a major funding source. Packaging $2 million or more of residential loans into a single block and issuing a government guarantee certificate (or a number of smaller certificates) based on the mortgages as collateral have become principal functions of the Government National Mortgage Association. Billions of dollars of otherwise nonmortgage-oriented funds are thus pumped into the market. Now the concept is expanding to use by institutional lenders—without a government guarantee (and usually without a guarantee of any kind by the issuer). Large banks, such as Bank of America (California), as well as rather small savings associations have adopted the mortgage-backed security concept and are issuing their own certificates. These are sold to other institutional investors, the general public, and, of course, to their own depositors.

In Colorado, a state without many large mortgage companies, the five major housing associations* formed a for-profit corporation to raise mortgage money through the sale of mortgage-backed securities. The Mortgage Corporation of Colorado began life in 1981 and obtained its first commitment from the Public Employees Retirement Association of Colorado (PERA), a target source as a mortgage investor for several Colorado lending institutions. PERA agreed to purchase $25 million in conventional mortgage-backed securities from the Colorado Mortgage Corporation. The initial money was allocated in 1982 through a bidding procedure that provided funds for 33 lenders. The Mortgage Corporation has good expectations of continuing its innovative methods of pulling mortgage money into Colorado, including the use of loan commitments from the Federal National Mortgage Association.

Another idea to expand available money for mortgage lending has been experimented with in California. This is for a government—in California it is the state—to allow its cash reserves to be placed on deposit with institutions that use the funds to make mortgage loans. In California, this has meant the savings associations. In many states there is a requirement that any deposit by the state must be collateralized by the banking institution with adequate securities to protect the state's funds. In California, this requirement was amended to allow mortgage notes held by the institution to serve as collateral.

---

*Colorado Mortgage Bankers Association, Savings and Loan League of Colorado, Colorado Association of Realtors, Colorado Association of Homebuilders, Colorado Bankers Association.

Future Real Estate Development

So closely intertwined is the housing industry with the mortgage-lending industry that the two are considered inseparable. However, the growth of very large multistate builders and developers has provided a few exceptions to this concept. Very large builders, such as U.S. Home, Kaufman and Broad, and others, operate on a scale that allows them to finance construction loans and even permanent residential loans through their own resources. These companies have the stability and size that enables them to sell bonds, stock, commercial paper, and other forms of securities in the open market. Several operate their own mortgage lending companies as subsidiaries. With access to money on their own market terms, these large companies can and do develop financing "gimmicks" in an effort to promote a particular house or subdivision. In a national market that requires traditional lenders to make 15 percent mortgage loans, the large builder might spring an advertising campaign around a 12⅞ percent loan—he may have found some lower cost money in a foreign country or may be absorbing the difference within the cost structure of the house. So the construction industry, particularly the housing segment, is developing a two-tier system: in the large urban growth areas where large builders are able to operate, the small builder may be subject to building cycles forced on him by the availability of mortgage money while the large builder remains relatively unaffected. However, financing alone is not the whole story of housing.

Change in our living patterns is a continuing process brought about by economic pressures plus the human desire for betterment. The increasing costs of housing are forcing urban construction into higher density structures such as apartments, townhouses, and condominiums. However, the impetus for urban growth is not for everyone. Statistics are showing an increase in the number of families and retired people moving to small communities with a more relaxed lifestyle. Development will continue to be needed in both large and small communities.

Small communities do not present a market of sufficient size to attract large builders and therefore will continue to be served by the individual entrepreneur. The large development companies can flourish in the metropolitan areas with a market for housing and other construction projects suitable to their size. In an industry that has been dominated by small independent companies, there will be no substantial change. A few builders have achieved national stature, more have reached prominence in a region of the country, but because of the localized nature of the product, the need for small innovative builders will continue.

Questions for Discussion

1. From whom and under what conditions did people borrow money prior to the Industrial Revolution?

2. How did the pre-Depression methods of financing real estate contribute to the collapse of the economy in the early 1930s?

3. What do you believe is the principal contribution of the Roosevelt Administration towards stabilizing the economy in 1933?

4. Why did the Federal Housing Administration find considerable resistance from private lenders to its insured loan program?

5. Describe a mortgage-backed security.

6. What is a *bond*?

Money and Interest Rates

No commodity is more widely used and less understood than money. In a limited sense, we know very well what money can do; its value lies primarily in our confidence that other people will accept the money in exchange for their goods and services. A brief reference to history shows that money has been with us in all civilizations as a means to improve the barter system of trading goods and services among people. Commodities of high intrinsic value have always been used in trade, including precious metals, gem stones, furs, and even salt and other spices. In fact, many areas of the world still use such standards today. Our modern business, however, floats on an intangible—the trust and confidence that individuals and nations place in currency and credit lines extended for bonds or other promissory certificates issued under a recognized government's authority. Certainly, the confidence placed in a government and its international trading power is indicated by the relative values placed on a nation's money in the realm of international trade.

As mortgage money becomes increasingly dependent on the financial markets as its source, it is important that the student of real estate finance understands how the government controls money supply and its consequent effects on the investment community. The experts who manage investment portfolios for large companies and institutions continually watch the Federal Reserve's (the Fed's) manipulation of monetary aggregates for signs of coming trends that may guide their investment decisions. For right or wrong, watching the weekly movement of money supply totals and anticipating how the Fed will react to the figures has become a key guide. It even has a name—"Fed watching." Unfortunately, for the careful analyst, the trends that follow certain actions by the Fed are no longer consistent because the expectations of the financial markets have become as important as the actions of the Fed itself. Since the perceptions of investors have often proven to be the reverse of what might normally be expected, yet another economic theory has arisen. It is called *rational expectations* and attempts to outguess the guessers! Let's look at the money supply and its management for clues as to how they affect the cost of mortgage money today.

The Monetary System

One of the major responsibilities of the Federal Reserve Bank is to manage the nation's money supply. This includes roughly the amount of currency in circulation plus the deposits within the banking system. The Federal Reserve Bank was established by Congress in 1913 as the national bank. It has a number of duties besides managing the money supply, including certain regulatory authority over national banks, monitoring and assisting the liquidity needs of these banks, issuing and policing credit regulations as may be required by Congress, enforcing the requirements of the Community Reinvestment Act, and serving as the banking arm of the United States Government. It operates as an independent agency under the direction of seven governors appointed by the president. The chairman of the board of governors is also appointed by the president and all have tenure; that is, they cannot be removed from office by the president as can a cabinet officer. Thus, the Fed operates with its monetary policies independently of Congress and the president.

The policies undertaken by the Fed to control the money supply are for the purpose of stabilizing and improving the nation's economy. It must activate its policies through a system of privately owned banks which do not always respond to the Fed's signals. For example, banks set the rate of interest charged to their customers independently of the Fed. Also, if a bank does not approve of a particular regulatory limitation on a certain type of loan, it may easily refuse to make any loans that fall in the unacceptable category. Credit is not rationed in this country, nor are private lenders required to make any specific kinds of loans by government edict. The banks are given guidelines in the form of regulations directed towards maintaining the solvency of the banking institution as well as protecting the general public. Interest rates could be set by law, but for years only one rate has been controlled, and that is the interest paid on various classes of savings accounts and savings certificates by the depository institutions. (As mentioned previously, the interest limits on savings deposits, Regulation Q of the Fed, are scheduled for gradual lifting and elimination by 1986.)

At the present time, about 5,250 commercial banks belong to the Federal Reserve System out of a total of 14,700 in the country. The banks within the system account for approximately 70 percent of the total banking assets, as all the larger banks are members. The authority of the Fed has been expanded recently through a change in the deposit reserve requirements under the Depository Institutions Deregulation and Monetary Control Act signed into law by President Carter on March 31, 1980. Over a period of several years the Federal Reserve has extended its reserve requirements to cover *all* depository institutions handling transaction accounts (generally checking accounts). The reserves are set at a uniform level and must be held on deposit with the Federal Reserve Bank at no interest. In addition to the reserve requirement, the Fed must exercise its influence through the use of restrictive regulations, a few banking signals on interest rates (but not control of them), and its management of the money supply.

The Fed has a number of problems in making effective use of its authority over the money supply, not the least of which is defining money itself. Also, the increasing use of electronic funds transfers results in a faster movement of funds. This increased movement of money means less money can accomplish more. Another important change in the banking system is the growth of nonregulated bank-type companies—those not directly subject to banking regulations. Such companies as American Express, Sears Roebuck, and Merrill Lynch have entered the financial services market and others are testing their entry into it.

Another problem involves the increasing flow of money between major trading countries, which has made action by the Federal Reserve less effective. Foreign governments can buy and sell U.S. government bonds and can make deposits or withdrawals from banks in this country in large blocks that distort normal trade movements. And the increase in the number of foreign banks in this country adds further complications.

Probably the biggest problem in the operation of the monetary system is that so many different agencies and people can exercise an influence on it. Ultimate control rests with Congress which has taxing and spending authority plus the power to borrow whatever is needed to cover any deficits. And the federal government's power to borrow money is unlimited. There are no legal, economic, or political restraints on how much the government will pay to raise the needed money. Thus, it has the ability to crowd out all other borrowers. The United States Treasury, operating under the direction of the politically appointed Secretary of the Treasury, is charged with the handling of the public debt.

How the Treasury funds and re-funds the federal debt has a strong influence on our monetary system and the availability of money in the private sector of the economy.

In spite of the many problems with the monetary system, it should be pointed out that over the years it has proven to be an effective one. So far, this system has been able to provide the capital needed for worthy projects. There have been delays in periods of tight money and disagreement over what is considered "worthwhile." But the mixture of free enterprise and government controls has managed to finance a nation of homeowners and an unparalleled growth in the nation's productivity.

Money Supply

The amount of money available at any one time for use in mortgage lending is dependent on the competition for this same money plus the amount of new money that is introduced into the system by the Federal Reserve Bank. It is the increase in the money supply that is so closely watched to determine the course of Federal Reserve policies. The theory is that an increase in the money supply stimulates the economy; no change or a decrease stifles it. While the activities for handling the money supply are complex and cloaked in secrecy by the Board, the basic cause and effect relationship is fairly simple.

The size of our total money supply and of the economy makes the problem appear almost beyond comprehension. For clarification, let us use a simplified example. First, remember that the value of money used today is represented by the goods and services that it can buy. If we have an economy with exactly 10,000 units of goods and services with an amount of money available to purchase these products totaling $1 million, each unit of goods and services would be worth $100. Now, by increasing productivity over several years, the economy has 20,000 units of goods and services for sale. But assume that *no increase* has been made in the available money. With twice as much to buy for the same amount of money, the price of each unit of goods and services drops to $50. If a different policy were used so that over the same period of time that our increased productivity supplied 20,000 units of goods and services, the money supply was subsequently increased to $3 million, then each unit would be worth $150. To maintain a stable pricing structure, a balance must be maintained between the money supply and the increase in productivity.

Measuring the Money Supply

To control the money supply, it is first necessary to define it so that a measurement can be made. Economists differ on the precise concept of money as well as the categories used for its measurement. Basically, money is an asset with commonly recognized value that can be readily exchanged for other goods and services. For its particular purpose, the Fed recognizes as money all currency in circulation and those money assets which represent immediate purchasing power for the holders. To distinguish some of the differences in the nature of this money, the Federal Reserve identifies four categories using the letter M as follows:

M_1 Currency in circulation, nonbank travelers checks, demand deposits in commercial banks and mutual savings banks, negotiable orders of withdrawal (NOW) accounts and automatic transfer service (ATS) at both banks and thrift institutions, and credit union share draft accounts. As of March, 1982, M_1 totaled $448.2 billion.

M_2 The total of M_1 plus savings and small denomination time deposits at all depository institutions, overnight repurchase agreements, and general-purpose money market mutual funds. As of March, 1982, M_2 totaled $1,865 billion.

M_3 The total of M_2 plus large denomination ($100,000 and over) time deposits at all depository institutions, term repurchase agreements at commercial banks and savings associations, and balances of institution-only money market mutual funds. As of March, 1982, M_3 totaled $2,235 billion.

L The total of M_3 plus other liquid assets such as Eurodollars held by U.S. residents, bankers acceptances, commercial paper, Treasury bills, and U.S. savings bonds. As of December, 1981, L totaled $2,643 billion.

Definitions of less well-known money terminology include the following:

Non bank travelers checks Those issued by companies such as American Express.

NOW accounts Savings accounts that can be withdrawn by writing withdrawal slips payable to third parties. Accounts that can be used to transfer money to other than the owner of the account (as is possible with a checking account) are called *transaction accounts*.

ATS accounts An interest-bearing savings deposit tied to a checking account within the same institution so that any checks written can be automatically covered by a transfer from the savings account into the checking account.

Share draft accounts A depositor in a credit union owns a "share" in the union's deposit assets and may be allowed to withdraw money by writing a checklike "draft" on the account.

Time deposit Any deposit that cannot be withdrawn immediately. Savings certificates represent deposits held for a specific period of time, as do certificates of deposit (C/Ds). Passbook savings accounts are not subject to immediate withdrawal; regulations allow the institution 30 days to honor a withdrawal, although the privilege is not exercised by any institution for fear of creating loss of depositor confidence.

Repurchase agreements Classified as a security rather than a deposit, it is simply another name for a savings certificate. For example, a depositor gives the bank, say, $10,000 in exchange for an agreement, a certificate in the amount of $10,000 which the banker agrees to buy back (that is, return the deposit amount plus interest) after a specified period of time.

Money market mutual funds A pooling of small sums of money into a common fund wherein the fund money is invested in large denomination amounts in higher yielding short-term investments. The idea began when large deposits (over $100,000) were deregulated as to the interest they could earn. The advantages of pooling small sums that might be earning a 5½ percent passbook savings rate into a large fund that could invest in a $100,000 certificate of deposit earning, say, 14 percent interest, attracted many investors. As of June, 1982, money market funds had exceeded $200 billion in total assets.

Eurodollars U.S. dollar deposits held in European banks. For statistical purposes, the market bases rates on such deposits held in London banks usually on amounts of $100,000 or more.

Bankers acceptances Negotiable bank-guaranteed credit instruments typically used to finance an import order.

Commercial paper High-grade unsecured promissory notes sold through dealers by major corporations in multiples of $1,000. One major issuer of commercial paper is the General Motors Acceptance Corporation (GMAC).

L Liquid assets.

Thrift institutions Savings associations and mutual savings banks; that is, those institutions initially organized to provide security for their depositors' assets.

Management of the Money Supply

The actual amount of money and credit available in this country is not directly controlled by either the Congress or the president. It is the responsibility of the Federal Reserve Bank. The Federal Reserve manages the nation's money through a system of 12 branches plus the commercial banks who are members of the system, a total of 5,250 banks at the end of 1981. In addition, since 1980, the Fed sets reserve requirements on all depository institutions handling transaction accounts (check-writing-type of accounts) which substantially increases its regulatory position in the banking community.

The control of the money supply itself gives the Federal Reserve Board a strong hand on the nation's economy. The crucial decisions on how much money will be added to the supply or withdrawn from circulation are made by the 12 people who comprise the Federal Open Market Committee. These are five presidents from different branch Reserve Banks and the seven governors of the Reserve Board. They meet the third Tuesday of every month in closely guarded secrecy to study indicators, receive reports, and argue among themselves as to what action should be taken. The decision is not announced to the public immediately but is transmitted to a small staff which operates out of the New York Federal Reserve Bank and implements the Open Market Committee's decisions.

If the decision is to increase the money supply, the operation is carried out through a small number of dealers and big banks who are licensed to trade in government securities. The Federal Reserve staff handling the operation contacts one or more of these dealers and gives them a check drawn on the Federal Reserve account to buy government securities. The dealer delivers the securities and deposits the check in a bank. The check is sent back to the Fed for collection. The Fed credits the bank which now has more money on deposit and thus more money to lend. As money becomes more plentiful in the banks, it should become cheaper and encourage business activity. This works most of the time.

But how can the Fed simply write checks like this? It is authorized by law to do so and has what amounts to an open-ended bank account. It can create money as it sees fit. Because of this power, it is easy to see why the federal government can never go bankrupt. States and cities may become insolvent or bankrupt but not the federal government. It is the authority to print money and create its own bank credits that gives the federal government its top of the list credit rating. Anyone buying a government bond, note, or bill knows that it will be paid off in full at due date simply by the government's printing the money to do so, if necessary.

The ideal for the Federal Reserve to aim for with its handling of the money supply is to increase the amount of available money exactly in proportion to the growth of our economy. There is a normal need for more money as the population grows and as business activity increases along with productivity increases. In practice it does not work out very smoothly. Many economists believe that the key to economic stability lies in how the money supply is increased and that it has to be used as a throttle mechanism for the economy. Because of its substantial power to speed up or slow down the pace of business activity with its money supply decisions, the Federal Reserve in the past has declined to announce its money supply decisions when they are made. In 1975, Congress required the Fed to announce its money supply goals in advance, which has reduced some of the speculation. But the announced goals have proven hard to reach. The steps taken to make adjustments in the money supply are hard to measure precisely, and the results of their moves lag behind the need to know.

A major change in Fed policy was announced on October 6, 1979, when the Fed abandoned its policy of keying money supply decisions to the federal funds rate as reflected by commercial banks in the New York market. Previously, the decision to add or withhold additional money to the base was based on whether or not the federal funds rate rose or declined. Since the federal funds rate is the interest charged by one bank to another for a short-term loan (sometimes as short as 24 hours), it was considered an accurate reflection of the cash reserves within the banking system. If this interest rate began to rise above the target levels that were considered currently adequate by the Fed, then money would be added to the system. Increasingly, it became obvious that this method of controlling the money supply was in itself creating some of the problems. A surge in the economy tends to drive interest rates upward, which includes upward pressure on the federal funds rate. As the rates rose, the Fed used this signal to inject additional money into the system, which in turn helped to accelerate the upward pressures. Further, the Fed's use of interest rates to determine money supply placed an unwelcome blame on the Fed for too high interest rates.

The basic change in Fed policy in its handling of money supply growth is to center the determination on the *quantity* of bank reserves. Thus, fluctuations in the money supply are determined more through direct controls rather than by an effort to manipulate interest rates. Some economists challenge this change of policy as one of the causes of high and erratic interest rates.

Tools Used by the Fed

Monetary policies, as determined solely by the Federal Reserve Board, are implemented within the banking system through several "tools." Sometimes the tools can be used very effectively either to slow economic activity or to increase it. At other times, actions taken by the Fed seem to produce conflicting results. Just what does the Fed do in its efforts to stabilize and provide for an orderly growth of the economy? It utilizes four major powers within its authority to manipulate the economy. These are discussed as follows:

1. *Money supply* As previously considered in this chapter, determining the amount of money available in the economy is a major, and probably the most closely watched, power exercised by the Fed.

2. *Open market operations* Open market operations allow the Fed to raise or lower the level of cash available within the banking system. If the Fed buys government bonds in the open market from private investors, there is no real increase in the amount of government bonds (that is, government debt) outstanding. However, if the Fed buys government bonds directly from the U.S. Treasury using its authority to issue checks, or credit, up to the federal debt limit, then there is an increase in government bonds outstanding. The latter procedure, buying bonds from the U.S. Treasury so that the government can pay its bills, is also known as *monetizing the debt.*

3. *Changes in reserve requirements* Prior to the passage of the Depository Institutions Deregulation Act of 1980, the Fed could set reserve requirements for only its member banks. Reserves are that portion of a depository institution's deposits that must be kept in reserve; that is, on deposit and not available for making loans to customers. In general, national banks in the past have been required to maintain substantially larger reserves than their state-chartered competitors. This was not well received by the national bank members of the Fed. The Deregulation Act of 1980 enlarged the Fed's authority to require all depository institutions handling transaction accounts to deposit reserves with the Fed interest-free. The rule is being implemented over several years, and its ultimate effect has not had time for full testing. The expectation is that any increase in reserve requirements by the Fed will have substantially greater impact on the banking system than before, as would any decrease in requirements. The less money an institution must hold in reserve, the more it has with which to make loans. One

advantage for those institutions that have recently been required to place deposits on reserve with the Fed is that they now have the right to borrow money from the Fed at the discount rate of interest. In banking terminology, the Fed's discount window is open to all who have reserves on deposit with it.

4. *Discount rate*   One of the more publicized tools that the Fed uses is the discount rate—that interest charged to institutions holding deposits with the Fed when they borrow money from it. Money borrowed from the Fed is considered for use mostly in emergency or unusual situations, not as a source of capital for making loans. Thus, the discount rate does not establish a true cost of funds for the banking system. It serves more as a signal to the banking community to indicate the Fed's position regarding interest rates. If the discount rate is increased, banks consider this a sign of higher interest rates to come and usually raise their own charges to customers. However, there is *no requirement* that the banking system follow the movement of the discount rate either up or down.

The United States Treasury

Responsibility for monitoring the federal debt and payment of government obligations rests with the United States Treasury. Since both the Treasury and the mortgage market seek borrowed money, there is competition between them. In years past, prior to 1965, both the Treasury and mortgage lenders tapped sources with long-term money to loan. These were savings deposits, insurance money, and some trust and pension fund assets. This is referred to as the *long-term market*, loans with terms of ten years or longer. It is also called the *capital market*.

In the decade from 1965 to 1975, the Treasury looked more to the short-term market, referred to as the *money market*, for funding. Congress did not restrict the interest rates that could be paid by the government for short-term loans as they did for long-term loans. One result of this policy was a decrease in the competition between the government and mortgage lenders for long-term money. After 1975, however, long-term money began to dry up, and both the government and mortgage lenders began to compete for short-term sources of funds. A brief history of how the federal government has handled its borrowing requirements over the years should prove interesting as a background for understanding our changing mortgage markets.

Prior to 1917, every new offering of Treasury securities required specific congressional authorization, including terms and conditions of each issue. During World War I, Congress granted some leeway to the Treasury in setting terms of new issues but insisted on setting the maximum interest rate—originally at 3½ percent, reflecting the congressional desire for low interest rates. In 1919, Congress gave the Treasury more flexibility by removing interest rate ceilings on securities that matured in five years or less but retained a 4¼ percent ceiling on new issues of longer term securities.

The restrictions provided little problem for the following half century. After all, the cost of long-term funds ranged from 2 to 6 percent through the massive economic fluctuations that occurred between 1865 and 1965. But as interest rates began to soar during the inflationary 1965–75 decade, the only way that the Treasury could sell new long-term issues was to ask Congress for higher interest rate ceilings: above 4¼ percent. Some increases were allowed for new issues during this period. Congress also changed the definition of "bond" maturity from five to seven years, and now to ten years. This effectively exempted a wider range of maturities from the ceiling and spurred the Treasury reliance on the shorter term Treasury "bills" and Treasury "notes."

The congressional restrictions on interest rates and investors' unwillingness to lend long-term money during a prolonged inflationary period have led to a continuing decline in the maturity of the federal debt. In 1946, the average maturity of the debt was more than nine years, and longer term issues (then defined as maturities of five years or more) accounted for 54 percent of the total. By 1980, the average maturity was less than three years and long-term issues accounted for only 10 percent of the total.

Selling Treasury Obligations

To whom does the United States Treasury sell its long-term and short-term obligations when it needs money? The answer to this question has an important bearing on the nation's economy. The market has only two principal buyers—(1) the general public, as private investors and (2) the Federal Reserve Bank. The purpose of the government's borrowing is to raise money with which to buy more goods and services. It thus competes with the general public for the same goods and services. Now if the government sells its securities to the general public, it effectively takes money out of their hands and prevents competition between the general public and the government for the same goods and services, which is essentially noninflationary.

But if the Treasury sells its obligations to the Federal Reserve Bank, which is a method used to increase the supply of money, there is no comparable reduction in the public's power to buy goods and services. The increase of money in government hands now competes directly with the general public for the same goods and services and presses all prices upward.

Other Government Influences on Money and Credit

While the Federal Reserve Board monetary policies and the deficit spending policies of the government are often singled out as the main cause of high interest rates and a resulting slowdown of the economy, there are other factors that must also be considered. These include the perception business people and consumers have of anticipated inflation plus the substantial overload that has been placed on the credit markets. The credit market basically comprises the supply of money available for loans but defies precise measurement because of the flexible nature of our banking system. The Federal Office of Management and Budget (OMB) must estimate the credit markets in its effort to determine the impact of federal spending on these markets and the resulting interest rates that the government will have to pay for its own borrowing.

To give the reader an idea of the size of this market, the OMB reported that in 1981 $408 billion was raised in U.S. credit markets. Of this amount the federal government took $142 billion, or 35 percent. The government demand for credit has proliferated since the 1960s. There are three kinds of government demands for borrowed funds, all of which compete with the private sector for available credit. The three are listed as follows:

1. Direct loans to the government.
2. Loans guaranteed by the government (such as FHA/VA).
3. Loans by government-sponsored enterprises.

During the 1960s, government borrowing—direct loans, loan guarantees, and loans by government agencies—accounted for 15 percent to 20 percent of all credit. In the 1970s, federal borrowing averaged 28 percent. By 1981, the figure had climbed to 35 percent ($142 billion out of $408 billion available). In 1982 the OMB estimated that credit supply would decline because of economic recession to $368 billion, of which the federal government would require $206 billion, or 56 percent. The breakdown of the $206 billion includes: $115 billion in direct loans by the public to the Treasury; $44 billion in loans guaranteed by the federal government, such as those for homeowners and small businesses; and $47 billion in loans by government-sponsored enterprises, including such agencies as the Federal Home Loan Mortgage Corporation and the Farm Credit Administration. The 1983 OMB estimate anticipates an increase in available credit to $458 billion, of which the federal share will be $212 billion, or 46 percent.

(It might be noted here that the all-time record for federal domination of the credit markets was set in 1944 according to the Federal Reserve Board. At the peak of World War II, the government borrowed $58 billion which amounted to 99 percent of the net available credit.)

Interest Rates

Investment money constantly reaches for the highest yield on comparable risks. So the setting of interest rates is very important in determining the direction that money will move. Although interest is the price paid for using another's money, the price does not work quite the way it does with other commodities. An increase in the price for money does not always discourage the borrower, nor will a decrease in the interest rate by itself bring a greater demand for lendable funds. Money simply does not respond to pricing pressures in a precise and predictable manner. Where other commodities maintain something of a balance between supply and demand through price adjustments in a relatively free market, the price of money is under too much regulation to float freely, and the economy operates too freely to accept regulated prices for money. The result is a blend of pressures that sets the interest rates.

The free market economy uses the basic forces of supply and demand to influence interest rates—as the demand for money increases, the cost will also increase. As the regulator of the economy with control of the monetary system, the government can establish interest rates in certain areas and pump money into programs in an effort to reduce interest costs. But neither the government nor bankers are able to set market rates of interest. The Congress could establish fixed rates of interest for various major categories of loans, but this would probably require fixing prices of many other commodities at the same time. So the Congress allows the free market system to establish interest rates. Through banking regulatory agencies, only the interest rates paid by banks and savings associations to their depositors are set by law. The Federal Reserve sets the *discount rate*, which is the interest rate charged by the Fed to its member banks if they borrow from the Fed.

Banks do business in a competitive market and are in the business of making a profit. They are compelled to seek the highest yields possible commensurate with the risk. But the bank's customers are free to shift their business to other banks if the bank overcharges for its loans.

So in a very real sense, banks are restricted in what they can charge by the forces of competition, not by any governmental authority.

For mortgage money, the most visible indication of free market action setting interest rates is shown by the frequent auctions for mortgage loan commitments held by both the Federal Home Loan Mortgage Corporation and the Federal National Mortgage Association. At these auctions, approved mortgagees from all over the country submit bids for mortgage loan money, at yields (interest rate plus discount) that each bidder feels will be competitive in his local area of operation. While not all primary lenders participate in these auctions, they do watch the results published each week as a major guide for their own interest charges. In the short-term money market, another major indicator rate is found in the weekly auctions of Treasury bills.

Interest Rate Indicators

There are a number of interest rates published daily in leading business magazines and newspapers and all give good clues as to the direction money costs are moving. Following are four rates that represent important indicators for the real estate mortgage business.

Treasury Bill Rate. The cost of short-term borrowing by the federal government is clearly determined each week at the auctions of Treasury bills. The bills are sold by the Federal Reserve Bank and can be purchased from the Bank or through authorized security dealers. The return on this type of investment is expressed as a *yield* because it is determined by the difference between the purchase price and face value of the bill. For example, in one auction,* 13-week bills were bought for an average price of 97.018. This means that a T-bill receipt in the face amount of $10,000.00 was purchased for $9,701.80. At maturity, 91 days later, the T-bill is redeemed for $10,000.00. Thus, the investor earns the difference between the purchase price of $9,701.80 and the redemption price of $10,000.00, or $298.20. The return (not an interest rate but expressed as a *yield*) amounts to 11.797 percent based on a $10,000.00 investment. However, since the investment was $9,701.80, rather than $10,000.00, the effective return amounts to 12.33 percent based on a 360-day year. The 12.33 percent return is called the *coupon rate*. The auctions for Treasury bills are open to anyone with investment cash (they have sold denominations as small as $1,000.00 but generally are limited to $10,000.00 denominations) and reflect the current short-term market accurately. As in all indicators, the trend, up or down, is an important guideline.

---

*On July 12, 1982.

Prime Rate. This is defined as the interest rate charged by a commercial bank to its most credit-worthy customers. Each bank may set its own prime rate by any method it chooses. Some use complicated formulas, and others depend on the wisdom of their board of directors. In practice most banks simply follow the lead of one of the major commercial banks. The prime rate is used more as a base upon which to float an interest rate for any class of loans than as an actual lending rate. A good example is a construction loan which may be quoted at 2 points over prime—if the prime rate is 10 percent, the construction loan will be 12 percent. If the prime rate moves up to 11 percent, the construction loan automatically is increased to 13 percent and calculated from the date the prime change is announced. Another direct effect of the prime rate on the mortgage field is that warehouse lines of credit held by mortgage companies with their commercial banker are usually quoted at prime or a point over prime.

FNMA Auction Yields. Every other Monday the Federal National Mortgage Association holds an auction for four-month commitments to buy home loans. The bidding is for commitments by Fannie Mae to buy mortgages during the commitment period if the originator selling the mortgages cannot get a better price elsewhere. The bid is expressed as a yield. At one auction* the average yield offered to FNMA for a commitment to purchase conventional loans was 17.180 percent. The result indicates that mortgage companies and other loan originators participating in this auction felt that they could make loans in their local market at a rate of 17.180 percent or a little better. Thus, yields quoted at these auctions tend to reflect lender expectations for home loan rates for the next four months. By 1982, a depressed real estate market, along with doubling of the FNMA commitment fee from 1 to 2 points, substantially diminished bidding activity in the biweekly auctions. Because of the thin market, the auction results are not as accurate a measure of mortgage rates as before. To maintain its loan purchases, FNMA turned to an administrative pricing system and negotiation for loans

FHLMC Auction Yields. Since 1977, FHLMC has used an auction procedure similar to that of FNMA for selling loan commitments. The auctions are held every Friday for immediate purchase commitments, twice a month for 6-month forward commitments, and once a month for 8-month forward commitments. Bidders at the FHLMC auctions are predominantly savings associations, and the results provide an accurate indication of their anticipated home loan interest rates. (*Note*: In making a comparison between FNMA and FHLMC auction results, there is a

---

*Auction held July 6, 1982.

built-in differential, which is the fee charged for servicing a loan. FHLMC uses a *net* basis in the yields quoted at their auctions; that is, no service fees are included. FNMA yields are quoted on a *gross* basis that includes a service fee of ³/₈ percent to the loan originator who is expected to service the loan for FNMA.)

Usury

Usury laws are state laws, not federal statutes, that limit the amount of interest that may be charged to various categories of borrowers. Until the 1970s, market interest rates remained generally below the various state limits, and there was little concern for this particular restriction. But as interest rates have continued to climb, lenders in some states found that the restrictive laws made it difficult, if not impossible, to continue orderly lending activities. The rising cost of money for lenders made it more and more difficult to make loans within the statutory limits and retain a safe operating margin. Further, states with higher interest limits were able to attract the big secondary market investors who are able to purchase mortgages anywhere. Many states were simply excluded from the national market for mortgage money by restrictive usury laws. Congress suspended certain state usury limits for the first three months of 1980. Then, on March 31 of that year, Congress preempted state usury limits for first-mortgage residential loans.

The historical concept of usury has a religious basis. In earlier societies, charging money for something other than the product of one's labor was considered sinful. Thus, lending money for profit was held to be a violation of religious doctrine by Christians through the Middle Ages. Even today certain Moslem faiths hold this belief and do not permit interest to be charged among the faithful. However, this belief does not apply to lending money to those outside the faith!

The more modern concept supporting usury laws is that the individual borrower should have some protection from the substantial power represented by a lender. In earlier times, and perhaps in some smaller communities today, the protection may be appropriate. But where mortgage loans are concerned, the growth of lending across state lines, coupled with the big national auction markets for loans, have made restrictive usury laws somewhat counterproductive.

Influences on Interest Rates

To sum up, the four basic influences on interest rates are listed as follows:

1. Supply of money.
2. Demand for money.

3. Monetary policies.
4. Fiscal policies.

Each of these influences is further discussed below.

Supply of Money. For lending purposes, we must understand those factors that influence the flow of funds into the large sources. One of these, the inclination to save a portion of one's earnings, both by individuals and corporations, for the "rainy day," is still quite strong. As this money flows into the great pools of private funds (commercial banks, thrift institutions, and life insurance companies), their capacity for lending more money obviously increases. As our economy has grown, the increase in savings has been correspondingly steady, although more so in some years than others. However, compared with European countries, United States savings rates (the percentage of income that people put into bank accounts, securities, insurance and mortgages) are much lower. The average savings rate for this country is a little over 6 percent of disposable income. West Germans squirrel away about 14 percent, the French 17 percent, the Italians 25 percent, and the British 14 percent. However, some of the savings are of an involuntary kind in the form of payroll-paid life insurance and pension programs.

Situations arise in which the movement of funds between various institutions causes periodic shortages of money in certain areas. The competitive efforts among savings associations, among banks, and between banks and savings associations to garner more deposits, mostly at each other's expense, may cause some changes in the availability of money for mortgage lending. For example, competition has surfaced in such ways as changes in interest rates offered for various types of deposits; higher yielding money market funds (some of which offer check-writing privileges); savings accounts held in foreign banks; and the introduction of a checking account procedure into savings associations. Whether or not savings will be allowed to accumulate in the banks, thrift institutions, and life insurance companies' portfolios also depends on the condition of business in general. In times of increasing inflationary pressures it is often necessary to draw against savings reserves to meet rising costs. Or inflation could cause withdrawals of cash to spend on major appliances or a car before prices increase further. The element of mass psychology is inherently involved in this area and complicates the problems of analysis and prediction.

So the supply of money available in the lender's hands at any given time for a specific loan depends not only on government policies and the business climate but also on the amount of money the lender has on hand to loan. The movement of money out of the traditional sources for mortgage money, regardless of the reason, reduces the ability of mortgage lenders to fund loans.

Demand for Money. The basic supply of money in the country does not fluctuate nearly as much as the demand. There are four major areas of demand covering both long-term and short-term needs that compete with each other for the available supply. These are listed as follows:

1. *Business borrowing* All forms of loans, inventory needs, tax requirements, long-term funds, and others.
2. *Consumer and personal loans* Installment loans, auto financing, personal requirements.
3. *Government financing* Federal, state, and municipal bond issues, short-term needs, government agency issues.
4. *Mortgage loans* All types: construction, development, income properties, housing, and industrial.

In a booming economy, all segments have needs that add to the upward pressures on interest rates in their efforts to attract the necessary financing. Regulations that previously restricted the interest rates that could be paid on bond issues by cities and states have been eased, and those issues have now become more competitive. Efforts to reduce demand by forcing acceptance of higher interest rates have not always been effective, however, because businesses can afford the higher rates if their competitors are forced to pay the same costs. The federal government is not restricted as to what interest it can pay in the bill and note markets, and Congress does not show concern for money costs when voting for a deficit spending program.

The lower end of the demand spectrum includes people on fixed incomes who are not always able to pay the extra interest costs required to purchase a car or new house. In a sagging economy, the lowering of interest rates does not in itself create much new demand for money. The inclination to borrow for an expansion of facilities or for an increase in inventory is neither strong nor urgent when business declines.

Monetary Policies of the Federal Reserve Bank. Monetary policies have been considered earlier as part of the subject of "money supply." In the past, control over the money supply was exercised through manipulation of the federal funds rate. In late 1979, the method was shifted to a more direct control over the money supply base itself.

Fiscal Policies of the U.S. Government. The manner in which the government handles its tax and spending programs comprises the fiscal policies. The effect on interest rates is substantial. Within ill-defined bounds, an increase in taxes, primarily the income taxes on persons and corporations, will take money out of the hands of people who would otherwise spend it for more goods, whereas a decrease in taxes should

TABLE 2-1

Terms and Yields in Primary and Secondary Markets
(In Millions of Dollars)

Item	1979	1980	1981	1981 Oct.	1981 Nov.	1981 Dec.	1982 Jan.	1982 Feb.	1982 Mar.	1982 Apr.
				Terms and yields in primary and secondary markets						
PRIMARY MARKETS										
Conventional mortgages on new homes *Terms[1]*										
1 Purchase price (thousands of dollars)	74.4	83.4	90.4	89.2	84.5	88.7	102.6	97.3	90.0ʳ	95.1
2 Amount of loan (thousands of dollars)	53.3	59.2	65.3	63.5	62.7	64.4	71.3	71.1	65.4ʳ	70.6
3 Loan/price ratio (percent)	73.9	73.2	74.8	73.0	77.3	75.3	73.5	76.5	75.7ʳ	77.7
4 Maturity (years)	28.5	28.2	27.7	27.4	23.4	27.7	27.4	28.1	27.4ʳ	28.8
5 Fees and charges (percent of loan amount)[2]. .	1.66	2.09	2.67	2.86	2.52	2.87	2.55	3.01	2.90ʳ	3.26
6 Contract rate (percent per annum)	10.48	12.25	14.16	15.04	15.68	15.23	14.66	14.44	14.93ʳ	15.08
Yield (percent per annum)										
7 FHLBB series[3]	10.77	12.65	14.74	15.65	16.38	15.87	15.25	15.12	15.67ʳ	15.78
8 HUD series[4]	11.15	13.95	16.52	18.05	16.95	17.00	17.30	17.20	16.80	16.65
SECONDARY MARKETS										
Yield (percent per annum)										
9 FHA mortgage (HUD series)[5]	10.87	13.42	16.29	17.43	15.98	16.43	17.38	17.10	16.41	16.31
10 GNMA securities[6]	10.22	12.55	15.29	16.54	15.10	15.51	16.19	16.21	15.54	15.40
FNMA auctions[7]										
11 Government-underwritten loans	11.17	14.11	16.70	18.13	16.64	16.92	17.80	18.00	17.29	0.0
12 Conventional loans	11.77	14.43	16.64	18.61	17.20	16.95	17.33	17.91	17.09	16.66

1. Weighted averages based on sample surveys of mortgages originated by major institutional lender groups. Compiled by the Federal Home Loan Bank Board in cooperation with the Federal Deposit Insurance Corporation.

2. Includes all fees, commissions, discounts, and "points" paid (by the borrower or the seller) to obtain a loan.

3. Average effective interest rates on loans closed, assuming prepayment at the end of 10 years.

4. Average contract rates on new commitments for conventional first mortgages, rounded to the nearest 5 basis points (from Department of Housing and Urban Development).

5. Average gross yields on 30-year, minimum-downpayment, Federal Housing Administration-insured first mortgages for immediate delivery in the private secondary market. Any gaps in data are due to periods of adjustment to changes in maximum permissible contract rates.

6. Average net yields to investors on Government National Mortgage Association guaranteed, mortgage-backed, fully modified pass-through securities, assuming prepayment in 12 years on pools of 30-year FHA/VA mortgages carrying the prevailing ceiling rate. Monthly figures are unweighted averages of Monday quotations for the month.

7. Average gross yields (before deduction of 38 basis points for mortgage servicing) on accepted bids in Federal National Mortgage Association's auctions of 4-month commitments to purchase home mortgages, assuming prepayment in 12 years for 30-year mortgages. No adjustments are made for FNMA commitment fees or stock-related requirements. Monthly figures are unweighted averages for auctions conducted within the month.

8. Includes some multifamily and nonprofit hospital loan commitments in addition to 1- to 4-family loan commitments accepted in FNMA's free market auction system and through the FNMA-GNMA tandem plans.

9. Includes participation as well as whole loans.

10. Includes conventional and government-underwritten loans.

Source: Federal Reserve Bulletin, June, 1982, p. A40.

serve as a spur to the economy. As for the spending side of the fiscal policy, a big deficit spending program is intended to increase a lagging economy and bring forth some inflationary pressures, whereas restricted spending programs should dampen business activity and slow down the economy. The economic interaction isn't quite so simple as suggested, however, since deficit spending creates the corresponding problem of raising the cash to finance the loss, which is done by selling more government bonds, thus soaking up lendable funds that might have been used for other purposes in the private sector of the economy.

Interest Rates on New Home Mortgages

Table 2-1 shows the changes that have occurred in residential mortgage rates, maturities, and average loan amounts over the four-year period 1979 to 1982.

Questions for Discussion

1. Describe the monetary system used in this country.

2. How does the Federal Reserve increase the money supply?

3. Describe two government agencies that can influence the market for mortgage money and how they can do so.

4. How does the Treasury raise money when it has to borrow?

5. Explain the major factors that influence interest rates.

6. Explain what is meant by *fiscal policies* and by *monetary policies*.

7. Identify the four major areas of demand for money.

8. How does a change in interest rates affect business borrowing?

9. Compare the going rates of interest on mortgage loans in your community with the latest FNMA auction yields. How do the rates charged by savings associations compare with mortgage company rates?

10. Suggest ways to improve our banking system.

Notes and Mortgages

Loans made with real estate as the collateral security can be traced back as far as the ancient Pharaohs of Egypt and the Romans of the pre-Christian era. Even then, some form of pledge or assignment of the property was used to ensure repayment of an obligation to the lender. The development over many centuries of this type of property assignment illustrates the interplay of individual rights, more specifically, the rights of a borrower as against the rights of a lender.

History and Development

The Mortgage as a Grant of Title to Property

In its earliest forms, a property pledge to secure a debt was an actual assignment of that property to the lender. During the term of the loan, the lender might even have the physical use of that land and was entitled to any rents or other revenues derived from the land pledged. Thus, the earliest form of land as security for a loan was the actual granting of title to the lender for the term of the loan.

Due to the primitive conditions of communication and transportation then in existence, the practice of granting title to property for a loan tended to foster a number of abuses by lenders. For example, a slight delay in payments, which might even be encouraged by the lender, easily created a default and forfeited the borrower's rights for any recovery of his land. Sometimes borrowers who felt they had been unjustly deprived of their property appealed to the king, or perhaps to an appointed minister, to seek a hearing for their grievances and to petition for just redress. And if it was subsequently determined that a wrong had been committed, the borrower might be given a chance to redeem his land with a late payment of the obligation. Thus the *right of redemption* came into being.

However, lenders were not happy with this redemption privilege and initiated a countermove by inserting a clause in future loan agreements that specifically waived the right of redemption. The borrower had to accept this clause or be denied the loan. As our civilization developed away from the unchallenged rule of an absolute monarch into written codes of law, the granting or refusal of redemption became a matter of law or of statute often referred to as *statutory redemption*. Variations in such laws among the states are substantial, going all the way from a total lack of redemption rights upon default up to two full years after default to pay off the loan and recover the property.

The Mortgage as a Lien

Another way in which land can be pledged as security for a loan is by means of granting a lien. A *lien* constitutes an encumbrance on property. It is a declaration of a claim to a parcel of land for some purpose that is recorded in the public record. In states where the lien form is prevalent, a pledge of land as security for a loan grants no title except under default of the obligation. So when a default does occur, the lender must convert his lien rights into an actual title to the property through court action, as the particular state may require.

While there is some variation in the precise usage of the lien as a form of pledge, and the limited assignment of title as another form of pledge, all property laws concerning mortgages can be classified into one form or the other. The advantages and disadvantages of each can be weighed as legal arguments, but for purposes of finance, it is important mainly to be aware of the existing differences and to know under what laws a particular property can be mortgaged.

Lenders have learned to live with various requirements and can obtain adequate security for their loans by adapting their pledges to the many different laws. For example, they have adjusted even to the unique law spelled out in the original constitution of the state of Texas protecting a family homestead from all creditors with just three exceptions: (1) a loan for purchase of the property, (2) mechanic's and materialmen's liens, and (3) property taxes.

State Laws Control Property Rights

Property rights in the United States are spelled out primarily under state laws, not by the federal government. Each state has written into its code of law specific rights that must be adhered to with regard to land-ownership in that state. The local variations and shadings in these laws reflect the background and origins of the particular region. In the East, for example, the great body of English parliamentary law and common law guided the New England and mid-Atlantic states in setting up their constitutions and subsequent statutes. In the South, on the other hand, the French legal codes were reflected in the Louisiana Territory and were especially evident in the growing city of New Orleans. In still another section of the country, the Southwest, Spanish heritage determined the laws, and these laws recognized Catholic religious ties in marriage as well as patriarchal protection of wife, children, and family relationships. As a result, community property statutes were enacted, and for many years special protections as well as special limitations regarding women's property rights were in force in this region of the country.

An attempt to cover such a broad field of law as real property rights on a national basis would be out of place in this text since it is a subject more properly handled by qualified attorneys, skilled in interpreting these rights according to the laws of each state. It can be pointed out, however, that most states have laws specifically limiting any conveyance of property rights solely to written agreements and all states require certain procedures to record conveyances of land in the public records. The result has been an increasingly accurate record of land titles, with a corresponding increase of protection for property owner's rights and those of any other interested parties.

The Mortgage and Promissory Note

There are certain basic instruments used in real estate loans that have essentially the same purposes throughout the country. The collateral pledge that has given its name to the entire field of real estate finance is the *mortgage*. A mortgage is simply a pledge of property to secure a loan. It is not a promise to pay anything. As a matter of fact, without a debt to secure, the mortgage itself becomes null and void by its own terms, or, as the French derivative of the word *mortgage* indicates, a "dead pledge." Due to the differences in state laws, the precise definition varies somewhat but for our purposes a mortgage can best be defined as a conditional conveyance of property as security for the debt recited therein, which can only be activated by failure to comply with its terms.

It is the promissory note, the actual promise to pay, which must accompany, or in some cases becomes a part of, the mortgage instrument, that is the real proof of the debt. It calls out the payment terms including the rate of interest. It is the note that defaults for nonpayment, not the mortgage instrument. The expression *mortgage default* is a technical misnomer. When the promissory note falls into default, the mortgage instrument is activated and becomes the means of protecting the lender's collateral.

In 1970, the Federal National Mortgage Association decided to expand its lending activities from exclusively FHA- and VA-underwritten loans into the larger area of conventional loans, that is to say, those loans without government underwriting. In order to provide a more uniform standard of collateral, the FNMA devised a mortgage instrument with a wider application than those previously used. No one form could be used throughout the country because of variations in state laws. To illustrate a few variations, Figure 3-1 shows the new "plain language" note as now required in New York. Figure 3-2 is the standard promissory note used in Texas, and Figure 3-3 illustrates a mortgage instrument designed for Michigan. Standard forms have been developed for every state.

When the Federal Home Loan Mortgage Corporation was established, it joined with FNMA in the development of standardized forms that would be acceptable to both of these organizations, including loan application forms and appraisal forms as well as the notes and mortgage instruments reproduced on the following pages.

Clauses Found in Mortgage Instruments

Identification of *parties* in the initial clause spells out the precise names of all parties involved, the borrower or mortgagor, and the lender or mortgagee. In many states a wife must join her husband to create a binding pledge on real property. As in all such legal instruments, the parties must be legally qualified (of legal age, of sound mind, and so on) to undertake the contract. It is important for the lender to make sure that *all* parties holding an interest in the title to any pledged property are a party to the mortgage pledge.

Identification of the *property* used as security must be accurately

NOTE

US $ .... , New York

City

.... , 19........

1. BORROWER'S PROMISE TO PAY

In return for a loan that I have received, I promise to pay ....
.... Dollars (this amount will be called "principal"),
plus interest, to the order of the Lender. The Lender is ....
.... I understand that the Lender may transfer this Note.
The Lender or anyone who takes this Note by transfer and who is entitled to receive payments under this Note will be
called the "Note holder."

2. INTEREST

I will pay interest at a rate of .... percent per year. Interest will be charged on that part of principal
which has not been paid. Interest will be charged beginning on the date of this Note and continuing until the full
amount of principal has been paid.

3. PAYMENTS

I will pay principal and interest by making payments every month. Each of my monthly payments will be in the
amount of .... Dollars
(US $ ....).

I will make my monthly payments on the .... day of each month beginning on .... ,
19......... . I will make these payments every month until I have paid all of the principal and interest and any other
charges, described below, that I may owe under this Note. If, on .... , I still owe
amounts under this Note, I will pay all those amounts, in full, on that date.

I will make my monthly payments at .... ,
or at a different place if required by the Note holder.

4. BORROWER'S FAILURE TO PAY AS REQUIRED

(A) Late Charge for Overdue Payments

If the Note holder has not received the full amount of any of my monthly payments by the end of ....
calendar days after the date it is due, I will pay a late charge to the Note holder. The amount of the charge will be
.... percent of my overdue payment of principal and interest.

(B) Notice From Note Holder

If I do not pay the full amount of each monthly payment on time, the Note holder may send me a written notice
telling me that if I do not pay the overdue amount by a certain date I will be in default. That date must be at least 30
days after the date on which the notice is mailed to me or, if it is not mailed, 30 days after the date on which it is
delivered to me.

(C) Default

If I do not pay the overdue amount by the date stated in the notice described in (B) above, I will be in default. If
I am in default, the Note holder may require me to pay immediately the full amount of principal which has not been
paid and all the interest that I owe on that amount.

Even if, at a time when I am in default, the Note holder does not require me to pay immediately in full as
described above, the Note holder will still have the right to do so if, at a later time, I am in default again.

(D) Payment of Note Holder's Costs and Expenses

If the Note holder has required me to pay immediately in full as described above, the Note holder will have the
right to be paid back for all of its reasonable costs and expenses. Those expenses include, for example, reasonable
attorney's fees.

5. BORROWER'S PAYMENTS BEFORE THEY ARE DUE

(A) Borrower's Right to Make Prepayments

I have the right to make payments of principal before they are due. Any payment made before it is due is known
as a "prepayment." A prepayment of only part of the unpaid principal is known as a "partial prepayment."

NEW YORK—1 to 4 Family—9/78—FNMA/FHLMC PLAIN LANGUAGE UNIFORM INSTRUMENT

FIGURE 3-1a (Continued)

If I choose to make a partial prepayment, the Note holder may require me to make the prepayment on the same day that one of my monthly payments is due. The Note holder may also require that the amount of my partial prepayment be equal to the amount of principal that would have been part of my next one or more monthly payments. If I make a partial prepayment, there will be no delays in the due dates or changes in the amounts of my monthly payments unless the Note holder agrees in writing to those delays or changes. The Note holder will use all of my prepayments to reduce the amount of principal that I owe under this Note.

(B) Prepayment Charge

I will pay a prepayment charge to the Note holder only if a percentage and a date are filled in below *and if I make the prepayment using money lent to me by a lender other than the Note holder.* [Strike italics if not applicable.]

During any twelve-month period ending on an anniversary of the date of this Note, I may make partial prepayments of up to $... without charge. This amount will be called the "free prepayment amount."

I will pay a prepayment charge if the total of my prepayments during any such twelve-month period is greater than the free prepayment amount. The prepayment charge will be a percentage of the amount by which my prepayments in any such twelve-month period are greater than the free prepayment amount. That percentage will be .... percent until .... ; it will change to .... percent on that date until .... ; and it will change to .... percent on that date until .... After the last date filled in above, there will be no prepayment charge.

6. BORROWER'S WAIVERS

I waive my rights to require the Note holder to do certain things. Those things are: (A) to demand payment of amounts due (known as "presentment"); (B) to give notice that amounts due have not been paid (known as "notice of dishonor"); (C) to obtain an official certification of nonpayment (known as a "protest"). Anyone else (i) who agrees to keep the promises made in this Note, or (ii) who agrees to make payments to the Note holder if I fail to keep my promises under this Note, or (iii) who signs this Note to transfer it to someone else (known as "guarantors, sureties, and endorsers"), also waives these rights.

7. GIVING OF NOTICES

Any notice that must be given to me under this Note will be given by delivering it or by mailing it addressed to me at the Property Address below. A notice will be delivered or mailed to me at a different address if I give the Note holder a notice of my different address.

Any notice that must be given to the Note holder under this Note will be given by mailing it to the Note holder at the address stated in Section 3 above. A notice will be mailed to the Note holder at a different address if I am given a notice of that different address.

8. THIS NOTE COVERED BY A MORTGAGE

A Mortgage, dated .... , protects the Note holder from possible losses which might result if I do not keep the promises which I make in this Note. That Mortgage describes how and under what conditions I may be required to make immediate payment in full of all amounts that I owe under this Note.

9. RESPONSIBILITY OF PERSONS UNDER THIS NOTE

If more than one person signs this Note, each of us is fully and personally obligated to pay the full amount owed and to keep all of the promises made in this Note. Any guarantor, surety, or endorser of this Note (as described in Section 6 above) is also obligated to do these things. The Note holder may enforce its rights under this Note against each of us individually or against all of us together. This means that any one of us may be required to pay all of the amounts owed under this Note.

Any person who takes over my rights or obligations under this Note will have all of my rights and must keep all of my promises made in this Note. Any person who takes over the rights or obligations of a guarantor, surety, or endorser of this Note (as described in Section 6 above) is also obligated to keep all of the promises made in this Note.

....

....
Property Address   *(Sign Original Only)*

FIGURE 3-1b

NOTE

US $ . . . ., Texas

City

. . . ., 19 . . . .

FOR VALUE RECEIVED, the undersigned ("Borrower") promise(s) to pay. . . . .
: . . . ., or order, the principal sum of
. . . . .Dollars, with
interest on the unpaid principal balance from the date of this Note, until paid, at the rate of. . . . .
. . . . .percent per annum. Principal and interest shall be payable at. . . . .
. . . . .in consecutive monthly installments of
. . . . Dollars
(US $ . . . .), on the. . . . . .day of each month beginning
. . . ., 19 . . . . Such monthly installments shall continue until the entire indebtedness
evidenced by this Note is fully paid, except that any remaining indebtedness, if not sooner paid, shall be due and
payable on. . . . .

If any monthly installment under this Note is not paid when due and remains unpaid after a date specified by a notice to Borrower, the entire principal amount outstanding and accrued interest thereon shall at once become due and payable at the option of the Note holder. The date specified shall not be less than thirty days from the date such notice is mailed. The Note holder may exercise this option to accelerate during any default by Borrower regardless of any prior forbearance. If suit is brought to collect this Note, the Note holder shall be entitled to collect all reasonable costs and expenses of suit, including, but not limited to, reasonable attorney's fees.

Borrower shall pay to the Note holder a late charge of. . . . . .percent of any monthly installment not received by the Note holder within. . . . . .days after the installment is due.

Borrower may prepay the principal amount outstanding in whole or in part. The Note holder may require that any partial prepayments (i) be made on the date monthly installments are due and (ii) be in the amount of that part of one or more monthly installments which would be applicable to principal. Any partial prepayment shall be applied against the principal amount outstanding and shall not postpone the due date of any subsequent monthly installments or change the amount of such installments, unless the Note holder shall otherwise agree in writing.

Presentment, notice of dishonor, and protest are hereby waived by all makers, sureties, guarantors and endorsers hereof. This Note shall be the joint and several obligation of all makers, sureties, guarantors and endorsers, and shall be binding upon them and their successors and assigns.

Any notice to Borrower provided for in this Note shall be given by mailing such notice by certified mail addressed to Borrower at the Property Address stated below, or to such other address as Borrower may designate by notice to the Note holder. Any notice to the Note holder shall be given by mailing such notice by certified mail, return receipt requested, to the Note holder at the address stated in the first paragraph of this Note, or at such other address as may have been designated by notice to Borrower.

The indebtedness evidenced by this Note is secured by a Deed of Trust, dated. . . . .
. . . ., and reference is made to the Deed of Trust for rights as to acceleration of the indebtedness evidenced by this Note.

. . . .

. . . .

. . . .

               Property Address   *(Execute Original Only)*

TEXAS —1 to 4 Family—8/79—FNMA/FHLMC UNIFORM INSTRUMENT

FIGURE 3-2

MORTGAGE

THIS MORTGAGE is made this . . . . day of . . . . ,
19 . . . . . between the Mortgagor, ...
. . . . , whose address is . . . .
. . . . (herein "Borrower"), and the Mortgagee, ...
. . . . , a corporation organized and existing
under the laws of . . . . , whose address is . . . .
. . . . (herein "Lender").

WHEREAS, Borrower is indebted to Lender in the principal sum of . . . .
. . . . Dollars, which indebtedness is evidenced by Borrower's note
dated . . . . (herein "Note"), providing for monthly installments of principal and interest,
with the balance of the indebtedness, if not sooner paid, due and payable on . . . .
. . . . ;

To SECURE to Lender (a) the repayment of the indebtedness evidenced by the Note, with interest thereon, the payment of all other sums, with interest thereon, advanced in accordance herewith to protect the security of this Mortgage, and the performance of the covenants and agreements of Borrower herein contained, and (b) the repayment of any future advances, with interest thereon, made to Borrower by Lender pursuant to paragraph 21 hereof (herein "Future Advances"). Borrower does hereby mortgage, grant and convey to Lender, with power of sale, the following described property located in the County of . . . . , State of Michigan:

which has the address of . . . . , ... ,
 [Street]   [City]
. . . . (herein "Property Address");
 [State and Zip Code]

TOGETHER with all the improvements now or hereafter erected on the property, and all easements, rights, appurtenances, rents, royalties, mineral, oil and gas rights and profits, water, water rights, and water stock, and all fixtures now or hereafter attached to the property, all of which, including replacements and additions thereto, shall be deemed to be and remain a part of the property covered by this Mortgage; and all of the foregoing, together with said property (or the leasehold estate if this Mortgage is on a leasehold) are herein referred to as the "Property".

Borrower covenants that Borrower is lawfully seised of the estate hereby conveyed and has the right to mortgage, grant and convey the Property, that the Property is unencumbered, and that Borrower will warrant and defend generally the title to the Property against all claims and demands, subject to any declarations, easements or restrictions listed in a schedule of exceptions to coverage in any title insurance policy insuring Lender's interest in the Property.

MICHIGAN—1 to 4 Family—6 75°—FNMA/FHLMC UNIFORM INSTRUMENT

FIGURE 3-3a (Continued)

UNIFORM COVENANTS. Borrower and Lender covenant and agree as follows:

1. Payment of Principal and Interest. Borrower shall promptly pay when due the principal of and interest on the indebtedness evidenced by the Note, prepayment and late charges as provided in the Note, and the principal of and interest on any Future Advances secured by this Mortgage.

2. Funds for Taxes and Insurance. Subject to applicable law or to a written waiver by Lender, Borrower shall pay to Lender on the day monthly installments of principal and interest are payable under the Note, until the Note is paid in full, a sum (herein "Funds") equal to one-twelfth of the yearly taxes and assessments which may attain priority over this Mortgage, and ground rents on the Property, if any, plus one-twelfth of yearly premium installments for hazard insurance, plus one-twelfth of yearly premium installments for mortgage insurance, if any, all as reasonably estimated initially and from time to time by Lender on the basis of assessments and bills and reasonable estimates thereof.

The Funds shall be held in an institution the deposits or accounts of which are insured or guaranteed by a Federal or state agency (including Lender if Lender is such an institution). Lender shall apply the Funds to pay said taxes, assessments, insurance premiums and ground rents. Lender may not charge for so holding and applying the Funds, analyzing said account, or verifying and compiling said assessments and bills, unless Lender pays Borrower interest on the Funds and applicable law permits Lender to make such a charge. Borrower and Lender may agree in writing at the time of execution of this Mortgage that interest on the Funds shall be paid to Borrower, and unless such agreement is made or applicable law requires such interest to be paid, Lender shall not be required to pay Borrower any interest or earnings on the Funds. Lender shall give to Borrower, without charge, an annual accounting of the Funds showing credits and debits to the Funds and the purpose for which each debit to the Funds was made. The Funds are pledged as additional security for the sums secured by this Mortgage.

If the amount of the Funds held by Lender, together with the future monthly installments of Funds payable prior to the due dates of taxes, assessments, insurance premiums and ground rents, shall exceed the amount required to pay said taxes, assessments, insurance premiums and ground rents as they fall due, such excess shall be, at Borrower's option, either promptly repaid to Borrower or credited to Borrower on monthly installments of Funds. If the amount of the Funds held by Lender shall not be sufficient to pay taxes, assessments, insurance premiums and ground rents as they fall due, Borrower shall pay to Lender any amount necessary to make up the deficiency within 30 days from the date notice is mailed by Lender to Borrower requesting payment thereof.

Upon payment in full of all sums secured by this Mortgage, Lender shall promptly refund to Borrower any Funds held by Lender. If under paragraph 18 hereof the Property is sold or the Property is otherwise acquired by Lender, Lender shall apply, no later than immediately prior to the sale of the Property or its acquisition by Lender, any Funds held by Lender at the time of application as a credit against the sums secured by this Mortgage.

3. Application of Payments. Unless applicable law provides otherwise, all payments received by Lender under the Note and paragraphs 1 and 2 hereof shall be applied by Lender first in payment of amounts payable to Lender by Borrower under paragraph 2 hereof, then to interest payable on the Note, then to the principal of the Note, and then to interest and principal on any Future Advances.

4. Charges; Liens. Borrower shall pay all taxes, assessments and other charges, fines and impositions attributable to the Property which may attain a priority over this Mortgage, and leasehold payments or ground rents, if any, in the manner provided under paragraph 2 hereof or, if not paid in such manner, by Borrower making payment, when due, directly to the payee thereof. Borrower shall promptly furnish to Lender all notices of amounts due under this paragraph, and in the event Borrower shall make payment directly, Borrower shall promptly furnish to Lender receipts evidencing such payments. Borrower shall promptly discharge any lien which has priority over this Mortgage; provided, that Borrower shall not be required to discharge any such lien so long as Borrower shall agree in writing to the payment of the obligation secured by such lien in a manner acceptable to Lender, or shall in good faith contest such lien by, or defend enforcement of such lien in, legal proceedings which operate to prevent the enforcement of the lien or forfeiture of the Property or any part thereof.

5. Hazard Insurance. Borrower shall keep the improvements now existing or hereafter erected on the Property insured against loss by fire, hazards included within the term "extended coverage", and such other hazards as Lender may require and in such amounts and for such periods as Lender may require; provided, that Lender shall not require that the amount of such coverage exceed that amount of coverage required to pay the sums secured by this Mortgage.

The insurance carrier providing the insurance shall be chosen by Borrower subject to approval by Lender; provided, that such approval shall not be unreasonably withheld. All premiums on insurance policies shall be paid in the manner provided under paragraph 2 hereof or, if not paid in such manner, by Borrower making payment, when due, directly to the insurance carrier.

All insurance policies and renewals thereof shall be in form acceptable to Lender and shall include a standard mortgage clause in favor of and in form acceptable to Lender. Lender shall have the right to hold the policies and renewals thereof, and Borrower shall promptly furnish to Lender all renewal notices and all receipts of paid premiums. In the event of loss, Borrower shall give prompt notice to the insurance carrier and Lender. Lender may make proof of loss if not made promptly by Borrower.

Unless Lender and Borrower otherwise agree in writing, insurance proceeds shall be applied to restoration or repair of the Property damaged, provided such restoration or repair is economically feasible and the security of this Mortgage is not thereby impaired. If such restoration or repair is not economically feasible or if the security of this Mortgage would be impaired, the insurance proceeds shall be applied to the sums secured by this Mortgage, with the excess, if any, paid to Borrower. If the Property is abandoned by Borrower, or if Borrower fails to respond to Lender within 30 days from the date notice is mailed by Lender to Borrower that the insurance carrier offers to settle a claim for insurance benefits, Lender is authorized to collect and apply the insurance proceeds at Lender's option either to restoration or repair of the Property or to the sums secured by this Mortgage.

Unless Lender and Borrower otherwise agree in writing, any such application of proceeds to principal shall not extend or postpone the due date of the monthly installments referred to in paragraphs 1 and 2 hereof or change the amount of such installments. If under paragraph 18 hereof the Property is acquired by Lender, all right, title and interest of Borrower in and to any insurance policies and in and to the proceeds thereof resulting from damage to the Property prior to the sale or acquisition shall pass to Lender to the extent of the sums secured by this Mortgage immediately prior to such sale or acquisition.

6. Preservation and Maintenance of Property; Leaseholds; Condominiums; Planned Unit Developments. Borrower shall keep the Property in good repair and shall not commit waste or permit impairment or deterioration of the Property and shall comply with the provisions of any lease if this Mortgage is on a leasehold. If this Mortgage is on a unit in a condominium or a planned unit development, Borrower shall perform all of Borrower's obligations under the declaration or covenants creating or governing the condominium or planned unit development, the by-laws and regulations of the condominium or planned unit development, and constituent documents. If a condominium or planned unit development rider is executed by Borrower and recorded together with this Mortgage, the covenants and agreements of such rider shall be incorporated into and shall amend and supplement the covenants and agreements of this Mortgage as if the rider were a part hereof.

FIGURE 3-3b *(Continued)*

7. Protection of Lender's Security. If Borrower fails to perform the covenants and agreements contained in this Mortgage, or if any action or proceeding is commenced which materially affects Lender's interest in the Property, including, but not limited to, eminent domain, insolvency, code enforcement, or arrangements or proceedings involving a bankrupt or decedent, then Lender at Lender's option, upon notice to Borrower, may make such appearances, disburse such sums and take such action as is necessary to protect Lender's interest, including, but not limited to, disbursement of reasonable attorney's fees and entry upon the Property to make repairs. If Lender required mortgage insurance as a condition of making the loan secured by this Mortgage, Borrower shall pay the premiums required to maintain such insurance in effect until such time as the requirement for such insurance terminates in accordance with Borrower's and Lender's written agreement or applicable law. Borrower shall pay the amount of all mortgage insurance premiums in the manner provided under paragraph 2 hereof.

Any amounts disbursed by Lender, pursuant to this paragraph 7, with interest thereon, shall become additional indebtedness of Borrower secured by this Mortgage. Unless Borrower and Lender agree to other terms of payment, such amounts shall be payable upon notice from Lender to Borrower requesting payment thereof, and shall bear interest from the date of disbursement at the rate payable from time to time on outstanding principal under the Note unless payment of interest at such rate would be contrary to applicable law, in which event such amounts shall bear interest at the highest rate permissible under applicable law. Nothing contained in this paragraph 7 shall require Lender to incur any expense or take any action hereunder.

8. Inspection. Lender may make or cause to be made reasonable entries upon and inspections of the Property, provided that Lender shall give Borrower notice prior to any such inspection specifying reasonable cause therefor related to Lender's interest in the Property.

9. Condemnation. The proceeds of any award or claim for damages, direct or consequential, in connection with any condemnation or other taking of the Property, or part thereof, or for conveyance in lieu of condemnation, are hereby assigned and shall be paid to Lender.

In the event of a total taking of the Property, the proceeds shall be applied to the sums secured by this Mortgage, with the excess, if any, paid to Borrower. In the event of a partial taking of the Property, unless Borrower and Lender otherwise agree in writing, there shall be applied to the sums secured by this Mortgage such proportion of the proceeds as is equal to that proportion which the amount of the sums secured by this Mortgage immediately prior to the date of taking bears to the fair market value of the Property immediately prior to the date of taking, with the balance of the proceeds paid to Borrower.

If the Property is abandoned by Borrower, or if, after notice by Lender to Borrower that the condemnor offers to make an award or settle a claim for damages, Borrower fails to respond to Lender within 30 days after the date such notice is mailed, Lender is authorized to collect and apply the proceeds, at Lender's option, either to restoration or repair of the Property or to the sums secured by this Mortgage.

Unless Lender and Borrower otherwise agree in writing, any such application of proceeds to principal shall not extend or postpone the due date of the monthly installments referred to in paragraphs 1 and 2 hereof or change the amount of such installments.

10. Borrower Not Released. Extension of the time for payment or modification of amortization of the sums secured by this Mortgage granted by Lender to any successor in interest of Borrower shall not operate to release, in any manner, the liability of the original Borrower and Borrower's successors in interest. Lender shall not be required to commence proceedings against such successor or refuse to extend time for payment or otherwise modify amortization of the sums secured by this Mortgage by reason of any demand made by the original Borrower and Borrower's successors in interest.

11. Forbearance by Lender Not a Waiver. Any forbearance by Lender in exercising any right or remedy hereunder, or otherwise afforded by applicable law, shall not be a waiver of or preclude the exercise of any such right or remedy. The procurement of insurance or the payment of taxes or other liens or charges by Lender shall not be a waiver of Lender's right to accelerate the maturity of the indebtedness secured by this Mortgage.

12. Remedies Cumulative. All remedies provided in this Mortgage are distinct and cumulative to any other right or remedy under this Mortgage or afforded by law or equity, and may be exercised concurrently, independently or successively.

13. Successors and Assigns Bound; Joint and Several Liability; Captions. The covenants and agreements herein contained shall bind, and the rights hereunder shall inure to, the respective successors and assigns of Lender and Borrower, subject to the provisions of paragraph 17 hereof. All covenants and agreements of Borrower shall be joint and several. The captions and headings of the paragraphs of this Mortgage are for convenience only and are not to be used to interpret or define the provisions hereof.

14. Notice. Except for any notice required under applicable law to be given in another manner, (a) any notice to Borrower provided for in this Mortgage shall be given by mailing such notice by certified mail addressed to Borrower at the Property Address or at such other address as Borrower may designate by notice to Lender as provided herein, and (b) any notice to Lender shall be given by certified mail, return receipt requested, to Lender's address stated herein or to such other address as Lender may designate by notice to Borrower as provided herein. Any notice provided for in this Mortgage shall be deemed to have been given to Borrower or Lender when given in the manner designated herein.

15. Uniform Mortgage; Governing Law; Severability. This form of mortgage combines uniform covenants for national use and non-uniform covenants with limited variations by jurisdiction to constitute a uniform security instrument covering real property. This Mortgage shall be governed by the law of the jurisdiction in which the Property is located. In the event that any provision or clause of this Mortgage or the Note conflicts with applicable law, such conflict shall not affect other provisions of this Mortgage or the Note which can be given effect without the conflicting provision, and to this end the provisions of the Mortgage and the Note are declared to be severable.

16. Borrower's Copy. Borrower shall be furnished a conformed copy of the Note and of this Mortgage at the time of execution or after recordation hereof.

17. Transfer of the Property; Assumption. If all or any part of the Property or an interest therein is sold or transferred by Borrower without Lender's prior written consent, excluding (a) the creation of a lien or encumbrance subordinate to this Mortgage, (b) the creation of a purchase money security interest for household appliances, (c) a transfer by devise, descent or by operation of law upon the death of a joint tenant or (d) the grant of any leasehold interest of three years or less not containing an option to purchase, Lender may, at Lender's option, declare all the sums secured by this Mortgage to be immediately due and payable. Lender shall have waived such option to accelerate if, prior to the sale or transfer, Lender and the person to whom the Property is to be sold or transferred reach agreement in writing that the credit of such person is satisfactory to Lender and that the interest payable on the sums secured by this Mortgage shall be at such rate as Lender shall request. If Lender has waived the option to accelerate provided in this paragraph 17, and if Borrower's successor in interest has executed a written assumption agreement accepted in writing by Lender, Lender shall release Borrower from all obligations under this Mortgage and the Note.

If Lender exercises such option to accelerate, Lender shall mail Borrower notice of acceleration in accordance with paragraph 14 hereof. Such notice shall provide a period of not less than 30 days from the date the notice is mailed within which Borrower may pay the sums declared due. If Borrower fails to pay such sums prior to the expiration of such period, Lender may, without further notice or demand on Borrower, invoke any remedies permitted by paragraph 18 hereof.

FIGURE 3-3c (*Continued*)

NON-UNIFORM COVENANTS. Borrower and Lender further covenant and agree as follows:

18. Acceleration; Remedies. Except as provided in paragraph 17 hereof, upon Borrower's breach of any covenant or agreement of Borrower in this Mortgage, including the covenants to pay when due any sums secured by this Mortgage, Lender prior to acceleration shall mail notice to Borrower as provided in paragraph 14 hereof specifying: (1) the breach; (2) the action required to cure such breach; (3) a date, not less than 30 days from the date the notice is mailed to Borrower, by which such breach must be cured; and (4) that failure to cure such breach on or before the date specified in the notice may result in acceleration of the sums secured by this Mortgage and sale of the Property. The notice shall further inform Borrower of the right to reinstate after acceleration and the right to bring a court action to assert the non-existence of a default or any other defense of Borrower to acceleration and sale. If the breach is not cured on or before the date specified in the notice, Lender at Lender's option may declare all of the sums secured by this Mortgage to be immediately due and payable without further demand and may invoke the power of sale hereby granted and any other remedies permitted by applicable law. Lender shall be entitled to collect all reasonable costs and expenses incurred in pursuing the remedies provided in this paragraph 18, including, but not limited to, reasonable attorney's fees.

If Lender invokes the power of sale, Lender shall mail a copy of a notice of sale to Borrower in the manner provided in paragraph 14 hereof. Lender shall publish and post the notice of sale and the Property shall be sold in the manner prescribed by applicable law. Lender or Lender's designee may purchase the Property at any sale. The proceeds of the sale shall be applied in the following order: (a) to all reasonable costs and expenses of the sale, including, but not limited to, reasonable attorney's fees; (b) to all sums secured by this Mortgage; and (c) the excess, if any, to the person or persons legally entitled thereto.

19. Borrower's Right to Reinstate. Notwithstanding Lender's acceleration of the sums secured by this Mortgage, Borrower shall have the right to have any proceedings begun by Lender to enforce this Mortgage discontinued at any time prior to the earlier to occur of (i) the fifth day before sale of the Property pursuant to the power of sale contained in this Mortgage or (ii) entry of a judgment enforcing this Mortgage if: (a) Borrower pays Lender all sums which would be then due under this Mortgage, the Note and notes securing Future Advances, if any, had no acceleration occurred; (b) Borrower cures all breaches of any other covenants or agreements of Borrower contained in this Mortgage; (c) Borrower pays all reasonable expenses incurred by Lender in enforcing the covenants and agreements of Borrower contained in this Mortgage and in enforcing Lender's remedies as provided in paragraph 18 hereof, including, but not limited to, reasonable attorney's fees; and (d) Borrower takes such action as Lender may reasonably require to assure that the lien of this Mortgage, Lender's interest in the Property and Borrower's obligation to pay the sums secured by this Mortgage shall continue unimpaired. Upon such payment and cure by Borrower, this Mortgage and the obligations secured hereby shall remain in full force and effect as if no acceleration had occurred.

20. Assignment of Rents; Appointment of Receiver; Lender in Possession. Omitted.

21. Future Advances. Upon request of Borrower, Lender at Lender's option prior to release of this Mortgage, may make Future Advances to Borrower. Such Future Advances, with interest thereon, shall be secured by this Mortgage when evidenced by promissory notes stating that said notes are secured hereby.

22. Release. Upon payment of all sums secured by this Mortgage, Lender shall prepare and file a discharge of this Mortgage without charge to Borrower, and shall pay the fee for recording the discharge.

IN WITNESS WHEREOF, Borrower has executed this Mortgage.

Witnesses:

. . . .
                                                                                                                                          —Borrower

. . . .
                                                                                                                                          —Borrower

STATE OF MICHIGAN, ...County ss:

The foregoing instrument was acknowledged before me this . . . .
                                                                                                                         (date)

by . . . .
                       (person acknowledging)

My Commission expires: . . . .

                    Notary Public, ...County, Michigan

This instrument was prepared by . . . .

──────────────── (Space Below This Line Reserved For Lender and Recorder) ────────────────

FIGURE 3-3d

described so as to distinguish it from any other property in the world (see Chapter 9). A street address is never acceptable, nor are boundary lines based on physical features, such as the "big live oak by the river bend." Accurate legal descriptions are normally used either by "metes and bounds" (a surveyor's description of boundary lines from a fixed starting point, thence proceeding in specific compass directions and distances around the property back to the starting point); or more commonly in urban areas, by lot and block taken from a subdivision plat registered and approved by a local governmental authority. An erroneous description of the property, even a typographical error, can render the mortgage instrument void but does not necessarily invalidate the promissory note.

Principal Amount Due

The mortgage instrument must define the property pledged as security for the initial amount of indebtedness. But the mortgage claim cannot exceed the value of the unpaid balance of the debt. As payments are made on the principal amount of the debt, the value of the mortgage pledge is correspondingly reduced. In this context, the word *estoppel* is sometimes used. Since the mortgage instrument may have a term of 20 or 30 years, and is recorded in the public records only in its original form, the question may arise as to the balance due at an interim point in the mortgage term. While most mortgage loans are repaid on a monthly installment basis and the reduction of principal due after each payment is accurately projected by an amortization table, breaks in the payment pattern can always occur. A greater reduction of principal may be made in any one year, or payments could be delinquent. The balance due becomes important when a mortgage loan is sold between lenders. At such time, an estoppel form may be required. This form is a statement of the balance due as of a specific date, acknowledged by the lender and the borrower, and in effect "stops" the subsequent purchaser of the loan from claiming any greater amount due from the borrower. Modern practice of trading in the secondary market places the responsibility of accurate reporting on the balance due with the seller of the loan, and the estoppel form is becoming obsolete.

Prepayment

A clause contained in many residential mortgages prior to 1972 and found today in most commercial mortgages calls for an additional premium to be paid to the lender if a loan is paid off before maturity. This particular privilege has caused many arguments and misunderstandings. From the lender's viewpoint, he is making a loan of, say, $65,000 for a period of 30 years at 14 percent interest. Under the terms of the promissory note, the borrower agrees to make certain monthly payments, which include both principal and interest. The 360 payments agreed to can amount to as much as $212,000 in interest for the lender over the 30-year period.* The lender can claim a contractual right to this interest, which has obvious value. Why should the lender then be required to forfeit this right to the interest? Earlier mortgages usually provided a compromise to this position by calling for a specific payment against the unearned portion of the interest at the time of early principal payment in order to obtain a release of the mortgage claim. This *prepayment premium*, or conversely, prepayment penalty from the homeowner's viewpoint, varies widely within the industry and may run 1 to 3 percent of the principal amount paid prematurely. A more common provision allows up to 20 percent of the original loan to be paid off in any one year without any premium for the unearned interest, plus 1 percent of any balance in excess of the 20 percent paid in the same year.

Commercial loans are not subject to the numerous limitations that may apply to residential loans. This is particularly true of prepayment penalties which are almost always found in commercial loans. An even more difficult restraint on prepayment is the *lock-in* of an interest charge for a specific number of years. For example, the mortgage note may call for the payment of *all interest* that may be earned for the first five, or ten, years of the term of the loan. So if a property is sold within this time period and refinancing is desirable, payoff of the existing loan may require the payment of a substantial interest penalty. High interest rates encourage lenders to include this kind of clause in an effort to offset any future decline in interest rates.

Conventional residential loans are more apt to contain a prepayment penalty clause, rather than a lock-in. If the uniform documents found in an FNMA/FHLMC conforming type of loan are used, there will be no penalty provision. And neither the FHA nor VA permits a prepayment clause to be applied. Watch for the provision in conventional loan instruments prepared by the lender itself. The reasoning behind the elimination of a penalty provision is that when a prepayment of principal is made, the lender can put the money back to work in a new loan and thus suffers no compensable loss.

Acceleration

One of the essential clauses in a mortgage instrument provides for the payment in full of the balance due; that is, the "acceleration" of each

---

*Monthly payment on a $65,000.00 loan for 30 years at 14 percent interest is $770.25. 770.25 × 360 = 277,290. To repay a $65,000.00 loan, the interest cost is $212,290 over a 30-year term.

monthly payment to the present date in case of a default in the mortgage terms. While there can be other possible reasons for a default in the mortgage terms, such as improper usage of the property or selling of the premises without specific permission of the mortgagee, the most probable cause of default is nonpayment of the debt secured. Without an acceleration clause, it is conceivable that a lender would be forced to foreclose his claim each and every month as the installment payments came due.

The acceleration clause is sometimes referred to as the *call clause*. This is not an accurate description. There are several clauses in a mortgage instrument that recite conditions which, if violated, can cause a default on the agreement and result in the calling of the loan. The acceleration clause simply makes it possible to call for the entire balance due at one time but is not in itself a condition that can cause default.

Right to Sell—Due-on-Sale Clause

As a general rule, mortgaged property can be freely sold by the owner or mortgagor, either with an assumption of the existing debt by the new buyer, or by paying off the balance due on the existing mortgage. In a sale the common assumption is that the original borrower remains liable on the obligation along with the new buyer. Some lenders may grant a release of liability to the original borrower, but they are under no obligation to do so.

When interest remained at lower and more stable rates, lenders were more cooperative in allowing sales and assumptions of their loans. But interest rates moved upward in the late sixties, more lenders eyed the loss of value in their older loans, which had been made at much lower rates. And many began to insert clauses in their mortgage instruments that required specific approval by the lender before the borrower could make any sale of the property that included an assumption of the loan. The price of that approval often proved to be an adjustment of the interest rate upward on the balance of the loan to a percentage rate closer to the then existing market rate. This interest adjustment is sometimes demanded without releasing the original borrower from the obligation.

The reservation of the right to approve a sale by the lender should not be confused with the term *interest escalation*, although this can be the result. More specifically, the escalation of interest can be called for in a promissory note when payments become delinquent or when default occurs. The purpose of increasing the interest in such cases is to help offset the increased costs to the lender in collecting a delinquent account or in undertaking foreclosure proceedings.

Since the late 1970s a number of legal challenges have been made and legislation has been passed that affects the right of a lender to increase the interest rate on an existing loan in the event the property is transferred and the loan assumed. These questions have been lumped under the name of *due-on-sale* clauses. (The FNMA/FHLMC uniform mortgage documents, Covenant 17, identify the item as "Transfer of the Property: Assumption.") The conflict stems from a lender's right, or obligation, to protect the loan collateral through periodic inspections and to make sure that the usage of the property and its occupancy is not detrimental to the property's value. As this right to approve a new occupant; that is, a new buyer, was extended to include the right to increase an interest rate upon the loan being assumed, homeowners found it more difficult to sell their property. And challenges in the court began.

The now famous *Wellenkamp v. Bank of America** case in California state courts denied the lender's right to increase an interest rate upon assumption without a variable interest rate agreement. An earlier case in California, *Tucker v. Lassen Savings and Loan*,** determined that the lenders position was not altered by the sale of the collateral property under a contract for deed (land contract) since the title remained in the name of the seller who was still liable under the loan agreement.

By 1982, the question had become further confused with about one-third of the states prohibiting or severely restricting through legislation or court decisions the right of a lender to change an interest rate upon the assumption of a residential loan. Added to this, federal regulators (in this case both the Federal Home Loan Bank Board and the Comptroller of the Currency) reiterated their long-held position that federally-chartered institutions are not subject to state laws that restrict their lending authority. Thus, federal charters could adjust interest rates when loans were assumed if the mortgage agreement provided for such an adjustment. Then, the United States Supreme Court agreed to hear the challenge of a homeowner to the lender's right to alter an interest rate in a fixed rate mortgage agreement. In its decision, handed down on June 28, 1982, the Supreme Court ruled that a federally-chartered institution *does* have the right to adjust an interest rate upon assumption, regardless of state law, provided the right to adjust is clearly stated in the mortgage agreement. Whether or not state legislatures and state courts will apply the federal rules to their state-chartered institutions is a matter that will only be determined over a longer period of time.

Insurance

Mortgages require property insurance coverage for the lender's protection. This is also termed *hazard insurance*. Principally, it includes fire

---

*August 25, 1978, 582 P. 2d 970.
** October 10, 1974, 34 Cal 3rd, 579.

and extended coverage and is required by the lender where any buildings are involved in an amount at least equal to that of the loan. To make certain that insurance payments are made, the lender generally requires a full year's paid-up insurance policy before releasing the loan proceeds, plus two months of the annual premium paid into an escrow account. Then with each monthly payment, one-twelfth of the annual premium must be paid. The original policy is held by the lender, and it is part of the lender's responsibility to maintain the coverage with timely payments made from the borrower's escrow account.

Insurance companies in most states have another requirement controlling the minimum amount of coverage that can be carried to establish full coverage in case of a loss. Since most fire losses are partial in extent, it is not unusual for a property owner to carry only partial insurance hoping that any fire would be brought under control before the damage exceeds the amount of insurance coverage. To distribute the cost of insurance more equitably over all policyholders, many insurance companies require that the insured maintain insurance of not less than a given percentage of the actual cash value of the building at the time of the loss. These clauses are known variously as *coinsurance clauses*, *average clauses*, or *reduced rate contribution clauses*. A common minimum amount of insurance to provide full coverage is 80 percent of the actual cash value of the building at the time of the loss. By carrying less than the agreed percentage of insurance, the property owner cannot collect in full for a loss but will have to bear a part of the loss personally. The insurance company will be liable only for such percentage of the loss as the amount of insurance carried bears to 80 percent of the actual cash value of the property at the time of the loss. The insurance company's liability may be expressed by the formula:

$$\frac{C}{R} \times L = A$$

Where   C = the amount of insurance carried
                    R = the amount of insurance required
                    L = the amount of the loss
                    A = the amount for which the insurance
                           company is liable

In periods of rapidly rising property values, any failure to maintain proper insurance coverage can expose the lender as well as the property owner to uninsured losses.

Another insurance problem to be considered in a mortgage involves determining just how the proceeds should be paid in case of an actual loss. Earlier mortgages required payment of the insurance money to the lender, who in turn decided how to apply the funds; that is, whether to permit the funds to be used for restoration of the property, which is the usual procedure on smaller losses, or to apply the insurance proceeds to the payoff of the loan. As time has passed, recent mortgages have given the borrower a stronger position in the distribution of insurance proceeds, as is apparent in the FNMA/FHLMC standard conventional mortgage covenants.

Taxes

Lenders long ago learned that the real first lien on any property is in the hands of the property taxing authority; that is, the agency that levies the *ad valorem* property taxes. It can be categorically stated that the full documented and properly recorded "first" mortgage instrument securing the lender's position takes only a poor second place to a tax levy. And in some states, this tax levy includes an assessment by a properly authorized neighborhood maintenance association!

It is evident then that the timely payment of property taxes becomes another essential requirement in mortgage loans. Lenders usually require that a cushion in an amount equal to two months of the annual taxes be paid into an escrow account by the borrower before the loan is funded. One-twelfth of the annual taxes is also added to each monthly payment of principal and interest. In this manner, the lender accumulates sufficient cash each year to pay the borrower's property taxes directly to the tax authorities and thus is protected against any tax priority lien on the pledged property.

In regard to federal taxes, these take priority over state laws regarding property and do carry lien rights and highest priority. However, federal taxes, including federal income taxes, become property liens only when they are filed as a delinquent assessment against an individual or corporation, not when the tax liability is incurred. A federal tax lien is a general lien and may apply to any and all property owned by the taxpayer. The *ad valorem*, or property tax, is a specific lien (applying only to the designated property liable for the tax) and becomes a lien against the property from the minute the taxing authorities levy the assessment.

Foreclosure

The right of the lender to foreclose on a property is limited by the terms of the mortgage instrument and by the applicable state laws. In general, foreclosure is the last recourse of the lender, often a costly procedure and usually an open admission that an error in judgment was made in making the loan. Lenders will normally put forth considerable effort to cooperate with a borrower who has unforeseen financial problems and needs some relief. But the lender must depend on the borrower to seek the relief, and this is more easily arranged before a serious delinquency occurs. Lenders have an obligation to their own investors, depositors, insurance policyholders, trust funds, and so on to exercise control over their borrowers' accounts and not allow a property mortgage note to slide into default so that such laxity would compromise the lender's security. When failure to comply with the terms of the note and mortgage occurs on the part of the borrower, generally due to nonpayment of the obligation, then the lender must seek foreclosure of the property.

The real purpose of a foreclosure is to sell the property under the authority of a court order, usually referred to as a *sheriff's sale*, and to distribute the proceeds to the various creditors holding claims on the property. Contrary to popular belief, in a foreclosure proceeding, the lender has no more right to take title to the property than anyone else.

Accordingly, the court orders a property to be sold in a foreclosure proceeding, and whoever offers the highest cash price at the subsequent public sale acquires a deed to the property by court order, in some places referred to as a *sheriff's deed*. In practice, the lender is allowed to submit a claim; that is, the balance due on the promissory note, as part or all of the cash offer for the property. In many states, the lender need not even offer the full amount of the claim if it is deemed too high.

In a foreclosure action, the proceeds realized from the sale of collateral are distributed to claimants in the order of an established priority. The handling of a foreclosure is unlike that of a bankruptcy. In a bankruptcy, the referee attempts to distribute the debtor's assets in an equitable manner between the secured claimants and the unsecured claimants. In a foreclosure procedure, the amount realized from the sale is used, first, to pay all administrative costs; second, to pay all property taxes in full; and then to pay each claimant what is due in order of lien priority. It is quite possible that the sale will result in insufficient funds to pay off even the first lien holder.

Because the lender has a claim against the property and can use that as payment in a foreclosure sale, the lender or an agent for the lender usually ends up taking title to the foreclosed property. If the claim against the borrower is not fully satisfied from the proceeds of the sale, then the lender can seek a deficiency judgment for the balance due. Some states do not permit deficiency judgments to be taken against homeowners.

The above considerations strongly suggest that the foreclosure is apt to be a difficult, distasteful, and discouraging procedure. The lender is faced with the costs of litigation, with the possibility of an unpleasant eviction, plus the risk of property damage through owner abuse or vandalism. In addition, the lender may have to pay the costs of renovating and maintaining the property plus payment of delinquent taxes and insurance. Foreclosure is seldom a satisfactory solution.

For the real estate agent, foreclosure is not a subject of likely in-volvement. It is a legal matter handled only by qualified attorneys. How prevalent is foreclosure? The desire to own and protect one's home is a very strong emotion, and the excellent record of mortgage loan repay-ment underlines this attitude. Over the years, about one-half of 1 per-cent of residential loans become involved with foreclosure. In the most difficult economic periods, such as 1982, loan delinquencies (over 30 days past due) ran about .055 percent of all outstanding residential loans.

Types of Mortgages

The most common forms of mortgage instruments have some important variations, namely, in how and when they are used. The underlying purpose of providing a pledge of property as security for a loan remains the same, however. Some of the principal variations are treated in the following discussion.

Deed of Trust

The *deed of trust* introduces a third party, a trustee, into the pledging instrument. Under these terms, the borrower actually makes an assign-ment (the wording is very similar to a warranty deed) of the property to the trustee but restricts the effectiveness of the assignment to when a default occurs under the mortgage terms. The trustee is normally select-ed by the lender with the right of substitution in case of death or dis-missal.

The deed of trust form is used in many areas and is almost univer-sally used in Texas as a means of simplifying "homestead" law proce-dures. It substantially reduces the problems of foreclosure, limiting the process to an action by the trustee, with proper notice and in accor-dance with prevailing laws, rather than by litigation conducted in a court hearing.

Open-end Mortgages

The open-end mortgage permits a lender to advance additional money under the same security and priority as the original mortgage. This type of mortgage is often employed in farm loans where the lender maintains continuing relations with his customer-borrower. As the borrower pays the mortgage principal down, he or she may wish to add a new barn or perhaps a new loading corral to the property. The additional loan can easily be accommodated under the terms of an open-end mortgage.

In some areas a borrower may elect to leave a minimal mortgage balance of, say, one dollar outstanding on the mortgage loan. This record of balance due, no matter how small, sustains the life of the mortgage instrument and, most significantly, its priority over any other subsequent lien except, of course, property taxes. This provision gives rural banks a means of making loans to their farm- or ranch-owning customers without the expense and delay of researching a title and recording a new mortgage instrument with each loan.

Construction Mortgages

A loan to build a house or other building is a *construction loan*, sometimes called *interim* financing. The security requirement is the same—a first lien on real property—but in this type of loan, proceeds are disbursed as the building is constructed. Under the construction mortgage, the borrower or builder draws a portion of the total loan at various stages or at set time intervals, such as monthly, for work completed. It takes a construction-wise lender to make sure his disbursement of funds does not exceed the value of a building at each stage of construction.

A construction loan is considered a high-risk loan. It carries high interest rates and is seldom intended to extend beyond three years. Commercial projects, such as a warehouse or apartment, usually require assurance of permanent financing or a *takeout commitment*; that is, an agreement by a reputable lender to make a permanent loan upon completion of the project.

Homebuilders frequently build for speculative sales, in which case the construction lender must look to the actual sale of the house to pay off the construction loan. This increases the risk for the lender who may require the builder to obtain a standby commitment for a permanent loan before commencing construction. For additional information, see "Construction Loans," Chapter 14.

Mortgages with Release Clauses

When money is borrowed for the purpose of land development, it is necessary to have specific release procedures to enable the developer to sell lots, or a portion of the land, and deliver good title to that portion. This is the purpose of a release clause. The conditions are stated so that the developer can repay a portion of the loan and obtain a release of a portion of the land from the original mortgage. In a subdivision of building lots, the developer would be required to pay a percentage of the sales price of the lot or a minimum dollar amount against the loan for each lot released. The lender would calculate the payoff so that the loan would be fully repaid when somewhere around 60 to 80 percent of the lots were sold.

Under regular mortgages, there is no provision to allow a partial sale of the property. So a development loan requires considerable negotiation to work out all the details necessary for success. The lender will want some control over the direction of the development; that is, lots must be developed and sold in an orderly manner that will not undermine the value of any remaining land. A time pattern must be negotiated to allow realistic limits on how fast the lots must be sold. The clause that permits the release of a portion of the mortgaged land is also called a *partial release* since the remainder of the land continues to be held as security for the loan.

Junior Mortgages

The term *junior mortgages* applies to those mortgages that carry a lower priority than the prime or first mortgage. These are *second* and even *third* mortgages.

The mortgage instrument carries no designation in its text describing its lien position. The order of priority, which determines the exact order of claims against a piece of property, is established by the time of the recording of that instrument. This becomes of extreme importance in a foreclosure proceeding. For example, if a property considered to be worth $50,000 carries a first mortgage for $30,000, and a second mortgage for $8,000, and that property is forced into a foreclosure sale that results in a recovery of $35,000 in cash after payment of legal fees—how, then, should the money be distributed? The priority of the liens exercises control, and assuming that no other liens, taxes, or otherwise, have shown priority, then the first mortgage holder is in a position to recover his full $30,000 from the $35,000 proceeds, and the remaining $5,000 is awarded to the second mortgage holder, leaving him $3,000 short of recovering his $8,000 loan. Due to the promissory note, the second mortgage holder may have a right to seek a deficiency judgment against the borrower to recover that $3,000. However, it becomes evident that the security of the land has been wiped out in the foreclosure sale and resulting settlement.

Later in this text, the subjects of recording and of title protection, as related to the question of establishing the priority of mortgage liens, will be discussed in more detail.

Purchase Money Mortgages

Primarily, a *purchase money mortgage* is a mortgage taken by the seller of a property as a part of the consideration. The designation is also used in some states with homestead laws to distinguish it from any other form of mortgage that would not carry the same lien rights. In this mortgage form, the proceeds of a loan are used to acquire the property.

Chattel Mortgages

Although we have been discussing mortgages primarily in terms of real property as security, the term *mortgage* can also be used to describe a pledge of personal property such as furniture or a car. This personal property can be referred to as *chattel*. Chattel, then, may be defined as a movable object—any property, exclusive of land or objects permanently attached to the land. With a chattel mortgage, the pledge of personal property as security for a loan can be similar to that for real property. It is the movable quality of the collateral and the difficulty of properly identifying an object such as a table or a washing machine that make the pledge a less secure procedure than it is in regard to real property.

Nevertheless, the form is widely used in small loan companies and for installment financing. Some states, it should be noted in this connection, use a conditional sales contract procedure for installment purchases that does not legally pass title to the chattel until it is fully paid for, thus eliminating the need for a mortgage pledge.

Package Mortgages

The *package mortgage* occurs in a hybrid form and attempts to include in the mortgage indenture both real property and personal property. It is used in residential loans when considerable built-in equipment is included with the house. Such a mortgage would list various household appliances, such as an oven, a range, a dishwasher, or disposal equipment, that might be considered attached to and a part of the real property, but that can be removed rather easily. By adding these various items to the mortgage as security, the lender may better protect his complete property loan. Although the procedure is often ignored or not enforced, it is definitely a violation of the mortgage terms to sell or dispose of a mortgaged range or dishwasher without the express consent of the mortgagee.

Blanket Mortgages

A mortgage is not limited to pledging a single parcel of land. Sometimes the security pledged for a loan may include several tracts of land. When more than one tract of land is pledged in the mortgage instrument, it is called a *blanket mortgage*.

Contract for Deed

In listing types of mortgages, a *contract for deed* would be considered out of place, except for the fact that many people believe this instrument to be similar to a mortgage procedure. It is not.

In essence a contract for deed is another method of selling real estate. It is exactly what its name implies, a contract for a deed, and no more. It is used to sell real property on an installment payment basis without delivering title to the property until payment has been made. Properly drawn, a contract for deed is enforceable against either signatory party, as is any contract under the state's codes providing for contracts. However, it is not a deed to real property and grants to the buyer only the rights of possession and enjoyment; and these rights exist only as long as the grantor holds control of the land. Some states, such as Ohio, provide for recording contracts for deed. Under these circumstances, the buyer acquires rights to the property being purchased that must be recognized by any subsequent claimant. The buyer holds what is called an *equitable title* to the property under contract. This means that there is a right to eventually accede to legal title when the contract terms are met.

If fully understood by both parties, the contract for deed can be helpful in transferring property usage when a buyer has temporary credit problems or the seller does not yet hold a fully marketable title. However, this form of contract has gained a poor reputation through abuses, failure to fully disclose the facts, and outright frauds. The real pitfall lies in the possible inability of the seller to deliver a valid title after full payment has been made. During the installment paying period, anything that might happen to the seller, such as a damage claim resulting in a heavy adverse judgment, a divorce causing property settlements, dissolution of a corporate seller through bankruptcy, or any lien filed against the property under contract, can defeat the intent of the contract and can cause the seller to be unable to deliver a good title. If the seller cannot produce a good title to the property at completion of payment, the buyer may have a claim for damages against the seller, but may have no direct claim to the property involved.

Contract for deed sales are most commonly used in the sale of resort-type lots and also in smaller rent houses where a tenant becomes a buyer if he completes the payments. In the latter case, the property owner may wish to give a tenant the right to buy the house, but because of some prior credit problems or inability of the buyer to meet the job tenure requirements of a mortgage lender, the owner does not want his land encumbered by the tenant-buyer if a default occurs.

In regard to the resort-type lot sales, there have been flagrant abuses in the past. In 1969, the Department of Housing and Urban Development established the Office of Interstate Land Sales Registration as a policing agency for developers of property containing more than 50 lots in any one development and less than five acres per lot. The thrust of the legislation is not to establish sales patterns or minimum lot requirements but to make sure the developer fully discloses the development plans and the legal status of the land title itself. And the buyer must acknowledge the receipt of all the information required, which also has the effect of protecting the developer against unwarranted claims from the buyer.

The terminology used to identify a contract for deed varies somewhat in different regions of the country and, in some cases, can be misleading. The most commonly used alternative names are *land contract* and *contract of sale*. Other terminology includes installment land contract; installment sales contract; agreement to convey; conditional land sales contract; and one that is even less descriptive—real estate contract. Whatever the name, the essence of the agreement is that the legal title to the property remains with the seller.

Mortgage Procedures

Again, the practices and procedures by which mortgage rights are established and protected vary among the states, but certain elements are common to all. In the following discussion, the common procedures and reasons for them will be considered.

Recording

Of all the statutes written regarding ownership of land, the incentives to record a transaction have had the greatest long-range effect on improving records of landownership. In fairly recent times and due to the lack of controlling legislation, courts have held that a valid title to land was actually passed by such procedures as a handwritten entry in the family Bible. How can a mortgage lender determine who really owns a piece of land? The answer lies in the recorded instruments of land transactions filed in the county records wherein the land is located. As the laws have made the recording of land transactions a necessary procedure and as our methods of handling this documentation have improved, the actual determination of proper title is becoming more and more accurate.

What is *recording*? In legal terms it is a form of notice—notice to the world—that a transaction of some kind has affected the title to a specific piece of land. Another form of legal notice is actual possession of the land, and historically, possession is the highest form of notice. The procedure for recording a transaction is to take the document to the record office of the county where the land is located and pay the fee for filing. The county officer responsible for the recording copies the instrument in its entirety for the record book and certifies on the original as to the time, date, volume, and page or pages that contain the record.

Most state laws that relate to instruments affecting land titles and the recording of them do not challenge the contractual rights of any parties to buy, sell, or encumber a piece of land. What they actually do is to declare anyland transaction invalid against a third party *only in regard to the title to land if it is not recorded*. For example, *A* can agree to sell ten acres of land to *B* and actually deliver a deed for the ten acres to *B*. The contract may be valid and the consideration (payment for the land) accepted, but actual title to the land is not secure until the deed has been recorded. If the seller *A*, in this example, should suffer a heavy casualty loss and be subjected to a court judgment against him before the deed to buyer *B* has been recorded, the ten acres of land would be subject to the claim of *A*'s new creditors since the title would still be in *A*'s name on the public record.

It is important to emphasize that the failure to record an instrument affecting land title does not invalidate the instrument insofar as the parties involved in the transaction are concerned. It places the burden on whichever party is asserting a claim to the land to give notice of his or her claim in the public records or lose the effectiveness of that claim against any other claimant. The rules apply to all instruments applicable to land titles, conveyances, claims, or debts against the land itself or against the landowner, and, of course, all mortgage instruments. Contracts for deed and leases are instruments affecting land title and can be recorded, but for various reasons of privacy or other interests often are not recorded.

State laws are usually lenient as to what instruments can be recorded, but most require that the signature to the instrument be acknowledged before a duly authorized officer of the state, such as a Notary Public, or be properly witnessed. Because any instrument affecting a title to land is a legal matter that can involve many state laws, it is customary, though not always required, that such an instrument be prepared by a licensed attorney. The preparation of any instrument conveying a land title is considered the practice of law in most states and, therefore, is restricted to that state's licensed attorneys. Few, if any, lenders would permit a loan to be made based on a mortgage instrument prepared by anyone other than a qualified attorney regardless of the requirements for recording.

Mortgage Priorities

The expression *first mortgage* or *second mortgage* is so commonly used that it is not unusual for a person to expect to find such an identification spelled out in the mortgage instrument. Such is not the case. The priority by which a mortgage or any other claim to land is established is by the time of recording. And this is determined not only by the day of recording, but by the time of that particular day.

In handling a mortgage instrument, the lender is most concerned about the proper priority of his security claim; that is, what prior claims, if any, could jeopardize the lender's claim to the land. Most lenders do not rely on the record alone but require an insuring agent to guarantee the priority of the claim backed by an insurance policy, called a *title policy*.

The statutory priorities given workmen and material suppliers in most states may be a source of additional problems for construction loan mortgages. For example, in a mortgage to secure construction money, any work permitted on the land prior to the recording means that a workman may have a claim on the land itself in case of nonpayment. Such a claim held by a workman or contractor need not be recorded to establish its priority, but there must be some positive proof that the work was accomplished before the mortgage was recorded. One method of establishing priority for the lender is to photograph the raw land, have the date of the picture certified, and retain the print as proof that the land was untouched prior to recording the mortgage.

Any claim to land that is of lower priority; that is, recorded or incurred at a later date, is said to be junior to the prior claim. Thus, as noted earlier, second and third mortgages are sometimes referred to as junior mortgages.

Subordination

Another method of establishing priorities for mortgage instruments is by contract. For various reasons it may be beneficial to the parties involved in a land transaction to establish a claim of lower value or lesser importance to another, a procedure called *subordination*.

An example might be a hypothetical case where a piece of land is sold to a developer who plans to erect an office building for lease to one of his customers. The seller of the land, for taxes or other reasons, prefers to take his payment in ten annual installments. But the developer needs to mortgage the land immediately with first priority for payment going to the mortgage lender for construction money to build the office building. In such a case, and assuming credit-worthiness of the developer, the land seller would agree specifically to subordinate the landownership claim to the lender's mortgage, securing the ten annual payments with a second mortgage.

Assumption

In periods of tight money and escalating interest costs, more homes are sold with assumption of existing loans plus seller-assisted secondary financing. The rights of a seller to offer his or her house with an assumption of the existing loan vary considerably and depend on the conditions agreed to in the mortgage instrument. As noted earlier in the discussion of the due-on-sale clause, federally-chartered lenders do have the right to increase interest rates on a loan assumption if the mortgage agreement clearly provides for such an adjustment. State-chartered institutions follow state laws, and these vary considerably on this matter.

What homeowners have successfully contended in some states is that an increase in the interest rate on a fixed interest loan creates an unreasonable restraint on the right of the owner to sell the property. In legal terminology, this restraint on a sale is called a *restraint on alienation*. Thus, a right-to-sell clause in a mortgage is sometimes referred to as the *alienation clause*. Most states prohibit any *unreasonable* restraint on alienation—a limitation that has been mostly concerned with discriminatory practices. For example, a restrictive covenant in a property deed that forbids any future sale to a female would most likely be classed as an unreasonable restraint on the owner's right to sell. The question of whether or not a lender's right to increase an interest rate with the power to otherwise deny the right to sell constitutes an unreasonable restraint is going through state courts for determination.

Another legal distinction that should be noted is the difference between selling a property with an *assumption* of an existing loan and selling *subject to* an existing loan. When a buyer assumes an existing loan, he or she becomes liable for all obligations, including payment, to the lender. This is not true of a sale made subject to an existing loan. When a transaction uses the terminology "subject to" an existing loan, then the buyer acknowledges the existence of a loan but accepts no obligation for its repayment.

Limitation Statutes

In the codes of law established by the various states, *time limitations* have been established on the validity of most claims or debts. These limitations may vary somewhat, but usually place time limits within which a creditor can file a claim for an open account, such as one to two years, and usually a longer limit within which a written promissory note can be recovered, perhaps five to ten years. Time limits for secured debts may be extended for even longer periods.

There are also limiting statutes imposed for general contractors and subcontractors filing claims for unpaid work and materials on construction projects. Failure to file a claim, usually in the form of a lien recorded in the county records, within the prescribed time limits, would make that claim invalid insofar as the land itself is concerned. It does not void the debt, however.

There are also time limitations in most states affecting title to real property. These have been established in an effort to clarify claims to ownership of land. The time limitations vary with what is called the "color of title" that can be asserted to the land claimed. Two factors are essential in establishing a valid claim to land over a period of time within the statutes of limitation: (1) actual possession and use of the land, and (2) possession and use considered adverse or use without the express consent of the opposing claimant.

An example of a short time limitation might be cited here. Let's assume, for instance, that a buyer purchases a house from the heirs of a family who previously owned the property. All the known heirs have agreed to the sale of the property and have joined in signing the deed; the purchaser has duly paid the full price agreed to. Then several years later someone claiming to be an heir comes forward to assert his interest in the house that was sold. Because a deed was delivered in good faith and the consideration was paid, the new claimant might be limited to three years within which his claim would be considered by the courts.

The longest time limits are usually granted in any transaction involving minor children or mentally incapacitated persons. Most states draw a line at 20 to 25 years and simply rule that possession of land for that period precludes anyone else asserting a claim against it.

The result of these limiting statutes is an effective scrubbing of the records after the prescribed number of years. Title insurance policies lapse after the maximum years within which claims can be filed. Many property owners are careful to establish their own property lines with special markers and to assert their own usage and ownership of land by restricting access to private roadways, and so forth, for perhaps one day a year, so as to prevent or offset the workings of time limitation statutes.

Land Titles

Ownership of land is a right. It is not a deed, it is not a title insurance policy, it is not living on the land. All of these characteristics are important evidences of ownership, but the right itself is broader and covers four definable areas:

1. *Possession* The right to occupy the land.
2. *Use* The right to work the land, which includes what may be grown, what minerals may be recovered.
3. *Enjoyment* The use and occupancy of the land free of harassment or interference.
4. *Disposition* The right to sell, lease, or otherwise dispose of the land.

In today's complex living patterns, the free and unfettered ownership of land that once existed in earlier rural areas is difficult to find.
Possession is about the only element of ownership that remains clearly
distinguishable, and even that has become more difficult to determine.

The usage of land is complicated by leases on mineral rights (oil,
gas, coal, and so on) and by restrictions set up by some state governments forbidding the use of water except by separate grants of water
rights, as well as by federal restrictions as to what can or cannot be
grown on the land. The enjoyment of the land is also subject to many
restrictions in urban areas, particularly in the form of zoning laws,
health and safety restrictions, and possible conflicts in neighborhood associations.

The rights to dispose of land are complicated by the practice of
bequeathing life estates, say, to a widow upon the death of a husband;
or by the assignment of property by will to a charitable foundation or
educational institution; or by a gift of land to a community for a specific use such as a park, with the land reverting back to the estate of the
former owner should his wishes be violated.

With all the complications in landownership, it becomes necessary
to find a way to establish where and in whose hands ownership and
control of the land actually lie. In order for a mortgage instrument to be
valid and to provide security for a loan, it is necessary that sufficient
rights to the land be pledged and that the pledge be made by the person
or persons holding the rights to do so. Loans are made against various
portions of real property ownership, such as oil production loans on oil
leases, development loans on mining claims, and crop loans on surface
and water rights. It rarely happens today that much more than a portion of the ownership rights is pledged, but that portion must include
the essential rights that would enable a lender to use the property as a
last resort in recovering the balance of his loan.

The area under study in this text is land development and the
buildings occupying the land, which would mean the ownership rights
to at least the surface, the access rights thereto, and protection against
infringement by any other user of rights to that land. The researching
of these rights of ownership to land is the special province of land title
companies, which are basically insurance companies. Title companies
sell insurance policies that guarantee to the purchaser a good title to a
certain piece of property. The guarantee is in the form of a promise to
protect the land title against any adverse claim or to pay the holder of
the policy the face amount (purchase price of the property) in cash,
should the title fail for any reason. At the time the initial owner's policy is issued, a second policy covering the same property may be purchased that makes a similar pledge of title protection to the lender or
mortgagee. The mortgagee's policy runs with the mortgage, that is, the

insurance is in the amount of the balance due on the mortgage note, automatically covers any subsequent holder of the note, and is in effect until the note is paid off. The owner's policy has different terms—it insures the owner for the face amount of the policy for a specified number of years, usually the statutory limit of the owner's possible responsibility for the title. The owner's policy continues to protect the owner even after the property has been sold because he or she still carries a responsibility to defend the title that may be passed on under a general warranty deed. The fact that a title policy may exist on a piece of property provides no protection at all for a new purchaser. The new purchaser can only be protected, title insurance-wise, with a new policy issued in his or her name.

A second method of obtaining title information and of determining the validity of a mortgage pledge is to employ an attorney to research the title. In this procedure, the attorney will order an abstract from an abstract or title company. The abstract is a certified collection of all instruments that have been recorded and, therefore, have affected the chain of title since the inception of that title. The inception of the title could be a land grant by a foreign monarch who once claimed the land, or more commonly by a state granting title to a purchaser, or it could be by quit claim deed from the federal government. From its original grant, the land may have been broken into many segments and passed through many hands, and the abstracts can be quite voluminous. The result of the research is an attorney's opinion on the title stating any adverse claims to the land that are exceptions to the title. The opinion will then identify those title problems that must be corrected, or "cured," before a mortgage can be made securely.

In certain areas of the country another method is employed to handle property titles, a method flowing from the Torrens Act procedure. This is a process whereby a state has adopted a program for recording title, mostly for urban property lots, by registering property title in the public record established for that purpose. The procedure is very similar to that used in registering the ownership of a car. Any sale of the property must be registered, and a new certificate of title is then issued by the state. The plan has some inherent advantages in minimizing legal expenses and title costs in the sale of property, but because of the complex nature of land ownership, this plan has not become too widespread in usage.

Accepting the fact that land titles in today's urban society are seldom completely clear, the mortgage lender has learned to live with certain kinds of exceptions. For instance, title insurance companies have standard clauses of exceptions that they customarily make in any insurance policy they issue. One of these exceptions has to do with the rights of anyone then in possession of the property. The title company does not physically inspect the property, leaving that to the buyers.

Since the seller is usually in possession of the property when it is sold, his rights are clearly determined when he signs a warranty deed granting title to the buyer. If a tenant is in possession, it is necessary to establish his rights before a sale is consummated.

Another standard exception made by the title company is in the zoning requirements or sometimes in regard to deed restrictions. The title company is not insuring any specific usage of the property; it is only making certain that the ownership rights of possession and disposition are clearly assignable.

The title-insuring policy will usually list any easements crossing the property, which are generally utility easements and street rights-of-way. The easements are exceptions to the insurance policy and are simply claims to the land, which are accepted as normal and necessary.

Often the title company will list certain requirements in the initial title opinion that involve a question of encroachments on the property lines, or perhaps a dispute among heirs, or a problem arising from a divorce settlement that is undecided. The requirements must be resolved to the satisfaction of the title company, or the insurance policy can be refused, or it can be issued with the unsatisfied requirement listed as an exception to the coverage.

What these questions involving title problems lead to is not always a completely clear title, but what is called a *merchantable* or *marketable* title. There can be exceptions or unsatisfied requirements, which, at the discretion of the mortgage lender, may be so unimportant or insignificant to the total property value that they can be ignored. The ultimate question is whether or not a knowledgeable buyer would be willing to accept the minor title defects in a subsequent sale should foreclosure become necessary.

In some states, such as Ohio, title companies offer a choice of assurances regarding the land title. A purchaser may require proof of title in the form of a *title guarantee* which is essentially a certification of the information on the subject property as recorded in the county office. The recorded description of the property is accepted, and a survey may not be required. If the purchaser requires that the title company also insure the title for a monetary value, an additional charge is made for such a coverage.

Questions for Discussion

1. What procedure is used in your state to handle a pledge of security for a mortgage loan?

2. What is the purpose of a promissory note? Of a mortgage instrument?

3. Distinguish between an *acceleration* clause and an *escalation* clause in a mortgage.

4. What is the underlying purpose of requiring a borrower to escrow money each month for the annual payment of property taxes?

5. List the costs to a lender that could be involved in a foreclosure action.

6. Describe what is meant by an *open-end* mortgage.

7. What is the principal risk for the buyer-borrower in a contract for deed?

8. Identify the two principal methods by which a lender can be assured that the mortgage pledge is made by the person or persons who have the legal rights to do so.

9. Why is an accurate property description important?

10. Discuss the rights of a lender and a homeowner in the matter of adjusting an interest rate when a loan is assumed.

Alternative Mortgage Instruments

For the past half century there has been one dominant mortgage design used in this country: the fixed interest rate, constant-level payment, fully amortized plan. This orderly system began to change in the mid-1970s when lenders and regulators became concerned for the future of mortgage lending and one of its principal purposes: the acquisition of houses. Rising housing costs and increasing interest rates could overwhelm the market. Two major problems were involved: first, lenders with fluctuating and rising costs of money needed a method to match their income more closely to their cost of funds; second, home buyers needed a method to enter the housing market at a lower initial cost than was permitted with the high-interest constant-payment mortgage.

To assist the lender, regulators approved a series of mortgage repayment plans that allows the lender to make periodic adjustments in the rate of interest charged for a long-term loan. These interest adjustment plans, generally known as *adjustable rate mortgages*, have proliferated. There are well over 250 different plans now in use throughout the country.

To assist the home buyer, another series of mortgage repayment plans has been developed which are known as *graduated payment mortgages*. The key element in the graduated payment plans is that the monthly payment amount is arbitrarily reduced during the early years of repayment with annual increases in the payment amount until the loan becomes fully amortized. The advantage is that the borrower is qualified as to payment amount vs. income level based on the lesser payment amount for the first year.

The whole series of new mortgage designs became known as *alternative mortgages*. Have the new mortgage plans replaced the older constant-level payment loan? No, but they are taking a larger share of the market. Still, over half of the residential loans being made are with fixed interest rates and for long terms of 25 to 30 years. There are several reasons for this. Mortgage money derived from the sale of securities, such as municipal bond programs, generally offers fixed interest loans. In addition, some lenders consider interest rates at or near peak levels and prefer to hold the higher rates rather than ride an adjustable rate when it slides downward. Still others simply find administrative problems too difficult in the fast changing market of alternative mortgage plans. When alternative procedures become more stabilized, more lenders may undertake them.

The first major move towards greater flexibility in loan repayments began with the variable rate mortgage, which found wide acceptance in California through state-chartered savings associations. Then, in 1974 the Federal Housing Administration started an experimental program with graduated payment mortgages that resulted in congressional approval to implement the program nationally as of November 1, 1976. In the meantime, the Federal Home Loan Bank Board (FHLBB) had begun its own research into new designs for residential mortgage instruments—the Alternative Mortgage Instruments Research Study. As a result of this study, the FHLBB approved the writing of four new mortgage designs for federally chartered savings associations effective January 1, 1979. The four new mortgages were (1) Variable Rate Mortgage (VRM); (2) Graduated Payment Mortgage (GPM); (3) Pledged-Account Mortgage (PAM); and (4) Reverse Annuity Mortgage (RAM). For the first time, national approval had been given for the writing of conventional loans with other than constant-level amortization payments. Later, on March 27, 1981, the Comptroller of the Currency gave approval for adjustable rate mortgages to be written by national banks. As both lenders and regulators saw the need for greater flexibility in mortgage repayment plans to meet buyer capabilities and to soften the impact of higher cost loans, new ideas proliferated. The following discussion examines the basic concepts around which the new mortgage designs have been created.

Alternative Mortgages

An alternative mortgage plan differs from the standard design in that it allows, or requires, variations in two repayment essentials that formerly were fixed. These are:

1. Interest rate.
2. Monthly payment amount.

Change of Interest Rate.   If the interest rate is changed during the life of a loan, the result can be a change in the term of the loan. This is because a change in the amount of interest due each month may result in an addition, or possibly a reduction, in the principal balance due. There are two ways a borrower may be asked to absorb a change in interest rate:

1. *Change in payment amount.*   The amount of the monthly payment may be adjusted, upwards or downwards, to reflect a change in the amount of the interest cost. That portion of the payment amount applied to principal reduction is not changed. Thus, the term of the loan holds constant.
2. *Change in the term of the loan.*   This means that any change in the rate of interest will be handled through a reallocation of the payment between principal and interest with no change in the monthly payment itself. With this method of handling a change in the interest rate, an increase in the rate may require an amount greater than the fixed monthly payment amount.* If so, the unpaid interest is periodically added to the principal balance due. To repay the increased principal amount, some repayment plans allow the term of the loan to be increased, usually limiting such an increase to a term not exceeding 40 years. When the principal balance due on a loan is increased rather than decreased with each payment, the result is called *negative amortization*.

Change in Monthly Payment Amount.   An adjustable rate mortgage can result in a change in the payment amount; for a graduated payment mortgage, it is a key element. It is the potential for substantial increases in some adjustable rate mortgages that causes concern and possible downstream problems for borrowers. With a graduated payment plan, the changes in monthly payment amount are predetermined, that is, fully disclosed at the time a loan is initiated. Following are the differences in how monthly payments are handled.

1. *Adjustable rate mortgages.*   If a change in interest rate could be absorbed within a constant monthly payment amount, the effect on a borrower would be minimal. However, most plans are not so

---

*Fully amortized long-term loans have little margin in the monthly payment amounts to reallocate between principal and interest. For example, in a 30-year loan, an interest increase of about ¼ percent wipes out any payment to principal. For a 40-year loan, a ⅛ percent increase in interest causes the entire payment to go for interest cost.

easily handled. As interest costs are increased or decreased, the change can be added or subtracted from the principal balance due. As pointed out earlier, the term of the loan could be changed to allow repayment over a longer or shorter period of time. An alternative method is for the payment amount to be adjusted at periodic intervals, like every three to five years, in an amount to fully amortize the loan in the remaining term.

2. *Graduated payment mortgages.* The graduated payment design is based on the idea that the monthly payment amount is changed (increased) each year until a payment sufficient to fully amortize the loan is reached. The amount of change each year is predetermined and must be stated in the mortgage agreement. The graduated payment concept can be offered in combination with an adjustable rate. However, when the combination is offered (called a Graduated Payment Adjustable Rate Mortgage—GPARM), the adjustable rate feature generally does not trigger until after the graduated increases are exhausted.

Further consideration will be given to just how the major alternative mortgage plans work in practice. In spite of the multitude of repayment plans now offered, the reader will find that there are some common practices and regulatory requirements that control the basic designs.

Adjustable Rate Mortgages

Adjustable rate mortgages are not new. Other free-world countries have wondered how we have been able to stick with fixed rates for so long. British mortgage lenders, called Building Societies, have offered only variable rate mortgages since 1932. Canada developed a pattern of short-term mortgage loans, like five years, that allows a lender to *renew* the note when it comes due and to make an adjustment in the interest rate. The renewal type of note has become known as the *Canadian Rollover*.

The early designs of adjustable rate mortgages contained limitations on the frequency and amount of each adjustment plus a "cap" on the total increase in interest rate permitted over the life of the loan. The first such design approved by the FHLB for federally chartered savings associations was called a *Variable Rate Mortgage (VRM)*. It was not very widely accepted by lenders primarily because the limitations rapidly proved too restrictive in an escalating interest market. Remember, no lender is required to make any kind of a loan. An "approved" mortgage plan only means that it is legal for a regulated lender to offer such a mortgage—the lender does not have to offer the plan, and many have not. The initial VRM design limited interest rate changes to a maximum of 0.5 percent per year and to not more than 2.5 percent over the life of the loan. Such caps have generally been increased or eliminated.

What kind of restrictions apply to lenders offering mortgages with adjustable interest rates? Do borrowers have any protection against unreasonable changes? The answer is a qualified yes. All regulated lenders must tie the periodic adjustment of interest rates to a published index—one that must be disclosed at the origination of the loan. Mortgage lenders generally do not have the freedom to adjust an interest rate on a float over prime rate as can be offered by a commercial bank to their consumer and business customers. Further, some mortgage lenders offer self-imposed restrictions to protect the borrower against what might be a catastrophic change in the payment amount.

Since the major protection offered the borrower in these adjustable rate plans is the use of an independent index (one not under the control of the lender), the concern of the borrower focuses on how the index is applied. The first concern is the selection of the index—is it volatile in its movements or is it stable and fairly reflects the mortgage market? And second, how is the movement of the index applied for the adjustment of an interest rate? While the lender can control what mortgage plan is offered, the borrower does have the freedom to examine more than one source. And a knowledge of how the procedures function is most important when considering which kind of loan to accept. Following are the principal elements affecting the costs of an adjustable rate mortgage.

Indexes

Regulated lenders (who supply almost all of the money used to make mortgage loans) may offer adjustable rate mortgages with interest adjustments tied to any index approved by their regulatory agency. While a number of indexes have been approved in the past few years, the following dominate the market. Five interest rate indexes are acceptable for adjustable rate mortgages sold to FNMA:

1. Six-month Treasury bills.
2. One-year Treasury securities.
3. Three-year Treasury securities.
4. Five-year Treasury securities.
5. Federal Home Loan Bank Board (FHLBB) series for closed loans on existing homes.

Three other interest rate indexes are widely used:

1. Cost of Funds - FSLIC insured institutions—all districts.
2. Federal National Mortgage Association biweekly FMS auction results for weighted average yield.
3. Federal Home Loan Bank Board series for newly built homes.

Comments on Indexes. It is difficult to select one index as "best" for either the borrower or the lender—it depends on a case-by-case need. The lender would be most interested in using an index that closely correlates with its own cost of funds. The borrower is most concerned about what the index will indicate at the point of an adjustment. When the adjustment period comes due—be it six months from origination of the loan, three years, of maybe five years—whatever the index shows at that time becomes the new interest rate for the next period. Generally, it can be said that the shorter the term of the index (like six-month Treasury bills), the more volatile it tends to be.

The Cost of Funds - FSLIC insured institutions index was picked up by regulatory authorities early as providing an accurate and close relation for the lender between its cost of funds and its mortgage loan rates. However, the trend of the index has been steadily upward and as passbook interest rates become deregulated, it may tend to move even higher. It is not an accurate reflection of the mortgage market. The FNMA biweekly Free Market System auction is a more accurate reflection of the mortgage market but tends to be a bit volatile. Also, the very low volume of activity in this auction has made it less representative than in prior years. FNMA itself does not offer its auction results as an acceptable index for their loan purchases.

Probably one of the more accurate indexes available for mortgage interest rates is the report from the Federal Home Loan Bank published monthly in its journal. Their Table S.5.1 provides national averages on conventional home mortgages as reported by all major types of lenders. The movement of this index is fairly stable and it is only 60 days delayed. (May results are reported in July, for example.) Table 4-1 is a reproduction from a recent issue of the *FHLB Journal* showing the manner in which the information is reported each month.

Application of the Index. Two lenders may select the same index. But the manner in which the index is applied to the rate adjustment can result in substantially different payment amounts. Following are the principal methods used to apply an index:

1. *Index as the rate.* The rate shown by the index at the adjustment period may be applied directly to establish the rate for the

Table 4-1

Example of an Interest Rate Index
Federal Home Loan Bank National Average Mortgage Rates

Mortgage Markets

Table S.5.1.—Terms on Conventional Home Mortgage Loans Made: National Averages for All Major Types of Lenders [1]

Period	Contract interest rate[2] (percent)	Initial fees and charges[3] (percent)	Effective rate[4] (percent)	Term to maturity (years)	Loan amount (thousands)	Purchase price (thousands)	Loan-to-price ratio (percent)	Percentage distribution of estimated number of loans by loan-to-price ratio class			
								70.0 percent or less	70.1-80.0 percent	80.1-90.0 percent	Over 90.0 percent
					All Loans						
1978	9.37	1.30	9.59	26.7	41.4	57.1	74.6	NA	NA	NA	NA
1979	10.59	1.50	10.85	27.4	48.2	67.7	73.5	33	43	18	7
1980	12.46	1.97	12.84	27.2	51.7	73.4	72.9	35	41	16	9
1981	14.39	2.39	14.91	26.4	53.7	76.3	73.1	36	38	16	11
1981											
May	14.01	2.29	14.49	26.2	51.3	71.6	73.9	33	39	18	11
June	14.32	2.32	14.82	26.0	54.5	78.0	72.7	35	40	16	9
July	14.57	2.47	15.10	26.9	55.8	79.6	73.1	33	40	16	11
Aug	14.88	2.53	15.45	26.2	55.1	79.4	71.9	38	39	16	8
Sept	15.14	2.48	15.70	25.6	53.4	76.8	72.0	40	36	16	9
Oct	15.35	2.44	15.89	25.9	52.7	77.9	70.1	43	32	14	11
Nov	15.75	2.52	16.37	24.6	53.1	76.6	73.2	37	35	12	16
Dec	15.41	2.55	15.98	26.2	54.6	78.0	72.0	41	33	15	12
1982											
Jan	15.13	2.46	15.69	26.1	57.5	83.5	71.7	38	37	15	10
Feb	15.03	2.52	15.60	26.3	57.7	82.0	73.8	33	35	19	13
Mar	15.03	2.78	15.67	26.3	56.1	78.8	73.9	32	38	18	12
Apr	15.35	2.90	16.00	26.3	55.3	78.1	73.9	33	37	17	14
May	15.50	2.56	16.11	23.1	49.2	74.4	68.6	41	32	13	14
				Purchase of newly built homes							
1978	9.33	1.39	9.56	28.0	46.0	62.8	75.2	29	42	19	11
1979	10.49	1.66	10.78	28.5	53.3	74.4	73.8	33	43	17	9
1980	12.26	2.09	12.66	28.1	59.1	83.2	73.2	34	41	16	10
1981	14.13	2.66	14.70	27.7	65.2	90.3	74.8	32	37	17	15
1981											
May	13.56	2.60	14.10	28.5	65.5	88.9	76.7	28	34	23	16
June	14.18	2.60	14.07	27.5	66.0	94.1	72.0	33	42	18	18
July	14.14	2.73	14.72	28.3	67.9	95.2	73.9	32	40	14	14
Aug	14.60	2.98	15.27	27.2	70.3	98.1	74.7	33	38	17	11
Sept	14.69	2.75	15.29	26.6	64.8	89.1	74.4	37	35	17	12
Oct	15.04	2.86	15.65	27.4	63.5	89.2	73.0	37	33	14	16
Nov	15.68	2.52	16.38	23.4	62.7	84.5	77.3	32	30	11	27
Dec	15.23	2.87	15.87	27.7	64.4	88.7	75.3	33	32	18	17
1982											
Jan	14.67	2.55	15.25	27.4	71.3	102.0	73.5	32	38	17	13
Feb	14.44	3.01	15.12	28.1	71.1	97.3	76.5	28	33	20	19
Mar	14.93	2.90	15.67	27.4	65.4	90.0	75.7	29	36	20	15
Apr	15.13	3.28	15.84	28.6	70.4	95.7	77.2	27	33	18	22
May	15.11	3.16	15.89	25.9	64.8	86.4	77.4	31	27	19	24
				Purchase of previously occupied homes							
1978	9.40	1.26	9.61	26.4	39.6	54.5	75.0	28	45	21	7
1979	10.63	1.44	10.89	27.1	46.4	64.8	74.0	31	43	19	6
1980	12.53	1.91	12.90	26.9	40.4	66.9	73.5	34	41	17	9
1981	14.51	2.27	15.00	25.9	47.7	68.5	72.9	36	38	16	10
1981											
May	14.19	2.17	14.66	25.4	44.8	63.5	73.0	34	40	17	9
June	14.40	2.22	14.88	25.3	49.3	70.8	73.1	35	39	17	9
July	14.77	2.36	15.28	26.3	50.2	72.4	72.9	32	40	18	10
Aug	15.03	2.31	15.54	25.7	48.1	70.3	70.9	39	40	14	7
Sept	15.38	2.40	15.93	25.2	47.2	69.4	71.2	39	37	16	8
Oct	15.47	2.42	16.01	25.7	48.1	71.9	70.9	41	34	15	10
Nov	15.80	2.52	16.38	25.4	46.0	70.1	70.8	40	39	12	9
Dec	15.53	2.30	16.04	25.3	48.1	70.0	70.6	44	33	14	8
1982											
Jan	15.37	2.44	15.92	25.3	47.6	70.0	70.6	42	35	15	9
Feb	15.22	2.31	15.73	25.5	50.3	72.7	72.7	36	36	17	12
Mar	15.07	2.71	15.65	25.8	50.5	71.1	73.4	32	39	17	11
Apr	15.39	2.73	16.00	25.3	47.8	69.1	72.5	34	40	16	10
May	15.57	2.33	16.11	22.3	42.9	69.3	65.1	46	32	12	10

[1] Savings and Loan associations, mortgage bankers, commercial banks, and mutual savings banks.

Source: *Federal Home Loan Bank Journal*, July, 1982

next period. For example, if the FHLB rate for existing home mortgages shows a contract rate of 15.57 percent, the new rate could be set at 15.5 percent (usually the rates are rounded to the nearest quarter or eighth percent but need not be). The direct application of an index rate is most likely to be used when the index reflects the current market. Examples would be the FNMA biweekly auction yields or the FHLB monthly reports on national average rates.

2. *Index plus.* An index may be stated as a control reference with the actual rate applied a point or two higher than the index. For example, if the FHLB monthly average for existing homes is 15.57 percent, the rate used by the lender at the adjustment period could be that rate plus one or two additional percentage points—maybe 16.67 percent or 17.67 percent. Any such addition to the index must be clearly stated in the mortgage contract.

3. *Movement of the index.* A fairly popular way of using an index is to consider only the movement of the index from the time of origination (or it could be from the point of last adjustment) to the time of the adjustment period. For example, if a mortgage calls for an annual adjustment, assume the origination date was May, 1981 and the adjustment period comes due in April, 1982. If the index applied is the FHLB existing home average rate (see Table 4-1), the contract rate during that period moved from 14.19 percent to 15.39 percent for a total increase of 1.20 percent. Now, to whatever the initial rate on the loan may be (and this rate is determined by the lender), the 1.20 percent increase is added. Thus, if the initial rate offered by the lender was 15 percent, the interest rate for the new adjustment period would be 16.20 percent. It should be noted that all regulations thus far have made rate increases *optional* for the lender, but rate decreases are *mandatory*. In other words, should an index rate decline, the lender must pass this reduction on to the borrower.

4. *Lesser of two indexes.* A lender may offer two indexes with the proviso that the lesser of the two applies at the adjustment period. This procedure has been used primarily by FNMA in its refinancing and resale programs to encourage early repayment of older, lower interest rate loans. The same procedure could also be used with the provision that the *greater rate* of the two indexes would be the one used at the adjustment period.

5. *Caveat.* In order to encourage the use of adjustable rate mortgages as well as to allow borrower qualification at lower payment amounts, some lenders are offering initial interest rates at substantially less than going market rates. Then, after a limited period of time, the rate adjusts to an index applied rate. It could mean a

large increase in the payment amount at the adjustment period. There is nothing wrong with this procedure and it is not intended to be tricky—it must be fully disclosed in the mortgage instrument. The important point is that the borrower (or the broker advisor) must carefully read the mortgage agreement and ask questions of the lender to reach a full understanding when necessary. Many of these procedures are so new and have undergone such frequent changes that some loan officers are not completely familiar with all the details involved.

Limitations on Changes (Caps). Regulatory authorities have tried to consider the potential for catastrophic increases in adjustable rate mortgage payments that could result in an unfortunate default for the home buyer. At the same time, there must be some reasonableness to the limits, otherwise few lenders would be willing to undertake the new mortgage design. Required limitations have centered on the following three aspects of adjustable rate loans:

1. *Mortgage payment amount.* The limitation on payment amount has to do with both the dollar amount and the frequency of changing the dollar amount. For the home buyer, perhaps overreaching a bit to acquire suitable housing, the dollar amount of payment is crucial. However, it is not a widely used limit. Generally, the rule for a particular mortgage design would limit an increase (or possibly a decrease as well) to not more than, say 10 percent, of the previous payment amount. The other limit on mortgage payment amount has to do with the frequency of change, or how often can the change be made. For example, in Texas, state-chartered savings associations may not change a payment amount more often than once a year, but they can change the interest rate every six months.

2. *Frequency of rate change.* Earlier regulations, particularly those applying to federally chartered institutions, offered plans that limited the frequency of rate changes to a range of from one to five years. Many states, and a number of approved federal plans, have now reduced the time span for change of rate to every six months. To illustrate some of the complexity in these rules, the following chart indicates how the Federal National Mortgage Association applies limitations differently for each of their five approved indexes. The frequency of mortgage interest rate adjustments depends on the index selected by the borrower:

| | Adjustment Intervals | |
Index	Standard ARMs	Graduated Payment ARMs
six-month Treasury bills	6 months	6 months
one-year Treasury securities	1 year	n/a
three-year Treasury securities	2½ years	3 years
five-year Treasury securities	5 years	5 years
FHLB series of closed loans	1 year	n/a

3. *Limits on rate swings.* The limit on rate swings applies to the rate change over the life of the loan. The original cap on swing set by the FHLB for their first variable rate mortgage was 2 1/2 percent. That is, the rate could not be increased more than 2 1/2 percent over the life of the loan. There was no limit on the amount of a decrease. Later, the FHLB came out with its Renegotiable Rate Mortgage plan that allowed a swing of not more than a 5 percent increase or decrease in the interest rate over the life of the loan. Many approved adjustable rate mortgage plans have now dropped this limit altogether. Thus, the amount of swing is subject only to the movement of the applicable index.

Graduated Payment Mortgage (GPM)

The graduated payment mortgage concept was first tested by the FHA as a method of allowing home buyers to pay lower initial monthly payments in the earlier years of a mortgage term, with payments rising in later years to a level sufficient to fully amortize the loan within a 30-year term. With a lower initial monthly payment, the buyer might qualify for a loan with a lower income, or conversely, be able to buy a larger house with the same income. An added requirement is that the buyer must show reasonable expectation of an increase in annual income so as to meet the annual increase in monthly payments.

An inherent problem with the GPM is that even a constant-level payment, long-term mortgage loan allows very little payment on principal in the early years. So, with only a modest reduction in the payment amount, any allocation to principal may easily be eliminated along with a portion of the interest payment due. For example, the constant-level payment on a $50,000 loan at 10 percent with a term of 30 years amounts to $438.79. The amount of this monthly payment allocated to pay off principal is about $25.00 during the first year. Thus, a reduction of the monthly payment below $413 per month would not allow for any reduction of principal, and would result in a probable accumulation of unpaid interest. When the graduated payment plan allows for payments so low that not all of the interest is paid, each year's unpaid interest is added to the principal balance for repayment in later years. For most of the plans currently in use, there is an accumulation of unpaid interest in the early years of the mortgage term; thus, the borrower ends the year with larger principal balances owing than when the loan was first undertaken. As mentioned previously, this is called *negative amortization*—the loan balance *increases* with each payment, rather than decreases. To avoid the possibility that the increasing amount of the loan balance could exceed the initial value of the property collateral, GPMs generally call for higher down payments than are necessary for constant-level payment plans. Down payments for this type of loan are calculated so the loan balance will not exceed the limits permitted, which are 95 per cent of the initial property value for conventional loans and 97 per cent of the initial value for FHA-type loans.

A legal qualification is necessary in some states for this type of loan. The act authorizing the FHA program specifically preempts any state law that prohibits the addition of interest to the principal of a mortgage loan insofar as it pertains to the manner in which the loan is repaid. This preemption is also claimed by federally chartered institutions that come under federal banking rules, not state rules.

The popularity of the FHA Section 245 GPM program has made the term *graduated payment mortgage* almost synonymous with FHA. (See Chapter 8 for more detail on the FHA Section 245 program.) What the FHLBB approved in 1979 was a *conventional* loan to be written with graduated payment terms. However, the FHLBB leaned heavily on the experience developed under the FHA program and has used FHA procedures to set the maximum limits for the conventional plans. Federally chartered savings associations are not required to offer a GPM, but if they elect to do so, whatever plan they offer cannot exceed authorized limits. As set by the FHLBB, these limits include a maximum annual increase in monthly payments for a five-year period of 7 1/2 percent and a maximum annual increase for a ten-year period of 3 percent. The loan-to-value ratio cannot exceed 95 percent during the term of the loan. Under the FHLBB rules borrowers have the right to convert a GPM to a standard mortgage form at the borrower's option. To convert the mortgage, a borrower must be able to meet the association's normal underwriting standards. In most cases, this would mean that the borrower's income must be sufficient to allow a constant-level payment. Also, no fees or penalties are permitted for the conversion, providing all other terms remain the same.

Approval to write a conventional mortgage permitting graduated payments was granted during a period of considerable market uncertainty. Savings associations at that time were not seeking new ways in which to loan their limited funds. Under more competitive market conditions, there would be greater interest in this mortgage form as it fulfills a need. Young families buying their first home do not have the benefit of an escalating equity interest in an existing house to trade with. So, permitting lower initial monthly payments enables more family incomes to qualify for loans.

Initial concern with the GPM concept centered on the requirement for larger down payments to qualify. Would families with limited incomes and in need of lower initial monthly payments be those capable of making larger down payments? In practice, many families have taken advantage of the FHA program and have been able to handle the down payment—some with savings, some with parental help. However, Congress took steps in 1979 to reduce the down payment requirements for FHA-GPM loans by recognizing the inflation-induced escalation in home values. The result is a new *Section 245(b)* program which is more fully explained in Chapter 8.

Pledged-Account Mortgage

For several years past, some state-chartered savings associations have been making mortgage loans using a pledged savings account to provide additional collateral. Funds are withdrawn from the pledged account each month to supplement the mortgage payments. Normally, no additional cash is required to establish the pledged account since it comes from the money the buyer would otherwise have used as a down payment. The purpose of the procedure is the same as that of the GPM: to establish a lower initial monthly payment that can be used to qualify a lesser income for a larger house.

As of January 1, 1979, federally chartered savings associations have been permitted to write pledged-account mortgages. No change has been made in the maximum permissible loan-to-value ratio at 95 percent, and loans over 90 percent LTVR must carry mortgage default insurance. The calculations used to administer the pledged-account payments must contain the net risk within the 95 percent limit. The balance held in the pledged account is considered a part of the loan collateral and thus reduces the net mortgage risk.

A pledged-account plan conceived by Allan Smith of Newtown, Pennsylvania, using the name *Flexible Loan Insurance Plan, FLIP mortgage*, and marketed as a computer program, provides a practical example of the calculations needed to implement the program. An example is used to illustrate the repayment plan. For this purpose, consider a house costing $70,000 and a cash requirement of the buyer for $20,000. Instead of paying all the cash to the seller, a portion is deposited in a pledged account with the lender and becomes a part of the collateral securing the loan. For this example:

To pledged account	$12,100
Paid to seller	7,900
Total cash requirement	$20,000

The $7,900 paid to the seller gives the following mortgage requirement:

Cost of house	$70,000
Cash paid to seller	7,900
Remainder borrowed	$62,100

The mortgage loan in the amount of $62,100 is paid with an initial combination of the buyer's monthly payments plus a monthly supplement withdrawn from the pledged account. The sum of the two each month equals the $735.81 payment needed to fully amortize the $62,100 loan at 14 percent in 30 years. Each month the lender withdraws a portion of the pledged account principal, adds the earned interest on the account, and applies the sum of the two to the mortgage payment. For this example, the buyer's payment and the supplement each month are calculated for a five-year supplemental period in the following manner:

Beg. of Year	Buyer's Monthly Pmt. for Yr.	PLUS	Pledged Acct. Principal	PLUS	Interest on Pledged Account	EQUALS	Total Monthly Payment
1	380.05		308.64		47.12		735.81
2	441.29		263.12		31.40		735.81
3	507.14		210.29		18.38		735.81
4	577.92		149.40		8.49		735.81
5	654.01		79.61		2.19		735.81
6	735.81		-0-		-0-		735.81

The lender initially holds as security for the loan a house worth $70,000 PLUS control of the pledged account which adds to the collateral in the amount of $12,132.73.* Thus the initial risk exposure of the

---

*Note: $32.73 must be added to the pledged account to make the five-year supplemental payments exactly balance.

lender is reduced to a loan-to-value ratio of only 71.38 percent. As the pledged account is reduced during the five years of withdrawals, the risk exposure climbs to a high (for this example) of 87.32 percent, well within the lenders risk limits. Following is the annual change in mortgage balance and loan-to-value ratio:

Beg. of Year	Mortgage Balance	Pledged- Account Balance	Net Mortgage Balance	Cost of House	Loan- to -Value Ratio
1	62,100	12,133	49,967	70,000	.7138
2	61,955	8,429	53,526	70,000	.7647
3	61,788	5,272	56,517	70,000	.8074
4	61,598	2,748	58,849	70,000	.8407
5	61,378	955	60,422	70,000	.8632
6	61,125	-0-	61,125	70,000	.8732

Why pledge a portion of the $20,000 cash requirement in a pledged account? Wouldn't it be better to use the entire $20,000 to reduce the mortgage loan to $50,000 (the $70,000 price of the house less $20,000 equals $50,000)? The answer is clear: a $50,000 loan at 14 percent interest for 30 years requires a monthly payment of $592.44. Using the FLIP calculation for a pledged-account mortgage, the initial monthly payment drops to $380.05.* Obviously, more borrowers could qualify at the lower monthly payment amount.

Buy-Down Mortgages

One of the more popular methods to arrange an alternative financing plan is for the seller, usually a home builder, to "buy down" the initial payment amounts. This is simply a variation on the normal discount procedure. The major difference is that a buy-down is a prepayment of interest costs for only a few years, whereas the discount is normally considered as prepayment of interest costs over the life of the loan.

Buy-downs can span any period, but generally are offered for periods of one to five years. The average buy-down, and the one acceptable for purchase by FNMA, is a three-year buy-down amounting to a 3 percent less-than-market rate the first year, 2 percent second, and 1 percent the third. The procedure is sometimes called "3-2-1." The purpose is the same as that achieved by graduated payment plans—to reduce the monthly payments for the buyer in the early years of loan repayment. Thus, a larger market of qualified buyers may be reached.

*Note: Figures in this example used with permission of FLIP Mortgage Corporation, Newtown, Pennsylvania 18940.

What the seller is actually doing is paying a portion of the interest cost in the early years. The following figures illustrate the cost reduction of interest on a $50,000 loan at a nominal interest rate of 16 percent with a 3-year buy-down. The *nominal rate* means that named on the note and is the only interest rate shown.

Example

First, consider the round figure cost of a buy-down:

To reduce the interest cost from 16 percent to 13 percent for the first year, the seller must pay 3 percent of the cost

$$.03 \times \$50,000 = \qquad \$1,500$$

For the second year, the cost is 2 percent

$$.02 \times \$50,000 = \qquad 1,000$$

For the third year, the cost is 1 percent

$$.01 \times \$50,000 = \qquad \underline{500}$$

Total cost of buy-down $3,000

With a portion of the interest paid in advance, the buyer makes reduced monthly payments in the following amounts:

1st year —$50,000 @ 13% = $553.10
2nd year—$50,000 @ 14% = $592.49
3rd year —$50,000 @ 15% = $632.22
4th year —$50,000 @ 16% = $672.38

The precise calculation of the cost of a buy-down is not always uniform as lenders vary somewhat in allowing for the time value of money. That is, money paid in advance earns the lender additional interest, and this can be used to reduce the cost of the initial buy-down payment.

Growing Equity Mortgages (GEM)

A fairly recent repayment plan that has attracted considerable attention is the *Growing Equity Mortgage*, sometimes called a *Graduated Equity Mortgage*. The basic idea is that the sooner one can repay the principal amount of a loan, the less the cost of interest. At interest rates in the range of 14 percent to 15 percent, a 30-year loan paid to maturity can result in interest costs alone of roughly three times the amount of principal borrowed.

The Growing Equity Mortgage provides a method to reduce the principal balance sooner than the 30-year plans. There are a number of variations on how this can be accomplished, but one popular plan calls for an increase in the monthly payment amount by 4 percent each year. *All* of the payment increase is applied to the reduction of the principal balance. Depending on the interest rate, the 4 percent annual increase in payment amount allows the loan to be paid off in about 15 years. The reduction in interest cost from that on a 30-year term loan is substantial.

Both the FHA and VA have approved this concept for early payment of a loan. The FHA acceptance comes under their Section 245(a) program (same as graduated payment mortgage plans) because it authorizes insurance on mortgages with varying rates of amortization.

Other Alternative Plans

Two other basic concepts need to be considered in the many variations now available in mortgage repayment plans. One is shared financing, and the other is borrowing against home equity with a reverse annuity mortgage.

Shared Appreciation Mortgage (SAM)

When home values show a prolonged appreciation in value, lenders may find it profitable to take a portion of the expected return of their money from the appreciation. In the late 1970s, the Federal Home Loan Bank explored the idea and considered allowing their regulated institutions to write such a mortgage and accept a portion of the appreciation as "contingent interest."

For example, if market rates are at a 15 percent level, the lender could offer to make a loan at 10 percent and take one-third of any appreciation in property value over, say, the next ten years. If the property is sold sooner, the lender is entitled to one-third of the appreciation at the time of sale. If the owner does not sell, the loan agreement could call for an appraisal at the end of ten years. Based on the appraised value, the lender could then claim one-third of any net increase (additions to property not included). Payment to the lender could be made in a lump sum cash payment, or it could be added to the loan balance and a new note written.

Obviously, in areas with declining property values, this concept would not be acceptable. Shared appreciation is different from a *shared equity* mortgage. The shared equity is an arrangement whereby two or more parties hold an ownership interest in the property. An example could be an employer joining with an employee to buy a house in a remote, or a high cost, area to assist in a job transfer. Normally, the employee is given an option to buy out the employer's portion within a limited number of years. Or, in case of a transfer, the employer could purchase the entire property at the appraised value.

Reverse Annuity Mortgage (RAM)

The reverse annuity is another of the mortgage forms approved by the FHLBB as of January 1, 1979. However, it does not finance the acquisition of real estate as the other forms do. Rather, the reverse annuity utilizes the collateral value of a home as a means of financing living expenses for the owner. The basic purpose is to assist older homeowners who are pressed to meet rising living costs with fixed retirement or pension forms of income. With the use of a reverse annuity, the increased value of the home may be utilized without the owner being forced to sell it.

Where state laws permit (the owner's homestead rights may preclude this form of mortgage), a lender can advance monthly installment payments to the homeowner, using a mortgage on the home as security. The FHLBB rules governing the writing of RAMs require extensive disclosures to reduce the possibility of misunderstandings by the homeowner. Among the requirements is that a seven-day rescission period be allowed the borrower should a change of mind occur. Another is that a statement must be signed by the borrower acknowledging all contractual contingencies that might force a sale of the home. Repayment of the loan must be allowed without penalties, and if the mortgage has a fixed term, refinancing must be arranged at market rates if requested at maturity of the loan.

Interest on this type of loan is added to the principal amount along with each monthly payment made to the borrower. For a savings institution, the monthly payout of loan proceeds with interest added to the principal presents an altogether different cash flow problem. The concept of reverse annuity is new and will require some years of testing before many institutions will decide to offer it.

Questions for Discussion

1. How does a graduated payment mortgage help a home buyer?

2. Explain why an increase in interest rate without a change in the payment amount alters the term of a loan.

3. What is the major constraint on lenders in setting new interest rates on an adjustable rate mortgage?

4. Discuss the quality of the major indexes cited in the text.

5. Describe how a lender uses the "movement of an index" in setting a new interest rate at the adjustment period.

6. What is *negative amortization* and why is it associated with graduated payment mortgages?

7. How does a pledged-account mortgage function and why is it beneficial for the home buyer?

8. Describe a buy-down mortgage.

9. What is a Growing Equity Mortgage?

Sources of Mortgage Money

No other major industry is so dependent on borrowered money as is the construction industry with its largest component, the housing industry. Because of this dependence, cyclical swings in the financial markets hit housing first, and perhaps, hardest. The long-term nature of mortgage loans and the past limitations on qualified sources have placed this industry at the whip end of financial cycles. Another industry heavily dependent on borrowed money is the automobile industry. However, auto financing is mostly short term and generally pays a substantially higher effective interest than do mortgage loans. The importance that the government places on the housing industry is indicated by the many programs and banking procedures that have been implemented to assist the industry in its efforts to combat the ups and down that plague stable operations.

To understand real estate financing it is necessary to examine the specific sources of mortgage money along with the incentives and constraints under which they operate. First, let's look at the distribution of the outstanding mortgage debt in this country by type of loan (Table 5-1). The total mortgage debt outstanding now exceeds $1.5 trillion and is growing each year. Where does this money come from? Almost all of it comes from private sources: individual and company savings in the form of all kinds of savings deposits, payments for life insurance, retirement programs, and pension funds. In this regard, one long-range problem facing the United States is the low rate of savings. People in this country squirrel away between 5 and 7 percent of their disposable income compared with two to three times that amount saved by people in

TABLE 5-1

Mortgage Debt by Type of Loan[1]
(as of March 31, 1982)

Loan Category	Percentage
Residential (1- to 4-family)	66
Commercial	18
Apartment	9
Farm	7
Total all debt	100%

[1]Percentages derived from Federal Reserve Bank figures.

the major free European countries. However, there has been a gradual shift in the manner in which private investment money, or savings, is moving into mortgage loans.

Financial Markets as a Money Source

Before examining the major lenders or primary sources of mortgage money, whom a borrower would contact to obtain a loan, it is important to consider where these sources currently obtain their lendable funds. For a number of reasons, the comfortable pool of savings deposits which once sought mortgage loans began to dry up in the late 1970s. Primary lenders turned to other sources, mostly the financial markets, for money to lend. Table 5-2 graphically illustrates the significant size of this shift.

TABLE 5-2

Source of funds	Percent of Mortgage Money Funded	
	1976	1981
Savings associations and mutual banks	75	36
Financial markets	2	45

Source: Interpolated from Federal Home Loan Bank tables.

Savings deposits with their regulated passbook rates (5½ percent for S & Ls, 5¼ percent for commercial banks at this writing, Regulation

Q, Federal Reserve Bank) have long provided the primary low-cost source of funds for residential loans. As Table 5-2 indicates this is now a declining source. However, to replace the short-fall from savings deposits there has been an increase in the participation of the financial markets (those people, companies, and institutions who invest in corporate and government securities). Tapping this source of funds has been handled primarily through the sale of mortgage-backed securities. What is a *mortgage-backed security*? It is a security which has as collateral a block of mortgage loans. The procedure is different from that used in a secondary market sale transaction. When a loan is *sold* in a secondary market sale transaction, the individual mortgage loan package is physically transferred to the possession of the purchaser. Thus, the purchaser acquires the risk and benefit accruing to each loan.

In a mortgage-backed security transaction, a number of loan packages, comprising a "block" of loans, are delivered to a trustee for safekeeping. They are not "sold." The lender seeking funds through this method then issues a security based on the block of mortgages which is the collateral. The security may be called a *bond*, a *participation certificate*, or just a *security*. The block of loans pledged to a trustee as collateral may amount to, say, $2 million. The securities issued based on this collateral may be in lesser denominations of, say, $5,000 or $10,000 for easier sale in the financial markets. What the investor in the security acquires is an interest in a *diversified block* of individual mortgage loans. The individual loans in the possession of the trustee pay monthly to that trustee. The trustee, who represents the security owners, is responsible for the timely distribution of the loan payments proportionately to the security owners. The flow of this money from the borrower, to the trustee, and then on to the security owner has developed the name *pass-through* security—the money passes through the trustee on to the security owner.

What does this mean for mortgage borrowers in the future? Essentially, the new source of money, call it the financial markets, will invest only if the return is competitive with other securities. So mortgage money no longer has the large pool of low-cost savings deposits to draw upon and must now compete with such other investment securities as corporate bonds, municipal bonds, and federal government bonds, notes, and Treasury bills for funds. Uncertainty in the financial markets has reduced the time span for which lenders are willing to place their money at risk in securities. Hence, short-term investments (less than three years), such as certificates of deposit, money market funds, and three-month and six-month Treasury bills, now compete with mortgage money for funds. With the federal government alone calling upon over half (up from roughly 30 percent in 1980) of the available funds in the credit market by 1982, the cost of mortgage money will be hard pressed to achieve lower rates without a decline in government borrowing.

The Primary Sources

The basic pools of mortgage money available in this country can be divided into major sources and lesser sources for purposes of discussion. The major sources are the large institutional lenders, meaning the regulated lenders such as savings associations, commercial banks, mutual savings banks, and life insurance companies. Several government agencies, such as the Federal Land Bank, the Farmer's Home Administration, and, more recently, the Government National Mortgage Association, participate in the mortgage market as sources of funds. The lesser sources, such as individuals, trusts, pension funds, and many others, will be considered later in this chapter. Even though mortgage companies have an important position within the industry, they are not considered a "source" in providing a reservoir of cash from which to make loans. Rather, mortgage companies serve as intermediaries between the major sources and the borrowing public. They are classed in financial terminology as "noninstitutional" lenders, and their importance is considered later in a separate chapter.

The distinction between the various categories of mortgage lenders is becoming much less precise than in prior years. The Monetary Control Act of 1980 has encouraged a merging of functions—savings associations are becoming more like commercial banks. Further, such companies as American Express, Sears, Roebuck, and Merrill Lynch are moving into the banking field outside the regulatory authorities. These newcomers to banking have money to lend on mortgages and can participate in the origination of mortgage-backed securities.

While the mortgage market has undergone significant changes, for the average borrower, the changes are not so obvious. The major sources still handle most of the loan originations, for it is they who have the expertise in loan underwriting. The average borrower will find the same lenders as in the past willing and capable of making mortgage loans. The big difference is that the lenders may, or may not, be using their own deposit assets to fund the loan. For the borrower it primarily means a higher cost loan.

Loan Volume by Major Lenders

Table 5-3 shows the four types of mortgage loans that the major lenders are most likely to make and gives the percentage of funds that these lenders have invested in each loan category. The figures represent the percentage of mortgage debt held by lenders, not the amount funded in any one year. Nevertheless, it gives an indication of the participation by each major class of lender.

TABLE 5-3

Mortgage Debt by Class of Lender[1]

Lender Source	Type of Mortgage Loan (by Percentage of Total)			
	Residential[2]	Commercial	Apartment	Farm
Savings associations	42	17	26	0
Commercial banks	17	32	11	8
Mutual savings banks	6	6	11	0
Life insurance companies	2	32	14	13
Federal and related agencies	7	0	10	44
Mortgage pools or trusts	14	2	8	8
Individuals and others	12	11	20	27
	100%	100%	100%	100%

[1]Percentages derived from Federal Reserve Bank figures as of March 31, 1982.
[2]Defined as 1- to 4-family housing.

Note in Table 5-3 that while savings associations still hold the dominant position in residential loans, they are declining somewhat in the overall market. Their problem has been that so much of their revenue-paying assets is in the form of old mortgage loans still paying 6 percent to 8 percent interest while the cost of funds has risen to nearly 11 percent. Commercial banks continue to reflect a fairly consistent level of participation in the mortgage markets, but their holdings are mostly in short-term mortgage loans. This short-term category is in construction loans and warehouse lines of credit extended to mortgage companies. Mutual savings banks have long favored mortgage loans, particularly FHA/VA loans, as a sound investment. However, like savings associations, they have been hurt by the mismatch between their revenue assets and their cost of funds and are moving into other investments. Life insurance companies are more interested in the higher yielding commercial loans, which may include participation incentives. But more recently they have been buying blocks of residential loans because the yields are higher than in past years.

Mortgage Debt Outstanding

One more statistical table is worth reviewing. Table 5-4 is a reprint of mortgage debt outstanding figures published monthly in the *Federal Reserve Bulletin*. It gives the dollar volume of mortgage loans held by the major sources over each of the past five years.

TABLE 5-4

Mortgage Debt Outstanding (In Millions of Dollars, End of Period)

Type of holder, and type of property	1979	1980	1981	1981 Q1	Q2	Q3	Q4	1982 Q1'
1 All holders	1,326,785	1,445,966	1,544,784'	1,468,053	1,499,066	1,525,599'	1,544,784'	1,559,620
2 1- to 4-family	880,369	961,340	1,021,140'	974,411	993,793'	1,010,838'	1,021,140'	1,029,059
3 Multifamily	128,167	136,953	141,271'	137,946	139,199	140,010'	141,271'	142,686
4 Commercial	235,572	255,655	280,566'	261,242	268,562'	274,719'	280,566'	284,099
5 Farm	82,677	92,018	101,807	94,454	97,512	100,032	101,807	103,776
6 Major financial institutions	938,567	997,168	1,044,037	1,007,240	1,023,793	1,036,880	1,044,037	1,045,187
7 Commercial banks[1]	245,187	263,030	286,626	266,734	273,225	281,126	286,626	291,426
8 1- to 4-family	149,460	160,326	172,549	161,758	164,873	169,378	172,549	175,326
9 Multifamily	11,180	12,924	14,905	13,282	13,800	14,478	14,905	15,126
10 Commercial	75,957	81,081	90,717	83,133	86,091	88,836	90,717	92,499
11 Farm	8,590	8,699	8,455	8,561	8,461	8,434	8,455	8,475
12 Mutual savings banks	98,908	99,865	100,015	99,719	99,993	99,994	100,015	98,500
13 1- to 4-family	66,140	67,489	68,200	67,619	68,035	68,116	68,200	67,086
14 Multifamily	16,557	16,058	15,962	15,955	15,909	15,939	15,962	15,611
15 Commercial	16,162	16,278	15,813	16,105	15,999	15,909	15,813	15,763
16 Farm	49	40	40	40	50	30	40	40
17 Savings and loan associations	475,688	503,192	518,350	507,556	515,256	518,778	518,350	515,125
18 1- to 4-family	394,345	419,763	432,978'	423,606	430,702'	433,750'	432,978'	430,084
19 Multifamily	37,579	38,142	37,684'	38,219	38,077	37,975'	37,684'	37,450
20 Commercial	43,764	45,287	47,688'	45,731	46,477'	47,053'	47,688'	47,591
21 Life insurance companies	118,784	131,081	139,046	133,231	135,319	136,982	139,046	140,136
22 1- to 4-family	16,193	17,943	17,382	17,847	17,646	17,512	17,382	17,332
23 Multifamily	19,274	19,514	19,486	19,579	19,603	19,592	19,486	19,674
24 Commercial	71,137	80,666	89,089	82,839	85,038	86,742	89,089	90,105
25 Farm	12,180	12,958	13,089	12,966	13,032	13,136	13,089	13,025
26 Federal and related agencies	97,084	114,300	126,112	116,243	119,124	121,772	126,112	128,725
27 Government National Mortgage Association	3,852	4,642	4,765	4,826	4,972	4,382	4,765	4,438
28 1- to 4-family	763	704	693	696	698	696	693	689
29 Multifamily	3,089	3,938	4,072	4,130	4,274	3,686	4,072	3,749
30 Farmers Home Administration	1,274	3,492	2,235	2,837	2,662	1,562	2,235	2,469
31 1- to 4-family	417	916	914	1,321	1,151	500	914	715
32 Multifamily	71	610	473	528	464	242	473	615
33 Commercial	174	411	506	479	357	325	506	499
34 Farm	612	1,555	342	509	690	495	342	640
35 Federal Housing and Veterans Administration	5,555	5,640	5,999	5,799	5,895	6,005	5,999	6,007
36 1- to 4-family	1,955	2,051	2,289	2,135	2,172	2,240	2,289	2,267
37 Multifamily	3,600	3,589	3,710	3,664	3,723	3,765	3,710	3,740
38 Federal National Mortgage Association	51,091	57,327	61,412	57,362	57,657	59,682	61,412	62,544
39 1- to 4-family	45,488	51,775	55,986	51,842	52,181	54,227	55,986	57,142
40 Multifamily	5,603	5,552	5,426	5,520	5,476	5,455	5,426	5,402
41 Federal Land Banks	31,277	38,131	46,446	40,258	42,681	44,708	46,446	47,947
42 1- to 4-family	1,552	2,099	2,788	2,228	2,401	2,605	2,788	2,874
43 Farm	29,725	36,032	43,658	38,030	40,280	42,103	43,658	45,073
44 Federal Home Loan Mortgage Corporation	4,035	5,068	5,255	5,161	5,257	5,433	5,255	5,320
45 1- to 4-family	3,059	3,873	4,018	3,953	4,025	4,166	4,018	4,075
46 Multifamily	976	1,195	1,237	1,208	1,232	1,267	1,237	1,245
47 Mortgage pools or trusts[2]	119,278	142,258	162,273	147,246	152,308	158,140	162,273	169,559
48 Government National Mortgage Association	76,401	93,874	105,790	97,184	100,558	103,750	105,790	108,645
49 1- to 4-family	74,546	91,602	103,007	94,810	98,057	101,068	103,007	105,769
50 Multifamily	1,855	2,272	2,783	2,374	2,501	2,682	2,783	2,876
51 Federal Home Loan Mortgage Corporation	15,180	16,854	19,843	17,067	17,565	17,936	19,843	23,959
52 1- to 4-family	12,149	13,471	15,888	13,641	14,115	14,401	15,888	18,995
53 Multifamily	3,031'	3,383	3,955	3,426	3,450	3,535	3,955	4,964
54 Farmers Home Administration	27,697	31,530	36,640	32,995	34,185	36,454	36,640	36,955
55 1- to 4-family	14,884	16,683	18,378	16,640	17,165	18,407	18,378	18,740
56 Multifamily	2,163	2,612	3,426	2,853	3,097	3,488	3,426	3,447
57 Commercial	4,328	5,271	6,161	5,382	5,750	6,040	6,161	6,351
58 Farm	6,322	6,964	8,675	8,120	8,173	8,519	8,675	8,417
59 Individual and others[3]	171,856	192,240	212,362'	197,324	203,841	208,807'	212,362'	216,149
60 1- to 4-family	99,418	112,645	126,070'	116,315	120,572	123,772'	126,070'	127,965
61 Multifamily	23,189	27,164	28,152'	27,208	27,593	27,906'	28,152'	28,787
62 Commercial	24,050	26,661	30,592'	27,573	28,850	29,814'	30,592'	31,291
63 Farm	25,199	25,770	27,548	26,228	26,826	27,315	27,548	28,106

1. Includes loans held by nondeposit trust companies but not bank trust departments.

2. Outstanding principal balances of mortgages backing securities insured or guaranteed by the agency indicated.

3. Other holders include mortgage companies, real estate investment trusts, state and local credit agencies, state and local retirement funds, noninsured pension funds, credit unions, and U.S. agencies for which amounts are small or for which separate data are not readily available.

NOTE. Based on data from various institutional and governmental sources, with some quarters estimated in part by the Federal Reserve in conjunction with the Federal Home Loan Bank Board and the Department of Commerce. Separation of nonfarm mortgage debt by type of property, if not reported directly, and interpolations and extrapolations when required, are estimated mainly by the Federal Reserve. Multifamily debt refers to loans on structures of five or more units.

Source: *Federal Reserve Bulletin*, June 1982, p. A41.

To restate a portion of the information provided in Table 5-4 in another form, take a look at the respective *increases* in mortgage loans held by each of the major lenders as shown in Table 5-5.

TABLE 5-5

Type of Holder	Percent Increase 1979 to 1982
All holders	17.5
Major financial institutions	11.4
Federal and related agencies	31.9
Mortgage pools	42.0
Individuals and others	26.3

Table 5-4 shows that major financial institutions still hold 67 percent of the outstanding mortgage debt and maintain a substantial lead over the nearest rival. But the present trend, as evidenced in Table 5-5, is greater growth in the other types of holders.

Savings and Loan Associations

Historically, the number one source for mortgage loans has been the savings and loan associations. Changing regulations and market conditions have forced a decline in their lending activity, but their primary purpose has long been to finance buildings. Indeed, many older institutions flourished under such names as "Building and Loan Association" or "Building Society."

The origin of this type of institution was loosely formed associations of people with common interests: farmers, storekeepers, religious groups, fraternal organizations, and others who pooled their capital to provide funds for building houses, improving land, or adding to their farms. The modern counterpart of these groups might be found in company credit unions, although there are differences in the types of loans made by credit unions compared with the earlier associations.

Until the 1930s the individual states regulated their own state-chartered savings associations as each deemed necessary. But the Depression of the 30s showed up many problems. Resources were restricted to local deposits, and the long-term loans allowed little liquidity or flexibility. In 1932 the federal government established the Federal Home Loan Bank system—still in operation today—which provides member associations a bank from which they can borrow money to meet emergency needs. In 1933 the Federal Home Loan Bank (FHLB) was authorized to issue federal charters to newly formed savings associations, charters that required certain standards of compliance and a supervised method of operations. A year later, in 1934, the Federal Savings and Loan Insurance Corporation (FSLIC) was established to provide deposit insurance, and all federally-chartered associations were required to belong and to comply with its rules. The insurance coverage now protects any one depositor up to the amount of $100,000.

Along with the efforts of the federal government to improve the savings associations, most states undertook reforms of all kinds to strengthen regulatory authorities and make more stringent lending laws for their own state-chartered institutions. Many states find it a good policy to follow the guidance of the Federal Home Loan Bank Board in order to establish a more uniform set of rules. The growing dependence on the secondary market for the sale of mortgage loans has increased the pressure toward more uniform standards, and unless other procedures are required by state policies, the lending institution tries to follow the more nationalized procedures.

State-Chartered Savings and Loan Associations

When the federal government created its own chartering authority for savings associations, it began the dual chartering system. A part of the confusion in what our lending institutions can and cannot do stems from this dual authority.

Before 1933 all savings associations were state-chartered and operated under whatever rules and administrative procedures the various state legislatures established. State-chartered associations now operate under a variety of rules. They may be either mutually owned by the depositors, or they may be stock corporations owned by stockholders. Further, state charters may be required to carry deposit insurance, or they may not. Some states operate their own insurance funds to protect the depositors; others may require compliance with the Federal Savings and Loan Insurance Corporation. State-chartered associations are permitted to become members of the FSLIC and to be insured by it. To be eligible, the association must also become a member of the Federal Home Loan Bank system and is subject to its supervision. Thus, the state-chartered association would be subject to the rules established by the FSLIC, subject to the supervision of the FHLBB, plus meet the requirements of the state regulatory authorities. In spite of the overlapping of authorities, many state charters elect to join the federal system because of the protection it provides for the depositor.

State regulatory bodies can and do set their own limitations on the types of loans that can be made, the amounts that limit any one type of loan, and the general mix of investments permitted to the associations under their jurisdiction. In practice the upper limits of loans are being set by the federal authorities—the FHLBB and the newer Federal Home Loan Mortgage Corporation, which purchases mortgage loans. The reason is to maintain a portfolio of loans that can be more easily converted to cash should the need arise.

Federally-Chartered Savings and Loan Associations

The authority granted to the Federal Home Loan Bank Board in 1933 to issue savings and loan association charters created a new pattern that is uniform across the country. All federally-chartered associations until 1975 had to be mutually owned by the depositors. They must be members of the Federal Home Loan Bank system and have the deposits insured by the FSLIC.

The general requirements that the Federal Home Loan Bank Board has imposed on its members are (1) an economically sound policy for mortgage loans, and (2) the condition that the interest rates charged be reasonable. The Board also requires that a portion of each association's assets be held in reserve; that is, not available for loans. The reserve requirement prior to 1971 amounted to 7½ percent of each association's deposits. In periods of tight money, the reserve requirement is reduced in an effort to increase the available cash for loans. In November, 1979 the requirement was lowered from 6 percent to 5.5 percent.

After many years of review, the Federal Home Loan Bank Board has recently taken some limited steps to permit a few mutually-owned savings associations to switch the form of ownership to that of a stockholder-owned corporation. From the depositor's viewpoint, a change to a stockholder form is important. Over the years these thrift institutions have built up substantial undistributed surpluses, which technically belong to the depositors. Since the individual depositors continue to change through the years, the proper allocation of the accumulated surplus to the current depositors is a major problem to any transition of ownership. From the lending viewpoint, the same rules and regulations would apply to the institution regardless of the form of ownership. A stockholder form of ownership might be considered more aggressive and could tend to channel loans into areas of higher yields.

Investment Policies of Savings Associations

Two important rules have guided savings and loan investment policies. One of these is the requirement that 80 percent of a savings association's assets be held in residential mortgage loans, as that is the purpose of federal charters. The other is a rule of the Internal Revenue Service that allows a savings association to transfer earnings to a nontaxable surplus account, providing that loans classified as commercial do not exceed 18 percent of the association's assets.

The tax rule was designed to assist the purpose of the savings associations. The pooling of the depositors' funds is intended to provide them with a source of money to purchase or improve their homes. By permitting any earnings to accumulate tax-free, the association's ability to assist its customers is increased, and this promotes the growth of the economy. If any of the earnings are distributed as a dividend to the association's owners, that distribution is taxed at the corporate level and also as income to the recipient. Consequently, many associations prefer to accumulate surpluses.

But surpluses have not always been enough to stabilize the inflow of funds when new deposits slow or reverse themselves into an outflow. From experiences learned in the 1969–70 credit crunch, the Federal Home Loan Bank Board made several changes in the regulations governing member associations to improve their ability to handle fluctuating market conditions. Rules limit the right of a depositor to withdraw from a passbook savings account held by a savings association without a 30-day prior notice. The protection offered by this rule is seldom utilized, as a refusal to permit immediate withdrawal today would most likely create the sense of panic that it is intended to restrain. However, it is this legal limitation on immediate withdrawal that gives an association a technical position to make the long-term loans that cannot be permitted with a commercial bank's demand checking accounts.

To give savings associations greater stability than the 30-day withdrawal notice was supposed to provide, the FHLB in 1971 created a savings certificate to pay 6 percent interest, which was a full 1 percent over the existing passbook rate, provided that the certificate was held for two years. The new savings form was very popular, and some areas of the country reported over half of their deposits were coming from the long-term certificates. Another practice that had a tendency to improve the savings associations' long-term stability of deposits was the increase of branch offices into the smaller communities and rural areas. The effect has been to attract depositors who keep their money in the association and ignore interest rate cycles.

The FHLBB also relaxed some of the restrictions on the types of loans that savings associations could make, allowing them to finance mobile homes and household appliances and to grant more liberal property-improvement loans. These are short-term loans for the most part and give the associations a more rapid turnover of their money and greater flexibility in their loan portfolio.

A Decade of Changes

Prior to the 1970s, savings associations generally made loans from their own deposit assets and made little effort to sell these loans. The liquidity of their loan assets (the ability to convert the asset into cash) had not been a great concern. The credit crunch of 1969–70 highlighted the need for greater flexibility for this major source of long-term mortgage loans. Consequently, in 1971 the Federal Home Loan Bank added a new federally-chartered corporation to its system—the Federal Home Loan Mortgage Corporation. The FHLMC, more popularly known as "Freddie Mac," was created for the purpose of *buying* loans from member (of the Federal Home Loan Bank System) savings associations. To raise the money for purchasing loans, the FHLMC sold its own mortgage-backed securities called *participation certificates* or PCs. How did the privately owned savings associations react to the new entry into the secondary market for mortgage loans? Some savings associations ignored the FHLMC and continued to loan only their own deposit assets, others sold a moderate amount of their loans, and some went all out with the sale of most every loan they made.

As the rules were changing to allow savings associations greater freedom with their handling of mortgage loans, the commercial bankers who had ignored mortgage loans in many parts of the country, began to show renewed interest in this particular market. Appeals were made to governmental authorities to allow commercial banks similar advantage to those held by savings associations. These were principally the right to pay a higher rate of interest on savings deposits and the deferment of income taxes on undistributed profit. In 1973 the interest differential that could be paid on passbook savings deposits was reduced from 1/2 percent to 1/4 percent when the permissible rate for savings associations was increased to 5 1/2 percent and that for commercial banks moved to a maximum of 5 1/4 percent. The 1/4 percent differential has been maintained since then and is applied to other types of savings accounts. At this writing, the advantage held by savings associations with a tax deferment on undistributed profits has not been allowed for commercial banks on their earnings made from long-term mortgage loans. Even so, the advantage has become somewhat moot as many savings associations burdened with older, low interest-bearing mortgage loan assets began to show losses by the early 1980s. Without profits, the tax deferment has become meaningless for the hard-pressed savings associations.

In the late 1970s, increasing interest rates again threatened the ability of savings associations to compete for funds with their fixed-rate passbook interest and a limited use of longer term certificates of deposit. The heavy withdrawals of money from savings associations for investment into other, more lucrative, forms of savings is termed *disinter-mediation*. When this occurs, savings associations must limit their loans and often find it very difficult to meet prior commitments for loans. To maintain the capability of savings associations to provide mortgage money, a number of new, longer term certificates of deposit were introduced. Some C/Ds formerly required minimum deposits (or purchases of the certificates) in $1,000 amounts; all have since been reduced to $100 minimum amounts. The range of terms offered runs from three months to eight years: the longer the term, the higher the interest rate. While these rates are subject to change, when the passbook rate (maximum rate) offered was 5½ percent, the longest certificate at eight years offered an 8 percent interest rate. Large certificates of deposit, defined as $100,000 or more, are not limited by rules as to interest that can be paid. The result has been very high rates (over 14 percent in 1982) that may fluctuate daily.

In addition, a new concept in savings certificates intended to compete directly for funds against the government's own Treasury bills, was authorized. Experience had shown that T-bills were one of the largest causes of disintermediation from the savings associations. When the yields offered by T-bills rose approximately 1½ percent above savings rates, the money started to flow out. To counteract this trend, savings associations and commercial banks can now offer *money market certificates*. The interest rate offered can be ¼ percent over the yield determined each Monday on the sale of 26-week Treasury bills. The minimum deposit required for a money market certificate is $10,000, which is the minimum denomination for a T-bill. In 1981 a new mini-certificate was approved in a minimum denomination of $7,500 with the rate and term tied to the three-month Treasury bill. A result of these moves has been to retain deposits within savings associations and available for mortgage loans, but at substantially higher costs.

Another relatively new method of attracting additional money into savings associations (and commercial banks) is the sale of mortgage-backed bonds or other mortgage-backed securities. In this procedure, a block of mortgages is pledged as collateral for the issuance of a mortgage-backed security, which is sold to the public as an investment. This procedure, as well as the issuance of large denomination certificates of deposit, is altering the character of savings resources in that more reliance is being placed on *borrowing* of funds by the association. The result is a broadening of the base for funds and an increase in the cost of money for use in making loans.

One rather obvious method of increasing the inflow of funds into savings accounts would be a relaxation of the Federal Reserve's Regulation Q, which sets the maximum rates for passbook accounts. The Deregulation Act of 1980 did authorize a gradual lifting of the interest rate limit over a six-year period and complete removal of the limit by 1986. However, there has been some delay in taking any action on this rate limitation. One of the problems facing regulators in allowing an increase is the detrimental impact on older savings associations, particularly in the stable northeast section of the country. For years savings associations did not have a market for their loans and customarily retained 100 percent of their mortgage notes. These older assets, still paying returns of 5 percent to 7 percent, are a threat to the stability of the institutions if limits on passbook rates are removed.

Lending Limits of Savings Associations

The lending powers of both federally- and state-chartered associations are limited by their respective regulatory agencies. In November, 1980, dollar limits that applied to Federal chartered institutions were dropped. Individual institutions often set their own dollar limits, with a lower limit for 95% loans. The "95 percent" means the amount of the loan in relation to the value of the property. Almost all types of loans consider the value of the property as the appraised value, or the selling price, whichever is the lesser. Federal regulations call for mortgage default insurance on any loan over 90 percent, but most lenders place this requirement on loans over 80 percent.

While state regulatory agencies exercise their own authority over lending limits, many choose to follow the guidelines established by the Federal Home Loan Bank Board for its member associations. As pointed out earlier, a large number of state-chartered associations have joined the Federal Home Loan Bank system, since it is much less confusing to follow a sound national policy when possible.

There are fewer dollar limits on the amount of money that may be loaned at ratios of 80 percent or less because the risk exposure of the lending institution is much lower. Some states have simply removed all dollar limits for their own chartered institutions, depending on the prudent judgment of the associations' lending officers to establish their own limitations.

Another limitation on loans is that no one borrower may have more than 10 percent of the association's net worth outstanding. Loans to officers and directors are prohibited by a 1976 FSLIC regulation, except for a personal residence.

A major consideration of most savings associations in establishing their own limits and guidelines is the pattern established for the purchase of loans in the secondary market. Both the Federal Home Loan Mortgage Corporation and the Federal National Mortgage Association have limiting requirements. The ability to sell a block of mortgage loans to either of these organizations at some future date gives an association's portfolio of loans a much greater flexibility. In addition to maximum dollar limitations for various types of loans, the secondary market purchasers are also concerned with the forms used for the note and mortgage instruments. Limitations also apply to the types of loans—the secondary market is not as strong for 95 percent loans as for the lower ratio loans. The market for resort, weekend, or second homes is not as good as for primary houses.

In the matter of geographical limits, some states still confine their thrift institutions to property loans within a maximum of 50 miles from an association's offices. Federal guidelines, which did limit member associations to loans within a radius of 100 miles of the lending institution's authorized servicing offices have been removed. Savings associations are restricted in the amount of money they can invest out of state. The long-time limit at 5 percent of their assets that could be invested out of state was raised several years ago to 10 percent and applies only to conventional loans. There is no limit on the amount of money any one institution can invest out of state in FHA- or VA-underwritten loans.

The need for making mortgage loans outside a local geographic area falls primarily on the large savings associations in the big eastern cities, in Chicago, and in some of the cash-heavy midwestern cities, and even in some of the smaller communities with good business activity but not a commensurate residential growth. In the past it has been these cash-surplus associations which provide much of the mortgage money for the growing sections of the country that have generally been short of lendable funds. And as purchasers of loans, these associations become a part of the secondary market.

Considering the large number of savings associations in this country, it should be noted that the majority are relatively small in assets— under $25 million—and restrict their lending to their local areas. These associations are usually active, enthusiastic participants in local community programs and take considerable pride in using their available funds to promote neighborhood growth.

Deposit Insurance

Of the 4,600 savings associations in this country, about 3,900 carry deposit insurance with the Federal Savings and Loan Insurance Corporation. The FSLIC is a federal agency and functions in a manner similar to the Federal Deposit Insurance Corporation which insures deposits in commercial banks. In several states, a state insurance agency insures deposits covering an additional 400 savings associations. The balance of the savings associations are either insured by private carriers or have no insurance. Insured associations generally display the emblem of the insuring agency in a prominent location.

What kinds of deposits are insured? All kinds of deposits in the insured institution are covered. This includes passbook accounts, savings certificates, individual retirement accounts (IRAs), Keough accounts, and certificates of deposit. However, there is a limit on the amount of coverage. At present the limit is set at a maximum of $100,000 for each account holder. This means an individual is insured up to $100,000 even though he or she may have more than one account in the insured institution totaling more than $100,000.

Cost of the insurance is paid for by the insured association. Over the nearly 50 years that the FSLIC has been in operation it has collected reserves of $6.5 billion which are invested in U.S. Treasury securities. As additional protection, the FSLIC can borrow (presently up to $750 million) from the U.S. Treasury, and it can require additional premiums to be paid by the insured savings associations.

Savings associations hold over $500 billion in savings deposits, most of which is insured by the FSLIC. While $6.5 billion may seem like an inadequate reserve for so large a deposit asset, there is little expectation that any more than a few associations would fail at any one time. The record has been excellent in that only a few institutions have ever been closed and only about $350 million has had to be paid to insured savers over the life of the FSLIC. The FSLIC carefully monitors its insured associations watching for signs of trouble. It can arrange for a merger with a solvent institution should this become necessary to avoid a failure.

Investment Table

Table 5-6 shows the distribution of the loan portfolio for savings and loan associations over the past four years. Real estate mortgages, which are, of course, the purpose of their charters, comprise 75 percent of their assets. Growth of total assets continues at a moderate rate, showing an increase of 18 percent in the 1979 to 1982 period. Note the decline in net worth beginning in 1981.

Mutual Savings Banks

Because the origins of mutual savings banks are so similar to that of savings and loan associations, they are included in the category of thrift institutions: savings and loan associations were organized for the specific purpose of savings intended for homeownership; mutual savings banks were organized simply to encourage saving with no specific usage in mind.

TABLE 5-6

Savings and Loan Associations' Selected Assets and Liabilities (In Millions of Dollars, End of Period)

Account	1979	1980	1981 July	Aug.	Sept.	Oct.	Nov.	Dec.	1982 Jan.	Feb.	Mar.	Apr.[p]
1 Assets	578,962	630,712	649,807	653,022	655,658	659,073	660,326	663,844	667,600	671,895	678,039	681,712
2 Mortgages	475,688	503,192	511,990	518,172	518,778	519,248	519,146	518,350	517,493	516,284	515,896	514,683
3 Cash and investment securities	46,341	57,928	57,817	58,932	59,530	61,517	61,369	62,756	64,089	66,585	67,758	68,050
4 Other	56,933	69,592	75,000	75,918	77,350	78,308	79,811	82,738	86,018	89,026	94,835	98,979
5 Liabilities and net worth	578,962	630,712	649,807	653,022	655,658	659,073	660,326	663,844	667,600	671,895	678,039	681,712
6 Savings capital	470,004	511,636	514,805	513,438	515,649	519,288	519,777	524,374	526,382	529,064	535,566	532,955
7 Borrowed money	55,232	64,586	79,704	83,456	87,477	86,108	86,255	89,097	89,099	89,465	91,013	93,752
8 FHLBB	40,441	47,045	57,188	60,025	61,857	62,000	61,922	62,794	62,581	62,690	63,639	65,242
9 Other	14,791	17,541	22,516	23,431	25,620	24,108	24,333	26,303	26,518	26,775	27,374	28,510
10 Loans in process	9,582	8,767	7,741	7,354	7,040	6,757	6,451	6,369	6,249	6,144	6,399	6,563
11 Other	11,506	12,394	16,556	18,275	15,307	17,506	19,101	15,612	18,356	20,145	18,574	22,435
12 Net worth	32,638	33,329	31,001	30,499	30,185	29,414	28,742	28,392	27,514	27,077	26,487	26,007
13 MEMO: Mortgage loan commitments outstanding	16,007	16,102	17,235	16,689	16,012	15,733	15,758	15,225	15,131	15,397	15,582	16,326

Source: *Federal Reserve Bulletin*, June 1982, p. A29

This latter type of bank exists mainly in the northeastern 18 states, plus Oregon, Washington, and Alaska, with 75 percent of the total assets located in just two states—New York and Massachusetts. All are state chartered, and all are mutually owned as the name implies. However, the depositor-owners have almost no voice in management. As presently organized, the mutual savings banks elect their first board of trustees. Subsequent vacancies are filled by the board itself, thus creating a self-perpetuating management.

Mutual savings banks are an outgrowth of a banking method originally popular with new citizens of foreign birth who did not understand or place much confidence in the pieces of paper used as checks. They felt more comfortable dealing in cash. Consequently, the savings banks provided a convenient depository for a savings account and/or cashing paychecks. There was no real need in the beginning for checking account service, and these banks still do not feature this type of demand deposit. However, steps taken by federal authorities to deregulate certain banking procedures have encouraged increased offering of check-type deposit accounts.

As controlled by the state regulatory bodies, mutual savings banks may belong to the Federal Deposit Insurance Corporation (the same as commercial banks) or to one of several state agencies that provide similar account deposit insurance. These insurance agencies exercise authority as to types of investments, limits on amounts for each, and require certain accounting procedures to be followed. They also run periodic examinations of the banks' records to assure that standards are being met.

Investment Policies of Mutual Savings Banks

Mutual savings banks have a wider choice of investments than savings associations. Where the associations are substantially limited to residential mortgages, the savings banks can buy bonds and make personal, educational, and other consumer-type loans. It is interesting to note that despite the latitude available for investments by this type of institution, the loan portfolios of all savings banks have shown a steady increase in mortgage lending since World War II. In the period immediately following that war, savings banks held approximately 30 percent of their investments in mortgage loans. An explanation of this relatively low percentage is suggested by the fact that foreclosures accompanying the Depression had left an unfavorable mark on mortgage loans, which was followed by the decreased building volume during the war years of 1941 through 1946. Both of these factors had encouraged heavy investments in government securities. By 1960, however, the investments in mortgages had jumped to a little over 70 percent of the total assets and by 1970 had moved above 75 percent. What accounts for this strong growth of investments in mortgages, which has more than doubled since the 1940s? The following four reasons can be cited:

1. The end of World War II brought a selling off of government bonds, depressing the yield from them as compared to mortgages.
2. Changes in the banking laws of the largest states controlling mutual savings banks permitted them to make out-of-state loans.
3. The housing industry expanded following World War II, greatly increasing the demand for mortgage money.
4. Mortgage lenders' attitudes generally changed toward acceptance of FHA and VA commitments, now considering them to be sound and valued procedures.

After 1970, mutual savings banks reduced the amount of their investments in mortgage loans and turned a bit more to securities, particularly corporate bonds, for the investment of their increasing deposits. As a result, mortgage loans dropped to about 60 percent of their total assets through the 1970s and to 55 percent by 1982. Unlike savings associations, which have shown a preference for conventional loans, the mutual savings banks invest heavily in FHA- and VA-underwritten loans. Approximately one-half of their mortgage loans are held in FHA-VA types because these are underwritten and can be made out of state without limits.

The impact of mutual savings banks on our mortgage money market is far greater than the rather regionalized base of their home offices would indicate. With the authority to make out-of-state investments, the savings banks located in areas of heavy deposits relative to loan demands for housing have been able to profitably channel money to the cash-short growth areas of the south, southwest, and west. The movement of this money to out-of-state investments has been handled through agreements with mortgage bankers and other savings institutions and will be more fully detailed in Chapter 7. The savings banks use both an immediate purchase procedure of buying large blocks of loans on a wholesale basis and a forward commitment method, which is a sales and service type of agreement with an agent, such as a mortgage banker, to purchase a block of loans of a specific type at an agreed interest rate over the next four to nine months.

Table of Mutual Savings Bank Investments

Table 5-7 shows a stabilizing of deposits in mutual savings banks and a gradual change in the investment of their assets. Mortgage loans have declined in dollar value and represent a smaller portion of the investment portfolio. This decline reflects a diversification of investments and a concern over the unsettled conditions in the real estate market.

TABLE 5-7

Mutual Savings Banks' Selected Assets and Liabilities (In Millions of Dollars, End of Period)

Account	1979	1980	1981	1981				1982				
				Sept.	Oct.	Nov.	Dec.	Jan.	Feb.	Mar.	Apr.	May
14 **Assets**	**163,405**	**171,564**	**174,578**	**174,761**	**175,234**	**175,693**	**175,258**	**175,728**	**175,938**	**175,763**	**174,776**	n.a.
Loans												
15 Mortgage	98,908	99,865	100,095	99,987	99,944	99,903	99,879	99,997	99,788	98,338	97,464	
16 Other	9,253	11,733	14,359	14,560	14,868	14,725	15,073	14,753	15,029	15,604	16,514	
Securities												
17 U.S. government	7,658	8,949	9,361	9,369	9,594	9,765	9,508	9,810	9,991	9,966	10,072	
18 State and local government	2,930	2,390	2,291	2,326	2,323	2,394	2,271	2,288	2,290	2,293	2,276	
19 Corporate and other	37,086	39,282	38,374	38,180	38,118	38,108	37,874	37,791	37,849	37,781	37,379	
20 Cash	3,156	4,334	4,629	4,791	4,810	5,118	5,039	5,442	5,210	5,412	5,219	
21 Other assets	4,412	5,011	5,469	5,547	5,577	5,681	5,615	5,649	5,781	5,869	5,852	
22 **Liabilities**	**163,405**	**171,564**	**174,578**	**174,761**	**175,234**	**175,693**	**175,258**	**175,728**	**175,938**	**175,763**	**174,776**	
23 Deposits	146,006	154,805	153,757	153,120	153,412	154,066	153,809	155,110	154,843	154,626	154,022	
24 Regular	144,070	151,416	151,394	150,753	151,072	151,975	151,787	153,003	152,801	152,616	151,979	
25 Ordinary savings	61,123	53,971	50,593	49,003	49,254	48,238	48,456	49,425	48,898	48,297	48,412	
26 Time and other	82,947	97,445	100,800	101,750	10?,818	103,737	126,889	121,343	120,740	120,282	118,536	
27 Other	1,936	2,086	28,494	27,073	25,769	24,806	2,023	2,108	2,042	2,010	2,043	
28 Other liabilities	5,873	6,695	10,156	11,125	1?,458	11,513	11,434	10,632	11,280	11,464	11,132	
29 General reserve accounts	11,525	11,368	10,665	10,516	10,364	10,114	10,015	9,986	9,814	9,672	9,622	
30 MEMO: Mortgage loan commitments outstanding	3,182	1,476	1,401	1,333	1,218	1,140	1,207	1,293	916	950	978	

Source: *Federal Reserve Bulletin,* June 1982, p. A29.

Commercial Banks

The largest of all lenders with the greatest total cash resources are the commercial banks. But in total investments they seldom carry over 10 to 12 percent of their portfolio in long-term mortgage loans. Before the Depression, commercial banks held a much larger proportion of their deposits in savings accounts, also called *time deposits,* as opposed to the demand deposits or checking accounts. After World War II, the growth of thrift institutions accounted for the greater portion of savings increases. The thrift institutions were permitted to pay a higher interest rate on their deposits, which fostered the movement away from the commercial banks. Being unable to compete for the longer term savings money, the commercial banks concentrated their efforts on the short-term loans they could make with their demand deposits.

In many small communities and rural areas, the commercial bank still represents the main source of all money, including mortgage money for farm loans. The banks make the longer term property loans in direct relation to the amount of savings deposits they hold. In large urban areas, most commercial banks refuse to make real estate loans for long terms, except, perhaps, as an accommodation to a good commercial customer or for some other appropriate reason such as a civic improvement. Even then, the term of such a loan would be in the 5-to-15-year bracket rather than the 20-to-30-year bracket. During the 1970s, the patterns changed somewhat as banking regulations tended to reduce the former competitive advantages of the thrift institutions and make long-term investments more attractive for the commercial banks.

In any type of loan, an obvious restriction is the size of the bank and its capitalization. There are about 14,700 commercial banks in the United States with resources averaging $25 million. The range in size is from less than $1 million in deposits to over $100 billion. Regulations limit any single loan of a bank to a percent of its total assets or not to exceed the net worth (the equity interest) of the bank. In addition, each bank will establish guidelines for its own loans based on its size, which will also include loan minimums. For example, a huge bank such as Chase Manhattan of New York will not consider some categories of loans, such as oil production loans, for less than $1 million, whereas a small local bank could not touch a $1 million loan but can make money on a personal loan for a thousand dollars.

Regulation of commercial Banks, State and National

Commercial banks operate under either state charters or national charters. The distinction to the public lies in the use of the word *national* in the name of the bank.

State-chartered banks operate under the authority of a state banking board or commission, and the rules have considerable variety. State charters in the past have granted greater leeway than national charters in regard to the type of loan, the term of the loan, the amount of the loan in relation to the collateral offered as security, and the dollar amount of the loan in relation to the bank's assets.

State banks can, and often do, become members of the Federal Reserve system and insure their deposits with the FDIC. If so, they become subject to the regulations and the audits of both the federal and state authorities.

The authority and responsibility of the state and federal banking agencies over the commercial banks can be listed as follows:

Comptroller of the Currency Has authority to grant national charters and to regulate and supervise the 4,700 national banks.

Federal Reserve System This is the government bank with authority to examine, supervise, and press corrective action when necessary over the 4,700 national banks and the 750 state-chartered banks that are members of the Federal Reserve System.

Federal Deposit Insurance Corporation Insures the deposits (up to $100,000 each) in 14,470 banks in the United States. The FDIC does not have examination responsibility over the 5,450 member banks of the Federal Reserve System. It does have examination responsibility over the 9,250 state-chartered banks that are insured by the FDIC and are not members of the Federal Reserve System. Its insurance activities do give the FDIC authority to take actions that will minimize the impact of bank failures on depositors of any insured bank.

State banking agencies Have the responsibility of regulating their own state-chartered banks. The degree of regulation and enforcement powers varies among the states, but most try to follow the patterns for investments and accounting procedures as established by federal authorities.

Reserve Requirements

One of the ways the Federal Reserve Bank controls the economy is by adjusting the reserve requirements for the banking system. Prior to 1980, the authority of the Fed in this matter was confined to member commercial banks. If the Fed opted to throttle back on an inflation-fueled economy, it could increase the reserve requirement. This action would force member banks to reduce the amount of their assets that could be profitably placed in loans. That is, a greater proportion of their assets would have to be placed on deposit, interest-free, with the Federal Reserve Bank. In practice, this kind of action antagonized bankers to the point that many state-chartered institutions elected to withdraw from the Federal Reserve System. (Only national charters are required to belong to the Fed.) Further, the limited impact of this action made the reserve requirements ineffective and a bit unfair. Consequently, one of the titles in the Monetary Control Act of 1980 drastically altered the application of reserve requirements. Over a period of several years, the Federal Reserve has expanded authority to phase in reserve requirements for *all* depository institutions that handle "transaction" accounts; that is, checking accounts. This includes deposits on which the depositor can make a withdrawal payable to a third party. Examples of such withdrawals include checks, drafts, negotiable orders of withdrawal (NOW accounts), and share drafts. Savings accounts with automatic transfer privileges to checking accounts and accounts subject to automated teller machines are classed as transaction accounts and are now subject to Federal Reserve requirements.

What this means is that all institutions handling transaction accounts will come under the Federal Reserve's reserve regulations. This includes not only the commercial banks, but savings associations, mutual savings banks, and credit unions, regardless of whether they are state or federal charters. The new reserve requirements call for 3 percent reserve on the first $25 million of transaction balances and 12 percent on all over $25 million. In addition, there is a reserve requirement for nonpersonal (other than an individual or sole proprietorship) time deposits in the amount of 3 percent. A *time deposit* is defined as one allowing the institution at least 14 days' notice prior to withdrawal, and the reserve rule applies to any such deposit with a maturity of less than four years. Because most of the institutions covered under the 1980 law are nonmembers of the Fed and not previously required to deposit reserves under their rules, the Fed is phasing in the requirement over eight years—from November 13, 1980 to September 2, 1987. The phase in calls for an increase in reserve by one-eighth of the full requirement each year. For member institutions that have been subject to higher reserve requirements in the past (up to 16¼ percent), the adjustment is being phased in over three and a half years allowing one-quarter of the difference between old and new reserve requirements to be adjusted for each year.

The immediate impact of these changes on real estate credit will not be very great. What it does is transfer an increased measure of control over all regulated lending institutions to the Federal Reserve Bank. How the Fed may exercise its expanded authority has yet to be determined.

Real Estate Investments of Commercial Banks

Insofar as real estate loans are concerned, the national banks have always been more restrictive in their regulations than have state-chartered banks. The historical precedent for this difference goes back to 1820. Prior to that time, national banks were not even permitted to make a mortgage loan. The rule has, of course, been changed to allow real estate loans, but generally with lower limits than most state-chartered banks can now permit.

Within their individual limitations, all commercial banks make real estate loans of some form or another. These loans can be generally classified in the following three catagories:

1. Direct mortgage loans.
2. Construction loans.
3. Mortgage warehouse line of credit.

Direct Mortgage Loans. While all commercial banks are now legally authorized to make loans using real estate as collateral, the incentives to make such loans vary considerably. Small rural banks are still the only source of such loans in many areas. In medium-sized towns and cities, the banks often use their capacity to make long-term loans as an attraction for other business. In large urban areas, the commercial banks find more profitable use for their money in short-term loans that give the portfolio more liquidity. But there are short-term mortgage loans that do attract commercial bank investments.

Some city banks will make short-term loans—three to five years—on raw land for a developer. These are usually limited to 65 percent of the land value and carry higher interest rates than, say, a home loan. Another type of short-term mortgage loan would be on a building fully leased with a fast payout assigned to the bank. For example, service stations can be handled with mortgage loans for up to 15 years, which are secured by a major oil company lease agreement.

Commercial banks often have customers or associated lending firms that are capable of making long-term loans and can lend assistance in accommodating a customer through referrals. A few banks have established real estate investment trusts, discussed later in this chapter, to provide long-term money for their customers outside of the bank's immediate deposit assets.

Another possible source of mortgage money under the control of most commercial banks is that held by their trust departments. In this field the bank acts as the manager of a trust and would not be investing deposits subject to demand withdrawals, nor would it be subject to the same banking regulations affecting deposits. However, most trusts are guided by the terms under which the money is placed in the bank's care, and the type of investment permitted may be restricted. Trust funds are usually held for specified terms and, as such, make a good source for mortgage money if the trust allows.

Construction Loans. Construction loans are a special form of real estate loan that will be discussed in greater detail in Chapter 14 on loan analysis, but should be noted here as one principal type of mortgage loan offered by some commercial banks. Because of the high risk and specialized construction knowledge required for these loans, not all commercial banks are qualified to handle them. The loans are short-term, generally 6 to 30 months, and return high rates of interest, such as one to five points over the prime rate.

Mortgage Warehouse Line of Credit. With many of the large commercial banks, the warehousing of mortgage loans for other lenders comprises a major portion of their real estate credit lines. The purpose is to provide immediate cash for a customer, such as a mortgage banker, to fund their loans at closing. After establishing a line of credit with the bank, the mortgage banker is able to pledge a note and mortgage obtained from the borrower as security for the cash to fund the loan. Since the mortgage company will be continually adding to the number of loans pledged with the commercial bank, and then periodically shipping groups of these loans on out to permanent investors, the practice has acquired the name of *warehousing*.

The credit lines can run from $1 to $10 million, depending on the strength of the mortgage company. Sale of these loans out of warehouse is usually made in blocks of $250,000 upward to $3 million. A warehouse line of credit will cost the mortgage company for money so borrowed an interest rate based on the prime rate, or perhaps 1 percent (one point) over prime with a term of 6 to 18 months. Warehousing as a mortgage company procedure is more fully covered in Chapter 7.

Table of Mortgage Loan Activity

Table 5-8 shows the mortgage loans held by commercial banks compared with their total loans and investments.

Community Reinvestment Act (CRA)

The Community Reinvestment Act, which took effect in November 1978, expands the concept that regulated financial institutions must serve the needs of their communities. The purpose of the Act is to re-

TABLE 5-8

Mortgage Loans Held by Commercial Banks
(In Billions of Dollars, Seasonally Adjusted)

Date	Total Loans	Mortgage Loans	Percent of Total
1977	891.1	175.1	19.6
1978	1,014.3	210.5	20.7
1979	1,149.4	248.3	21.5
1980	1,237.0	260.6	21.0
1981	1,316.3	285.7	21.6
1982 (June)	1,368.7	297.3	21.7

Source: *Federal Reserve Bulletin*, June 1982, p. A15.

quire all regulated financial institutions to publicize their lending services in their own community and to encourage participation in local lending assistance programs. Enforcement of the requirements is handled by federal regulators—the examiners who regularly review each institution's loan records and procedures. The penalty for failure to comply is a limitation on approvals for expansion that may be required from federal regulatory authorities by the offending institution. The Act applies to all federally-regulated financial institutions and is subject to interpretation by each of the regulatory authorities. Initially, the guidelines and examination procedures were defined jointly by the Federal Home Loan Bank Board, the Comptroller of the Currency, the Federal Reserve Board, and the Federal Deposit Insurance Corporation.

What the Act requires is that each institution undertake four new procedures, listed below:

1. *Define the lender's community.* Each lender must prepare a map of the area that it serves, which is the neighborhood from which it draws its deposits and into which it makes loans.
2. *List types of credit offered.* A list of credit services available from the institution must be submitted to the regulators and made available to the public. The Act is directed towards publicizing methods of borrowing, rather than saving money.
3. *Public notice and public comments.* Each institution covered by this Act must post a notice in its place of business stating that the institution's credit performance is being evaluated by federal regulators and further, that the public has the right to comment on the institution's performance and to appear at open hearings on any request for expansion.
4. *Report on efforts to meet community needs.* A periodic report

must be made on the efforts of the institution to ascertain the credit needs of its community and how it is attempting to meet those needs.

The regulatory authorities admit that compliance with the Act is determined primarily by the judgment of the federal examiners. Guidelines have been issued to provide examples of compliance, such as holding seminars to inform the public as to how they can borrow money, studies made of the community to determine credit needs, and participation in at least some of the many federal housing and loan assistance programs now offered.

Life Insurance Companies

Life insurance companies rank fifth in the nation's total investments by sources, and they have long had a substantial interest in real estate financing—both as an investment in the ownership or equity position and in the making of direct mortgage loans. At one time, life insurance companies equaled the total investments of savings associations in the amounts of their mortgage loans. But life insurance companies were not organized primarily for the purpose of providing mortgage money, as were the savings associations. Their primary interest in using their substantial investment funds has been to provide the highest yield possible commensurate with the safety of their policy-holders' money. And this has dictated some flexibility in the movement of their investments from time to time for better returns.

Casualty insurance companies—those that handle fire coverage, automobile insurance, and a host of other types of hazard insurance—have tremendous premium incomes but are not required to maintain the larger permanent reserves demanded for the life insurance companies. Therefore, casualty companies hold their reserves in short-term investments due to the need for liquidity to pay claims. They negotiate practically no mortgage loans and are not a source for our consideration.

Like all sources of mortgage money, the life insurance companies must possess a predictable or controllable cash inflow and outflow with a large pool retained for investment. These companies fully meet this requirement because they have established the need for life insurance protection as a way of life and thus continue to enjoy steady growth of their premium income. The reserves held to assure policyholders that their contracts will be honored upon reaching a specified age, or upon death, provide a multibillion-dollar pool of investment capital that also produces a continuing profit for the life insurance company to reinvest.

The outflow of cash is about as predictable as the inflow. What many would consider an uncertain problem is the payment of death benefits; but carefully compiled mortality tables show quite accurately the average rates of death, and on the large number of policyholders that insurance companies deal with, the payment of benefits for any period is readily calculable. Small companies usually reinsure their life insurance contracts with the large companies, and even large companies will spread the risk of a large policy with several other insurance companies.

One of the least predictable outflows of cash for an insurance company comes from the right of policyholders to borrow up to the amount of the cash value of their policy at a low rate of interest. Repayment of such a loan carries a first claim on the insurance proceeds and is a secure investment for the company. But a sudden demand by policyholders for cash can strain a life insurance company's resources and force liquidation of some other portion of its investment portfolio. Demands for loans by policyholders follow money cycles; for example, in periods of tight money, more policyholders seek the relatively lower cost policy loans.

In the United States there are over 1,900 life insurance companies and a few from Canada selling policy contracts. They range in size from companies with a very few million in assets to the multibillion dollar giants that have become household words, such as Prudential, Metropolitan Life, and Equitable.

Regulation of Life Insurance Companies

All insurance companies are under the control of state regulatory bodies. There are no federal charters for insurance. Consequently, the life insurance companies are required to adhere to policies that do vary from state to state, but the regulations are generally directed toward protecting the investing public.

The state regulations usually set limits on the types of investment that are permissible, the percent of total portfolio that may be kept in stock, or bonds, or mortgage loans, or the amount of liquidity that must be maintained for each policy dollar outstanding; and most states establish limits on the maximum amount of any one loan or any one property. Some states have limited their own chartered insurance companies to investments within their own states, and others have placed limits on out-of-state companies selling insurance within their state, unless proportional investments are made within the state. Restrictive investment policies based on geography are giving way to regulations designed more for the safeguarding of the policyholder's dollar.

For the most part, state regulations and governing commissions are well conceived and show good intentions to foster sound investment policies. But not all states are able to administer regulations and to police the actual operations as well as a legislature may have intended. Some state insurance boards have been created with substantial investigative capacity but little real authority to correct an abuse if it is discovered. Over the years there have been a few spectacular failures that might have been prevented. Fortunately, the very great majority of life insurance companies are soundly managed and are far more cautious with their policyholders' money than the state might require. Loan applications are carefully scrutinized and objectively judged. A few companies will even refuse to permit their own sales representatives to present a loan application from an individual who also wishes to buy life insurance—the loan underwriters want no pressure exerted on their judgment from the sales personnel.

Investment Policies

The normal pressure on life insurance companies to seek maximum yield from their investments, commensurate with the safety of the money, increased with the introduction of variable annuity policies. This type of life insurance provided for increases in dividends or in the total value of the policy based on the yields from the company's investments. The policy is an effort to compete with the growing interest of mutual funds as a personal investment. Whereas in the past, insurance companies moved their investments from, say, stocks and bonds into mortgage loans or other forms of securities, or vice versa, in order to achieve the highest yields, the pressure increased to do something more.

Many company investment managers had watched the real estate projects that they had made possible with mortgage loans at interest rates of 4 or 5 percent grow in value as land escalated in the 1950s and 1960s, while the insurance company earned only a nominal interest rate in return. Thereafter, the larger companies with greater resources in personnel began to direct their money and their talents into outright ownership and development of real estate as an investment procedure. During periods of scarce money, insurance companies as well as other lenders found they could increase yields by demanding a part of the equity interest—the so-called piece-of-the-action stipulation. One way companies have used to protect their investments from inflationary trends is to calculate debt service based on current market rentals for income properties, then take, perhaps, a quarter of any rental income increases that are made.

Another method commonly used by insurance companies expand-

ing their real estate investments is to join with an experienced development company as a partner. Metropolitan Life Insurance Company of
New York City joins with such developers as Trammel Crow of Dallas
and Kenneth Schnitzer of Houston to acquire land and build projects
such as the Allen Center in Houston projected at a half-billion dollars.
Business Men's Assurance of Kansas City, Mo., in addition to making
some direct mortgage loans, joins with developers as partners for large
commercial ventures, builds housing projects for resale to owners, and
builds hotels and motels for the purpose of leasing them to qualified operators such as the Marriott Hotel chain. Prudential uses real estate af-
filiates to build large urban complexes such as the $150 million
residential and commercial complex in the Detroit suburb of South-
field. A few states, fearing the movement of the insurance giants into
too much ownership of properties, have enacted restrictive laws to limit
the trend; that is, Texas does not permit an insurance company to own
an apartment building except as acquired through foreclosure.

For the individual borrower, there is little access to an insurance
company for a loan such as can be found by walking into a savings and
loan office. This is possible with some of the smaller insurance companies, but the larger ones must deal in larger loans or blocks of smaller
loans. The volume of money that a company such as Northwestern Mutual Life of Milwaukee must handle with over $2 billion in real estate
loans outstanding makes it impractical to deal directly with, say, a
$50,000 house loan.

Life insurance companies have in the past maintained their own
lending offices in selected locations, and a few still do. Lately, the trend
has been more toward working through correspondents or loan representatives. In the handling of direct mortgage loans, the companies can and
do make forward commitments to mortgage bankers for specific classes
of home loans. Many of the small and medium-sized companies find
home loans in their operating territory to be both profitable investments
and beneficial to their own company growth.

For the individual borrower, there is little access to an insurance
company for a loan such as can be found by walking into a savings and
loan office. This is possible with some of the smaller insurance companies, but the larger ones must deal in larger loans or blocks of smaller
loans. The volume of money that a company such as Northwestern Mutual Life of Milwaukee must handle with over $2 billion in real estate
loans outstanding makes it impractical to deal directly with, say, a
$50,000 house loan.

The investment portfolios of life insurance companies will continue to be influenced by the need for greater yields. Long-term mortgage loans are sound investments for the companies and should always
be of interest to them when the yields are competitive with other forms
of investment. But yield and security alone are not the only goals; there
is also a desire to maintain a particular balance with a company's overall
investments. Thus, a higher return from one type of investment would
not attract all of a company's money at that time. Looking ahead, it is
not likely that states will enact more restrictive legislation to direct an
insurance company's investments so as to press more money into the
mortgage lending field.

Table of Life Insurance Company Investments

Table 5-9 shows the distribution of life insurance company investments. Roughly one-half are held in business-type securities—stocks and bonds. From 1979 to 1982, the percentage of assets held in mortgages declined slightly from 27 percent to 26 percent of total assets.

Federal and State Governments

In addition to the private sources of money discussed so far, several federal and state government agencies provide funds for making direct mortgage loans or purchasing them from other lenders.

A few states have established housing agencies with authority to make direct mortgage loans to assist home buyers, and many more are seeking ways to encourage more lendable funds in their states. Money for this purpose is raised by the sale of bonds and with the assistance of various programs developed by the Department of Housing and Urban Development. All states have pension funds and most have specialized trust funds of some kind. These are being utilized increasingly to provide capital for development within the state and to improve housing for its people.

In North Dakota, the state itself owns the Bank of North Dakota. It was established in 1919 by a group of farmers as a service organization and to avoid using out-of-state bankers who they felt were overcharging for loans. By 1981 the bank held over $853 million in resources and led the nation in providing financial assistance to college students. Long-term home loans have been available for many years, but this type of credit was temporarily suspended in late 1982. The bank relies heavily on public deposits with the state government accounting for 75 percent of the deposits. It has been efficiently managed by an Industrial Commission, operates as one of the most profitable banks in the country, and has attracted the attention of several other states.

Tax-Exempt Bonds

When a state or municipality sells bonds to finance their various operations, the interest paid on these bonds is exempt from federal income taxes. As a result, the bonds attract higher income investors who gain from the tax-exempt feature. The availability of this lower cost money

TABLE 5-9

Investments of Life Insurarce Companies (In Millions of Dollars)

Account	1979	1980	1981					1982				
			Aug.	Sept.	Oct.	Nov.	Dec.	Jan.	Feb.	Mar.	Apr.	May^p
31 Assets..............................	**432,282**	**479,210**	**503,994**	**506,585**	**509,478**	**515,079**	**519,281**	**521,354**	**525,331**	**526,573**	**530,014**	
Securities												
32 Government................	338	21,378	23,691	23,949	24,280	24,621	25,200	25,310	26,157	26,847	27,322	
33 United States.........	4,888	5,345	7,359	7,544	7,670	7,846	8,321	8,578	9,204	9,887	10,236	
34 State and local......	6,428	6,701	6,865	6,904	7,033	7,129	7,148	6,968	7,063	7,043	7,069	
35 Foreign..............	9,022	9,332	9,467	9,501	9,577	9,646	9,731	9,764	9,890	9,917	10,017	n.a.
36 Business...............	222,332	238,113	250,186	250,371	250,315	253,976	255,632	254,978	257,614	257,318	257,452	
37 Bonds................	178,371	190,747	203,016	204,501	205,908	208,004	209,194	208,587	211,686	212,685	213,217	
38 Stocks..............	39,757	47,366	41,170	45,870	44,407	45,972	46,438	46,391	45,928	44,633	44,235	
39 Mortgages.............	118,421	131,080	135,928	136,516	136,982	137,736	138,433	139,046	139,596	139,777	140,259	
40 Real estate...........	13,007	15,033	17,429	17,626	17,801	18,382	18,629	19,157	19,276	18,999	19,472	
41 Policy loans..........	34,825	41,411	45,591	46,252	47,042	47,731	48,275	48,741	49,092	49,535	50,083	
42 Other assets.........	27,563	31,702	31,169	31,971	33,058	32,633	33,112	34,122	33,288	34,097	35,426	

Source: *Federal Reserve Bulletin*, June 1982, p. A29.

has encouraged its use for mortgage loans. Generally, two classes of municipal bonds have been used to raise money for mortgage lending: (1) to finance industrial development in the community, encouraging industry to bring jobs to the local people; and (2) to provide an additional source of money at lower cost to assist people buying homes.

As interest rates escalated in the late 1970s, tax-exempt municipal bonds became one of the very few ways to obtain lower cost loans, and their use multiplied. Since the tax-exempt nature of the money caused a possible loss in tax revenues and there was some question as to whether or not financing homes was a true purpose of the tax exemption, the federal government and the Internal Revenue Service decided to take a closer look at the matter. The result has been a series of tax rulings that for awhile closed the door on this kind of financing. What the IRS did was to set requirements for qualification of such bonds as tax exempt. One requirement was that at least 20 percent of the funds so raised must be used to finance housing for low-income families. While the purpose was good, the investment bankers who sell the bonds concluded that there was not sufficient assurance that the money could be properly allocated, and if not, the exempt status would be forfeited. One of the problems in the allocation of the funds was the question of qualification. With the escalation in the cost of housing, would it still be possible for lower income families to meet the qualification standards? Modifications have been made in the requirements as of this writing to permit a limited sale of tax-exempt securities for the purpose of financing mortgage loans.

States, counties, and municipalities have all become involved in this kind of financing to varying degrees. The methods used vary from making direct loans through a housing agency to handling the money through established, approved mortgage lenders. The loans that can be made are generally limited to middle and lower income families and have limits on dollar amount, term, and repayment methods. Because the source of the money is from securities offering a fixed rate of interest, the mortgage loans also offer fixed rates, rather than adjustable rate plans.

The federal government has felt a need to assist the people in their living and housing requirements and has long maintained programs of direct loans for such purposes. While a number of agencies provide financing and direct grants of money to assist farmers and ranchers, small businesses, minority businesses, disaster victims, and displaced families, the three most active agencies making direct loans based on real estate mortgages are the Federal Land Bank, the Farmers Home Administration, and the Government National Mortgage Association, discussed in the following paragraphs.

Federal Land Bank

Established in 1916 to provide funds to farmers and ranchers—funds that were not always available in the private sector—the Federal Land Bank system has provided many billions of dollars for the purchase and improvement of farms and ranches. Initially, financing was obtained as an agency of the federal government. Over the years, government advances have been fully repaid and the Federal Land Bank is now owned by over 500 Federal Land Bank Associations. The Associations are cooperative credit organizations owned by local borrower-members. It is the local associations that assist farmers in need of a loan, screen and approve acceptable loan applications, and forward the applications to the district Federal Land Bank. Approved loans are guaranteed by the local Associations.

The Federal Land Bank system operates through 12 district offices. Funding for the loans is now arranged through the sale of Consolidated Systemwide Bonds by the Federal Farm Credit Banks. This agency combines the requirements of the 13 Banks for Cooperatives and the 12 Federal Intermediate Credit Banks with the needs of the Federal Land Bank to make consolidated bond offerings. The bonds are not federal government obligations, nor are they guaranteed by the government, but in financial markets they are handled as government "agency" issues. Proceeds of each sale are allocated among the various districts as the need requires.

Loans are limited to 85 percent of the appraised value of the property with a maximum term of 35 years. Since the local Association guarantees the loan as well as administers the repayment, there is a strong incentive to work with the farmer-borrower in the enforcement of repayment schedules. The special nature of farm and ranch loans requires some flexibility in collections, and the borrower is dealing with his own peers who best know the local circumstances affecting repayment.

Farmers Home Administration

The Farmers Home Administration was established in 1946 as a part of the Department of Agriculture for the purpose of making and insuring loans to farmers and ranchers. The program's intent is to provide credit for the purchase and improvement of farms as well as rural community rehabilitation programs for low-income and elderly persons unable to obtain credit elsewhere. The FmHA is authorized to borrow money from the U.S. Treasury and from the Federal Financing Bank to obtain funds for its loans. Also, the agency can sell participations in mortgage pools to raise additional funds.

The home loan program under Section 502 is limited to rural areas or towns with a population of 10,000 or less, and to low- and moderate-income families who are unable to qualify for home financing in the private market. There are a few areas in the country with towns up to 20,000 population that have the special qualifications that permit this type of FmHA financing. Loans can be made up to 100 percent of the appraised value of a house for a family with an Adjusted Family Income (AFI) of not more than approximately $20,000 per year. The maximum permissible AFI is changed periodically as the economy requires, and it does vary in different sections of the country. The calculation for qualification within the AFI limits is as follows: Compute 95 percent of the gross family earnings, less $300 for each minor dependent child living at home. For example, The Adjusted Family Income of a family earning $22,000 per year with four minor children at home can be determined in the following manner:

Annual earnings	$22,000
Less: 5% adjustment	1,100
Less: 4 × 300	1,200
Adjusted Family Income	$19,700

Since the calculated AFI is less than the maximum $20,000 permitted, the family would qualify to make a loan application. If the AFI is $15,000 or less, the family may receive an interest subsidy or credit, provided their housing costs (mortgage payment, insurance, and taxes) exceed 20 percent of their adjusted income.

Evaluation of the loan application is handled in a manner similar to other lending agencies and requires a complete financial statement, a history of family income, and a credit report. Each loan is reviewed periodically to determine if the borrower's financial condition has improved to the extent that the loan could be handled by a private lending institution.

For single-family housing, the FmHA will make loans on new or existing structures. However, the living area cannot exceed 1,200 square feet. The maximum amount of a loan permitted for this size house is determined by the applicant's ability to repay the loan. A realistic limit now ranges from $30,000 to $36,000 for this type of loan.

The FmHA, under its Section 515 program, can make loans for the construction of new multifamily projects or the rehabilitation of older ones. The program is restricted to communities of less than 20,000 population. Further, a market survey must show a need for additional housing, particularly for the elderly and low-to-moderate-income families.

Government National Mortgage Association

This is a newer agency of the federal government under the Department of Housing and Urban Development (HUD), created in 1968 to carry a portion of the financing chores previously handled by the Federal National Mortgage Association. The Government National Mortgage Association, GNMA or "Ginnie Mae," sells bonds, as do other federal agencies, to raise funds for direct mortgage loans. This agency also has authority to borrow money from the United States Treasury when authorized for specific purposes. And it is the agency that handles direct subsidies for housing programs as appropriated by Congress, GNMA has used its authority to guarantee blocks of mortgages in order to attract more private capital into the mortgage lending field. The impact of this government agency is far broader than the capacity to make some direct loans, and as such, the organization and programs will be discussed in greater detail in Chapter 8.

Federal National Mortgage Association

FNMA (Fannie Mae) should no longer be considered a source of money under the direction of the federal government as it has been publicly owned and listed on the New York Stock Exchange since 1970. However, as a quasi-public organization it still has strong ties to the federal government and a commitment to various government programs. The bonds it sells to finance purchases of residential mortgage loans are still classed in the financial community as agency issues. With its Free Market System of handling mortgage loan offerings from approved lenders throughout the country, FNMA provides an interesting guide to the fluctuations in mortgage interest rates. As a major factor in the secondary markets, buying and selling mortgage loans, the FNMA organization and methods will be more fully covered in Chapter 6.

Federal Housing Administration and Veterans Administration

The FHA and VA are included in this discussion of the sources of mortgage money only to dispel the thought that they are. Neither agency makes loans as a continuing practice. The VA does actually make loans in special circumstances. What these two agencies do is, in the case of the FHA, to issue an insurance policy protecting the lender against a default by the borrower and, in the case of the VA, to issue a certificate guaranteeing a specific portion of a loan to enable a veteran to acquire housing without a down payment if desired. Both agencies are of sufficient importance in real estate finance to warrant separate coverage, which will be found in Chapter 8.

Lesser Sources

Lesser sources of mortgage money are identified not so much by their own sizes as by their investments in mortgage loans. While lesser sources do not compare in dollar volume of mortgage loans with the more traditional major sources, they are important in the variety that they offer. This is particularly true in periods of tight money when it becomes necessary to explore new possibilities for mortgage loans. Many of the lesser sources work with mortgage companies for their public contact, while others place money with the larger lending institutions, which in turn handle the loan originations. The patterns are not uniform across the country and should always be explored within a given local area.

Pension and Trust Funds

The purpose of a *pension* fund is to accumulate cash and hold it in such a manner that it will assure an annual or monthly payment to an individual worker upon retirement or upon reaching a certain age. The purpose of a *trust* fund is to protect an asset over a period of time so as to achieve a specified purpose. While the reasons for creating a trust fund are different from those of a pension fund, the manner in which both funds are held and the need for delivering the assets upon maturity give both a similarity insofar as their possible use as sources of mortgage money.

Both pension and trust fund administrators are guided by the cardinal rule of security for the asset. No pressure exists for them to achieve maximum yields, nor do state or federal laws exercise much control over the type of investments a trust may make. A good administrator is obligated to protect the body of the assets and make sure the funds can be delivered when pledged to do so. Consequently, these assets have tended to be invested in high-grade stocks and bonds, which represent minimum risk and a ready market when they have to be sold for cash. Lately, some of this money is finding its way into the long-term mortgage market as the yields are good and the security is generally acceptable.

As sources of mortgage money, both pension and trust funds represent a near ideal situation in the predictability of inflow and outflow of funds that are needed for any long-term investment. The inflow of cash is easily determined by the agreements establishing the fund, and the outflow is an integral part of that agreement.

Pension Funds. Pension funds date back nearly one hundred years, but only recently have they become a factor in real estate financing. The quarter century from 1945 to 1970 showed tremendous growth in corporate pension funds, both insured and noninsured, along with federal, state, and local government pension funds, union funds, and funds of fraternal groups. As recently as 1940, pension funds totaled only $2.4 billion. By the end of 1981, the amount had increased to over $600 billion. The number of employees covered under these plans has increased in the same period from 4.3 million to 45.5 million persons.

Pension funds can be divided into *insured* or *uninsured* plans. The insured pension plans are those offered by most large insurance companies. The employer, perhaps with a participating contribution from the employee, pays the premium directly to the insurance company, which is responsible for making future payouts to the employee when due. There is uaually the added protection of life insurance coverage, and the insurance carrier is obligated to invest the premium payments just as with any other insurance policy.

The majority of pension funds fall into the category of being privately managed and are not underwritten by an insurance company. It is this category of pension plan that brought on some abuses and failures to make the payments to employees when due. Several years of government probing into the question resulted in the enactment of the Employee Retirement Income Security Act in 1974 (also known as the Pension Reform Act). As a part of ERISA, Congress also created the Pension Benefit Guaranty Corporation, chaired by the Secretary of Labor and whose directors also include the Secretary of the Treasury and the Secretary of Commerce. It is the purpose of PBGC to provide mandatory contingent employer liability insurance, at least until such insurance can be provided in the private sector. A small premium is paid by the subscribing pension fund which insures employee benefits at termination.

The Pension Benefit Guaranty Corporation has the right to examine the pension plans insured with them and to take corrective action if proper payments are not being made into the fund, or the investments are causing jeopardy to the future benefits for the employees. The PBGC can create liens on the employer's property for collection of the contingent payments.

No requirements have been established for the investment of the pension fund money—only that it be prudent and give proper protection to the employees' interest in the fund. The major effort that the government has made to channel pension fund money into real estate mortgages is through the Government National Mortgage Association. GNMA issues a certificate that guarantees a block of mortgage loans called a *mortgage-backed security.* Payment of principal and interest is guaranteed by the government on these securities, and this makes an attractive investment for a pension fund.

In the past few years there has been an increase in pension fund investment directly into the acquisition of high-quality real estate projects. One method that has proven attractive is for an insurance company with real estate expertise, such as Prudential Life, to set up separate investment accounts for the pension funds they manage. Then these accounts pool a portion of their assets to make major acquisitions. Thus, no one pension fund is at risk on just one project; their investments are spread over a number of properties in different growth areas of the country.

Trust Funds. Because trust funds are a practical means of accomplishing a person's objectives in spite of death, and because they hold a means of reducing tax liabilities in estate planning, their usage has grown substantially, and the accumulated assets in the hands of trust administrators have multiplied. Trust funds are usually specific in the purpose to be accomplished and provide guidelines and restrictions as to the ways in which the assets may be invested. Since these funds are essentially a form of private property, there is not much public interest in control or regulation of investments other than for the tax angles involved.

What motivates trust fund administrators is the security of the investment and a fair return. The growing size of the accumulated funds and the near absolute control on withdrawals make long-term mortgage loans practical investments. Mortgage-backed securities, the growing flexibility of the secondary market, the advantages of private mortgage insurance, and the attractive yields over the long term have all added to the appeal of mortgage loans for trust funds. While many funds are administered by competent individuals who may not have expertise in mortgage loans, a growing number of trusts are handled by commercial banks whose trust departments have access to persons of broad experience in this type of loan.

Individuals

The earliest lenders were wealthy individuals. In today's market the terms of mortgage loans are much too lengthy for most individuals to undertake. With a few exceptions, almost all primary mortgage lending by individuals has a motive other than as an investment to earn a return of interest. Some individuals make mortgage loans to assist a member of their family or perhaps a valued employee or associate. By far the largest investment by individuals in mortgage loans stems from a seller accepting a second mortgage as a partial payment for his house or land. The motive is to make a sale rather than an investment. In some areas, such as California, second and even third mortgages are sold to brokers or other individuals at substantial discounts, which increases the yields sufficiently to make an attractive investment.

As investors, individuals come under no specific regulations as to how they must lend money. A mortgage loan must comply with the real estate laws governing such transactions plus the usury laws that limit the amount of interest that can be charged.

Individuals can make mortgage loans on any type of property: residential or commercial, raw land, or development work. Some mortgage companies represent individuals who want to make investments in certain types of property. Due to the lack of regulation, there is no sound statistical basis for establishing the actual volume of mortgage loans held by individuals.

Real Estate Investment Trusts (REITs)

A relatively new source of mortgage money was encouraged in 1960 when Congress passed the Real Estate Investment Trust Act. The purpose of the Act was to provide more capital to satisfy the growing demand for long-term investment money by opening the field to the individual small investor. In order to encourage a person to buy shares in a corporation that qualified itself as a real estate investment trust, Congress exempted the trust from income taxes, provided that at least 90 percent of the profit be distributed each year as dividends. Also, the income must be derived from real property investments to qualify for the tax exemption. However, the dividends are taxable to the investor.

The idea was not enthusiastically received at first, but by 1970 many investment trust issues were placed on the market and sold very well. The trusts are formed primarily by leading banks and insurance companies, and many are traded on the nation's stock exchanges. A few of the well-known companies operating in this field are Massachusetts Mutual Mortgage, Northwestern Mutual Life Mortgage, Bank American Realty, Equitable Life Mortgage, MONY Mortgage, Mortgage Trust of America, and many others.

Most of the trusts are controlled by a board of trustees responsible for the integrity of the fund. Actual management of the investment portfolio is contracted to a professional money-management team. The management company is paid a fee for its services, usually about 1 percent of the total assets per year. The managers are all experienced lending officers who have worked with or are well known to the sponsoring bank or insurance company.

The original purpose of Congress in passing the law was to enable smaller investors to participate in the ownership, or equity, of real estate. Since then, two types of REIT's have developed, one making equity type investments, the other favoring the making of mortgage loans for development projects. The profit of equity REITs is derived mostly from the operation of income-producing properties they buy. In the late 1960s, a newer concept developed known as the mortgage type. These newer trusts specialize in the financing of properties and make their profits from the interest income on their mortgages. They operate under the same tax incentives as the equity type.

It was the mortgage type of REIT that created the surge in popularity between 1969 and 1971. Underwriters encouraged banks and insurance companies to establish the trusts because the shares could be easily sold and made good underwriting fees. Loans were easy to make in the real estate boom period of the early 1970s. The REITs borrowed heavily from banks and other lenders to support their demand for more money to lend to construction and development projects. Developers often found a source of mortgage money plus a partner in the REITs to build apartments, office buildings, and shopping centers. Between 1969 and 1973, the relatively new industry increased its assets from about $1 billion to nearly $20 billion.

Serious problems began to surface by 1974 after the bank prime rate had soared past 12 percent and some construction loans on large projects were reaching 18 percent interest rates. The unanticipated high interest costs faced by many of the builders (most construction loans pay interest rates that float from 1 to 6 points over the prime rate) consumed the construction money before the projects could be completed and many failures resulted. By 1975 some of the largest REITs in the country were reporting as much as 25 percent of their loans "not accruing interest"; that is a more optimistic way of describing loans in default. The sagging record forced REIT stock prices down to less than book value in some cases and destroyed the market for any new issues. At the same time, major lenders were withdrawing their support for the *REITs* and many of them faced the same bankruptcy procedures that their builders had faced earlier.

Only a few of the REITs have actually been forced out of business, more have sought mergers with larger REITs, but most of them have survived the shakeout as they became the equity owners of properties forced into foreclosure and those properties recovered value in the reviving market. The original purpose is still sound—to provide capital for real estate projects and to enable the small investor to participate in large, well-managed projects. Those REITs that became too heavily involved in mortgage loans were often forced into an equity position. But it may be a long time before REITs can again sell new stock issues to raise additional capital.

Miscellaneous Other Sources

In different parts of the country various types of companies and institutions have established themselves as sources of mortgage funds, usually limiting the geographic area in which they will loan money. In the following paragraphs the most important of these sources are identified.

Mortgage Bankers.   While the great majority of mortgage banking companies operate as a service industry handling funds for other major sources of money, a few of the larger companies have generated their own funds for lending through the sale of mortgage bonds. In the pre-Depression days of the 1920s, the sale of mortgage bonds was quite popular, but the Depression brought many of these issues and their sponsoring companies into collapse.

As the industry has reestablished itself, the sale of mortgage bonds to investors has started to grow again. In the hands of the established mortgage bankers, these funds have provided another source of money for both residential and commercial loans.

Title Companies.   Because title companies have a close association with and considerable knowledge of the mortgage industry, a few of them have developed direct loan departments or subsidiary companies that handle loans. These affiliated companies act both as primary sources in lending their own funds or those raised from the sale of mortgage bonds, and as correspondents or agents for other major lenders.

Endowment Funds, Universities, Colleges, Hospitals.   As a group, endowment funds prefer to maintain their assets in high-grade stocks and bonds that have a good record for security, are considered to be more liquid, and, most importantly, require less administrative attention than a portfolio of mortgage loans. However, many endowments are passed on in the form of land and other real property, and these have required more expertise in the mortgage loan field. The endowment funds can and do assist in the development of their own land by experienced developers, and they are increasing their activities in mortgage lending with such encouragements as the GNMA mortgage-backed security.

Foundations.   Foundations have been established primarily by corporations or by wealthy families as a means of continuing charitable or other purposes through the use of income earned from the foundations' investments. The attitude of foundations toward mortgage lending is somewhat similar to that of the endowment funds. They are primarily interested in investing in high-grade stocks and bonds but are not adverse to mortgage loans, particularly if a purpose of special interest to the foundation can be served.

Foundations have been under substantial legal attack as to their tax obligations and sometimes for the controversial use of their tax-free funds. However, they do represent a limited pool of investment capital that can be used in the mortgage market.

Fraternal, Benevolent, and Religious Associations. Over the years some fraternal, benevolent, and religious organizations have accumulated substantial pools of investment money, which are generally little known and very seldom advertised. The administration of these funds is usually handled on a sound economic basis with security of the loan of more importance than the yield. Some of these organizations limit their lending to their own members and will provide low-cost loans to qualified members in good standing.

Credit Unions. Many credit unions have long had the authority to make intermediate-term mortgage loans for the periods of up to 10 or 12 years. A big change occurred in the competitive position of credit unions with regard to long-term mortgage loans when Congress passed a law in 1977 authorizing federally-chartered credit unions to make first mortgage loans with up to 30-year terms. In 1978, the National Credit Union Administration (NCUA) implemented the law and further authorized federally-chartered unions to sell their loans in the secondary market. In order to qualify for making the 30-year loans, federally-chartered unions must show a minimum of $2 million in assets. Many state-chartered credit unions have benefited from policies of expanded state lending authority based on the federal requirements.

Credit unions are restricted to making loans only to their own members. And because of the more complex nature of a mortgage loan (as compared, say, with a car loan), the lack of experienced personnel within credit unions has hampered growth. However, the larger unions are capable of maintaining trained personnel in this field and can now offer full-service residential mortgage loans.

Questions for Discussion

1. Discuss the steps that have been taken to improve the liquidity of a savings association loan portfolio.

2. What role does the Federal Home Loan Bank play in the banking system?

3. Why have mutual savings banks increased their investments in real estate loans even though they are not legally required to do so?

4. Discuss the reasons insurance companies are looking more for ownership interests in real estate rather than making direct mortgage loans.

5. Why do insurance companies have such a wide variation in their lending practices?

6. How does the Federal Land Bank raise funds for making loans?

7. Explain the basic lending policies of the Farmers Home Administration for home loans.

8. What efforts are being made to attract pension and trust fund money into the real estate mortgage market?

9. Describe the type of loans preferred by commercial banks.

10. Are there any good sources of mortgage money available in your locality outside of the regulated lending institutions?

11. What new mortgage lending authority has been given to credit unions?

12. Describe the efforts that have been made to better enable savings associations to compete for the saver's dollar.

13. Discuss the purpose of the Community Reinvestment Act.

14. By what means are the traditional sources of mortgage money obtaining lendable funds through borrowing techniques?

Secondary Markets

In years past, mortgage loans carried the distinctive imprint of the local lender as well as local laws, attorneys, and customs. Because of this, mortgage loans were difficult to sell, that is, to convert to cash. One result of this lack of liquidity has been that a number of lenders, particularly savings associations, still hold older, lower interest-paying mortgage loans in their portfolios. Considerable progress has been made since the early 1970s towards creating a national market for mortgage loans. This market has become known as the *secondary market*. It comprises those institutions, companies, and investors who *purchase* mortgage loans, that is, loans they do not originate. There are now many business concerns and individuals involved with the purchase of these loans; participation in the secondary market is not limited to the two corporations whose primary purpose is the purchase of mortgage loans. These two, the Federal National Mortgage Association and the Federal Home Loan Mortgage Corporation, are key operators in the market but comprise only a portion of it. However, both will be examined in this chapter because of their leadership in this secondary market field.

Origins of Secondary Markets

To make a loan more salable, some means are needed to provide standardized procedures and a method to protect the secondary market investor. The government has succeeded in doing just this with its insured FHA programs and guarantees of VA loans. In this type of loan, the government agencies have established certain standard forms and

131

procedures that are known and accepted by the lenders. And most important, the government agencies provide that necessary common denominator of protection to the lender in the individual insurance commitment.

However, even this was not always the case. When the FHA was initially established, the government effort was not accepted at face value by private investors, and it became necessary to establish a market for government-underwritten loans. Thus the Federal National Mortgage Association was born, and with it the first step toward creating a national market for mortgage loans, the secondary market.

The precise delineation between the primary and secondary markets for mortgage loans is difficult to draw as there is an overlap. The clearest line can be made at the origination of the loan, which would be the primary lender. Lenders who buy or take a mortgage loan that they did not originate are considered to be the secondary market.

Procedures Used in Secondary Markets

Now note the difference in terminology at this point. The originator of a loan speaks to customers, who are the *borrowers*, in terms of *loaning money* and expresses the cost of the borrowed money as interest plus *points* of discount and fees. Once the originator closes the loan to the borrower, the note and mortgage instrument become marketable paper that can be assigned—and the terminology changes. The mortgage note is now a salable commodity and is negotiated as such. The originator of the loan becomes a *seller*, and the large lending institutions that deal in the secondary market for mortgage loans are called *purchasers*. When a mortgage loan is thus offered for sale, the potential purchaser is interested in only one factor of loans of similar type, size, and quality, and that is the *net yield*.

Pricing Loans To Adjust Yields

Since the interest rate on the loan or loans held by the originator have already been established, the only way a seller can change the yield to a purchaser is to adjust the *price* of the loan. For example, if the mortgage note is for $10,000 at 7 percent interest, the yield would be 7 percent. If the seller must offer a higher yield than 7 percent in order to attract a purchaser, he must sell the loan for less than $10,000, that is, discount the face value in order to increase the yield. By selling the $10,000 loan for, say $9,500, the purchaser is putting up less cash but still collects the originally agreed interest and principal payment applicable to the $10,000 loan at 7 percent, hence, a greater return or yield for the $9,500.

The principal balance due on an existing mortgage loan normally changes each month, so therefore the price is quoted as a percentage figure. The price is that percent of the loan balance for which the loan is sold. One hundred is, of course, par. If we were quoting the $10,000 loan mentioned above to sell for $9,500, the price would simply be 95." This indicates a 5 percent reduction in whatever the principal balance due on the mortgage note may be, or a 5-point discount.

In times of falling interest rates, a loan calling for a higher than current market interest can sell for a premium—at say 102 percent or even 104 percent of its face value. Examples of prices and yields are shown in Table 6-1 to illustrate their relationship.

TABLE 6-1

Price Yield Table Calculated at 7 Percent Interest for Term of 30 Years

Price	Discount	Yield if Prepaid 8 Yrs.	Yield if Prepaid 10 Yrs.	Yield if Prepaid 12 Yrs.	To Maturity
102	+2 (Premium)	6.66	6.71	6.74	6.81
100	0	7.00	7.00	7.00	7.00
96	4	7.70	7.61	7.54	7.41
92	8	8.44	8.24	8.12	7.85

A simple reading of the table shows that the length of time a loan is outstanding has a direct effect on the yield for that loan. Since loans vary considerably in the time for payoff, it is necessary to use some standard. Records of loan payoffs indicate a steadily decreasing length of time due largely to the increased moving that families do. Most mortgage loans are simply refinanced with each sale or after several sales. The average life of a 30-year loan is now under nine years. For simplification, most lenders use a twelve-year term to calculate the actual yield.

Growth Factors of Secondary Markets

The strongest impetus toward establishing a truly national market for mortgage loans must be credited to (1) the Federal National Mortgage Association, (2) the growth of private mortgage insurance fostered by the 1971 change in banking regulations, and (3) establishment of the Federal Home Loan Mortgage Corporation. In considering these three major influences in the development of secondary mortgage markets, the largest and most experienced single operator is the Federal National Mortgage Association. After the background and operations of FNMA are examined, the practices used by FHLMC will be reviewed.

Federal National Mortgage Association

Origin and Purpose of FNMA

By 1938, it had become obvious that private lenders were not looking with much favor on the four-year-old FHA concept of government-insured commitments to assist a credit-worthy but cash-short family in buying a home. Consequently, on February 10, 1938, the National Mortgage Association of Washington was formed as a subsidiary of the Reconstruction Finance Corporation, which then changed on April 5, 1938, to the Federal National Mortgage Association, referred to as FNMA, or Fannie Mae. The groundwork had been laid by Congress under Title III of the original FHA Authorization Act.

The basic aims of the Federal National Mortgage Association as determined by the chartering act and subsequent revisions to 1968 included:

1. Establishing a market for the purchase and sale of first mortgages.
2. Providing special assistance on certain residential mortgages and housing programs as designated by the President and by Congress.
3. Managing and liquidating the mortgage portfolio in an orderly manner with minimum adverse effect on the market and minimum loss to the government.

Money needed for the purchase of mortgages was derived from the sale of notes and debentures to private investors. While these FNMA obligations were subject to the approval of the Secretary of the Treasury, they were not guaranteed by the government. Some additional capital was raised by the requirement to purchase FNMA stock in the amount of one-half of 1 percent of every commitment sold. (The present requirement is to purchase stock in the amount of one-fourth of 1 percent of the mortgages delivered.) Operating money was raised through certain fees charged on the purchase of mortgages and through part of the discounts taken.

The initial concept of FNMA embodied the idea that it would serve as a secondary market primarily for buying and selling first mortgages, but over the years the portfolio steadily increased as selling of loans lagged behind. Congress has, from time to time, ordered Fannie Mae to make mortgage purchases to stimulate a lagging economy or to assist in financing new government lending programs as stipulated in the FNMA purposes outlined previously, since these programs were not readily acceptable to private investors as mortgage investments.

Finally, FNMA was charged with the task of management and liquidation, including the handling and disposition of the substantial accumulation of first mortgages in such a manner as not to upset the capital market or cause a loss to the government.

FNMA as Private Corporation

A major change was made in the FNMA establishment when it was transformed into a "private corporation with a public purpose" by Act of Congress in September 1968. Roughly, the FNMA entity was partitioned by this Act in such a way that the first of its three functions —that of maintaining a secondary market—was retained. The other two functions—special assistance programs, and management and liquidation of mortgages—were transferred to a newly formed body corporate without capital stock known as the Government National Mortgage Association (GNMA or Ginnie Mae), designed to operate as a part of the Department of Housing and Urban Development.

This FNMA-government relationship is unique and has been developed by a number of rules, chartering stipulations, and organization methods, such as:

1. Five of FNMA's 15 directors are appointed by the President of the United States.
2. The HUD Secretary is given regulatory authority to set Fannie Mae's debt limit and its ratio of debt to capital.
3. The HUD Secretary may require that a reasonable portion of the mortgages purchased be related to the national goal to provide adequate housing for low- and moderate-income families.
4. The Secretary of the Treasury has been given authority to buy FNMA debt obligations up to $2.25 billion, which greatly enhances its credit position.
5. While FNMA is a private corporation and its debts are not obligations of the government by its chartering act, FNMA obligations are lawful investments for fiduciary, trust, and public funds under the control of the federal government.

Operations

The Federal National Mortgage Association operates from its headquarters in Washington, D.C., with five regional offices in Dallas, Atlanta, Los Angeles, Chicago, and Philadelphia. The regional offices have authority to negotiate loan purchases within their area and serve as bases for all regional operations.

In order to sell a loan to FNMA, it is first necessary to qualify as an approved seller. Most mortgage companies, some savings and loan associations, and some insurance companies have found it beneficial to be able to do business with FNMA. An approval by the FHA and the VA have been normal prerequisites but do not in themselves qualify a mortgagee for FNMA—a complete file on the capitalization, background, and experience of the qualifying company and its key personnel is required.

All companies doing business with FNMA automatically become stockholders, as one of the requirements is that the seller purchase stock with one-quarter of 1 percent fee on each commitment. And the stock must be retained by the mortgagee at one-quarter of 1 percent of its total loans being serviced for FNMA.

FNMA Purchases of Loans

When it started in 1938, FNMA was authorized to purchase only FHA loans. Then in 1944, VA loans were added, and in February 1972, FNMA made its first purchase of a conventional loan. Considerable work and public hearings preceded the approval to buy conventional loans as they lacked the standard procedures and underwriting that characterized FHA/VA type loans. In cooperation with the Federal Home Loan Mortgage Corporation, FNMA developed standardized forms and procedures for conventional loans, which has created a new class of mortgages, now called *conforming*—conforming to FNMA-FHLMC maximum limitations.

FNMA buys mortgage loans in several ways. Until 1981, the dominant method was through a biweekly bidding procedure called the *Free Market System (FMS)* auction. Under the FMS auction, any lender qualified to do business with FNMA (called a *seller/servicer*) can submit a competitive bid offering a specific *yield* to FNMA for a promise by FNMA to buy loans up to a maximum dollar amount over the next four months. These promises are *forward loan commitments*. Smaller lenders can bid at these auctions on a noncompetitive basis (up to a maximum commitment of $500,000) and accept the weighted average yield resulting from that auction. Through this auction procedure, many loan originators, particularly mortgage companies, have been able to assure themselves of money to lend so long as the FNMA yield requirements are met.

In order to make a competitive bid system successful, there has to be some consistency, or standardization, in the kinds of loans available. In the past, FNMA offered to sell commitments through their auctions on three types of loans: (1) conventional or conforming, (2) standard FHA/VA, and (3) FHA/VA graduated payment plans. At this writing, the three types are still handled in a biweekly auction, but the market has been so weak that few loans are being purchased in this manner. The weak market has resulted, of course, from high interest rates and housing costs, plus the fact that FNMA now requires a two-point commitment fee, increased from one point in 1982.

In 1981 FNMA offered to buy adjustable rate mortgage loans and announced eight plans with differing indexes; some offered interest rate or payment caps that would be acceptable to them. FNMA also agreed to consider the purchase of blocks of loans through negotiation with loan originators. The result of these actions has been a proliferation of mortgage loan plans. In 1982, FNMA held over *200 different kinds* of adjustable rate mortgage loans in its portfolio.

Like savings associations that have been in business for a number of years, FNMA also holds a substantial amount of its investments in older, lower interest paying mortgage loans. Many of these loans are not paying enough interest to cover the current cost of money to FNMA. Thus, some losses have been sustained. In an effort to overcome this problem and also to give broader assistance to the home buying market, FNMA has greatly expanded the kinds of loans it will buy. Most are purchased through negotiation with an originator. The key requirement always is that the block of loans submitted to FNMA for purchase must not only meet their basic eligibility requirements, but must also produce a yield that meets the current market standard. FNMA has been so active in purchasing mortgage loans that they can now claim to hold one of every twenty residential loans, or 5 percent of the entire market.

Partly as a review of the variety of mortgage loans now active on the market and partly to indicate the scope of FNMA's activities, the following summary is presented. These are the categories of loans being purchased by FNMA:

1. *Mandatory Delivery Commitments*
    a. *General.* Mandatory delivery commitments of one or two months can be purchased for FHA/VA level payment, FHA/VA graduated payment, conventional fixed rate and adjustable rate whole mortgages secured by one- to four-family properties. Conventional fixed rate second mortgages are also

eligible. Adjustable rate mortgages must be originated under one of the eight standard plans (see Chapter 4) to be eligible for purchase.

    b. *First and second mortgage participations.* Commitments for one or two months can be purchased for participations in fixed rate conventional first or second mortgages.

2. *Optional Delivery Commitments*

    a. *FMS auctions.* Four-month optional delivery commitments can be purchased through the biweekly auctions for standard FHA/VA, FHA/VA graduated payment, and conventional fixed rate first mortgages.

    b. *Adjustable rate mortgages.* Four-month commitments can be purchased for each of the eight standard plans on a negotiated basis.

    c. *First mortgage participations.* Two-month commitments can be purchased for participation interests ranging from 50 percent to 95 percent in pools of fixed rate conventional first mortgages.

3. *Standby Commitments*

    a. *General.* Nine- to twelve-month standby commitments can be purchased for fixed rate and adjustable rate mortgages. When exercised the standby is converted to a mandatory one- or two-month delivery commitment at which time the FNMA posted yield then in effect is specified.

FNMA Sources of Money

Where does FNMA obtain the millions of dollars it needs to purchase mortgage loans? It uses several methods of raising cash. One is through the sale of *debenture bonds* in the financial markets. Debenture bonds are unsecured promises to pay and have been widely used by FNMA. Because of its high credit standing and its close ties to the federal government, FNMA has been able to sell this kind of security rather easily. However, none of FNMA's debt is secured by a government guarantee.

Another, and more recent method, is the sale of mortgage-backed securities. FNMA can block up loans from its own portfolio and pledge them as collateral to secure a mortgage-backed issue of securities. The money obtained from the sale of the security can then be used to buy more mortgage loans.

FNMA will even offer their approved seller/servicers a commitment for a guaranteed pass-through security if backed by conventional fixed rate one- to four-family first mortgages. The minimum issue is $1 million. Two options are available:

1. If the seller/servicer assumes the risk of foreclosure losses, the guarantee fee paid to FNMA is 25 basis points monthly. (A basis point is 1/100 of 1 percent.)
2. If FNMA assumes the risk of foreclosure losses, the monthly guarantee fee is 35 basis points.

One of the ongoing problems faced by FNMA is that most of its money now comes from short-term debt issues—those of three years or less. And this money is used to finance long-term loans which average a life of about 12 years. Thus, as current market interest rates fluctuate, the portfolio earnings of FNMA can suffer substantial losses. One method FNMA is using to offset possible losses is to increase its service activities for which it can charge fees. The offer to issue guarantee pass-through securities for their seller/servicers, as explained above, is an example of a service for which FNMA collects a fee.

Federal Home Loan Mortgage Corporation

The credit crunch of 1969–1970 highlighted a problem within the savings associations during periods of tight money. Many depositors simply withdrew their money for investments of higher yields than the fixed rates offered on savings accounts. The outflow of cash could easily exceed the repayments of loans outstanding and make any new loans impossible for an association to make. The Federal Home Loan Bank could not provide sufficient capital to give all the relief that might be needed with loans to members, so an additional agency was created. In the Emergency Home Finance Act of 1970, Congress authorized the Federal Home Loan Mortgage Corporation to *purchase* residential mortgages from members of the Federal Home Loan Bank and other approved financial institutions.

FHLMC Purchases of Loans

As a part of the Federal Home Loan Bank system, the FHLMC organized its purchase procedures to fit the needs of its member savings associations. Since the concept of selling loans was not basic to the intent and purpose of most savings associations, it has taken some time for FHLMC to develop into a major operator in the secondary market. In its early years, FHLMC set the price at which it would purchase loans by administrative decision based on a careful analysis of the market. The required yield for selling loans to FHLMC was published each week. Since 1977, the acceptable yield has been determined by auction in much the same way that FNMA handles its FMS auction.

The differences in FNMA and FHLMC auction procedures stem from basic differences in their markets. FNMA deals primarily with mortgage companies needing to pass their loans on to an ultimate lender. Savings associations, on the other hand, are the major market for FHLMC and they have their own deposits with which to make mortgage loans. The result is that FHLMC purchases primarily immediate commitments; that is, loans that have already been made, rather than forward commitments, which are FNMA's stock-in-trade.

Because FHLMC deals mostly with the savings association market, it is more apt to purchase a participation in a mortgage loan. That is, FHLMC purchases a partial interest in each one of a block of loans offered by a savings association. While both FNMA and FHLMC can purchase loan participations, the example used is the FHLMC procedure. Figure 6-1 illustrates the form used to sell a participating interest in conventional mortgages that are available for immediate delivery. FHLMC limits participations to a minimum of 50 percent and up to a maximum of 85 percent of the loan amount.

FHLMC allows both competitive and noncompetitive bids at auctions, which are held more frequently than FNMA auctions. Initially, bidding at FHLMC auctions was limited to member savings associations and other approved lending institutions. A nonmember is currently charged an additional ½ percent commitment fee to participate.

1. *Competitive bids.* Auctions are held every Friday for immediate purchase commitments, twice a month for six-month forward commitments, and once a month for eight-month forward commitments. Qualified bidders can make up to five competitive offers, each at a different yield, with the aggregate of all offers not exceeding $3 million.
2. *Noncompetitive bids.* Noncompetitive offers are limited to a maximum of $500,000 with a minimum of $100,000 at any one auction. The average weighted yield at each auction is assigned to the noncompetitive bids.

In its auctions FHLMC uses a *net* basis for quoting yields; that is, no service charges are included in the bid. In the FNMA auction a ⅜ percent (.375 percent) service fee for the bidder is included in the bid. In comparing the published results between the two types of auctions, it is necessary to adjust for the service charge.

EXHIBIT B

FHLMC Form 57

The Mortgage Corporation
Federal Home Loan Mortgage Corporation

IMMEDIATE PURCHASE CONTRACT
HOME MORTGAGES
CONVENTIONAL PARTICIPATION PROGRAM

Sale: The undersigned Seller hereby offers to sell to the Federal Home Loan Mortgage Corporation ("The Mortgage Corporation" or "FHLMC") undivided interests in Home Mortgages, on the terms stated below and in accordance with the Purchase Documents, as defined in the Sellers' Guide Conventional Mortgages as in effect on the date of this offer, all of which are fully incorporated herein by reference.

Servicing: The undersigned Seller hereby agrees to service all mortgages sold hereunder, in accordance with the Purchase Documents as in effect on the date of this offer, all of which are fully incorporated herein by reference.

Required Yield for Participation in Conventional Home Mortgages as of Date of Offer:_____Percent
(TO 3 DECIMAL PLACES)

Participation % Offered (85% maximum-50% minimum)	Aggregate Principal Amount	FHLMC's Participation Interest (Contract Amount)
_____ % (×)	$_____ (=)	$_____

Nonmember Fee: $_____enclosed, if applicable.

Seller's FHLBB Docket No.
or FDIC Certificate No.:_____

_____
SELLER

Date of Offer:_____, 19____

_____
ADDRESS

By _____(Seal)
AUTHORIZED REPRESENTATIVE

This contract is signed pursuant to a telephone offer: Yes_____No_____

Offer Hereby Accepted by
The Mortgage Corporation

Federal Home Loan Mortgage Corporation

Date of Acceptance:_____

By _____(Seal)
VICE PRESIDENT

Purchase Contract No.:_____

Required Delivery Date:_____

or ☐ Offer Declined by The Mortgage Corporation

Seller's FHLMC Seller/
Servicer No.:_____

Date of Declination:_____

FHLMC-57 4/76

FIGURE 6-1

FHLMC Sources of Money

While the FHLMC is owned by the Federal Home Loan Bank system and has access to funds raised through the sale of bonds, it also uses two other procedures to raise cash for the purchase of mortgages.

1. *Mortgage Participation Certificates*, also called PC's, are sold every business day through any of the five regional offices of FHLMC in denominations of $100,000, $200,000, $500,000, and $1,000,000. Each PC represents an undivided interest in a large, geographically diversified group of residential mortgages and is unconditionally guaranteed by FHLMC. PC's pay principal and interest every month and have produced excellent yields.
2. *Guaranteed Mortgage Certificates*, called GMC's, are similar to PC's in quality, denominations, and guarantee, and are aimed for institutions that prefer payment of interest every six months and of principal once a year.

The popular opinion that any agency representing a governmental operation is pumping out money for the benefit of banks or savings associations to use for loans should again be dispelled. There are some subsidy programs, but the beneficiaries are the people, such as those in lower income circumstances with living needs. The Federal Home Loan Mortgage Corporation is not a subsidy operation, and it is expected to raise money in the open market in competition with all other long- and short-term borrowers. Hence, it can only purchase mortgages from the offers presented that will meet the existing market requirements. It does provide an additional outlet for a savings association to achieve some needed liquidity, but always at a price.

Table of Secondary Mortgage Market Activity

Table 6-2 gives the dollar value of mortgage loans acquired by the Federal National Mortgage Association and the Federal Home Loan Mortgage Corporation. Both organizations *purchase* mortgages from loan originators and operate as a part of the secondary market.

An examination of this table points out several interesting facts about the mortgage market of the early 1980s. First, the overall volume of mortgage loans purchased by FNMA and FHLMC is still increasing each year but at a much slower pace. Second, FNMA is selling almost none of its loans in contrast to FHLMC which shows sales of loans equal to, or greater than, their purchases. Third, the FNMA free market system auction that formerly provided excellent clues to future mortgage interest rates has declined in volume to become an almost negligible factor.

TABLE 6-2

FNMA and FHLMC Activity
(In Millions of Dollars)

Item	1979	1980	1981	1981 Dec.	1982 Jan.	Feb.	Mar.	Apr.	May	June
FEDERAL NATIONAL MORTGAGE ASSOCIATION										
Mortgage holdings (end of period)										
13 Total	48,050	55,104	61,412	61,412	61,721	62,112	62,544	63,132	63,951	65,008
14 FHA/VA-insured	33,673	37,365	39,977	39,977	39,937	39,926	39,893	39,834	39,808	39,829
15 Conventional	14,377	17,725	21,435	21,435	21,784	22,185	22,654	23,298	24,143	25,179
Mortgage transactions (during period)										
16 Purchases	10,812	8,099	6,112	655	430	519	604	755	1,006	1,223
17 Sales	0	0	2	0	0	0	0	0	0	0
Mortgage commitments[1]										
18 Contracted (during period)	10,179	8,083	9,331	1,272	813	1,202	1,881	2,482	1,550	1,583
19 Outstanding (end of period)	6,409	3,278	3,717	3,717	3,536	3,857	4,990	6,586	7,016	7,206
Auction of 4-month commitments to buy										
Government-underwritten loans										
20 Offered	8,860.4	8,605.4	2,487.2	59.2	41.5	41.7	45.7	7.0	35.7	33.1
21 Accepted	3,920.9	4,002.0	1,478.0	27.0	30.8	23.4	29.6	0.0	7.4	7.4
Conventional loans										
22 Offered	4,495.3	3,639.2	2,524.7	84.4	31.7	28.6	65.0	29.5	37.8	59.0
23 Accepted	2,343.6	1,748.5	1,392.3	48.0	11.5	13.6	32.3	22.0	23.0	33.1
FEDERAL HOME LOAN MORTGAGE CORPORATION										
Mortgage holdings (end of period)[2]										
24 Total	4,035	5,067	5,255	5,255	5,240	5,342	5,320	5,274	5,279	5,295
25 FHA/VA	1,102	1,033	990	990	987	984	981	979	976	973
26 Conventional	2,933	4,034	4,265	4,265	4,253	4,358	4,339	4,295	4,303	4,322
Mortgage transactions (during period)										
27 Purchases	5,717	3,723	3,789	1,140	1,628	1,228	1,479	2,143	1,214	1,581
28 Sales	4,544	2,527	3,531	1,158	1,629	1,115	1,564	2,177	1,194	1,562
Mortgage commitments[3]										
29 Contracted (during period)	5,542	3,859	6,974	203	3,280	565	2,523	2,824	2,692	3,166
30 Outstanding (end of period)	797	447	3,518	3,518	5,033	4,336	5,461	6,041	7,420	8,970

[1] Includes some multifamily and nonprofit hospital loan commitments in addition to one- to four-family loan commitments accepted in FNMA's free market auction system, and through the FNMA-GNMA tandem plans.
[2] Includes participation as well as whole loans.
[3] Includes conventional and government-underwritten loans.
SOURCE: Adapted from *Federal Reserve Bulletin*, August, 1982 p. A40.

Points and Discounts

The use of points in discounting loans stems from the need to sell these loans in the secondary market. Hence, a closer examination of the methods and reasons is presented here.

The definition of *points* used in this text refers to the term as a unit of measurement. Thus, the word *point(s)* can be used to identify various fees, such as the origination fee for processing a loan; or it may be used to refer to the costs of private mortgage insurance; or it can be used in reference to the discount. A point is simply 1 percent of the loan amount.

The word *point*, as used to express a discount, is the percentage that must be added or subtracted from the face value of a loan in order to decrease or increase the yield to a competitive amount. Discounts are increasingly being asked on conventional loans as a method to obtain an increase in yield without showing an increase in interest rate. To the borrowing public, the expression is more closely associated with the fixed-interest loans underwritten by the FHA and VA. In financial circles, a discount is converted to a "price" for a loan in order to facilitate trading. The price helps determine the yield.

For this purpose, *yield* can be defined as the return to the investor in percent of the price paid for the note. *Discount* is the difference between the face value of the note and the price the investor paid for the note. Yield includes both the interest earned and the discount taken. So to express the discount as a part of the yield, it must be converted to an annual percentage rate. The discount is a one time charge: a lump sum taken at the time the loan is funded. To determine how much this adds to each year's earnings, or yield, the discount must be spread over the life of the loan. But what is the life of the mortgage loan? While most residential loans, including FHA- and VA-supported loans, are granted for a term of thirty years, the realistic life of the loan is approximately ten to twelve years. That is to say, within ten years the average loan is paid off, usually by resale and refinancing. So FNMA and FHLMC use a time span of twelve years to determine the yield value of a discount.

The free market system offerings (FNMA) are made in terms of a yield, usually carried to three decimal places. The accepted yield can be converted to a discount mathematically, or more easily, by means of a standard conversion table. Table 6-3 shows several typical yield figures and the sequence of steps shows the fixed interest rate for the note, the price that is used to achieve the yield, and the discount needed to achieve the price.

The mortgage banking industry is able to use the FNMA free market system yields as solid criteria from which to base its own handling

TABLE 6-3

For a Yield Amount	At Interest Rate	Price Must Be	Points to Achieve
9.500	9.500	100	0
9.800	9.500	97.45	2.55
10.600	9.500	91.12	8.88

of individual mortgage loans. For example, a mortgage company is making mortgage loans at 9½ percent, which is competitive in its current market, and must meet a yield of 9.800 percent in order to sell the loans. Using Table 6-3, we determine that the price must be 97.45, which requires a discount of 2.55 points to achieve. The mortgage company would probably ask a discount of 2¾ points as a rounded-out figure if the market is strong. Added to the quoted discount is the brokerage fee and the charge for mortgage insurance. Loan originators using the FNMA yields as a guide to trends would be watching for an upward or downward movement to further influence their decision as to what discount they might need in order to be making loans at a price, or yield, at which they could be sold.

It should be borne in mind that the normal brokerage fee of 1 to 1½ points is not to be confused with the charge for discount points. Charges for discounts, on the whole, are passed on by the mortgage company to the ultimate lender. The brokerage, or finance fee, is the remuneration earned by the mortgage company for soliciting, processing, and arranging the funding of the loan. Another term for this charge is *origination fee*.

Private Mortgage Insurance

One of the essential elements needed to facilitate free trading in mortgage loans is some standard of reliability. The fact that home loans and other property loans are so local in their nature has prevented many investors from moving very far geographically to invest in conventional mortgages. The FHA and VA proved that investors would cross state lines and assist the cash-short growth areas of the country if they had some assurance of protection against problems incurred in foreclosing a remote property.

The idea of providing insurance against a default in mortgage payments must be credited to the federal programs instigated by the FHA in 1933. It was some years later, during the 1950s, that several entrepreneurs began testing the market for the same type of insurance sold by private insurance companies. Progress was slow at first, and the independents did not really take hold in the mortgage industry until 1971. In that year the regulatory authorities expanded lending limits for conventional residential loans and required the use of default insurance coverage. Federally chartered savings and loan associations were permitted to make loans up to 95 percent of appraised value, compared to 90 percent previously, provided that the higher ratio loans were insured. The result was a tremendous growth in private mortgage insurance.

One major insuring company, Mortgage Guaranty Insurance Corporation (MGIC, picking up the acronym Magic'') based in Milwaukee, increased its loan coverage volume to $2.8 billion in 1971 and then to $7.5 billion in 1972 with about 40 percent of the coverage in 95 percent loans. The private sector topped the FHA coverage in that year and has retained its lead in the field.

Both private mortgage insurance (PMI) and the FHA insure against the same basic risk; that is, default by the borrower in making mortgage payments. However, there is a difference in the coverage: FHA insures the full amount of a loan; PMI offers a selection of coverages—the highest covers the top 25 percent of the loan. In practice, depending on the coverage and the circumstances, it is fairly common for the private insurance carrier to pay off the full amount of the mortgage loan (rather than 25 percent) in case of foreclosure and to assume the responsibility for disposition of the property. It is this relief from the problems of foreclosure, rehabilitation, and resale of properties, also found in the FHA and VA programs, that has increased the acceptability of default insurance by all lenders. Since the risk for the insurance company is loan repayment, the evaluation centers on the credit-worthiness of the borrower and the quality of the property offered as collateral.

There are only about 15 companies capable of selling this type of specialized insurance coverage, and they all work through loan originators: the mortgage companies, savings and loan associations, commercial banks, and other lending institutions. The loan originator must first qualify with the insurance company as an acceptable lender. The insurance carrier normally requires that each mortgage loan undergo evaluation by its own underwriting group before a certificate of coverage is issued. A request for coverage includes submitting (1) a property appraisal made by a professional appraiser approved by the insurance company; (2) a copy of the loan application; (3) a credit report on the borrower; (4) several verifications; and (5) any other data helpful in analyzing the loan. Once the necessary documents and information have been submitted, processing of the application tends to move quickly and is usually completed within 24 hours.

The essence of the insurance certificate is that in case the mortgage loan is defaulted and taken through foreclosure, the insurance company will pay off up to 25 percent of the loan. This means an exposure for the lender of 71.25 percent of the value on a 95 percent loan, and 67.5 percent on a 90 percent loan. The advantage to the lender is obvious in reducing risk to a more practical level wherein full recovery might be made even through an early foreclosure proceeding. The advantage to the borrower lies in being able to borrow a larger percentage of the value than previously obtainable in terms of a conventional loan.

Coverage Offered

Private insurance companies offer a variety of coverages for default mortgage insurance. While the basic coverage is for residential property, many types of commercial property loans can also be insured. These include loans for hotels, motels, shopping centers, office buildings, warehouses, and others. Qualification for commercial loan coverage is based more on an individual case study than on the limiting parameters used to qualify residential loans. Residential loans that can be insured include primary residences, second or leisure homes, multifamily properties, mobile homes (if permanently secured and classed as realty), and modular housing. Insurance can be obtained on participation loans and on junior liens within certain limiting conditions. An important recent addition to the coverage offered by private mortgage insurance companies is a policy for seller-financed loans, both first and second mortgages. Each insurance company sets its own maximum dollar limits on the amount of an insurable loan and usually sets a minimum requirement for borrower's equity.

While the FHA limits the term of its coverage to maturity of the loan, PMI offers a variety of shorter terms from 3 to 15 years. The cost varies with the length of the term. Also, PMI offers a choice of coverage from 10 percent of the initial loan amount up to 25 percent. Separate policies are offered for standard coverage, for FHLMC and GNMA coverage, and for FNMA coverage.

If a mortgage lender anticipates selling loans to FHLMC, GNMA, or FNMA, there are minimum requirements for the amount of private mortgage insurance as detailed in Table 6-4.

TABLE 6-4
Minimum PMI Coverage

	Loan-to-Value Ratio	
Loan Purchaser	Over 80% to 90%	Over 90% to 95%
Federal Home Loan Mortgage Corp.	17%	22%
Government National Mortgage Assoc.	17%	22%
Federal National Mortgage Assoc.	12%	16%

Florida

Standard Plans

MGIC

Annual Premium Plans — Single Premium Plans

MGIC Coverage	Loan-to-Value	Reduces Original Exposure To	1st Year Premium	Renewal Options Constant Years 2-10	Renewal Options Standard Years 2-Term	Close For Less Option	3 Yrs.	4 Yrs.	5 Yrs.	6 Yrs.	7 Yrs.	10 Yrs.	15 Yrs.
35%	91-95%	62%	1.50%	.24%	.25%								
	86-90%	59%	1.10%	.24%	.25%								
	81-85%	55%	.90%	.24%	.25%								
	80% & under	52%	.70%	.24%	.25%								
30%	91-95%	67%	1.25%	.24%	.25%	.40%	1.60%	1.65%	1.75%		2.25%	2.75%	3.00%
	86-90%	63%	.90%	.24%	.25%	.33%	1.20%	1.25%	1.40%		1.90%	2.40%	2.65%
	81-85%	60%	.70%	.24%	.25%	.30%	1.15%	1.20%	1.35%		1.65%	2.05%	2.30%
	80% & under	56%	.50%	.24%	.25%	.28%	.90%	.95%	1.10%		1.40%	1.75%	2.00%
25%	91-95%	72%	1.00%	.24%	.25%	.36%	1.35%	1.40%	1.50%	1.75%	2.00%	2.375%	2.50%
	86-90%	68%	.65%	.24%	.25%	.30%	.95%	1.00%	1.25%		1.60%	2.00%	2.375%
	81-85%	64%	.50%	.24%	.25%	.28%	.90%	.95%	1.20%		1.40%	1.70%	
	80% & under	60%	.35%	.24%	.25%		.70%	.75%	.90%		1.10%	1.45%	
22%	91-95%	75%	.80%	.24%	.25%	.34%	1.10%	1.15%	1.30%		1.80%	2.30%	2.40%
	86-90%	71%	.55%	.24%	.25%	.29%	.85%	.90%	1.20%		1.50%	1.90%	2.30%
	81-85%	67%	.45%	.24%	.25%	.27%	.75%	.80%	1.10%		1.30%	1.60%	
20%	91-95%	76%	.75%	.24%	.25%	.32%	1.05%	1.10%	1.25%	1.50%	1.75%	2.20%	2.30%
	86-90%	72%	.50%	.24%	.25%	.28%	.75%	.80%	1.10%		1.40%	1.80%	2.25%
	81-85%	68%	.35%	.24%	.25%	.26%	.70%	.75%	1.00%		1.20%	1.50%	
	80% & under	64%	.25%	.24%	.25%		.55%	.60%	.70%		1.00%	1.30%	
17%	86-90%	75%	.40%	.24%	.25%	.27%	.65%	.70%	.80%		1.00%	1.50%	2.00%
	81-85%	71%	.30%	.24%	.25%	.25%	.55%	.60%	.70%		.90%	1.20%	
	80% & under	67%	.20%	.19%	.20%		.45%	.50%	.60%		.80%	1.00%	
16%	91-95%	80%	.625%	.24%	.25%	.30%	.95%	1.00%	1.20%		1.60%	2.10%	2.20%
12%	86-90%	80%	.25%	.24%	.25%	.24%	.55%	.60%	.70%		.90%	1.20%	
	81-85%	75%	.15%	.14%	.15%		.45%	.50%	.60%		.80%	1.00%	
	80% & under	71%	.14%	.13%	.14%		.40%	.45%	.50%		.70%	.90%	

NOTES

(1) The standard renewal rate is based on the outstanding loan balance at the time of renewal. The constant renewal rate is based on the original loan amount.

(2) The annual renewal premium under the constant plan for years 11-term is .125% of the original loan amount.

(3) Five-year renewals are available as an option to the annual renewals in the 10 and 15 year programs. The five-year renewal rates are .50% of the principal balance.

(4) For seasoned loan rates see your MGIC operating manual.

(5) For CFL Options, the initial premium rate and the rate for the first 9 renewals are the same, based on the original loan amount. For years 11-term the rate is .125% of the original loan amount.

(6) The same premium plans apply to both owner and non-owner occupied 1-4 family dwellings.

Adjustor Plans

Annual Premium Plans — Single Premium Plans

Minimum Coverage	Loan-to-Value	1st Year Premium	Renewal Options Constant	Renewal Options Standard	Close For Less Option	3 Years	5 Years	10 Years
25%	91-95%	1.15%	.375%	.35%	.50%	1.95%	2.45%	3.70%
20%	86-90%	.70%	.375%	.35%	.44%	1.45%	1.95%	3.20%
20%	81-85%	.45%	.375%	.35%	.40%	1.20%	1.70%	2.95%
20%	80% & under	.35%	.375%	.35%		.95%	1.45%	2.70%

NOTES

(1) Coverage is the greater of the minimum coverage percentage or the claim amount in excess of 75% of the original market value of the property collateralized by the loan.

(2) Standard annual renewal rate is available for all premium plans and is applied to the outstanding loan balance at time of renewal.

(3) Constant annual renewal is available only for annual premium plans and is applied to the original insured loan balance upon renewal.

(4) The CFL premium rates, initial and renewals, are applied to the original insured loan balance.

Form #01-0670 (1 82)

FIGURE 6-2

Any of these policies can be purchased on either an annual premium plan or as a single premium. However, under the single-premium plan, the term of the coverage is limited to whenever the loan is paid down to 80 percent of its original amount or 15 years, whichever comes first.

Premiums Charged

Since PMI does not actually insure the full amount of a mortgage loan, the premiums charged are generally somewhat less than the FHA charges. Also, most states exercise their own controls over insurance rates and there can be some variation in the different states. PMI offers both a single-premium payment plan and an annual payment plan. Payment of the initial premium is made at the time a loan is closed and is usually deducted from the proceeds of a loan for direct payment to the insurance company. A good example of the variety of coverages offered and the premiums charged can be found in Figure 6-2, which is a reprint of a sample application form used for PMI. The premium amount is expressed as a percent of the initial loan amount.

In practice, it is the lender who selects the coverage required and thus determines the premium to be paid by the borrower.

Questions for Discussion

1. Without a national mortgage exchange, how are mortgages traded in the United States?

2. Explain the relationship between the price and the yield on a mortgage loan.

3. Why does the FNMA free market system provide a guide to the cost of mortgage money nationally?

4. Explain the role of the Federal Home Loan Mortgage Corporation and how it operates.

5. What is the purpose of a discount on a loan?

6. Define the term *point*.

7. List the different charges that can be required for a mortgage loan which can be quoted in points.

8. How does private mortgage insurance work?

9. Compare the most recent weighted average yields accepted by FNMA with local interest rates and discounts.

Mortgage Companies

Historical Background

From its origin as a brokerage-type service arranging loans, the mortgage banking industry has grown to a major business, handling well over half the mortgage loans in this country. As early as 1914, the people in this business formed a trade organization, known as the Farm Mortgage Bankers Association, indicating the original emphasis placed on farm loans. The name was changed to its present title of Mortgage Bankers Association of America in 1923, and it now has members from every state and a large permanent staff.

The Association serves as a communications and information center for the industry. Educational programs are sponsored to keep the many persons employed by mortgage bankers up-to-date on an ever-changing business. And a constant effort is being made to improve the methods and procedures of the industry.

In the early years of this century, mortgage bankers arranged for the sale of their own bonds and used these funds to buy small home and farm mortgages. Because of the thrift-conscious nature of these farmers and homeowners, mortgages were amazingly free of defaults and provided a widely used medium of investment.

The 1920s brought an increase in mortgage company financing of income properties such as office buildings, apartments, and hotels, perhaps with the firm conviction that a mortgage loan was as secure as gold. And the mortgage companies even referred to the small denomination bonds that they sold to the general public for mortgage financing as *gold bonds*.

However, the Depression, triggered by the collapse of prices on the nation's largest stock exchange in October 1929, showed up many basic weaknesses in the mortgage loan system. In the next two to three years most of the mortgage companies that had issued their own bonds as well as those that had guaranteed bonds for other development companies were faced with massive foreclosures. Unable to meet their obligations, they were forced into bankruptcy.

From these ruins has arisen a far more enlightened and professionally sound industry—one that today not only arranges for permanent financing of all types of mortgage loans, but also uses its own resources to fund the loans initially, sometimes handles the interim or construction financing, and finally services or administers the repayment of the loan for the permanent investor.

Mortgage Brokers

There is a significant difference between the services offered by *loan brokers*, and those offered by *mortgage bankers* working within the mortgage industry. Brokers limit their activity to serving as an intermediary between the client-borrower and the client-lender. While brokers are capable of handling all arrangements for the processing, or *packaging*, of the loan, they do no funding and have no facilities to service or administer a loan once it has been made. There are some loan-wise individuals who prefer to work on their own as brokers and carry their loan applications to a mortgage banker for verification and funding. They earn a portion of the normal one point finance fee plus an application fee.

Other types of mortgage brokers are companies operating on a national scale who primarily arrange purchases and sales of mortgage loans between originators and investors, or between investor and investor, and in so doing, greatly aid the free flow of mortgages across state lines in the private mortgage market. These brokers seldom originate a loan and do not service them. They are a part of the secondary market in some of their operations.

Another distinction that may be made between a mortgage broker and a mortgage banker is that the broker works mostly with commercial loans, while the banker is able to handle residential loans in addition to commercial loans. Large commercial loans are normally funded directly by the lending institution, say, an insurance company, and the monthly payments on debt service go directly to the lender.

Occasionally, a mortgage banker, or even a savings association, will broker a loan for a customer. Money may not be readily available through regular channels, or the loan request may be for something that the lender cannot handle with its own funds. The lender may then turn to other sources and earn a brokerage fee for handling the loan. This type of extra service is more commonly found in small communities.

The lines between a broker, a mortgage banker, and a lender are not always clearly drawn, as brokerage service may be handled by any one of them. Brokerage is essentially the service of processing the loan information for the borrower and arranging for a lender to make the loan. Good brokerage work is done by professionals who respect the confidential nature of the information they must obtain and who earn their fees by knowing which lenders are presently seeking certain types of loans.

Mortgage Bankers

The *full-service* facility offered by the mortgage banker today developed from both the need for a new approach after the Depression collapse and from the desire of the Federal Housing Administration to conduct its programs in conjunction with private industry. The economic pressures of 1930–1931 had dried up lendable funds, construction had been halted, and many banks had closed their doors. The shortage of available funds made the mortgage banker an intermediary for the only remaining sources of cash—cash from insurance companies, from a few large savings banks, and from the Federal National Mortgage Association. And the growth of the FHA brought the need for more servicing or loan administration by the mortgage bankers. More than half the mortgage companies operating today were founded after World War II, and in the 1950s four-fifths of all federally underwritten loans held by life insurance companies, savings and loans, and FNMA were serviced by mortgage bankers. The upward trend has continued, and if the government ventures further into the field of real estate financing, it undoubtedly will move through the channels that it helped to create— channels that have helped the government programs to succeed; that is, the mortgage banking industry.

Qualifications of a Mortgage Banker

At present there are no federal requirements regarding the qualifications or licensing of an individual or a company handling mortgage loans, and few states have established requirements. In most areas any individual meriting the confidence of a lending institution could assist in arranging a loan, thereby earning a fee for his or her services. In practice, however, most mortgage companies and lenders require more concrete proof of ability and integrity.

Some mortgage companies went into business initially to handle only conventional loans for various investor-clients and not FHA or VA loans. Those companies that specialize in large commercial loans have no real need of approval from FHA, nor do they feel compelled to comply with its regulations. Most mortgage companies, however, feel that a prime requisite for successful loan negotiation is to hold an FHA-approved certificate. The reason for this is that the home loan market, previously dominated by the FHA, is considered to be the most solidly reliable field, the "bread and butter" field, so to speak. In addition, many institutional lenders use the FHA certification of approval as one method of determining the reliability of potential correspondents.

The FHA requires a minimum capitalization of $100,000 (a sum now considered small within the industry), plus relevant details on the background and qualifications of the officers, directors, stockholders, and owners who will control and set policies for the mortgage company. It also requires that offices be made available for serving the general public and that no other business be conducted in those offices. Once the FHA has issued its charter of acceptance, the mortgage company becomes an *approved mortgagee* within the circle of companies qualified to handle federally underwritten commitments. Only approved mortgagees may present loan applications to the FHA for insured commitments. And in turn, the FHA depends heavily on its approved list of mortgage companies to prepare each application properly so as to include the relevant data needed for expeditious processing. Thus the FHA can rely on all information and verifications, the security of any cash required to be escrowed, and the prompt payment of any fees to be collected because it has already carefully examined the company and its official personnel before issuing its approval. A deliberate violation of an FHA requirement could result in the cancellation of the mortgage company's qualifications as an approved mortgagee.

As will become apparent in later chapters, the powerful role of the FHA in real estate finance began diminishing in early 1971, accelerated by a tightening of regulations brought on by abuses caused by a few groups and individuals. At about this same time, the private mortgage insurance business was boosted, and its activities became serious competition. Despite the fall from a dominant position, however, the FHA acceptance charter held by a company or institution remains an important credential of a mortgage company's qualifications to transact loans.

Mortgage Company Operations

Although mortgage companies vary widely in their methods, the business organization common to most operates by means of three basic divisions:

1. Administration.
2. Loan servicing.
3. Loan acquisition.

The administrative group supervises and directs all operations and usually seeks out and maintains contacts with its sources of money—the lending institutions. The development of stable, continuing relations with a group of investors is a source of pride with the mortgage companies. And there is always more than one investor, since it is not considered good business for either the mortgage company or the lender to maintain an exclusive arrangement. Lenders are in and out of the market as their particular needs fluctuate, while the mortgage company must maintain a steady supply of funds. The mortgage company officers must know which sources are available for loans and what particular type each lender prefers.

Loan servicing includes the record-keeping section that maintains the customers' or borrowers' accounts. Larger companies have converted much of this accounting to computerized methods for more efficient handling. One part of the records involves the escrow section, which holds the required insurance and tax deposits. Escrow personnel must maintain a continuous analysis of taxes and insurance costs for each property to assure the company that sufficient money will be available when needed to pay the taxes and insurance premiums. Another responsibility of the servicing section is to assure prompt payment of monthly accounts and to send out notifications on delinquencies and in case of a default. All lenders insist on knowing the account status and depend on the mortgage company to use diligence in keeping their accounts current. Laxity in this area could jeopardize a lender's rights in a foreclosure action.

The loan acquisition group, the division best known to outsiders, consists of the loan representatives or supervisors who make the contacts with potential borrowers, real estate agents, banks, accountants, and others in order to seek out the best loans and to handle the actual application for a loan. A loan processor usually works with one of these representatives to maintain the files and to help collect the information required on both the property and the borrower in putting together the complete loan package.

Loan Package

Basically, a loan package is all of the data needed to properly evaluate the property and to analyze the borrower as a credit risk. It is the information assembled by the mortgage banker to substantiate a loan. The following is a list of the ordinary requirements that a loan representative would assemble in preparing a house loan package.

Information required on the property

1. Earnest money contract on the sale, which should provide legal description of the property, and any special terms.
2. An appraisal by a qualified person.
3. A land survey by a registered surveyor.
4. A title opinion from the title company who will issue the title insurance.

Information required on the borrower (mortgagor)

1. Information questionnaire covering legal names, address, children, employment (for both borrower and co-borrower), assets and liabilities, and income and expenses (including fixed payments).
2. Verifications of employment.
3. Verifications of assets and debts.
4. Credit report from accepted agency.
5. Letters of explanation if unusual circumstances are involved.

The mortgage company then adds to this assemblage a covering letter or a report (FHA and VA have a special analysis form). The pertinent details are summarized with an analysis of the borrower's income, subtracting calculable living expenses and installment or monthly payments already committed, to show the cash available for debt retirement. Lenders each have varying requirements as to how this analysis should be presented, and the mortgage company is expected to know precisely what is needed.

For large loans, the same general information is required but in much greater depth. Usually this borrower is a corporation or partnership, and the loan package would require complete company information, financial statements, and corporate resolutions, if applicable. If the loan involves a project to be constructed, the package must include complete plans and specifications plus an assurance of the contractor's capability. A completion bond is required of the contractor under FHA procedures but is not always used in conventional financing. There is a growing list of certifications needed, such as the status with labor unions, nondiscrimination pledges, impact on the neighborhood statements, and new environmental requirements. Any special participation agreements required by the lender must be worked out in advance of the loan commitment.

A loan package assembled for initial closing under FHA procedure with multifamily projects includes 30 to 40 separate instruments, with all plans and data, and is often assembled under the guidance of an attorney who has specialized in such requirements and can knowledgeably represent the sponsor to the FHA and its attorneys at the closing.

Money Commitments

There are a number of ways for money to be promised or committed to a loan. The nomenclature for basic procedures may differ in some parts of the country, but the intent and purpose are similar and can be classed under the following categories of commitments.

Forward Loan Commitment (Sales and Servicing Contracts)

Since most mortgage bankers represent various institutional investors, some form of understanding or agreement is used to spell out the terms. Such an agreement between a lender and a mortgage company is called a *sales and servicing contract*. The agreement describes the type of loan and the conditions under which the lender will accept a loan and also states the services that must be provided by the mortgage company along with the fees charged for these services.

The lender, by terms of the agreement, offers to provide a specified amount of money to the mortgage company for certain classes of loans at a fixed interest rate. The mortgage company is allowed a service charge for handling collections, providing the escrow services, paying taxes and insurance, and for representing the lender if problems occur during the transaction. This service charge, which varies from one-tenth of 1 percent to one-half of 1 percent of the loan depending on the amount of servicing required, is a direct addition (*add-on*) to the interest rate. For example, presuming that a lender, such as an eastern savings and loan association, agrees to accept a mortgage company's loans for an interest rate of $13\frac{1}{2}$ percent and the mortgage company requires $\frac{3}{8}$ percent for servicing the loan, then the quotation submitted by the mortgage company to the borrower would be an interest rate of $13\frac{7}{8}$ percent. In this example the $13\frac{1}{2}$ percent rate is referred to as *net* to the lender. The lender then sets up a time limit during which the mortgage company may exercise its rights under the commitment, which usually extends from three to six months. This type of commitment can be termed a *forward* commitment, and depending on the relationship between the mortgage company and the lender, it is not unusual for the lender to require a commitment fee.

The commitment fee, when required, is usually 1 percent (or one point) of the total commitment payable upon issuance of the agreement by the lender. Generally this fee is refundable when the commitment is fully used. However, if the mortgage company does not use the full amount of the commitment, it may be required to forfeit a portion of the fee. For example, if a mutual bank makes a $1 million commitment to the M Mortgage Company for four months and the mortgage company deposits $10,000 as a commitment fee, then if at the end of the four-month term, only $750,000 of acceptable loans have been made, the mortgage company may have to forfeit the unfulfilled portion of the fee, or $2,500.

Under the forward commitment procedure, a mortgage company may be allowed to submit loans one at a time to the prime lender, but since this is a burdensome procedure, most agreements call for a minimum amount, say $250,000, in a group of loans at any one time. Unless the mortgage company has considerable capital of its own, it will resort to a *warehouse* line of credit with a local commercial bank to carry the loans until the minimum shipping package has been reached.

Immediate Commitments

Another method employed, and one that accounts for the greatest volume of commitment money, is the immediate or direct purchase of loans from the mortgage company by an institutional lender. Under this procedure the mortgage company funds large volumes of loans with their own capital and credit lines and periodically offers the loans in multimillion dollar blocks to the institutional investor. Immediate delivery usually means within 90 days.

A lender with surplus money to invest will tend to accept a lower net interest rate on a large block of loans where it is possible to make an immediate purchase. In this manner the lender's money is earning interest sooner. Under a forward commitment procedure, the lender may be reluctant to tie up money for future months since interest rates may change.

The large blocks of loans available by means of immediate purchase procedures are of greater interest to the big investors who must move their money in wholesale lots. Most large investors will not undertake a purchase of less than $1 million in loan totals from any single mortgage company.

Mortgage companies are generally able to retain the servicing contracts for residential loans when they are passed on to the institutional lenders regardless of the type of commitment—forward or immediate purchase. The amount of the servicing fee is determined in advance with the forward commitment but can vary somewhat with an immediate purchase commitment. With the latter, the servicing fee to be earned by the mortgage company would amount to whatever the differential is between the interest rate at which the loan was made to the borrower and the net rate acceptable to the secondary lender.

In the large commercial loans, the servicing may be passed on to the secondary lender, or a fee for this service may be negotiated with the mortgage company.

Future Commitments

While some of the terms used to describe the various types of money commitments are not always consistent in various parts of the country, probably the most confusing is the difference between a forward commitment and a future commitment. The *forward* commitment, as described in the preceding section, states a maximum amount for the commitment, then provides for the use, or withdrawal, of that money *during the term* of the commitment. The *future* commitment is a pledge of money, all of which will be made available at a *later specified date*. The future commitment may use terminology such as "on or before July 31, 19__"; or it could provide a time span such as "not before 18 months nor later than 24 months from the date of this commitment agreement." It is the future commitment that is used in making a permanent loan for a building yet to be constructed.

Delivery of the mortgage under a future commitment may, or may not, be mandatory. If delivery of the mortgage is not mandatory, the holder of the commitment may find a lower cost source of money for the permanent loan elsewhere and simply forfeit the commitment fee.

A future commitment almost always costs a nonrefundable commitment fee, which is negotiable. Normally it will be one to two points. The reason for the fee is that the lender is agreeing to have money available for a loan, perhaps one or two years from the date of commitment, and usually at a fixed rate of interest, and the lender feels entitled to a fee for this promise to deliver. As interest rates have become more volatile, future commitments are tending to be tied to a leading indicator of the capital market rather than held to a fixed rate.

It might be well to recall here that the long-term capital market fluctuates far more slowly than the short-term money market. The long-term investor is more interested in the *average* return on the total investments and thus can accept small increases and decreases in periodic new investments. The movement of rates, upward or downward, affects only a small portion of the overall portfolio at any one time. These investments over or under the average return are the *marginal* investments.

Take-out or Stand-by Commitments

A take-out or stand-by commitment is actually a backup promise to make a loan. It is more popular in periods of tight money and can be applied to any kind of a loan on a projected building, residential property, or income property. It is a commitment that is really not intended to be utilized but is available if needed.

To illustrate a take-out commitment in operation let us assume that an apartment builder wants to build in a tight money situation. The city appears to be overbuilt with apartment units and with decreasing occupancy and the major lenders have withdrawn from further apartment loans for the time being. However, the builder owns a piece of land in an area of the city that is growing and that shows a real need for more apartment units. In such a case the builder might seek stand-by financing in the form of a take-out commitment from a mortgage company, a real estate investment trust, or another type of lender. A take-out commitment is issued at a higher than market interest rate and lasts for a longer term than the average construction loan commitment. The builder may be allowed three to five years to exercise the rights. To obtain this type of commitment, the builder must pay from two to four points in cash at the time the commitment letter is issued. This assurance of a permanent loan, even though it is at uneconomical rates, is used as a backup to obtain a construction loan.

The real idea of the take-out commitment is to enable a builder to proceed with the construction of a building, allowing perhaps a year to achieve good occupancy, and with a proven income, then obtain a more reasonable permanent loan and simply drop the higher cost take-out commitment. The builder would, of course, forfeit the initial commitment fee. The idea has worked well when everything clicks and the market analysis has proved accurate. It has also caused some disasters when it hasn't worked.

The idea of take-out commitments has moved into the field of house construction loans as a better protection to the construction lender than a speculative house loan. A commitment for residential house loans would be made at 80 percent of the appraised value of the finished house (usually the same amount as the construction loan itself), to be exercised within one year and at a cost of one point, payable when issued. Sometimes the mortgage company that issues the take-out will allow a portion of the commitment fee to apply on the origination fee if the mortgage company also handles the home buyer's permanent loan. Unlike a take-out commitment for a commercial project, the take-out on a house loan is used by the issuing mortgage company to help secure the *permanent* loan when the house is sold. The borrower then would be the new house buyer.

Permanent Loan

The permanent loan is the final mortgage loan with repayment extended over many years. It can be made from a future commitment or an immediate one. Conventional loans are made for a period of time extending to 30 years, while some federally underwritten loans extend to terms up to 40 years.

Commercial projects should have a permanent loan assured (or a valid take-out loan commitment as above) before a construction loan will be released. The construction lender wants to know how he or she will be repaid when the building is completed. Only a few builders are financially strong enough to give this assurance without a loan commitment to support them. If a builder is capable of handling the construction costs with personal resources, it is far easier to obtain permanent financing upon completion of the project when the building can be inspected and the income potential more easily ascertained. Such a strong builder would also save paying the commitment fee that would be necessary if the permanent financing were handled as a future commitment rather than as an immediate one.

The permanent loan for a single-family residence is made to the buyer, which may be in the form of a future commitment made prior to actual construction, or more commonly, as an immediate commitment for an existing house.

Warehousing of Mortgage Loans

In order to accumulate the volume of mortgages needed to satisfy a sales and service contract or to work with immediate sales of blocks of mortgage loans, the mortgagee (mortgage company) must use its own cash to make the initial funding of a loan at closing. Or, as most mortgage companies do, it borrows short-term money at a local commercial bank to provide the cash.

As mentioned in Chapter 5 on commercial banks, warehouse lines are established by mortgage companies on a fully secured basis; that is, each loan advanced by the commercial bank is secured by a note and mortgage assigned to the bank by the mortgage company.

While the credit-worthiness and capabilities of the mortgage banking company will have been fully cleared by the commercial bank before a line of credit is established, there is still a concern as to what will become of the accumulated loans as interest rates fluctuate. If the commercial bank accepts, say $1 million in home loans, which were made at a 13 percent interest rate, and the rate then begins to climb upward to 14 percent, can the loans be sold without a loss? The answer, of course, is negative unless the loans have previously been committed at a price to yield 13 percent.

Under these conditions, the small mortgage companies seek to protect themselves and their warehouse line with a forward commitment; that is, a sales and service contract with a major lender, or, perhaps, an FNMA commitment. As discussed earlier in this chapter, the commitment by a permanent lending source to accept a fixed amount of certain types of loans over a period of four to six months not only assures the mortgage company of its sale of loans but provides assurance to the commercial bank that the loans in warehouse will be liquidated at an established price.

It is by means of this assurance to the small mortgage companies, and to some of the giants, that the Federal National Mortgage Association has played such a dramatic role. If a small mortgage company is simply unable to find any lenders willing to furnish a forward commitment because they themselves are short of cash, the mortgage company can then turn to FNMA and acquire, for example, a $200,000 commitment under the free market system procedure by making a noncompetitive offering (see Chapter 6) and accepting the weighted average yield. If the yield required by the loan commitment is, say 15 percent, then the mortgage company knows that it must offer its loans to borrowers at a combination of interest rate and discount that equals at least a 15 percent yield. Otherwise, the loan cannot be sold profitably by the mortgage company.

The large mortgage companies are capable of playing a different game with their warehouse lines. In the multimillion dollar business of handling large blocks of residential loans and some commercial loans, the commercial banks know that their large mortgage company customers are quite capable of selling big blocks of loans and absorbing substantial losses, if necessary, in an adverse market. Medium to large mortgage companies may have lines of credit at one or more banks totaling from $10 million to $100 million. As the mortgage company makes loans each day and places them in the warehouse line, one or more of the company's officers will be watching the secondary market and discussing possible loan sales with the large lenders. This procedure is somewhat like a speculation game, for when the market is right the mortgage company may sell off $10 or $20 million in loans at a price that provides a slight additional profit to the mortgage company. In these large volumes, a very slight movement of loan prices has a tremendous effect on the gain (or loss) on the sale.

In view of all this shifting around of the actual note and mortgage, what happens then to the people who borrowed the money to buy a house? They are relatively unaffected and, in most cases, do not know about the movement of the note. This is because the responsibility for the proper servicing of the loan is normally held by the originator of the loan who handles the collections and escrows the necessary tax and insurance money as an agent for the holder of the note. The originator earns a service fee for this work and provides a continuity to the borrower who continues to make monthly payments to the same office.

Other Sources of Income for Mortgage Companies

Mortgage companies often furnish other services in addition to their mortgage loan work, and these are usually affiliated with the building industry. The more common of these activities are:

Insurance. The sale of hazard insurance is closely associated with mortgage financing and is often handled by the mortgage company or an affiliated agency.

Appraising. Most mortgage companies have qualified appraisers on their staffs as a service to both their customers and their lenders.

Real estate sales. Since many mortgage company loan representatives are also qualified real estate brokers, the sale of real estate is an easy step. However, this represents direct competition to some of the mortgage company's best customers—the other real estate brokers—and is not practical in many cases.

Construction. Some mortgage companies have developed very competent construction divisions and will build both residential housing and commercial buildings for their own use as investments or for sales to others.

Land development. One of the methods used to move a step ahead of the competition is for a mortgage company to buy land for subdivision development and make the lots available to builders. In this manner the mortgage company can usually retain a first refusal look at all loans and other services that may be required in the new development.

The Future of Mortgage Companies

Mortgage companies have reached their present high position in the lending field by performing two principal services: (1) a service to borrowers in processing sometimes difficult loan applications and making sure the funds are available to them at closing, and (2) a service to lenders who are too large and remote to undertake processing and servicing of small individual loans. The method used by mortgage companies is to actively solicit loan applications through personal contact, through sales and service to the real estate industry, and through the home buyers. But the key to their continuing success lies more in their ability to find lenders willing to work with them and to provide the money for the loans, rather than on their proven sales ability. In periods of tight money, the small mortgage company can easily find itself short of funds and dependent on the higher cost sources, which could be mainly the Federal National Mortgage Association. As savings associations continue to grow and spread through their branches into the smaller communities, some have become more aggressive and sales minded in their approach to lending. The increase in activity of the secondary market and the growing acceptance by savings associations of selling some of their loans have fostered an increase in competition. Mortgage companies without direct affiliation to actual sources of money are finding it more difficult to compete in a fluctuating market. Many have recognized the trend, are broadening their field of activities into other related businesses, and/or are taking steps to acquire, or be acquired by, a bank, a bank holding corporation, or a savings association.

The changing market in mortgage money is offering several new opportunities for mortgage companies to expand their lending activities. The source of funds represented by the sale of mortgage-backed securities in financial markets is available to mortgage companies in most states. A segment of this market source, the sale of municipal bonds to raise money for mortgage loans, is open to mortgage companies as well as to institutional lenders. And, as will be discussed later in Chapter 12, "Seller-Financed Home Mortgages," two new developments in 1982 offer expanded markets and increased revenues for mortgage companies. One is the entry of private mortgage insurance companies into the field of default insurance. Mortgage companies now offer default insurance to home sellers who finance all or a part of their home sale. And the other is the expansion of FNMA's loan purchase activity to include seller-financed mortgage loans. Both the insurance and the sale of a seller-financed loan must be handled by an approved mortgage lender. In other words, home sellers can now have the benefit of professional advice and competent loan processing by working with approved lenders, which includes most of the mortgage companies.

Questions for Discussion

1. What does the FHA require in the way of qualifications in order for a mortgage lender to receive an approved mortgagee certificate?

2. Name the three basic divisions of operations in a mortgage company and describe what each does.

3. Describe a loan package as assembled by a mortgage company, including what information it must contain.

4. Does your state have any statutes or agencies regulating the mortgage banking industry? If so, how do they function?

5. Describe a forward commitment for money and how it is used by a mortgage company.

6. Define a *service fee* and a *commitment fee*.

7. What are the advantages of an immediate money commitment over a forward commitment for the mortgage company? For the institutional lender?

8. Describe a *take-out commitment*.

9. For what reasons would a mortgage company borrow money from a commercial bank on a warehouse line of credit?

Federal Government Programs

Introduction

There are many federal programs that give assistance to people buying homes, rehabilitating homes, suffering from natural disasters, and in need of decent housing. Only a few of these programs are considered in this chapter. First, the loan insurance programs of the Department of Housing and Urban Development are examined. Then the Veterans Administration is considered with a look at some of the methods they use to help veterans obtain housing. Because both HUD and the VA offer similar programs, they have recently achieved more uniform procedures for loan qualification which both agencies are able to work with. The qualification methods and the uniform instruments now used for application, appraisal, and verification are explained in a separate section. And finally, the general operations of the Government National Mortgage Association is covered.

Department of Housing and Urban Development/Federal Housing Administration

The Federal Housing Administration was one of several score agencies spawned during the Depression to help resolve the economic problems that plagued this nation. It is one of the very few that has survived, and it has proved its value over five decades of operation.

The reasons for which the FHA was formed in 1934 are still valid today, although the area of operations has expanded tremendously from the initial assistance program for home buyers. The purposes for the FHA are (1) to encourage wider homeownership; (2) to improve housing standards; and (3) to create a better method of financing mortgage loans. All of these aims have been realized, even beyond original hopes. This was done without making a single loan, simply by sound use of government credit to insure mortgage loans. From its initial widespread rejection by many private lenders, a government-insured commitment now is readily salable to a large number of investors. Even in the tightest money markets, there has always been funding available for a government-insured loan.

When the FHA stepped into the housing picture in 1934, houses had been financed for 50 to 60 percent of their sales price on a first mortgage of three to five years, with a second mortgage and even a third mortgage at increasingly higher interest rates. By offering to insure a single large loan up to 80 percent of value (an extremely high ratio in those days), the FHA was able to insist that the down payment be made in cash, permit no secondary financing, and command a moderate interest rate. The loans were for long terms—up to 20 years at first—and were fully amortized over the life of the loan. Equal monthly payments were charged for principal and interest. Escrow accounts were established for hazard insurance and for taxes, to collect one-twelfth of the yearly cost each month. Each of these monthly payments also included a fee of ½ percent of the unpaid mortgage balance annually to cover the cost of mortgage default insurance. Most of these features were later incorporated into the loan guarantee program of the Veterans Administration and have now become normal procedure for conventional loans as well. While none of these ideas actually originated with the FHA, this agency gave them wide usage for the first time and thus brought about a sweeping reform in the field of residential financing.

Over the years, modifications have been made in the mortgage amounts that may be insured, both by the introduction of new programs and by raising the limits on existing programs. Changes in the down payment requirements have the most immediate effect on home buyers in the low- and middle-income brackets with limited cash reserves. But with the changing market for housing, the FHA has found that buyers have a considerable ability to handle the higher down payments required with graduated payment mortgage programs. Other features have been added to the basic programs. The term of the loan commitment is 75 percent of the remaining useful life of the property to a present maximum of 30 years. In certain instances, a 35-year commitment can be approved if the house was constructed under HUD/FHA inspection procedures. And by 1982 several new repayment plans were being encouraged that utilize 15-year or less terms, thus substantially reducing the total interest cost.

The authority to specify maximum permissible interest rates for an insured loan has been granted to the Secretary of Housing and Urban Development. Adjustments are made in the published rate periodically to maintain a reasonable relationship with market interest rates on conventional loans. The workings of the free market further adjust this published rate to a competitive yield through a discount on the loan.

As the FHA gained strength in its housing assistance, more titles and sections were added to its program. While the FHA has over 50 different programs to offer in its portfolio of assistance to home loans, improvement loans, and multifamily project loans, our concern is primarily with loans for single-family residences. Under the assistance programs for home loans, the FHA has special help for servicemen, civilian employees of the armed services, and disaster victims, as well as programs in experimental housing, urban renewal, and condominium housing.

All programs are implemented by the issuance of a Certificate of Insurance, which protects the lender against default. The differences between the programs are based on the kind of property and the qualifications of the individual who needs the help. There may be lower cash requirements and, in certain programs, an actual subsidy of interest costs. Also, the property must meet certain parameters to qualify for an insured commitment.

Until several years ago, the FHA had been required to analyze each loan on the basis of its economic feasibility and to limit its insured commitments solely to those families who presented a reasonable credit risk. The care with which the FHA has exercised its authority over the years is indicated by the fact that it has, in the past, returned over two-thirds of its insurance fees to the Federal Treasury.

In the last fifteen years Congress has seen fit to recognize a growing social need for housing and has introduced a number of new programs through the HUD/FHA which are based not only on economic feasibility but also on a family's need for housing. This country has long supported various types of public housing built by government agencies and rented to lower income families for well below market rents. Public housing of this sort has not worked out very successfully, and in 1965 Congress altered the direction of the program to place the problem in the hands of private business. Money previously allocated to support public housing was now to be used to subsidize private developers with the expectation that they could do a more effective and efficient job. The programs to activate these social objectives have been channeled through the FHA with the first funding for such a project as far back as 1966.

In January 1973, the Secretary of HUD announced a suspension of all government-subsidized housing programs pending a reevaluation. Abuses and profiteering had been uncovered in some areas, and the Nixon administration felt a better method of giving assistance might be found. Meanwhile, a reduction in spending would be more helpful. By January 1976, housing shortages and high costs continued to plague the home buyer and President Ford ordered the release of the remaining assistance money that had been impounded three years earlier. Public policy has fluctuated in regard to subsidized housing programs since that time, but some assistance continues. Housing for the elderly, the handicapped, and for lower income families still has subsidy assistance programs but at a much lower level of funding than previously.

Change of Identification

Since its origin, the Federal Housing Administration has built a long list of good credits with its many contributions to the housing industry and financial assistance programs. The initials *FHA* have special meaning to those in the industry. However, as a part of the Department of Housing and Urban Development, the FHA identification is being phased out and replaced by *HUD*, or, in this period of transition, by *HUD/FHA*. The forms used for loan qualification are now identified by a HUD number rather than an FHA designation.

HUD/FHA Terminology and Basic Procedures

To handle qualification of borrowers and the property offered as collateral, the HUD/FHA follows certain procedures as detailed in their *Underwriter's Guide*. There are some words and phrases with special meaning in the world of HUD/FHA loan qualification. For example, a conventional lender measures the loan amount against the property value. With an FHA loan, the closing costs are added to the property value resulting in a sum called *value for mortgage insurance purposes*. The conventional lender focuses its cash requirement on a *down payment*; the FHA looks at the *cash required to close*. The purpose of qualification procedures is the same, whether FHA, VA, or conventional, and that is to qualify the borrower and the property. Nevertheless, to understand FHA procedures, it is necessary to understand the language.

Value for Mortgage Insurance Purposes

The amount of mortgage insurance available under any of the FHA insurance programs is limited to a percentage of the value of the property that will be used as collateral for the loan as well as limitations imposed by each of the various programs. In calculating the *value for mortgage insurance purposes*, the FHA adds its estimates of property value and closing costs. In this manner the borrower is able to include a portion of the closing costs in the loan amount. Closing costs may include the HUD/FHA application fee, a lender's origination fee (limited to 1 percent of the loan amount), costs of the title search, legal fees to prepare the necessary closing instruments, and miscellaneous costs, such as notary fees, recording costs, and a credit report.

Prepaid Items

The FHA distinguishes between closing costs and prepaid items. In most programs, prepaid items must be paid in cash by the borrower. Prepays include the escrow deposits required for insurance premiums and property taxes plus the mortgage insurance premium. The FHA requires that at least one month of the costs for these prepaid items be held in escrow and permits the lender to accept two months in advance. (Property hazard insurance requires one full year paid in advance plus one month of premium held in escrow by the lender.)

Secondary Financing with HUD/FHA Insured Commitments

In July 1980, the strict rule against permitting any second mortgage financing was relaxed a bit. In the past, HUD/FHA has permitted no secondary financing on property offered as collateral for an insured commitment. Now, secondary mortgages are permitted under the following conditions:

1. With prior approval of the Commissioner (Assistant Secretary for Housing—Federal Housing Commissioner), the mortgaged property may be subject to a secondary mortgage held by a federal, state, or local government or instrumentality.
2. Any required monthly payments under the HUD-insured mortgage plus the second mortgage may not exceed the mortgagor's ability to pay.
3. The borrower's total indebtedness secured by the property may be less than, equal to, or more than the estimated value of the property. (One exception is Section 235 interest subsidy program mort-

gages where total indebtedness may not exceed the HUD estimate of property value.)

4. Borrowers and mortgagees must disclose the secondary financing on Form HUD-92900, Application for Mortgage Approval.

5. If the borrower is required to amortize the loan, the estimated monthly payment will be included in the mortgagor's recurring charges and total fixed obligations.

Other Rules

Under FHA rules, the property value, that is, the value of the house itself, is the *lesser* of the FHA appraised value or the acquisition price. It should be noted that one of the stipulations in an FHA commitment is that the borrower has the right to rescind the contract with no penalty if the contract price exceeds the FHA appraisal. However, the buyer-borrower has the option to proceed with the purchase of a house at more than the FHA appraised value but must pay the excess amount in cash. HUD/FHA generally does not permit the buyer-borrower to pay a loan discount, since it could be classed as a fee for the use of a government benefit, rather than a method used in financial markets to adjust the yield of a fixed interest investment. Exceptions are now being made to this longstanding rule. With the introduction of the negotiated loan commitment in 1982, HUD/FHA allows the borrower to pay discount points if agreed to by all parties involved (seller, borrower, and mortgagee). Also, the new refinance program to allow borrowers to take advantage of lower interest rates also allows the borrower to pay discount points.

Program Details

There are now over 50 different programs offered by HUD/FHA. Their utilization varies somewhat across the country according to local situations. Some programs have become inactive due to loan limitations or qualification standards that no longer fit the changing housing market. This section examines the qualifications needed and the restrictions placed on several of the more popular programs.

1. Section 203(b)—Home Mortgage Insurance (including the special assistance offered veterans).
2. Section 203(k)—Rehabilitation Home Mortgage Insurance.
3. Section 234(c)—Mortgage Insurance for Condominiums.
4. Section 245—Graduated Payment Mortgages.
5. Title 1—Home Improvement Loan Insurance.

Section 203(b)—Home Mortgage Insurance

The basic 203(b) program authorized in the initial act of 1934 is still the most widely used home mortgage insurance program. Experience gained from this program has been used extensively in the development of many succeeding plans. As with all HUD/FHA programs, the property to be acquired and used as collateral for the loan must meet applicable standards. While there are no special requirements for the individual borrower, he or she must have a good credit rating and demonstrate an ability to make the required investment as well as handle the monthly mortgage payments.

Mortgage Limits. HUD/FHA no longer applies a standard limit on loan amount for the entire country. The Housing Act approved in April 1980 set the maximum loan amount at 95 percent of the median price of all new housing in the local area not to exceed $90,000 for single-family houses. The precise determination is made by FHA field offices.

Maximum Insured Commitment. As described above, the insured commitment is a percentage of the value for mortgage insurance purposes (which is the value of the property plus closing costs). The various programs offered differ in which percentages are used and how they are applied. Following are limits currently in effect for the Section 203(b) program:

1. For property approved prior to construction or completed more than one year:
   97 percent of the first $25,000 plus 95 percent of the value in excess of $25,000.
2. For a nonoccupant mortgagor:
   85 percent of the loan amount available to an owner-occupant. The amount may be reduced depending on the rental income from the property
3. For property not FHA approved prior to construction and less than one year old:
   90 percent of the value including closing costs. (This limit also applies to veteran applicants.)

Section 203(b)(Veteran). Under 203(b),HUD/FHA has a special concession for qualified veterans—it allows an insured commitment of 100 percent of the first $25,000 instead of the insured commitment of 97 percent it allows for nonveterans. The program is valuable because it has a broader application than the one available under the Veterans Administration. The basic differences are:

1. The FHA qualifications requires 90 days of active duty. The VA has longer time spans of required service at different periods of time such as hot war, cold war distinctions. (See VA requirements later in this chapter.)
2. The FHA does not require owner occupancy for veterans to qualify, while the VA does. VA limits its benefit to one house at a time, to be occupied by the veteran.
3. The FHA does not take into consideration any prior commitment of the veteran's entitlement, while the VA must deduct any previous usage of the entitlement if the loan has not been paid off or assumed by another veteran acceptable to the VA.

The special rules that apply to a qualified veteran for determining the maximum insured commitment are:

1. 100 percent of the first $25,000, or $25,000 plus prepaid expenses less $200, whichever is less.
2. 95 percent of the value in excess of $25,000.

Example of 203(b) Insured Commitment (Non veteran).

$$\text{Value of property and closing costs} = \$57,800$$
$$.97 \times 25,000 = 24,250$$
$$.95 \times 32,800 = \underline{31,160}$$
$$55,410 \text{ rounded down to } \underline{\$55,400}$$
$$\text{cash required} = \$\ 2,400$$

(Insured commitment is always rounded down to nearest $50 amount.)

Section 203(k)—Rehabilitation Home Mortgage Insurance

To help restore and preserve the nation's existing housing stock, a major revision of the old 203(k) program was implemented in June 1980. Unlike any other HUD-insured program, 203(k) combines a purchase money mortgage with a construction loan. The new revision offers an insured commitment (same limits as 203[b]) that allows the purchase of an existing house over one year old, plus sufficient additional money to rehabilitate the property. The program is limited to one- to four-family dwellings and can be utilized as follows:

1. To purchase and rehabilitate a dwelling and the real property on which it is located.
2. To refinance existing indebtedness and rehabilitate such a dwelling.

A single insurance commitment combines the funds needed to purchase the property or refinance existing indebtedness, the costs incidental to closing, and the money needed to complete the proposed rehabilitation. The money allocated to rehabilitation must be escrowed at closing in a Rehabilitation Escrow Account. This fund includes any money allocated to the contingency reserve as determined by the HUD Construction Analyst, but the contingency cannot exceed 10 percent of the cost of rehabilitation. This account must be kept separate and cannot be used to pay taxes or insurance. Further, the account must pay interest each month to the borrower at not less than 5 percent per annum.

If the 203(k)-insured commitment involves insurance of advances, which would be normal when rehabilitation is required, then a Rehabilitation Loan Agreement must be executed by the lender and the borrower. As a part of this agreement, there must be an Inspection and Release schedule which details the amount of escrowed money that can be released at each stage of completion.

Before any release of funds can be made by the lender holding the escrow account, an inspection must be made to determine satisfactory completion of the work to that stage. Inspection is made by HUD-approved fee inspectors from a list provided by the HUD field office. The number of inspections required will vary with the complexity of the rehabilitation but cannot exceed four plus the final one.

While the program does not specifically list it, Section 203(k) can be used to convert existing single-family homes into multiple unit dwellings for up to four families.

Section 234(c)—Mortgage Insurance for Condominium Housing

HUD/FHA insures mortgages for the purchase of individual family units in multifamily housing projects (234[c]). They also insure loans for the construction or rehabilitation of housing projects intended for sale as individual condominium units (234[d]). A condominium is defined as joint ownership of common areas and facilities by the separate owners of single-family dwelling units in the project. To be acceptable for FHA insurance, the project must include at least four dwelling units and it must be approved by FHA. At least one other unit in each project must be acquired under the government-underwritten program. One person may own as many as four units financed with HUD/FHA-insured mortgages, provided he or she lives in one of them.

Before a loan can be insured for a single condominium, the entire project must meet HUD/FHA minimum standards just as a new subdivision must meet compliance standards. The agreement under which a homeowners association may function comes under scrutiny as does the rights of the developer. Questions such as "When does the developer vacate the premises?" become more important with a condominium as it affects control of the common areas. Under FHA requirements, the developer may not claim a right of first refusal to offer condominiums for resale.

Mortgage Limits and the Insured Commitment. Both the maximum amount of mortgage loan permitted and the calculation of the maximum insured commitment are determined on the same basis as that of the 203(b) program described earlier in this section.

Section 245—Graduated Payment Mortgage

Several years of experimental testing provided the groundwork for HUD/FHA to offer an insurance program for graduated payment mortgages approved nationally in November 1976. The purpose of the program is to reduce monthly payments in the early years of the mortgage term so that families with lower income and reasonable expectation of future increases can qualify for suitable housing in a higher cost market. Acceptance of the program has been very favorable and is enabling many young families to purchase their first home. The key benefit for the applicant is that income qualification is based on the monthly payment required for the first year.

Section 245 is limited to owner-occupant applicants—there are no other special qualifications. As in other programs, the applicant must have a good credit record, demonstrate ability to make the required down payment, and be able to handle the monthly mortgage payments. There is one additional requirement—the applicant must have a reasonable expectation of an increased annual income in future years. Initially, the program was targeted for first-home buyer families but was not so limited. Later, in August 1980, Congress approved an expansion of the program with two new payment plans designated as Section 245(b) —the initial payment plans were designated 245(a). The purpose of the two new plans is to reduce the down payment requirements. Section 245(b) is limited to the first-home buyer, who is defined as anyone not owning a house in the past three years.

The lower monthly payments in the early years under most of the HUD/FHA Section 245 plans are insufficient to pay anything on principal and not all of the interest due each month. Consequently, each year the unpaid interest is added to the principal balance due. Since the loan balance is increased, rather than reduced or amortized, the result is called *negative amortization*. Because the increase in the loan balance could exceed the value of the property, HUD/FHA has a limit on the amount of increase.

Section 245(a). Initially, the FHA offered to insure graduated payment mortgages with five different repayment plans. These are differentiated by the rate of payment increases each year and the duration of the escalation period. Three plans offer 2½, 5, and 7½ percent annual increases for the first five years; two plans offer 2 percent and 3 percent increases for the first ten years. Stated another way, the initial monthly payment amount is so calculated that it can be increased each year at a fixed, or predetermined, rate so as to reach a constant-level payment amount by the sixth year for the five-year plans and by the eleventh year for the ten-year plans. The amount of the monthly payment, the mortgage insurance premium, and the down payment required, depend on the interest rate and the term of the loan. To simplify the calculation of these amounts, the FHA has published a series of tables that give factors to be used in the calculation of payment requirements. The calculation method and an example is given later in this section.

Section 245(b). In August 1980, two new repayment plans were added to the GPM program to allow lower down payments for first-home buyers.

The new plans allow higher insured commitments (lower down payments) than is required for the 245(a) plans. The loan balance, which increases in the early years of most GPM plans, had been limited under the older 245(a) plans to 97 percent of the *initial* appraised value plus closing costs (which is the value for mortgage insurance purposes). This meant that the plan allowing the lowest initial monthly payment (called Plan III) required the highest amount of down payment. To help overcome this obstacle for first-home buyers, Congress authorized the Section 245(b) plans. 245(b) increases the maximum insured commitment amount to 97 percent of the *projected* value of the property. The projected value is calculated by increasing the property value 2½ percent each year for five years. However, the principal obligation added cannot exceed 113 percent of the initial value plus closing costs.

Like Section 245(a) repayment plans, 245(b) plans use special tables of factors prepared by FHA for the calculation of insured commitments, monthly mortgage payments, and monthly mortgage insurance premiums. The two 245(b) plans offer yearly graduations in payment amounts as follows:

First plan 7½ percent increases for 5 years.

Second plan 4.9 percent increases for 10 years.

Borrower Qualification for 245(b). There are some interesting, and difficult, restrictions on qualification for 245(b) for first-home buyers. The borrower must be *unable* to qualify for existing 245(a) plans or any other HUD/FHA mortgage program. Field offices report that many applicants seeking 245(b) plans end up with qualification for some other program. To determine qualification for 245(b):

1. Total housing expense must be calculated as required under the 203(b) program (Line [j], Section III of the Mortgage Credit Analysis Worksheet). If the housing expense exceeds 38 percent of net effective income, the applicant may be eligible for 245(b).
2. Calculate the maximum mortgage available under 245(a), Plan III. If borrower does not have sufficient cash or other assets readily convertible to cash to meet the Plan III requirements, the applicant may be eligible for 245(b).

Mortgage Limits.   The maximum amount of the insured commitment (equals the loan amount) for Section 245 is the same as that applied to Section 203(b) commitments. These limits are now determined by the HUD field offices at 95 percent of the median price of all new housing in the local area, not to exceed $90,000 for single-family houses. Two components of Section 245 plans make it possible for the loan amount (that is, the principal balance due on the loan) to increase. These are the negative amortization features (adding unpaid interest to the principal balance each year) and the Section 245(b) calculation of a projected property value. Thus the loan balance can increase to an amount greater than the initial authorized maximum loan amount. This possibility is recognized and does not constitute a violation of the National Housing Act, so long as the down payment computations are made in accordance with Section 245 instructions.

Calculating the 245(a) Insured Commitment.   In order to comply with the requirements, it is necessary to make two separate calculations to establish the correct maximum insured commitment. Since the insured commitment almost always becomes the amount of the loan, the difference between the commitment and the contract price is the required down payment. The first calculation that determines the insured commitment, called Criterion I in the example below, is the same as that required for Section 203(b) qualification. The second calculation, Criterion II, is in accordance with the Section 245 formulas. The *lesser* of the two calculations is the amount of the insured commitment. Under Criterion II for the nonveteran applicant, the procedure is to take 97 percent of the property value (including closing costs) and divide the result by the highest outstanding balance factor for the applicable plan and interest rate. Different procedures apply for veterans and for property constructed without FHA prior approval or less than one year old.

Example of 245 Computation for Insured Commitment.   Assume a property value of $49,000 plus closing costs of $1,000 for a total value for mortgage insurance purposes of $50,000. The loan requested is a 30-year term at 9½ percent and the plan selected is Plan III, which has payments increasing at 7½ percent for the first five years. From the FHA tables, the highest outstanding balance factor is 1049.5206.

Section 245(a) Plan III:

Criterion I: 97% of $25,000   = $24,250
                 95% of $25,000   =   23,750
                                        $48,000 maximum loan

Criterion II: 97% of $50,000   = $48,500
                 $48,500 ÷ 1049.5206 = $46.2116
                 $46.2116 × 1,000   = $46,212 maximum loan

Lesser of I or II (rounded down)   = $46,200

Required down payment $50,000   − $46,200 = $3,800

To calculate monthly payment of principal and interest:
Loan amount: $46,200—9½ percent, 30-year term, Plan III

Year	Initial Loan in Thousands	×	Factor	=	Monthly Payment
1	46.2		6.3719		294.38
2	46.2		6.8498		316.46
3	46.2		7.3635		340.19
4	46.2		7.9158		365.71
5	46.2		8.5094		393.13
6	46.2		9.1476		422.62

To calculate mortgage insurance premium: The monthly mortgage insurance premium can also be calculated from tables furnished by the FHA. Since the mortgage balance due increases each year during the initial term, so does the cost of the mortgage insurance. When the monthly mortgage payments increase to the point that a reduction is made in the balance due, then the mortgage insurance premium reduces each year in the same manner as for the other FHA programs.

Title 1—Home Improvement Loan Insurance

One of the popular programs offered by HUD/FHA is insurance on loans to finance home improvements. The money may be used for major or minor improvements, alterations, or repairs of individual homes and nonresidential structures, whether owned or rented. Lenders determine the eligibility for these loans and handle the processing themselves. The smaller loans in this category are usually handled as unsecured personal loans (recording of a mortgage instrument is not required).

Any credit-worthy property owner is eligible for a Title 1 loan. Loans may also be made to tenants for improvement of leased apartment units, providing the lease term is at least six months longer than the term of the loan.

Negotiated Interest Rate Program

One of the more important innovations in HUD/FHA programs has been the introduction of a negotiated interest rate as of August 1982. HUD will insure mortgages on most of their single-family programs at interest rates that exceed the maximum published rate providing certain conditions are met. Section 245 GPM and the experimental housing program are excluded from this program.

Following are the principal requirements:

1. The interest rate is freely negotiable between borrower and lender. HUD maximum rate limitations do not apply.
2. The borrower may pay discount points, or they may be paid by any other party to the transaction. The borrower may pay a commitment fee to the lender.
3. The loan must be for a single-family dwelling to be occupied by the borrower.
4. The lender must commit itself to close the loan under the negotiated terms at any time up to thirty days after the Application for Mortgage Insurance (HUD 92900) is accepted for processing by the HUD field office. The commitment may be extended by mutual agreement and may initially provide for a longer term.
5. HUD underwriting will be based on the terms of the negotiated rate agreement, and the negotiated rate will be reflected in the firm commitment. The mortgage will still be insured if closed at a lower rate than that negotiated. However, the discount paid by the borrower can be no higher than that specified in the agreement.

Veterans Administration

The popularly called GI Bill of Rights was passed by Congress in 1944. It was designed to give returning World War II veterans a better chance upon resuming civilian life than their fathers had after World War I. While the initial bill, and subsequent additions, provided numerous other benefits such as hospitalization, education, employment training, and unemployment benefits, our interest here will be confined to the home loan section.

Section 501 of the act provides for a first mortgage real estate loan that is *partially* guaranteed by the Veterans Administration and is subject to strict rules covering all phases of the loan: the borrower, the lender, the property, the interest, the term and loan amount, plus collections and foreclosures. The primary interest of the VA is to aid the veteran, and to this end the rules are directed.

Unlike the FHA that *insures* up to 97 percent of some loans, the Veterans Administration *guarantees* a portion of the loan, which in effect constitutes a reasonable down payment for the lender. Since the VA does not require a veteran to pay any portion of the closing costs, forbids him to pay any discount, and eliminates the need for a down payment, many veterans can move into their houses with no cash requirements. In the beginning, Congress set the maximum guarantee at $2,000, which proved to be much too small. Over the years these limits have been increased periodically to improve the assistance program and to recognize inflationary pressures. In 1980 the present limits were set at 60 percent of the loan or a maximum of $27,500, whichever is least, less any portion of a veteran's entitlement already used.

Eligibility of Veteran

One of the first steps in determining the qualifications of an applicant for a VA guaranty is to check eligibility. The requirements have been changed somewhat over the years and now call for a period of active duty in accordance with the following schedule in order to qualify:

Period of Time	Days of Active Duty
September 16, 1940 to July 25, 1947	90
July 26, 1947 to June 26, 1950	181
June 27, 1950 to January 31, 1955	90
February 1, 1955 to August 4, 1964	181
August 5, 1964 to May 7, 1975	90
May 8, 1975 to present	181

In addition, surviving spouses of persons who died as a result of service are also eligible.

For any veteran considering the purchase of a home, it is a good idea to ask the Veterans Administration to confirm eligibility. This is done by submitting VA Form 26–1880, Request for Determination of Eligibility and Available Loan Guaranty Entitlement.

The Loan Guaranty Entitlement

The amount of money that the VA will guarantee for the veteran is called an *entitlement*. The present limits of the entitlement are 60 percent of the loan amount or $27,500, whichever is the least. If both a husband and wife are eligible veterans, the guarantee may be twice the amount but cannot exceed 60 percent of the loan amount. The entitlement may be only partially used with a balance remaining that may be applied to the purchase of another home. The amount of the entitlement has been increased as follows:

Original act, 1944	2,000
December 28, 1945	4,000
July 12, 1950	7,500
May 7, 1968	12,500
December 31, 1974	17,500
October 1, 1978	25,000
October 7, 1980	27,500

Each increase has added entitlement to all eligible veterans. An example of how this increase works is the situation of a veteran who purchased a home in 1973. At that time the guaranty was $12,500. Subsequent increases to $27,500 have opened a new $15,000 of entitlement for the veteran to use in 1983, even if the previous loan has not been paid off.

Restoration of Entitlement.   So long as the Veterans Administration remains obligated to the mortgagee, the veteran's entitlement remains pledged and unavailable to the veteran for any further use. If the property is sold and the loan assumed by the new buyer, the VA has no way of obtaining a release from the lender who undertook the loan originally. So the VA continues to hold that portion of the veteran's entitlement that was originally pledged for the loan. There are now two ways that the veteran can regain the use of the guaranty privilege or restore the entitlement. These are:

1. Pay off the loan through sale of the property. Restoration of the entitlement cannot be obtained by simply paying off the loan, unless the veteran also moves out. Under a VA guaranty, a veteran can only own one house which must be his or her residence.
2. Under a provision of the Veterans Housing Act of 1974 a new procedure was added which is Substitution of Entitlement. To qualify

under this provision, the veteran can sell his or her home on an assumption basis, but only to another qualified veteran. The purchasing veteran must: (a) have the same amount or more of entitlement as the selling veteran; (b) meet the normal income and credit requirements; and (c) agree to permit the entitlement to be substituted.

For many years the VA also required that there be a compelling personal reason for the sale such as a job transfer in order to restore a veteran's entitlement. This is no longer necessary.

Release of Liability

When a veteran sells his or her home and the VA loan is assumed, the veteran remains liable unless he or she asks for a release. The home can be sold to anyone—veteran or nonveteran—and the veteran seller may still be released from the VA obligation.

The release of liability needs a special application, but the law does require the VA to grant the release if the veteran meets the following three requirements: (1) the loan must be current; (2) the purchaser must qualify from the standpoint of income and be an acceptable credit risk; and (3) the purchaser must agree to assume the veteran's obligations on the property. It is a good idea for a veteran to make the sale of the house contingent upon the VA acceptance of the purchaser and a release of liability if the sale involves assumption of the GI loan. While the law specifies no time limit for obtaining the release of liability, once a sale is closed the veteran will find little interest from the new purchaser in helping secure the release.

The reason that a release of liability does not automatically restore the veteran's entitlement to a full guarantee again is that the VA remains liable under the original contract of commitment to the mortgagee. Only a payoff of the loan removes this exposure for the VA.

Other VA Requirements and Procedures

The concern of the Veterans Administration is to make sure that the veteran is assuming an obligation within his or her financial capability, that the property is fairly represented, and that the appraised value (CRV) is fully disclosed. As mentioned earlier, the VA is offering a program of assistance to the veteran as part of the nation's expression of gratitude for service. It would miss the mark if the veteran were burdened with an impossible debt load or with a grossly misrepresented house. It is with these guidelines in mind that the VA underwriter analyzes the information submitted for approval of a home loan guaranty.

In order to assure the veteran that the home loan will be properly handled and that the government guaranty will not be abused, the VA has a number of specific requirements relating to the loan and how it is handled. Essential areas of VA concern are as follows:

The Lender. To protect against an unscrupulous lender, the VA distinguishes between *supervised* and *nonsupervised* lenders. A supervised lender is one who is subject to periodic examination and regulation by a federal or state agency. Savings and loan associations, commercial banks, and insurance companies would all qualify as supervised lenders. As such, they can process loans on an *automatic* basis. In this procedure, the supervised lender takes all the necessary steps to qualify a borrower, asks for a VA appraisal, and then makes its own underwriting decision. If favorable, the information is submitted to the VA in a Loan Report which the VA is obliged to honor with the issuance of a guaranty certificate.

A nonsupervised lender is anyone who does not qualify as a supervised lender. Mortgage companies, fraternal associations, and individuals would be some examples of nonsupervised lenders. In order to obtain a certificate of guaranty from the VA, the nonsupervised lender would first have to obtain approval from the VA to make a loan to the veteran applicant and would have to submit all required information to the VA office for their underwriting approval.

A third category of lender, which was established by the Veterans Housing Act of 1974, is a nonsupervised lender who qualifies for automatic loan processing. Mortgage companies that handle a large number of VA loans are listed in this category. If the VA qualifications are met, the nonsupervised lenders may submit their own approved applications for guaranty in the form of a Loan Report and receive the same automatic issuance of a VA guaranty certificate as a supervised lender.

Interest Rates. In 1975, Congress gave the Administrator of Veterans Affairs the authority to set the maximum rate of interest that would be permitted to a lender under a VA guaranty commitment. The law states that the Administrator should set the rate after consultation with the Secretary of Housing and Urban Development who sets the interest rate for the HUD/FHA programs. In practice, any change in rates is usually announced simultaneously by the Administrator and the Secretary. Adjustment of the interest rate follows the conventional market rather than leads it. While there is no fixed rule, in practice, the FHA/VA rate moves within a range of about ½ to 1½ percent below the current conventional market rates. Any rate change triggers an adjustment in the discount points to match market yield requirements.

Many other considerations enter into a decision to change the fixed rates besides the general conditions in the conventional market.

One of these is the condition of the home building industry, another is the money market in general and its future trends, and not the least of considerations is the current political climate.

Funding Fee.   Since its origin the VA home loan program has been handled as a part of the VA's ongoing commitment of service to the veteran. There has been no charge for processing the loan application or for issuing the guaranty certificate. Effective in October 1982, the VA now charges ½ percent of the loan amount as a funding fee. It is payable at closing and may be included in the amount of the loan. There are a few exceptions. For example, the fee is not paid by veterans receiving compensation for service-connected disabilities or surviving spouses of veterans who died in service or as a result of service-connected disabilities. The fee applies to all types of VA-guaranteed loans including interest rate reduction refinancing loans, home improvement loans, graduated payment mortgages, growing equity mortgages, and loans with buy-down plans.

Amount of the Loan.   The maximum loan that can be approved by the VA for issuance of its guaranty is the amount of the Certificate of Reasonable Value—the VA-appraised value. If the price exceeds the appraised value, the additional amount must be paid in cash by the borrower. Regardless of the amount paid for a house, the VA guaranty on the loan remains limited to $27,500 or 60 percent of the loan amount, whichever is the less. Any additional risk associated with a large loan is placed on the lender. The secondary market has set a practical limit on the amount of a VA loan—both FHLMC and FNMA will not purchase a VA loan larger than four times the veteran's entitlement. So, if a veteran has a $27,500 entitlement, the maximum loan that could be sold to FNMA is $110,000.

Term of the Loan.   A GI home loan can be obtained for up to 30 years. Shorter terms are approved by the VA if required by the lender and accepted by the veteran. The veteran has the right to repay all or any part of the principal balance due on the loan at any time with no additional interest charges or penalties.

Loan Servicing.   The administration of a GI loan is not prescribed by the VA. The approved lenders are expected to follow the normal standards and practices of prudent lenders. The VA expects the veteran-obligor to meet the obligations fully and on time. However, the VA does encourage reasonable forbearance on the part of the lender with the enforcement of its collections. The lender is required to notify the VA of a default within 60 days after nonpayment of an installment. Failure to file the default notice within the prescribed time limits can result in a reduction of the guaranty allowed for the lender.

Once the notification of default has been filed, there is no time limit on when the lender must take action to foreclose on the property. If foreclosure does become necessary, the VA must first appraise the property and set a "specified value." This value becomes the minimum amount for which the property can be sold which serves as a protection for all parties involved. If a foreclosure does occur and the VA must pay a claim for the veteran as a result, the veteran then becomes indebted to the government for the amount of the claim.

The Property as Collateral.   The VA guaranty applies to the veteran's residence. The residence may be one to four units, but the veteran must live in one of them. The residence may be a farm but it must be personally occupied by the veteran. The VA is normally lenient in accepting a house with some deficiencies so long as the veteran certifies knowledge of any shortcomings and still expresses a desire to buy the property. The basic requirements are that the house be safe, sanitary, and structurally sound.

The VA appraisal has shifted somewhat from an evaluation "as is" to a value that includes any required rehabilitation. The present approach is similar to the one used by the FHA. Since November 1981, the VA has utilized the property valuation shown on HUD Form 92800-5 (HUD Conditional Commitment) as a basis for issuing a VA Certificate of Reasonable Value (CRV).

Mobile Home Loans

The Veterans Housing Act of 1970 and 1974 authorized the VA to guarantee loans made by private lenders to veterans for the purchase of new and used mobile homes. The same rule applies with the mobile home as with a house—it must be occupied by the veteran as a residence. The unit so acquired may be a single-wide or a double-wide, and the authorization to guarantee also covers a suitable lot for a mobile home.

Effective October 1, 1978, the former VA loan maximum for mobile home loans was eliminated in favor of a new procedure that follows the same pattern as a regular house loan. The guaranty amounts to 50 percent of the loan amount, or $20,000 (as of October 1980), whichever is the lesser. This is not an additional entitlement for the veteran as the privilege is reduced by the amount of any entitlement already committed.

The maximum term permitted for a single-wide mobile home loan and for a lot loan is 15 years 32 days. For a double-wide mobile home, the maximum term is 20 years.

The maximum interest permitted on a mobile home loan is adjusted periodically as may be needed, but in practice it has remained fairly stable because it follows the higher yields of installment loans. The rate for the lot loan is limited to a simple interest rate the same as for a VA house loan. As in other guaranteed loans, once the interest rate has been established for the loan, it cannot be changed during the life of the loan.

The same rules that apply to regular VA house loans regarding a veteran's entitlement and liability for repayment also apply to the mobile home loan.

VA Policies and Practices

Several of the guiding policies of the Veterans Administration are of interest. One is that, although the guaranty on a home loan is specifically limited and the VA is legally responsible only to that limit, in practice, should foreclosure become necessary, the VA pays off the balance due on the loan and takes title to the property. If the lender elects to reconvey the property on a defaulted loan, the VA is obligated to accept it. It is this assurance to the lender that he or she will not be burdened with the problems of handling property in foreclosure that has encouraged the wide acceptance of the VA programs by private lenders.

Another policy that can be misunderstood is the term of employment required for a veteran to be approved. Since many veterans need housing almost immediately after being discharged from service, it is difficult to show a long employment record with private industry. No rigid requirements for length of time on a job exist. The criterion is more that of the underwriter's judgment on the type of work the veteran is doing. If it is a continuation of a general field of expertise that may have been learned in the service, that would satisfy the stability of income guidelines. For example, a control tower operator in the service may continue this type of work as a civilian and have no trouble qualifying for loan approval. But a jet pilot starting out as an insurance sales representative might have a problem convincing the VA underwriter that he or she can make a reasonable living in the new field of endeavor.

The VA performs a very useful service with its assistance program and has helped many veterans find suitable housing. The program is not a gift—the veteran is expected to make full payment of the loan. It is the VA's job to assure themselves that the veteran has a reasonable chance to make the repayment. It is an underwriting philosophy with the VA that in marginal cases, the mortgagee (lender) will be asked to develop more information on the applicant and the property that might permit the resolution of any doubt to be made in the veteran's favor.

Qualifying for a Loan

For several years the VA and HUD/FHA have been expanding the area of cooperation between them with acceptance by the other of appraisals and procedures. A big step towards common procedures was taken in January 1982 when a new application form was released that combines HUD Form 92900, VA Form 26-1802a, and the FmHA Home Loan Guaranty form. The new form is reproduced in Figure 8-1 and is followed by reproductions of the new forms to be used for verification of deposits and verification of employment. In addition, both VA and HUD now use a standard form for requesting an appraisal: HUD Form 92800-1, VA Form 26 1805. This form is reproduced in Figure 8-4.

Qualifying the Applicant

In the past, qualification of a borrower's income as to whether or not he or she could meet the financial obligation of the loan was handled in two slightly different ways. Essentially, the FHA measured the housing expense (principal, interest, taxes, insurance, maintenance, and utilities) at a not to exceed limit of 38 percent of the borrower's effective income and total fixed expenses (which includes housing expense plus installment and other fixed obligations) at a not to exceed limit of 53 percent. The VA approach to qualification, called the *residual* method, adds basic monthly housing costs including mortgage payment, maintenance and utilities, plus a cost of living allowance that depends on the size of the family. If the sum of housing expenses plus cost of living does not exceed the net effective income, the applicant qualifies insofar as income is concerned. The cost of living amount varies in different parts of the country and is derived from a local cost of living index. To give a better idea of how this is calculated, the following breakdown for Houston is given:

Houston Cost of Living Index
(Revised May 1982) for a Low Budget Family of Four

Food	$4,479
Transportation	1,625
Clothing	1,041
Personal care	452
Medical care	1,682
Other family consumption	624
Subtotal	$9,903

Divided by 12 = $825 monthly

VA Application for Home Loan Guaranty ☐	USDA-FmHA Application for FmHA Guaranteed Loan ☐	HUD/FHA Application for Commitment for Insurance under the National Housing Act ☐	1. AGENCY CASE NUMBER ▲	2A. LENDER'S CASE NUMBER	2B. SECTION OF THE ACT (HUD Only)

3. NAME AND PRESENT ADDRESS OF BORROWER *(Include ZIP Code)*

6A. BORROWER: *If you do not wish to complete Items 5B or 5C, please initial in the space to the right.*   INITIALS

5B. RACE/NATIONAL ORIGIN
▲1 ☐ WHITE, NOT HISPANIC   4 ☐ ASIAN OR PACIFIC ISLANDER
2 ☐ BLACK, NOT HISPANIC   5 ☐ HISPANIC
3 ☐ AMERICAN INDIAN OR ALASKAN NATIVE

5C. SEX
▲1 ☐ MALE
2 ☐ FEMALE

4A. NAME AND ADDRESS OF LENDER *(Include ZIP Code)*

6A. SPOUSE OR OTHER BORROWER: *If you do not wish to complete Items 6B or 6C, please initial in space to the right.*   INITIALS

6B. RACE/NATIONAL ORIGIN
▲1 ☐ WHITE, NOT HISPANIC   4 ☐ ASIAN OR PACIFIC ISLANDER
2 ☐ BLACK, NOT HISPANIC   5 ☐ HISPANIC
3 ☐ AMERICAN INDIAN OR ALASKAN NATIVE

6C. SEX
▲1 ☐ MALE
2 ☐ FEMALE

4B. ORIGINATORS' I.D. *(HUD Only)*   **4C. SPONSOR'S I.D.** *(HUD Only)*

7. PROPERTY ADDRESS INCLUDING NAME OF SUBDIVISION, LOT AND BLOCK NO., AND ZIP CODE

8A. LOAN AMOUNT $	8B. INT. RATE %	8C. PROPOSED MATURITY YRS. MOS.

DISCOUNT: *(Only if borrower to pay)* ➡   8D. PERCENT %   8E. AMOUNT $

VA ONLY: Veteran and lender hereby apply to the Administrator of Veterans Affairs for Guaranty of the loan described in this application under Section 1810, Chapter 37, Title 38, United States Code to the full extent permitted by the veteran's entitlement and severally agree that the Regulations promulgated pursuant to Chapter 37, and in effect on the date of the loan shall govern the rights, duties, and liabilities of the parties.
HUD/FHA ONLY: Mortgagee's application for mortgagor approval and commitment for mortgage insurance under the National Housing Act.

SECTION I - PURPOSE, AMOUNT, TERMS OF AND SECURITY FOR PROPOSED LOAN

9A. PURPOSE OF LOAN – TO:
▲1 ☐ PURCHASE EXISTING HOUSE PREVIOUSLY OCCUPIED
2 ☐ FINANCE IMPROVEMENTS TO EXISTING PROPERTY
3 ☐ REFINANCE
4 ☐ PURCHASE NEW CONDO. UNIT
5 ☐ PURCHASE EXISTING CONDO. UNIT
6 ☐ PURCHASE EXISTING HOME NOT PREVIOUSLY OCCUPIED
7 ☐ CONSTRUCT A HOME - PROCEEDS TO BE PAID OUT DURING CONSTRUCTION
8 ☐ HUD ONLY – FINANCE COOP-PURCHASE

9B. HUD ONLY – BORROWER WILL BE
▲1 ☐ OCCUPANT   5 ☐ ESCROW COMMITMENT
2 ☐ LANDLORD
3 ☐ BUILDER
4 ☐ OPERATIVE BUILDER

10. VA ONLY – TITLE WILL BE VESTED IN:
☐ VETERAN   ☐ VETERAN AND SPOUSE
☐ OTHER *(Specify)*

11. LIEN: ☐ FIRST MORTGAGE   ☐ OTHER *(Specify)*

12. ESTATE WILL BE: ☐ FEE SIMPLE   ☐ LEASEHOLD *(Show expiration date)*

13. IS THERE A MANDATORY HOMEOWNERS ASSOC.? *(If "Yes," complete Item 14F.)* ☐ YES ☐ NO

14. ESTIMATED TAXES, INSURANCE AND ASSESSMENTS

		15. ESTIMATED MONTHLY PAYMENT	
A. ANNUAL TAXES	$	A. PRINCIPAL AND INTEREST	$
B. AMOUNT OF HAZARD INSURANCE ON SECURITY		B. TAXES AND INSURANCE DEPOSITS	
C. ANNUAL HAZARD INSURANCE PREMIUM		C. OTHER	
D. ANNUAL SPECIAL ASSESSMENT PAYMENT			
E. UNPAID SPECIAL ASSESSMENT BALANCE			
F. ANNUAL MAINTENANCE ASSESSMENT		TOTAL	$

SECTION II - PERSONAL AND FINANCIAL STATUS OF APPLICANT

16. PLEASE CHECK APPROPRIATE BOXES. IF ONE OR MORE ARE CHECKED, ITEMS 18B, 21, 22 AND 23 MUST INCLUDE INFORMATION CONCERNING BORROWER'S SPOUSE *(or former spouse if box "D" is checked).* IF NO BOXES ARE CHECKED, NO INFORMATION CONCERNING THE SPOUSE NEED BE FURNISHED IN ITEMS 18B, 21, 22 AND 23.

A. ☐ THE SPOUSE WILL BE JOINTLY OBLIGATED WITH THE BORROWER ON THE LOAN.

B. ☐ THE BORROWER IS RELYING ON THE SPOUSE'S INCOME AS A BASIS FOR REPAYMENT OF THE LOAN.

C. ☐ THE BORROWER IS MARRIED AND THE PROPERTY TO SECURE THE LOAN IS LOCATED IN A COMMUNITY PROPERTY STATE.

D. ☐ THE BORROWER IS RELYING ON ALIMONY, CHILD SUPPORT, OR SEPARATE MAINTENANCE PAYMENTS FROM A SPOUSE OR FORMER SPOUSE AS A BASIS FOR REPAYMENT OF THE LOAN.

17A. MARITAL STATUS OF BORROWER	17B. MARITAL STATUS OF COBORROWER OTHER THAN SPOUSE	17C. MONTHLY CHILD SUPPORT OBLIGATION	17D. MONTHLY ALIMONY OBLIGATION	18A. AGE OF BORROWER	18B. AGE OF SPOUSE OR COBORROWER	18C. AGE(S) OF DEPENDENT(S)
1 ☐ MARRIED 3 ☐ UNMARRIED 2 ☐ SEPARATED	1 ☐ MARRIED 3 ☐ UNMARRIED 2 ☐ SEPARATED	$	$			

19. NAME AND ADDRESS OF NEAREST LIVING RELATIVE *(Include telephone number, if available)*

20A. CURRENT MONTHLY HOUSING EXPENSE $

20B. UTILITIES INCLUDED? ☐ YES ☐ NO

21. ASSETS		22. LIABILITIES *(Itemize all debts)*		
		NAME OF CREDITOR	MO. PAYMENT	BALANCE
A. CASH *(Including deposit on purchase)*	$		$	$
B. SAVINGS BONDS - OTHER SECURITIES				
C. REAL ESTATE OWNED				
D. AUTO				
E. FURNITURE AND HOUSEHOLD GOODS				
F. OTHER *(Use separate sheet, if necessary)*		JOB-RELATED EXPENSE *(Specify)*		
G. TOTAL	$	TOTAL	$	$

23. INCOME AND OCCUPATIONAL STATUS			24. ESTIMATED TOTAL COST	
ITEM	BORROWER	SPOUSE OR COBORROWER	ITEM	AMOUNT
A. OCCUPATION			A. PURCHASE EXISTING HOME	$
			B. ALTERATIONS, IMPROVEMENTS, REPAIRS	
B. NAME OF EMPLOYER			C. CONSTRUCTION	
			D. LAND *(If acquired separately)*	
C. NUMBER OF YEARS EMPLOYED			E. PURCHASE OF CONDOMINIUM UNIT	
			F. REFINANCE	
D. GROSS PAY	▲ MONTHLY $ HOURLY $	▲ MONTHLY $ HOURLY $	G. PREPAID ITEMS	
			H. ESTIMATED CLOSING COSTS	
E. OTHER INCOME *(Disclosure of child support, alimony and separate maintenance income is optional.)*	▲ MONTHLY $	▲ MONTHLY $	I. DISCOUNT *(Only if borrower permitted to pay)*	
			J. TOTAL COSTS *(Add Items 24A through 24I)*	
NOTE — If land acquired by separate transaction, complete Items 25A and 25B.			K. LESS CASH FROM BORROWER	
25A. DATE ACQUIRED	25B. UNPAID BALANCE $		L. LESS OTHER CREDITS	
			M. AMOUNT OF LOAN	$

VA FORM 26-1802a, JAN 1982
HUD FORM 92900.1

SUPERSEDES VA FORM 26-1802a, APR 1979, WHICH WILL NOT BE USED.
HUD FORM 92900, JUL 1980, MAY BE USED FOR HUD PURPOSES.

VA/HUD COPY 1

Figure 8-1

Form Approved
OMB No. 63R-1062

VETERANS ADMINISTRATION AND U.S. DEPARTMENT OF HOUSING AND URBAN DEVELOPMENT
HUD COMMUNITY PLANNING AND DEVELOPMENT
HUD HOUSING - FEDERAL HOUSING COMMISSIONER

REQUEST FOR VERIFICATION OF DEPOSIT

PRIVACY ACT NOTICE STATEMENT - This information is to be used by the agency collecting it in determining whether you qualify as a prospective mortgagor for mortgage insurance or guaranty or as a borrower for a rehabilitation loan under the agency's program. It will not be disclosed outside the agency without your consent except to financial institutions for verification of your deposits and as required and permitted by law. You do not have to give us this information, but, if you do not, your application for approval as a prospective mortgagor for mortgage insurance or guaranty or as a borrower for a rehabilitation loan may be delayed or rejected. This information request is authorized by Title 38, U.S.C., Chapter 37 *(if VA)*; by 12 U.S.C., Section 1701 et seq., *(if HUD/FHA)*; and by 42 U.S.C., Section 1452b *(if HUD/CPD)*.

INSTRUCTIONS

LENDER OR LOCAL PROCESSING AGENCY: Complete Items 1 through 8. Have applicant(s) complete Item 9. Forward directly to the Depository named in Item 1. DEPOSITORY: Please complete Items 10 through 15 and return DIRECTLY to Lender or Local Processing Agency named in Item 2.

PART I - REQUEST

1. TO *(Name and Address of Depository)*	2. FROM *(Name and Address of Lender or Local Processing Agency)*

I certify that this verification has been sent directly to the bank or depository and has not passed through the hands of the applicant or any other party.

3. Signature of Lender or Official of Local Processing Agency	4. Title	5. Date	6. Lender's Number *(Optional)*

7. INFORMATION TO BE VERIFIED:

Type of Account and/or Loan	Account/Loan in Name of	Account/Loan Number	Balance
			$
			$
			$
			$

TO DEPOSITORY: I have applied for mortgage insurance or guaranty or for a rehabilitation loan and stated that the balance on deposit and/or outstanding loans with you are as shown above. You are authorized to verify this information and to supply the lender or the local processing agency identified above with the information requested in Items 10 through 12. Your response is solely a matter of courtesy for which no responsibility is attached to your institution or any of your officers.

8. NAME AND ADDRESS OF APPLICANT(S)	9. SIGNATURE OF APPLICANT(S)

TO BE COMPLETED BY DEPOSITORY

PART II - VERIFICATION OF DEPOSITORY

10. DEPOSIT ACCOUNTS OF APPLICANT(S)

Type of Account	Account Number	Current Balance	Average Balance for Previous Two Months	Date Opened
		$	$	
		$	$	
		$	$	
		$	$	

11. LOANS OUTSTANDING TO APPLICANT(S)

Loan Number	Date of Loan	Original Amount	Current Balance	Installments *(Monthly/Quarterly)*	Secured by	Number of Late Payments within Last 12 Months
		$	$	$ per		
		$	$	$ per		
		$	$	$ per		

12. ADDITIONAL INFORMATION WHICH MAY BE OF ASSISTANCE IN DETERMINATION OF CREDIT WORTHINESS: *Please include information on loans paid-in-full as in Item 11 above)*

13. Signature of Depository Official	14. Title	15. Date

The confidentiality of the information you have furnished will be preserved except where disclosure of this information is required by applicable law. The completed form is to be transmitted directly to the lender or local processing agency and is not to be transmitted through the applicant or any other party.

Replaces Form FHA-2004-F, which is Obsolete

VA 26-8497a/HUD-92004-F-6234 (7-80)

Figure 8-2

VETERANS ADMINISTRATION,
U.S.D.A., FARMERS HOME ADMINISTRATION, AND
U.S. DEPARTMENT OF HOUSING AND URBAN DEVELOPMENT
(Community Planning and Development, and
Housing - Federal Housing Commissioner)

REQUEST FOR VERIFICATION
OF EMPLOYMENT

INSTRUCTIONS

LENDER OR LOCAL PROCESSING AGENCY (LPA): Complete Items 1 through 7. Have the applicant complete Item 8. Forward the completed form directly to the employer named in Item 1. EMPLOYER: Complete either Parts II and IV or Parts III and IV. Return form directly to the Lender or Local Processing Agency named in Item 2 of Part I.

PART I - REQUEST

1. TO: (Name and Address of Employer)

2. FROM: (Name and Address of Lender or Local Processing Agency)

3. I certify that this verification has been sent directly to the employer and has not passed through the hands of the applicant or any other interested party.

_____

(Signature of Lender, Official of LPA, or FmHA Loan Packager)

7. NAME AND ADDRESS OF APPLICANT

4. TITLE OF LENDER, OFFICIAL OF LPA, OR FmHA LOAN PACKAGER

5. DATE

6. HUD/FHA/CPD, VA, OR FmHA NO.

I have applied for a mortgage loan or a rehabilitation loan and stated that I am/was employed by you. My signature in the block below authorizes verification of my employment information.

8. EMPLOYEE'S IDENTIFICATION

SIGNATURE OF APPLICANT

PART II - VERIFICATION OF PRESENT EMPLOYMENT

EMPLOYMENT DATA

9. APPLICANT'S DATE OF EMPLOYMENT

10. PRESENT POSITION

11. PROBABILITY OF CONTINUED EMPLOYMENT

13. IF OVERTIME OR BONUS IS APPLICABLE, IS ITS CONTINUANCE LIKELY?

OVERTIME ☐ Yes ☐ No
BONUS ☐ Yes ☐ No

PAY DATA

12A. BASE PAY (Current)

$_____ ☐ Annual $_____ ☐ Hourly
$_____ ☐ Monthly $_____ ☐ Weekly
$_____ ☐ Other (Specify)

12B. EARNINGS

Type	Year to Date	Past Year
BASE PAY	$	$
OVERTIME	$	$
COMMISSIONS	$	$
BONUS	$	$

FOR MILITARY PERSONNEL ONLY

Type	Monthly Amount
BASE PAY	$
RATIONS	$
FLIGHT OR HAZARD	$
CLOTHING	$
QUARTERS	$
PRO PAY	$
OVERSEAS OR COMBAT	$

14. REMARKS (If paid hourly, please indicate average hours worked each week during current and past year)

PART III - VERIFICATION OF PREVIOUS EMPLOYMENT

15. DATES OF EMPLOYMENT

16. SALARY/WAGE AT TERMINATION PER ☐ YEAR ☐ MONTH ☐ WEEK

BASE PAY	OVERTIME	COMMISSIONS	BONUS
$	$	$	$

17. REASONS FOR LEAVING

18. POSITION HELD

PART IV - CERTIFICATION

Federal statutes provide severe penalties for any fraud, intentional misrepresentation, or criminal connivance or conspiracy purposed to influence the issuance of any guaranty or insurance by the VA Administrator, the U.S.D.A., FmHA Administrator, the HUD/FHA Commissioner, or the HUD/CPD Assistant Secretary.

19. SIGNATURE

20. TITLE OF EMPLOYER

21. DATE

Previous Editions May be Used until
Supply is Exhausted

HUD-6233/92004-g; VA 26-8497; FmHA-410-5 (12-80)

RETURN DIRECTLY TO LENDER OR LOCAL PROCESSING AGENCY

Figure 8-3

RESIDENTIAL APPRAISAL REPORT

| HUD Section of Act | 1. CASE NUMBER |

2. PROPERTY ADDRESS *(Include ZIP Code and county)*

3. LEGAL DESCRIPTION

4. TITLE LIMITATIONS AND RESTRICTIVE COVENANTS

1. ☐ CONDOMINIUM 2. ☐ PLANNED UNIT DEVELOPMENT

5. NAME AND ADDRESS OF FIRM OR PERSON MAKING REQUEST/APPLICATION *(Include ZIP Code)*

6. LOT DIMENSIONS:

1. ☐ IRREGULAR: SQ/FT   2. ☐ ACRES:

7. UTILITIES (✓)	ELEC.	GAS	WATER	SAN. SEWER
1. PUBLIC				
2. COMMUNITY				
3. INDIVIDUAL				

8. EQUIP.	1. RANGE/OVEN	4. CLOTHES WASHER	7. VENT FAN
	2. REFRIG.	5. DRYER	8. W/W CARPET
	3. DISH-WASHER	6. GARBAGE DISP.	9.

9. BUILDING STATUS	10. BUILDING TYPE	11. FACTORY FABRICATED?	12. NUMBER OF UNITS	13A. STREET ACCESS	13B. STREET MAINT.
1. ☐ PROPOSED 3. ☐ UNDER CONSTR.	1. ☐ DETACHED 3. ☐ ROW	1. ☐ YES 2. ☐ NO		1. ☐ PRIVATE	1. ☐ PRIVATE
2. ☐ SUBSTANTIAL REHABILITATION 4. ☐ EXISTING	2. ☐ SEMI-DETACHED 4. ☐ APT. UNIT			2. ☐ PUBLIC	2. ☐ PUBLIC

14. STRUCTURE	15. DESCRIPTION *(Complete only one Item)*	16. UNDERGROUND WIRE?	17. CONSTR. WARRANTY INCLUDED?
1. ☐ FRAME 2. ☐ MASONRY 3. ☐ CON-CRETE	7. ☐ SPLIT FOYER 8. ☐ BI-LEVEL 9. ☐ SPLIT LEVEL OTHER *(Enter No. of Stories)* ▶	1. ☐ YES 2. ☐ NO	1. ☐ YES 2. ☐ NO

18. NEIGHBORHOOD DATA

A. CHECK ONE:	B. PRESENT LAND USE				
1. ☐ URBAN	D. BUILT-UP	%	H. TYPICAL RENT	I. TYP. BLDG. AGE	
2. ☐ SUB-URBAN	E. OWNED	%	$ /MO.	YEAR(S)	
	C. ANTICIPATED LAND USE	F. RENTED	%	J. PRICE RANGE	
3. ☐ RURAL	G. VACANT	%		

ITEM	DESCRIPTION	COND. *(Observed)*
19. BUILDING DATA FOUNDATION		
ROOF		
EXT. WALLS		
INT. WALLS		
FLOORS		
HTG. SYSTEM		
PLUMBING		
INSULATION		
ELEC. *(Amps)*		

20. OFFSITE IMPROVEMENTS	21. STREET SURFACE	22A. FEDERAL FLOOD HAZARD MAP ISSUED?	22B. PROPERTY IN SPECIAL FLOOD HAZARD AREA?
1. ☐ CURB 3. ☐ GUTTER		1. ☐ YES 2. ☐ NO	1. ☐ YES 2. ☐ NO
2. ☐ SIDE-WALK 4. ☐ STORM SEWER			

23. EVIDENCE OF:	24. UNIT RATING *(Check (✓))*	GOOD	AVG.	POOR
1. ☐ DRY ROT 3. ☐ SETTLEMENT	A. GENERAL CONDITION			
2. ☐ TERMITES 4. ☐ DAMPNESS 5. ☐ NO EVIDENCE	B. ROOM SIZES AND LAYOUT			
25. ESTIMATED REMAINING LIFE	C. ADEQUACY OF CLOSETS/STORAGE			
▶ YEAR(S) 1. ☐ ECO-NOMIC 2. ☐ PHYSICAL	D. KITCHEN CABINETS/WORKSPACE			

1. ☐ % BSMT. 1. ☐ CENT. AIR COND. 1. ☐ FIREPLACE
2. ☐ SLAB 2. ☐ WALL AIR COND. 2. ☐ REC. ROOM
3. ☐ CRAWL SP. NO. OF UNITS: 3. ☐

ITEM	SUBJECT PROPERTY	COMPARABLE NO. 1	COMPARABLE NO. 2	COMPARABLE NO. 3
ADDRESS				
PROXIMITY TO SUBJ.				
DATA SOURCE				
TYPE OF FINANCING AND SALE PRICE		$	$	$

26. MARKET DATA ANALYSIS	ITEM	DESCRIPTION	DESCRIPTION	(+) ADJ.	DESCRIPTION	(+) ADJ.	DESCRIPTION	(+) ADJ.
	ROOM COUNT	TOTAL LIVING AREA *(Square feet)*	ROOMS BDRMS BATH TOTAL S.F.	ROOMS BDRMS BATH TOT.S.F.	$	ROOMS BDRMS BATH TOT. S.F.	$	ROOMS BDRMS BATH TOT. S. F.	$
	DATE OF SALE							
	LOCATION							
	SITE/VIEW							
	DESIGN AND APPEAL							
	CONSTR. QUALITY							
	AGE/CONDITION							
	BSMT./BSMT FIN. RMS.							
	FUNCTIONAL UTILITY							
	AIR CONDITIONING							
	ENERGY EFFIC. ITEMS							
	STORAGE							
	PARKING FACILITIES							
	COMMON ELEMENTS AND MONTHLY ASSESSMENT							
	OTHER *(e.g. Fireplace, kitchen equipment, remodeling, etc.)*							
	TOTAL NET ADJUSTMENT		ENTER (+) OR (−) $		ENTER (+) OR (−) $		ENTER (+) OR (−) $	
	INDICATED VALUE		$		$		$	

RECONCILIATION

27A. INDICATED VALUE BY MARKET DATA APPROACH ▶ $

27B. INDICATED VALUE BY INCOME APPROACH *(If applicable)* ECON. MRKT. RENT TIMES GROSS RENT MULTIPL. $ /MO. X ▶ $

27C. IND. VAL. BY COST APPROACH *(If appl.) (Attach calculations.)* ▶ $

28. ESTIMATED LAND VALUE $

29. LEASE DATA *(Complete if applic.)*

A. ANNUAL GROUND RENT CAP. AT % = $
B. VAL. OF LEASED FEE $
C. VAL. OF LEASEHOLD EST. $

30. DOES PROP. CONFORM TO APPLICABLE MINIMUM PROPERTY REQUIREMENTS?
1. ☐ YES 2. ☐ NO *(If "No," explain in Item 32.)*

31. APPRAISAL IS MADE:
1. ☐ AS IS 2. ☐ SUBJECT TO COMPLETION PER PLANS/SPECS. 3. ☐ SUBJECT TO REPAIRS, ALTERATIONS, ETC.

32. ADDITIONAL COMMENTS *(Include repairs necessary to make property conform to applicable MPR's. Attach separate sheet if necessary.)*

33. FINAL RECONCILIATION/ESTIMATED VALUE

NOTE: No determination of reasonable value may be made unless a completed appraisal report is received (38 U.S.C. 1810 (VA ONLY)).
I CERTIFY that (a) I have carefully viewed the property described in this report, INSIDE AND OUTSIDE, so far as it has been completed; that (b) it is the same property that is identified by description in my appraisal assignment; that (c) I HAVE NOT RECEIVED, HAVE NO AGREEMENT TO RECEIVE, NOR WILL I ACCEPT FROM ANY PARTY ANY GRATUITY OR PAYMENT OTHER THAN MY APPRAISAL FEE FOR MAKING THIS APPRAISAL (HUD/VA ONLY); that (d) I have no interest, present or prospective, in the applicant, seller, property, or mortgage; that (e) in arriving at the estimated value I have not been influenced in any manner whatsoever by the race, color, religion, national origin, or sex of any person residing in the property or in the neighborhood wherein it is located. I understand that, if I am a fee appraiser, violation of this certification can result in my removal from the fee appraiser's roster.

| 34A. SIGNATURE OF APPRAISER *(Enter I.D. No. for HUD cases only)* | 34B. DATE | OFFICE USE ONLY *(Reviewer's I.D. No. − HUD cases only)* |

VA FORM 26-1803, AUG 1980
HUD 92800-3 FmHA 1922-8

VA/HUD/FmHA FILE COPY 5

Figure 8-4

U.S. DEPARTMENT OF HOUSING AND URBAN DEVELOPMENT
HOUSING — FEDERAL HOUSING COMMISSIONER
MORTGAGE CREDIT ANALYSIS WORKSHEET

CASE NUMBER

SECTION I — LOAN DATA

1. NAME OF BORROWER AND CO-BORROWER	2. AMOUNT OF MORTGAGE	3. CASH DOWN PAYMENT ON PURCHASE PRICE
	$	$

SECTION II — BORROWER'S/CO-BORROWER'S PERSONAL AND FINANCIAL STATUS

4. BORROW-ER'S AGE	5. OCCUPATION OF BORROWER	6. NO. OF YRS. AT PRESENT ADDRESS	7. ASSETS AVAILABLE FOR CLOSING	8. CURRENT MONTHLY RENTAL OR OTHER HOUSING EXPENSE
▲				

9. IS CO-BORROWER EMPLOYED?	10. CO-BORROWER'S AGE	11. OCCUPATION OF CO-BORROWER	12. NO. OF YEARS AT PRESENT EMPLOYMENT	13. OTHER DEPENDENTS
			▲	(a) Ages_____ (b) Number_____

SECTION III — ESTIMATED MONTHLY SHELTER EXPENSES (This Property)

14. TERM OF LOAN (Months)

7. SETTLEMENT REQUIREMENTS

FUTURE MONTHLY PAYMENTS	14. TERM OF LOAN		
15. (a) Principal and Interest	$	(a) Existing Debt (Refinancing ONLY)	$
(b) FHA Mortgage Insurance Premium	$	(b) Sale Price (Realty ONLY) ▲	$
(c) Ground Rent (Leasehold ONLY)	$	(c) Repairs and Improvements	$
(d) TOTAL DEBT SERVICE (A + B + C) ▲	$	(d) Closing Costs ▲	$
(e) Hazard Insurance	$	(e) TOTAL ACQUISITION COST (A + B + C + D) ▲	$
(f) Taxes, Special Assessments ▲	$	(f) Mortgage Amount	$
(g) TOTAL MTG. PAYMENT (D + E + F) ▲	$	(g) Borrower(s)' Required Investment (E minus F)	$
(h) Maintenance and Common Expense ▲	$	(h) Prepayable Expenses ▲	$
(i) Heat and Utilities	$	(i) Non-Realty and Other Items	$
(j) TOTAL HSG. EXPENSE (G + H + I) ▲	$	(j) TOTAL REQUIREMENTS (G + H + I) ▲	$
(k) Other Recurring Charges (explain)	$	(k) Amount paid ☐ cash ☐ other (explain)	$
(l) TOTAL FIXED PAYMENT (j + K) ▲	$	(l) Amt. to be paid ☐ cash ☐ other (explain) ▲	$
		(m) TOTAL ASSETS AVAILABLE FOR CLOSING	$

SECTION IV — MONTHLY EFFECTIVE INCOME

SECTION V — DEBTS AND OBLIGATIONS

		ITEM	✓	Monthly Payment	Unpaid Balance
17. Borrower's Base Pay ▲	$	25. State and Local Income Taxes		$	$
18. Other Earnings (explain)	$	26. Social Security/Retirement			
19. Co-Borrower's Base Pay ▲	$	27.			
20. Other Earnings (explain)	$	28.			
21. Income, Real Estate	$	29.			
22. TOTAL MONTHLY EFFECTIVE INCOME ▲	$	30.			
23. Less Federal Tax	$	31.			
24. NET EFFECTIVE INCOME ▲	$	32.			

SECTION VI — BORROWER RATING

34. Borrower Rating		33.	TOTAL	$	$

35. Credit Characteristics	
36. Adequacy of Eff. Income	
37. Stability of Eff. Income	
38. Adequacy of Available Assets	

39. FINAL	SECTION VII — RATIOS
☐ Approve Application	40. Loan to Value Ratio _____ %
☐ Reject Application	41. Total Payment to Rental Value _____ % ▲
	42. Debt Service to Rental Income _____ % ▲

43.
☐ Ratio of Net Effective Income to:

Total Housing Expense _____ %

Total Fixed Payment _____ %

44. REMARKS (Use reverse, if necessary)   First Time Home Buyer? ☐ Yes ☐ No

45. SIGNATURE OF EXAMINER	46. DATE

FORWARD TO MANAGEMENT SYSTEMS WITH HUD-92800-8

HUD-92900-WS (5-81)

Figure 8-5

From these figures the Houston Field Office for HUD/FHA recommended that $270 per month be allocated per adult and $140 per month be allocated for each child. This results in a total of $820 for a family of four. (See following example for application.)

HUD/FHA now accepts both methods of calculating borrower income qualification. That is, it accepts either the percentage guidelines or the residual method and applies whichever method offers qualification for the applicant. HUD/FHA uses a Mortgage Credit Analysis Worksheet (reproduced in Figure 8-5) prepared by a credit examiner from information submitted on the mortgagee's application (Form 92900). The credit examiner is required to adjust such income, expense, and tax figures necessary to meet HUD/FHA-underwriting requirements. Following are examples of the two methods of calculating qualification:

Percentage Guidelines
Monthly Basis

Applicant's total income		$2,400	
Less: Federal taxes		300	
Net effective income			$2,100
The following expenses are measured as a percentage of the net effective income.			
Housing expenses:			
Principal and interest	$530		
Taxes and insurance	125		
Maintenance and utilities	120		
Total housing expense (not over 38%)		$775	
Add fixed obligations:			
Car payment	$240		
Other installments	165		
Total fixed obligations		$405	
Total housing expenses plus fixed obligations (not over 53%)			$1,180

In this simplified example, the housing expense in the amount of $775 is 36 percent of the net effective income and therefore would qualify at this point. Adding the fixed obligations of $405 brings the total obligations to $1,180. That amounts to 56 percent of the net effective income and is cause for disqualification (limits are 38% and 53%).

Residual Method
Monthly Basis

Applicant's total income		$2,400
Less: Federal taxes		300
Net effective income		$2,100
The following expenses are added together and must be less than the net effective income in order to qualify.		

Housing costs:

Principal and interest	$530
Taxes and insurance	125
Maintenance and utilities	120
Car payment	240
Other installments	165

Add family cost of living figured at $270 per month per adult and $140 for each child.

For family of 4	820	
Total costs		2,000
Residual		$100

Using the same basic figures as those in the percentage guidelines method, the family in this example would now qualify for the loan.

HUD/FHA and VA Approval of Alternative Payment Plans

With the substantial changes that have occurred in the past few years in the methods that can be used to repay mortgage loans, both the HUD/FHA and the VA have offered greater flexibility in the kinds of mortgages that qualify for underwriting commitments. Most of the basic repayment plans described earlier in Chapter 4 are now eligible for both VA- and HUD/FHA-insured commitments providing the requirements of the two agencies are met. This includes builder or seller buy-downs, growing equity mortgages, and shared appreciation mortgages. The trend in some mortgage designs towards shorter than 30-year terms with larger monthly payments that substantially reduce total interest costs are being encouraged.

Refinancing of Existing Loans

Both the VA and HUD/FHA permit borrowers' to refinance existing loans if it is possible to obtain a reduced interest rate. The VA limits its program to the owner-occupied dwelling of the veteran applicant. Both agencies permit the refinancing to include the balance due on the existing loan plus closing costs and discount points.* The total amount of the new loan cannot exceed the original amount of the loan being refinanced. Nor can the term of the new loan exceed that of the original

*The VA will not allow closing costs and discount points to be added to the amount refinanced in Texas because of state homestead laws.

loan term. Refinancing is also permitted on mobile home or manufactured housing loans.

Government National Mortgage Association

In the partitioning of the Federal National Mortgage Association in 1968, the Government National Mortgage Association was established as a part of the Department of Housing and Urban Development. GNMA presently operates from a single office in Washington, D.C. and, under a service agreement, uses all of the FNMA regional offices to handle its field requirements. For these services a fee is paid to FNMA. GNMA is authorized to develop programs as may be directed in the following two areas: (1) special assistance projects and (2) management and liquidation.

Special Assistance Projects

The broad commission granted by the charter act of the GNMA for special assistance projects gives the president of the United States authority to direct GNMA to make purchase commitments on certain types and categories of home mortgages as he may determine. GNMA is authorized to buy such mortgages as are insured under other government programs and as may be committed by the Secretary for Housing and Urban Development. Further, GNMA carries special authority to make mortgage purchases in housing programs for the armed services, in emergency areas, for below market interest rate mortgages, for construction advances, and under the "Tandem Plan," it is empowered to subsidize discounts on government-insured mortgages.

Tandem Plan. One of the important methods that GNMA has used to render special assistance to the housing market in times of tight money and high discounts on federally underwritten fixed-interest loans, is to provide a subsidy for payment of a portion of the discount. This is handled under the tandem plan, which means that GNMA works in conjunction with the private lenders as a support mechanism rather than as a competitive purchaser of mortgages.

In its initial concept, the tandem plan was directed at specific programs that the government felt worthy of extra help. With the sharp declines in construction and the real estate market generally in 1973–74, GNMA broadened its programs to provide assistance for all home buyers. A limited amount of subsidy money was provided by Congress to pay the discounts necessary to reduce interest rates for any buyers on a first-come basis. The way this has been handled is for GNMA to offer to sell large blocks of commitments for money which must be loaned at fixed interest rates. For example, GNMA might offer to buy loans totaling $500 million with interest set at 10 percent for a price of 98.5. Since GNMA does not have a large field organization, these offers are handled through FHLMC and FNMA. As soon as such an announcement is made, a local originator such as a savings association, would immediately contact FHLMC requesting an allocation of the special program funds for their own use. (A mortgage company would probably make contact with FNMA.) The allocations exhaust the funds available for any one program and the originators must then wait for the next special program that may or may not become operational.

The tandem plan is a method whereby GNMA makes a commitment to a lender to buy a mortgage at a future date providing the loan is made at a predetermined interest rate which is lower than the prevailing market. GNMA then resells the loan at whatever discount is needed to meet the market rate, absorbing the difference between the purchase and selling prices. In this manner the government pays a portion of the cost of a loan in the amount of discount needed, but does not invest the massive amounts of cash that have been needed for previous plans of outright purchase of low interest rate mortgages.

Management and Liquidation of Loan Portfolio

Under the management and liquidating portion of GNMA operations, the Association carries the burden of orderly liquidation of the FNMA portfolio as of October 31, 1954. It has been in the interest of the government to transfer these older mortgages into private financing channels as rapidly as possible and return the funds to the Treasury. Another major function under this section is the authority granted to GNMA to guarantee securities issued itself, or by any other issuer approved for this purpose, in the form of a full government guaranty.

Mortgage-Backed Securities. In an effort to provide greater liquidity to its own pool of mortgages and to tap the growing source of funds in the hands of pension and trust funds, GNMA devised a method to issue a separate certificate of guaranty covering a specific block of FHA, VA, or Farmers Home Administration mortgages, or combinations of these federally underwritten mortgages. The block of mortgages for this purpose can be assembled by a mortgage banker, or a group of them, or by any other approved lending institution in a minimum amount of $2 million. After examination of the block of mortgages by GNMA, if all are found to be in order, a certificate of guaranty is issued for the entire block. For a purchaser of the guaranty certificate, the purpose is to provide a security of a quality similar to a government bond and paying a slightly higher yield for a long term.

After the first four years of operations in this type of certificate, GNMA had guaranteed and sold over $7.5 billion of such securities. In the beginning of the program, most of the purchases had been made by thrift institutions. But, by fiscal year 1974, over 80 percent of these securities were being purchased by pension funds and other nonmortgage-oriented institutions at a rate of over $3 billion per year.

As the program grew, the guaranty certificates were offered in smaller denominations (as low as $25,000 units) to attract a broader range of investors. All certificates represent an interest in a diversified block of government-underwritten mortgages and have attracted considerable interest in the big short-term financial markets. Trading in "Ginnie Maes" has escalated into speculative trading in Ginnie Mae futures on the Chicago Board of Trade. More recently, graduated payment mortgages, or GPM (called "Jeeps" in the financial markets rather than the first acronym that came out—"Gipem"), have reached the market bringing considerable activity for slightly higher yields. In 1982 (2nd quarter), GNMA mortgage pool securities had exceeded $111 billion compared with about $4 billion in direct mortgage purchases.

Sources of Money. As a branch of the federal government, GNMA has several methods that it may use to provide money for its purchase of mortgages. These are as follows:

1. *The United States Treasury.* The Chartering Act for GNMA authorizes the Association to issue its obligations and the Secretary of the Treasury to purchase these obligations which are redeemable within five years and at interest rates determined by the Secretary of the Treasury.

2. *Appropriations by Congress.* From time to time, Congress appropriates money to assist home buyers, displaced families, and victims of natural disasters. The housing assistance is in the form of direct subsidies and low interest loans. When GNMA handles such programs, it is under the specific direction of Congress and limited to the amount of money appropriated for that purpose. The money used for the purchase of mortgages under the tandem plan is appropriated by Congress. The intention of this plan is to subsidize the discount necessary to provide home buyers with less than market interest rates.

3. *Sale of Securities.* As an agency of the government, GNMA is authorized to issue guaranty certificates and sell securities to investors and the general public.

GNMA is expected to be self-supporting in its operating expenses. The money comes from fees collected on its mortgage transactions, not from the Federal Treasury.

Continuing Role of GNMA. As an agent of the federal government, GNMA will continue to exercise considerable influence over real estate financing through its various moves in the residential mortgage market. The government effort is in the direction of (1) minimizing the fluctuations in mortgage money that directly affect the ability of the housing industry to operate on a stable basis, and (2) providing the housing the country needs. It can be generally stated that with each successive recession since the depression years of the 1930s, the swings have been a little less violent. While complete stability may neither be obtainable nor desirable, the role of GNMA will continue to be directed toward reducing the cycles and to provide various forms of assistance when money rates climb and the market falls off.

In striving to reduce the extent of housing cycles, GNMA provides the government with one more tool to utilize.

Questions for Discussion

1. How has the FHA achieved the goals for which it was established?

2. What are the present limits on an HUD/FHA-insured commitment for a single-family residence under Section 203(b).

3. Discuss the guidelines used by the HUD/FHA and VA in determining the effective income of a loan applicant.

4. In the HUD/FHA settlement requirements, what rules apply to the handling of the down payment? Closing costs?

5. Explain the difference between the loan commitments made by the VA and the HUD/FHA.

6. Distinguish between the release of liability for a veteran and the restoration of entitlement.

7. What is a mortgage-backed security as conceived by GNMA and how does the program operate?

8. Describe the tandem plan used by GNMA to subsidize discount points so as to reduce interest rates for home buyers.

9. Is the graduated payment mortgage used extensively in your community?

Property Appraisal

Property Appraisals

One of the major factors controlling the actual amount of a real estate loan is the appraised value. In the not too distant past a loan officer or other official of a lending institution would determine property value based on personal knowledge and experience in the area. Only in the past few decades has the skill of the professional appraiser been recognized as a valuable addition to the proper analysis of a mortgage loan.

Today, we have at least six professional organizations of appraisers whose members may earn certain designations indicating superiority in a given field of work. The requirements differ somewhat but all are based on a minimum prescribed level of education and experience plus passing some rather difficult tests. The organizations and designations granted are listed as follows:

- *American Institute of Real Estate Appraisers (AIREA)*
  RM—Residential Member
  MAI—Member, Appraisal Institute (highest designation)
- *American Society of Appraisers (ASA)*
  ASA—American Society of Appraisers
- *Society of Real Estate Appraisers (SREA)*
  SRA—Senior Residential Appraiser
  SRPA—Senior Real Property Appraiser
  SREA—Senior Real Estate Analyst (highest designation)

- *Appraisal Institute of Canada (AIC)*
  AACI—Accredited Appraiser Canadian Institute
- *National Association of Independent Fee Appraisers*
  IFA—Independent Fee Appraiser Member
  IFAS—Independent Fee Appraiser, Senior Member
  IFAC—Independent Fee Appraiser, Counselor
- *National Association of Review Appraisers*
  CRA—Certified Review Appraiser, Senior Member

Of these organizations, two are older and better known within the industry. One is the American Institute of Real Estate Appraisers which was organized under, and requires an applicant to be a member of, the National Association of Realtors. The other is the Society of Real Estate Appraisers which developed primarily from the savings and loan group of staff appraisers.

Definition of an Appraisal

An appraisal may be defined as an estimate of the value of an adequately described property as of a specific date, which is supported by an analysis of relevant data. An appraisal is an evaluation of ownership or leasehold rights. Appraisals can be delivered in three forms: (1) a letter form that describes the main points, (2) a standard form such as the combined FHLMC-FNMA appraisal report illustrated in Figure 9-1, or (3) a narrative report that goes into considerable analytical detail to substantiate the findings.

Principles of Appraising

How do appraisers approach their problems? What are they looking for in determining values? What analytical details should lenders or borrowers expect to find in written appraisals?

Principles of Appraiser's Analysis. First, let us look at the broad theory behind a professional appraiser's analysis. There are certain principles that guide their thinking in evaluating property. Most important among these are the following:

1. *Supply and demand.* The same theory underlying all economic practice is that scarcity influences supply and that what people want controls the demand.

RESIDENTIAL APPRAISAL REPORT

File No. _____

Borrower	Census Tract _____ Map Reference _____
Property Address	
City	County _____ State _____ Zip Code _____
Legal Description	
Sale Price $ _____ Date of Sale _____ Loan Term _____ yrs	Property Rights Appraised ☐ Fee ☐ Leasehold ☐ DeMinimis PUD
Actual Real Estate Taxes $ _____ (yr) Loan charges to be paid by seller $ _____	Other sales concessions _____
Lender/Client	Address
Occupant _____ Appraiser _____	Instructions to Appraiser

NEIGHBORHOOD

Location	☐ Urban	☐ Suburban	☐ Rural
Built Up	☐ Over 75%	☐ 25% to 75%	☐ Under 25%
Growth Rate ☐ Fully Dev.	☐ Rapid	☐ Steady	☐ Slow
Property Values	☐ Increasing	☐ Stable	☐ Declining
Demand/Supply	☐ Shortage	☐ In Balance	☐ Over Supply
Marketing Time	☐ Under 3 Mos.	☐ 4–6 Mos.	☐ Over 6 Mos.

Present Land Use ___% 1 Family ___% 2–4 Family ___% Apts ___% Condo ___% Commercial ___% Industrial ___% Vacant ___%

Change in Present Land Use ☐ Not Likely ☐ Likely (*) ☐ Taking Place (*)
(*) From _____ To _____

Predominant Occupancy ☐ Owner ☐ Tenant ___% Vacant

Single Family Price Range $ _____ to $ _____ Predominant Value $ _____

Single Family Age _____ yrs to _____ yrs Predominant Age _____ yrs

	Good	Avg.	Fair	Poor
Employment Stability	☐	☐	☐	☐
Convenience to Employment	☐	☐	☐	☐
Convenience to Shopping	☐	☐	☐	☐
Convenience to Schools	☐	☐	☐	☐
Adequacy of Public Transportation	☐	☐	☐	☐
Recreational Facilities	☐	☐	☐	☐
Adequacy of Utilities	☐	☐	☐	☐
Property Compatibility	☐	☐	☐	☐
Protection from Detrimental Conditions	☐	☐	☐	☐
Police and Fire Protection	☐	☐	☐	☐
General Appearance of Properties	☐	☐	☐	☐
Appeal to Market	☐	☐	☐	☐

Note: FHLMC/FNMA do not consider race or the racial composition of the neighborhood to be reliable appraisal factors.

Comments including those factors, favorable or unfavorable, affecting marketability (e.g. public parks, schools, view, noise) _____

SITE

Dimensions _____ = _____ Sq. Ft. or Acres ☐ Corner Lot

Zoning classification _____ Present improvements ☐ do ☐ do not conform to zoning regulations

Highest and best use ☐ Present use ☐ Other (specify) _____

	Public	Other (Describe)	OFF SITE IMPROVEMENTS	
Elec.	☐		Street Access: ☐ Public ☐ Private	Topo _____
Gas	☐		Surface _____	Size _____
Water	☐		Maintenance: ☐ Public ☐ Private	Shape _____
San. Sewer	☐		☐ Storm Sewer ☐ Curb/Gutter	View _____
	☐ Underground Elect. & Tel.	☐ Sidewalk ☐ Street Lights	Drainage _____	

Is the property located in a HUD Identified Special Flood Hazard Area? ☐ No ☐ Yes

Comments (favorable or unfavorable including any apparent adverse easements, encroachments or other adverse conditions) _____

IMPROVEMENTS

☐ Existing ☐ Proposed ☐ Under Constr. No. Units _____ Type (det, duplex, semi/det, etc.) _____ Design (rambler, split level, etc.) _____ Exterior Walls _____

Yrs. Age: Actual _____ Effective _____ to _____ No. Stories _____

Roof Material _____	Gutters & Downspouts ☐ None	Window (Type) _____ ☐ Storm Sash ☐ Screens ☐ Combination	Insulation ☐ None ☐ Floor ☐ Ceiling ☐ Roof ☐ Walls

☐ Manufactured Housing

Foundation Walls _____

BSMT: ___% Basement ☐ Outside Entrance ☐ Concrete Floor ___% Finished

Floor Drain _____ Finished Ceiling _____
☐ Sump Pump Finished Walls _____
Finished Floor _____

☐ Slab on Grade ☐ Crawl Space Evidence of: ☐ Dampness ☐ Termites ☐ Settlement

Comments _____

ROOM LIST

Room List	Foyer	Living	Dining	Kitchen	Den	Family Rm.	Rec. Rm.	Bedrooms	No. Baths	Laundry	Other
Basement											
1st Level											
2nd Level											

Finished area above grade contains a total of _____ rooms _____ bedrooms _____ baths. Gross Living Area _____ sq. ft. Bsmt Area _____ sq. ft.

Kitchen Equipment: ☐ Refrigerator ☐ Range/Oven ☐ Disposal ☐ Dishwasher ☐ Fan/Hood ☐ Compactor ☐ Washer ☐ Dryer

HEAT Type _____ Fuel _____ Cond. _____ AIR COND. ☐ Central ☐ Other _____ ☐ Adequate ☐ Inadequate

INTERIOR FINISH & EQUIPMENT

Floors	☐ Hardwood ☐ Carpet Over _____ ☐ _____
Walls	☐ Drywall ☐ Plaster ☐ _____
Trim/Finish	☐ Good ☐ Average ☐ Fair ☐ Poor
Bath Floor	☐ Ceramic ☐ _____
Bath Wainscot	☐ Ceramic ☐ _____

Special Features (including energy efficient items) _____

ATTIC: ☐ Yes ☐ No ☐ Stairway ☐ Drop-stair ☐ Scuttle ☐ Floored

Finished (Describe) _____ ☐ Heated

CAR STORAGE: ☐ Garage ☐ Built-in ☐ Attached ☐ Detached ☐ Car Port

No. Cars _____ ☐ Adequate ☐ Inadequate Condition _____

PROPERTY RATING

	Good	Avg.	Fair	Poor
Quality of Construction (Materials & Finish)	☐	☐	☐	☐
Condition of Improvements	☐	☐	☐	☐
Room sizes and layout	☐	☐	☐	☐
Closets and Storage	☐	☐	☐	☐
Insulation—adequacy	☐	☐	☐	☐
Plumbing—adequacy and condition	☐	☐	☐	☐
Electrical—adequacy and condition	☐	☐	☐	☐
Kitchen Cabinets—adequacy and condition	☐	☐	☐	☐
Compatibility to Neighborhood	☐	☐	☐	☐
Overall Livability	☐	☐	☐	☐
Appeal and Marketability	☐	☐	☐	☐

Yrs. Est. Remaining Economic Life _____ to _____ . Explain if less than Loan Term.

FIREPLACES, PATIOS, POOL, FENCES, etc. (describe) _____

COMMENTS (including functional or physical inadequacies, repairs needed, modernization, etc.) _____

FHLMC Form 70 Rev. 7/79   ATTACH DESCRIPTIVE PHOTOGRAPHS OF SUBJECT PROPERTY AND STREET SCENE   FNMA Form 1004 Rev. 7/79

FIGURE 9-1(a)

VALUATION SECTION

Purpose of Appraisal is to estimate Market Value as defined in Certification & Statement of Limiting Conditions (FHLMC Form 439/FNMA Form 1004B). If submitted for FNMA, the appraiser must attach (1) sketch or map showing location of subject, street names, distance from nearest intersection, and any detrimental conditions and (2) exterior building sketch of improvements showing dimensions.

COST APPROACH

Measurements		No. Stories		Sq. Ft.
___ x ___ x ___				
___ x ___ x ___				
___ x ___ x ___				
___ x ___ x ___				
___ x ___ x ___				

Total Gross Living Area (List in Market Data Analysis below) _____

Comment on functional and economic obsolescence: _____

ESTIMATED REPRODUCTION COST – NEW – OF IMPROVEMENTS:

Dwelling _____ Sq. Ft. @ $ _____ = $ _____
_____ Sq. Ft. @ $ _____ = _____
Extras _____ = _____
Special Energy Efficient Items _____ = _____
Porches, Patios, etc. _____ = _____
Garage/Car Port _____ Sq. Ft. @ $ _____ = _____
Site Improvements (driveway, landscaping, etc.) = _____
Total Estimated Cost New . . . . = $ _____
Less   Physical | Functional | Economic
Depreciation $ ___ | $ ___ | $ ___ = $ (_____)
Depreciated value of improvements . . . . . . = $ _____
ESTIMATED LAND VALUE = $ _____
(If leasehold, show only leasehold value)
INDICATED VALUE BY COST APPROACH . . . $ _____

The undersigned has recited three recent sales of properties most similar and proximate to subject and has considered these in the market analysis. The description includes a dollar adjustment, reflecting market reaction to those items of significant variation between the subject and comparable properties. If a significant item in the comparable property is superior to, or more favorable than, the subject property, a minus (-) adjustment is made, thus reducing the indicated value of subject; if a significant item in the comparable is inferior to, or less favorable than, the subject property, a plus (+) adjustment is made, thus increasing the indicated value of the subject.

MARKET DATA ANALYSIS

ITEM	Subject Property	COMPARABLE NO. 1		COMPARABLE NO. 2		COMPARABLE NO. 3	
Address							
Proximity to Subj.							
Sales Price	$	$		$		$	
Price/Living area	$	$		$		$	
Data Source							
Date of Sale and Time Adjustment	DESCRIPTION	DESCRIPTION	+(-)$ Adjustment	DESCRIPTION	+(-)$ Adjustment	DESCRIPTION	+(-)$ Adjustment
Location							
Site/View							
Design and Appeal							
Quality of Const.							
Age							
Condition							
Living Area Room Count and Total	Total|B-rms|Baths	Total|B-rms|Baths		Total|B-rms|Baths		Total|B-rms|Baths	
Gross Living Area	Sq.Ft.	Sq.Ft.		Sq.Ft.		Sq.Ft.	
Basement & Bsmt. Finished Rooms							
Functional Utility							
Air Conditioning							
Garage/Car Port							
Porches, Patio, Pools, etc.							
Special Energy Efficient Items							
Other (e.g. fireplaces, kitchen equip., remodeling)							
Sales or Financing Concessions							
Net Adj. (Total)		☐ Plus; ☐ Minus	$	☐ Plus; ☐ Minus	$	☐ Plus; ☐ Minus	$
Indicated Value of Subject			$		$		$

Comments on Market Data _____

INDICATED VALUE BY MARKET DATA APPROACH $ _____

INDICATED VALUE BY INCOME APPROACH (If applicable) Economic Market Rent $ _____ /Mo. x Gross Rent Multiplier _____ = $ _____

This appraisal is made ☐ "as is" ☐ subject to the repairs, alterations, or conditions listed below ☐ completion per plans and specifications.

Comments and Conditions of Appraisal: _____

Final Reconciliation: _____

Construction Warranty ☐ Yes ☐ No   Name of Warranty Program _____ Warranty Coverage Expires _____

This appraisal is based upon the above requirements, the certification, contingent and limiting conditions, and Market Value definition that are stated in

☐ FHLMC Form 439 (Rev. 10/78)/FNMA Form 1004B (Rev. 10/78) filed with client _____ 19___ ☐ attached.

I ESTIMATE THE MARKET VALUE, AS DEFINED, OF SUBJECT PROPERTY AS OF _____ 19___ to be $ _____

Appraiser(s) _____

Review Appraiser (If applicable) _____
☐ Did ☐ Did Not Physically Inspect Property

FHLMC Form 70 Rev 7/79   REVERSE   FNMA Form 1004 Rev 7/79
                              43570-1 SAF Systems and Forms

FIGURE 9-1(b)

2. *Substitution.* The value of replaceable property will tend to coincide with the value of an equally desirable substitute property.

3. *Highest and best use.* It is the use of the land at the time of the appraisal that will provide the greatest net return. This requires the proper balance of the four agents of production (labor, coordination, capital, and land) to provide the maximum return for the land used.

4. *Contribution.* This principle applies to the amount of value added by an improvement, such as an elevator in a three-story building, or the value added to a building lot by increasing the depth of that lot.

5. *Conformity.* To achieve maximum value the land use must conform to the surrounding area. An overimprovement, such as a $200,000 house built in a neighborhood of $60,000 homes, will lower the value of the larger house.

6. *Anticipation.* Since value is considered to be the worth of all present and future benefits resulting from property ownership, the anticipation of future benefits has to be evaluated.

With the theory of the appraisal principles as a background to guide the analysis, the appraiser presents information in a logical sequence. The narrative report, which is the most comprehensive form of appraisal, uses the following pattern and guidelines:

Description of the Property. The property should be defined in accurate legal wording, and the precise rights of ownership must be described. The rights may be a leasehold interest, mineral rights, surface rights, or the full value of all the land and buildings thereon.

The Date and Purpose of the Appraisal. Appraisals can be made for times other than the present, such as when needed to settle an earlier legal dispute. The date of the appraised value must be clearly shown. Also, the purpose of the appraisal should be stated as it will influence the dominant approach to value. In professional appraisals there is no such thing as the buyer's or seller's value—this is not a "purpose" as identified here. An example of purpose would be to estimate value for an insurance settlement, which would involve a cost approach to value as claims are adjusted on the basis of cost. If the purpose is a condemnation action, the most relevant approach would be the market value.

The Background Data. While the standard form and simple letter report will not provide any economic background data, the narrative report discloses the economic information as clues to value. An overall study of the market region, which may be as large as an entire state, is made. The focus is then brought down to the local area—the town or the portion of a city where the property is located. From there the analysis narrows to the specific neighborhood and then to the actual site under appraisal.

The Approaches to Value. Appraisers use three common approaches to determine value: (1) cost, (2) market, and (3) income. All approaches should be used wherever possible, and all should reach approximately similar values, although these values are seldom the same. In certain appraisals, only one approach may be practical, such as valuing a city hall building for insurance purposes. In this analysis only a cost approach would be practical as there is not much buying or selling of city halls to provide market data, nor is there a true income from the building itself to provide figures for an income approach. A single-family residence may appear to lack any income for analysis, but certain neighborhoods have sufficient houses being rented to provide enough data to reach an income approach conclusion. The three approaches to value are discussed in greater detail later in this chapter.

Qualifying Conditions. If in the analysis of the property, the appraiser discovers any material factors that will affect the property's value, these can be reported as further substantiation of the conclusion.

Estimate of Value. This is the real conclusion of the study, the figure most people turn to first when handed a finished appraisal. Each of the approaches to value will result in a firm dollar valuation for that approach. Then, it is the purpose of this estimate to explain why one of the approaches to value is favored over the others. For example, with an income property such as a motel, the value judgment would rest most heavily on the income analysis. The final conclusion is a single value for the property and represents the considered knowledge and experience of the appraiser making the report.

Certification of the Appraiser and His or Her Qualifications. The professional appraiser certifies to his or her opinion by signature and disclaims any financial interest in the property being appraised that could influence a truly objective conclusion. A recitation of the appraiser's educational background, standing within the profession as indicated by professional ratings, and previous experience such as appraisals previously made and for whom, serves to substantiate the quality of the appraisal for the underwriting officer.

Addendum. Depending on the need for clarification, the appraisal will include maps of the area under consideration with the site pointed out, plus the location of comparable properties referred to in the analysis. Charts may be used to indicate such things as the variables in a market analysis. Photos of the actual property are usually mandatory.

Three Approaches to Property Values

In order to understand more clearly the use of the three approaches to value, which is the essence of an appraisal, each is discussed below.

Property Value as Determined by Cost Approach

The cost approach is developed as the sum of the building reproduction costs, less depreciation, plus land value. The reproduction costs can be developed the same as a builder would prepare a bid proposal by listing every item of material, labor, field burden, and administrative overhead. Reproduction cost estimates have been simplified in active urban areas through compilation of many cost experiences converted to a cost per square foot figure. The offices of active appraisers collect such data in depth for reference.

Depreciation, by definition, detracts from the value and must be deducted from the reproduction costs. Depreciation consists of three separate types:

1. *Physical deterioration.* The wear and tear of the actual building—this is the type most commonly associated with the word *depreciation.* Examples would be the need for repainting, a worn-out roof needing new shingles, and rotting window casements. These are *curable* items and under the breakdown method should be deducted from value as a rehabilitation cost. All other items of physical deterioration are *incurable,* that is, not economically feasible to repair. An illustration would be the aging of the foundations or of the walls, and this kind of deterioration should be charged off as a certain portion of the usable life of the building. Another method of handling physical deterioration, in contrast to the breakdown method, is the engineering or observed method wherein each major component of the building is listed, and a percent of its full life is charged off. This method recognizes that each major component of a building may have a different life and the percentage of depreciation would vary at any point in time.

2. *Functional obsolescence.* Equally as important as physical deterioration is that category of loss in value resulting from poor basic design, inadequate facilities, or outdated equipment. These elements, too, can be curable or incurable. An example of incurable functional obsolescence would be a two-bedroom, one-bath house, which was very popular at the end of World War II, but now is a hard item to sell in today's more demanding market. There could be an excess of walls or partitions in an office building, which would cost money to remove and modernize, but would be curable. Lack of air conditioning in a hotel or office building is another example of curable functional obsolescence.

3. *Economic obsolescence.* The third type of depreciation has a more elusive quality and really is not in the building at all. Economic obsolescence is that set of factors outside and surrounding the property that affect the value, requiring the determination of the plus or minus effect of these forces. Some are very obvious influences—a new freeway bypassing an existing service station, the construction of an undesirable industry in an area adjacent to residential property, or the bridging of a stream to open new land for development. The more difficult problem is ascertaining economic impact of the long-term rise or fall of a specific neighborhood. While landowners are able to exercise some voice in protest or encouragement of these outside forces, for the most part what is done with neighboring properties is not controllable and is not curable. And it will always be a force that will affect the value of an individual property.

The third factor to be considered under the cost approach is the value of the land. Lately, almost all land has been marked by a steady appreciation in value. But economic factors can adversely affect land value as well as favorably influence it. Normally, land value can be determined through an examination of recent sales of similarly located properties—the same basic method as used under a market approach to value. However, there are sometimes specific reasons for changes in the appraised value of land. Buildings can and do deteriorate, while the land itself can continue to increase in value due to the same outside factors noted in economic obsolescence above. For example, as urban areas expand, certain intersections become more and more valuable, new throughways and freeways concentrate greater flows of traffic, and huge shopping centers add to the value of all surrounding land. As the suburban sprawl moves outward, former farm land increases in value when it is converted into residential subdivisions; or, as another example, in some older sections of a city the land can become more valuable than the building. The building itself may represent such poor usage of the land that it becomes a liability to the property value, and its removal costs can be deducted from the stated value of the land. By ascertaining these fluctuations in land value, the appraiser can bring a cost analysis into step with a changing market value.

Property Value as Determined by Market Approach

Also known as a sales-comparison approach, the value by market approach is determined by prices paid for similar properties. Since no two properties are ever precisely comparable, much of the analysis under this method concerns itself with the detailing of major characteristics and whether these add to or subtract from the value of the property. These details of comparison cover items such as date of sale, location of property, size of lot, type of materials used in construction, and many other factors that the appraiser considers relevant.

The market approach represents one of the most important analyses, as the true worth of any property is the actual amount for which it can be sold. And to this end, accurate information on the present market is essential.

Some confusion does exist in the use of sales prices and asking prices. The appraiser is primarily concerned with completed sales and with sales uncomplicated by extraneous pressures such as forced sales, estate disposals, or transfers within a family. The asking or offering price is considered by most to represent a ceiling or maximum value for the property. Appraisers usually recognize the inherent inaccuracy of an asking price, especially one set by homeowners. This figure is often arrived at by adding the original purchase price, plus the full cost of all improvements that have been made, plus the selling commission, plus the owner's amateur notion of general market appreciation. But every so often an owner actually receives such a sales price from a willing buyer, and this makes the professional feel a bit foolish!

Property Value as Determined by Income Approach

Because the income approach looks at the actual return per dollar invested, it is the most important method for any investment property.

When people buy investment property they normally expect to recover, or *recapture* in appraisal terminology, their money with a profit. They do this from two sources: (1) the annual earnings (excess income over all costs) and (2) the proceeds from a resale at the end of the term of ownership, called the *residual value*.

Thus, value of property by the income approach is derived by capitalizing the present worth of an income stream and adding a lump sum residual at the end of the holding period.

Capitalization is achieved by dividing the stabilized income by the rate of return to equal value:

$$\frac{\text{Income}}{\text{Rate of return}} = \text{Value}$$

$$\frac{16,000}{.08} = \$200,000$$

or a reciprocal method,

$$\frac{100}{8} = 12.5 \qquad 12.5 \times 16,000 = \$200,000$$

Obviously there are many variables to consider in achieving the rather simple illustration above. The income itself is a projection of what the property can reasonably be expected to produce. The rate of return can and should be a composite rate reflecting perhaps one or two mortgage notes to be assumed plus the expected return on the equity investment. One can readily see the importance an appraiser must place in the selection of a rate of return—since a slight variation in this figure produces a wide variation in the calculated value.

The value of the residual added to the capitalized value of the income stream is an estimate of the property value at the end of an expected holding period. This may be 5, 10 or 25 years later and could include the expectation of appreciation from inflation.

It requires knowledge and experience to support a realistic figure of this kind. Many income evaluation techniques now include more complex analysis of the present worth of future cash flows. This method is also known as a *discount analysis;* that is, future cash flows are discounted to their worth today.

Surveys

One of the recurring problems in passing land titles and in making sure that a lender is actually receiving a mortgage on the proper land is the identification of that land. Improper identification of the property to be mortgaged, through field error or typographical error, will invalidate the mortgage instrument. It is to physically identify a parcel of land that a survey is made. A survey is an accurate measurement of the property, not a legal description of it.

An example of an error in property description occurred in a motel loan several years ago. In this case, the property described in the mortgage was identified by the perimeter of the building, rather than by the boundaries of the land on which the building stood. The parking areas surrounding the building, which provided the only access to the premises, were not included in the mortgage indenture. When it became necessary to foreclose, the mortgagee learned that he did not have access to the property!

A survey for our purposes is the physical measurement of a specific piece of property certified by a professionally registered surveyor. In processing a mortgage loan, no lender will accept any measurements other than a professional's, as it is a precise business and the loan package requires an accurate description of the land being mortgaged.

When a licensed surveyor defines a piece of property, it is customary to drive stakes or iron rods into the ground at the corners and to "flag" them with colored ribbons. It is not unusual for a lending officer to physically walk the land, checking the corner markers, thus satisfying himself as to the shape of the parcel, and whether or not there might be any encroachments that would infringe on the mortgage lien. However, the prime responsibility in locating encroachments belongs to the surveyor, which is one of the reasons why a survey is necessary.

Legal Descriptions

A completed survey is a map showing each boundary line of the property with its precise length and direction. A survey should not be confused with the legal description of a piece of land. A legal description describes property in words, while a survey describes by illustration. Legal descriptions are most commonly found in the following three forms.

Lot and Block

The best known type of legal description is that found in incorporated areas that have established procedures for land development. A subdivider, in obtaining city approval to build streets and connect utilities, submits a master survey of the entire block of land, showing how the subdivision is broken into *lots*, which are then numbered and grouped into *blocks* for easier identification. Once the subdivision plat is accepted, it is recorded in the county offices and becomes a readily available legal reference to any lot in the plan.

For lending purposes, where the need is to identify a specific property over a period of 30 or even 40 years, the recorded subdivision plat is a much better method than a street address. Street names change and numbers can be altered, but the lot and block numbers remain secure because they are recorded. It may be argued that a street address gives a much better picture of where a property lies in discussing various houses or properties, but such identification is not sufficiently accurate to be acceptable to a lender. The common method of clearly identifying property in real estate transactions is, first, to give the legal description, followed by a phrase such as "also known as," and then to provide the street address. To illustrate, a property identification might be spelled out as, "Lot 6, Block 9, Nottingham Addition, Harris County, Texas, also known as 1234 Ashford Lane, Houston, Harris County, Texas."

Metes and Bounds

When recorded plats are not available for identification of land (and sometimes when plats *are* available), it becomes necessary to use an exact survey of the boundary lines for complete identification. This might be true of a recorded lot that has a stream or river as one boundary—the precise boundary being subject to change through erosion or realignment.

The method used is to define a starting corner with proper references to other marking lines, then note the direction in degrees and the distance to the next marking corner, and so on around the perimeter of the property back to the starting point. These descriptions can be quite lengthy and involved. An example of the wording used to describe several boundary lines might be: ". . . and thence along said Smith Street south 61 degrees 32 minutes 18 seconds west 948 and 25/100 feet; thence continuing along said Smith Street south 64 degrees 45 minutes 51 seconds west 162 and 80/100 feet to the point of beginning."

It is obvious that considerable accuracy is required to figure the necessary directions down to a second of a degree and to measure the distances over highly variable and often rough terrain in order to close the boundaries properly. Such a description is acceptable only if certified by a registered surveyor.

In some rural areas, land is identified in the form of metes and bounds by the use of monuments. A *monument* may be something tangible such as a river, a tree, rocks, fences, or streets; or intangible such as a survey line from an adjoining property. Physical monuments such as these are subject to destruction, removal, or shifting, and do not provide lasting identifications for long-term loans.

Geodetic or Government Survey

As long ago as 1785, the federal government adopted a measurement system for land based on survey lines running north and south, called *meridians*, and those running east and west, called *base lines*. The system eventually applied to 30 western states with the exception of Texas. A number of prime meridians and base lines were established. Then the surveyors divided the areas between the intersections into squares, called *checks*, which were 24 miles on each side. These checks were further divided into 16 squares, each measuring 6 miles by 6 miles, called *townships*. The townships were then divided into square mile units (36 to a township), called *sections*, which amounted to 640 acres each. These sections were then divided into halves, quarters, or such portions as were needed to describe individual land holdings. An example is shown in the diagram below.

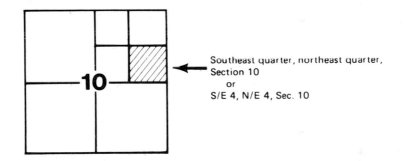

Southeast quarter, northeast quarter, Section 10
or
S/E 4, N/E 4, Sec. 10

During the growth years of our country, much of our western land was laid out in this fashion by contract survey crews. Marking stakes were duly placed to identify the corners, and these stakes are frequently used today. The fact that many of the surveys accumulated errors, including the failure to close lines, has created some confusion that concerns principally the oil and mining companies today who are attempting to identify leases, and ranchers claiming property lines against a neighbor.

However, these faulty descriptions have not constituted a serious problem for lending institutions. Land described, for example, as "Section 16, Township 31 north, Range 16 east, New Mexico Prime Meridian," could effectively handle a farm or ranch loan, and a minor inaccuracy in describing such a tract would not undermine the basic security of the collateral.

In pledging property where there is the possibility or probability that some slight inaccuracy has occurred as to the exact amount of land involved, it is customary to use a qualifying term such as "comprising 640 acres, more or less." Any variation in property size should be considered in the light of what might be termed "reasonable." A few acres out of line among 640 acres would not matter a great deal, but a few feet in a downtown city property could well be of critical importance.

Questions for Discussion

1. Define an *appraisal*.

2. What qualifications does a mortgage lender require for an appraiser? Identify the leading professional designations for appraisers.

3. What is meant by the *highest and best use* of land?

4. Describe each of the three principal forms in which appraisals can be presented. What are the advantages of each?

5. List the eight steps or sections normally found in a narrative form of appraisal.

6. Describe each of the three approaches to value and give examples of the type property for which each would be most applicable.

7. Name the three categories of depreciation associated with real property. What is the function of each?

8. How would you capitalize an income stream so as to show a property value? What is the *residual value*?

9. Distinguish between a *survey* and a *legal description*.

10. Give an example of a typical legal description made by lot and block numbers.

Analyzing
Borrowers

Most home loans are made to individuals or to individual coborrowers. It is the borrower who is expected to repay the loan, usually from personal income, rather than from property-related income. So the lender looks first to the strength of the borrower. The analysis of a borrower is concerned with an individual who has certain rights to privacy under the laws. However, the lender feels an obligation to determine the true credit-worthiness of the borrower to whom he is being asked to lend money—usually money that belongs to other individuals. In the past few years the laws have changed to provide new, and more equitable, guidelines for the granting of credit. Questions that might lead to discriminatory decisions have been eliminated from applications, and the lender is expected to base the analysis on strict financial comparisons. The procedures followed by the FHA and VA in evaluating a borrower have been covered in Chapter 8. This chapter will examine methods used for conventional loans; first, the evaluation of the individual home buyer, then information on credit reports, and finally, some of the problems in analyzing corporate borrowers.

Equal Credit Opportunity Act

The basis for an analysis of the borrower starts with the loan application. In 1974, Congress passed the Equal Credit Opportunity Act (ECOA), which prescribed limits on the information that may be asked for by a lender in the application for a loan. The Act was implemented under the direction of the Federal Reserve Board and administered by the Consumer Affairs Office of the Federal Reserve. Initially, the Act prohibited discrimination in the granting of credit on the basis of sex and marital status. On March 23, 1976, the ECOA was amended to expand the prohibition against discrimination in credit transactions to include race, color, religion, national origin, sex, marital status, age, receipt of public assistance income, and the exercise of rights under the Consumer Credit Protection Act, of which the ECOA is a part.

The restrictions covering information on sources of an applicant's income do not apply if the applicant expects to use that income as a means of repaying the loan. For example, no questions may be asked regarding alimony, child support, or maintenance payments unless the borrower plans to use this money to make the loan payments. No discounting of income is allowed because of sex or marital status or because income is derived from part-time employment. In regard to a credit history, an applicant must be permitted to show evidence that facts in a joint report do not accurately reflect his or her individual ability or inclination to repay the loan. If credit is denied, the lender must provide the reasons for denial upon request of the applicant.

The Act preempts only those applicable state laws that are inconsistent with the federal requirements. Lenders in states that may impose additional requirements, such as additional prohibitions as to what may be on a loan application, must also comply with the state laws. It should be noted that the requirement of the Act for separate liability for separate accounts (married persons can demand that separate credit records be maintained in either a married or a maiden name) cannot be changed by state laws. However, any action taken by a creditor in accordance with *state property laws* directly or indirectly affecting creditworthiness will not constitute discrimination.

In general, the new laws do not specify how or to whom loans should be made, but do call for lenders to be much more specific with reasons for the rejection of a loan applicant. Generalizations and categories of persons not eligible for credit are no longer permissible. For example, a married person who is separated can no longer be categorized as not acceptable for credit, but must be considered as an individual and judged by the same standards as any other person. There will continue to be a difference in the standards that a lender may use for long-term mortgage credit as opposed to a short-term installment type of credit but the standards must be applied uniformly to all applicants.

The Loan Application

A mortgage loan application offers information for qualification of both the borrower and the property. If the loan is residential, the information requested in the application must conform with the requirements of ECOA. For this purpose, the Federal Reserve Bank has prepared model application forms for five different kinds of credit, one of which is residential real estate. Although use of the Federal Reserve model form is not required, most lenders have followed the design closely so as to conform with applicable laws.

In order to accommodate their own analysis requirements, the Federal National Mortgage Association and the Federal Home Loan Mortgage Corporation cooperated in preparing a modification of the Federal Reserve design. Their form is a standard for conforming loans submitted to them for purchase. It is reproduced in Figure 10-1. While it is not a mandatory form, many lenders have adopted it as it meets current federal requirements and there is always the possibility that the loan could be sold to either FNMA or FHLMC later.

The information required in the residential loan application may be summarized as follows:

1. Identification of the borrower (and coborrower).
2. Employment and income data.
3. Anticipated monthly housing expenses.
4. Cost of house, down payment, financing requested.
5. List of assets and liabilities.
6. Credit references.
7. Applicant's certification as to accuracy of information.

If the loan is for commercial property, the lender is more likely to use its own form because considerably more information is needed. Since most commercial loans are expected to be repaid from the property income rather than from the borrower's personal income, specific information is needed on that income. Either a record of past profitability or a reasonable projection (a pro forma statement) on the anticipated income and expenses is required.

RESIDENTIAL LOAN APPLICATION **SAN JACINTO SAVINGS ASSOCIATION**

MORTGAGE APPLIED FOR	☐ Conventional ☐ FHA ☐ VA	Amount $	Interest Rate %	No. of Months	Monthly Payment Principal & Interest $	Escrow/Impounds (to be collected monthly) ☐ Taxes ☐ Hazard Ins. ☐ Mtg. Ins. ☐

Prepayment Option

SUBJECT PROPERTY

Property Street Address		City	County	State	Zip	No. Units

Legal Description (Attach description if necessary)		Year Built

Purpose of Loan: ☐ Purchase ☐ Construction-Permanent ☐ Construction ☐ Refinance ☐ Other (Explain)

Complete this line if Construction-Permanent or Construction Loan ➠	Lot Value Data	Original Cost	Present Value (a)	Cost of Imps. (b)	Total (a + b)	ENTER TOTAL AS PURCHASE PRICE IN DETAILS OF PURCHASE.
	Year Acquired	$	$	$	$	

Complete this line if a Refinance Loan		Purpose of Refinance	Describe Improvements [ ] made [ ] to be made
Year Acquired	Original Cost	Amt. Existing Liens	
	$	$	Cost: $

Title Will Be Held In What Name(s)	Manner In Which Title Will Be Held

Source of Down Payment and Settlement Charges

This application is designed to be completed by the borrower(s) with the lender's assistance. The Co-Borrower Section and all other Co-Borrower questions must be completed and the appropriate box(es) checked if ☐ another person will be jointly obligated with the Borrower on the loan, or ☐ the Borrower is relying on income from alimony, child support or separate maintenance or on the income or assets of another person as a basis for repayment of the loan, or ☐ the Borrower is married and resides, or the property is located, in a community property state.

BORROWER				**CO-BORROWER**			
Name		Age	School Yrs ___	Name		Age	School Yrs ___
Present Address	No. Years ___ ☐ Own ☐ Rent			Present Address	No. Years ___ ☐ Own ☐ Rent		
Street				Street			
City/State/Zip				City/State/Zip			
Former address if less than 2 years at present address				Former address if less than 2 years at present address			
Street				Street			
City/State/Zip				City/State/Zip			
Years at former address ☐ Own ☐ Rent				Years at former address ☐ Own ☐ Rent			

Marital Status ☐ Married ☐ Separated ☐ Unmarried (incl. single, divorced, widowed)	DEPENDENTS OTHER THAN LISTED BY CO BORROWER NO AGES	Marital Status ☐ Married ☐ Separated ☐ Unmarried (incl. single, divorced, widowed)	DEPENDENTS OTHER THAN LISTED BY BORROWER NO AGES
Name and Address of Employer	Years employed in this line of work or profession? ___ years Years on this job ___ ☐ Self Employed*	Name and Address of Employer	Years employed in this line of work or profession? ___ years Years on this job ___ ☐ Self Employed*
Position/Title	Type of Business	Position/Title	Type of Business
Social Security Number***	Home Phone	Business Phone	Social Security Number***	Home Phone	Business Phone

GROSS MONTHLY INCOME				**MONTHLY HOUSING EXPENSE****	PRESENT	PROPOSED	**DETAILS OF PURCHASE** Do Not Complete If Refinance	
Item	Borrower	Co-Borrower	Total	Rent	$	$	a. Purchase Price	$
Base Empl. Income	$	$	$	First Mortgage (P&I)			b. Total Closing Costs (Est.)	
Overtime				Other Financing (P&I)			c. Prepaid Escrows (Est.)	
Bonuses				Hazard Insurance			d. Total (a + b + c)	$
Commissions				Real Estate Taxes			e. Amount This Mortgage	( )
Dividends/Interest				Mortgage Insurance			f. Other Financing	( )
Net Rental Income				Homeowner Assn. Dues			g. Other Equity	( )
Other† (Before completing, see notice under Describe Other Income below.)				Other:			h. Amount of Cash Deposit	( )
				Total Monthly Pmt.	$	$	i. Closing Costs Paid by Seller	( )
				Utilities			j. Cash Reqd. For Closing (Est.)	$
Total	$	$	$	Total	$	$		

DESCRIBE OTHER INCOME

☞ B–Borrower C–Co-Borrower NOTICE:† Alimony, child support, or separate maintenance income need not be revealed if the Borrower or Co-Borrower does not choose to have it considered as a basis for repaying this loan.

		Monthly Amount
		$

IF EMPLOYED IN CURRENT POSITION FOR LESS THAN TWO YEARS COMPLETE THE FOLLOWING

B/C	Previous Employer/School	City/State	Type of Business	Position/Title	Dates From/To	Monthly Income
						$

THESE QUESTIONS APPLY TO BOTH BORROWER AND CO-BORROWER

If a "yes" answer is given to a question in this column, explain on an attached sheet.	Borrower Yes or No	Co-Borrower Yes or No	If applicable, explain Other Financing or Other Equity (provide addendum if more space is needed).
Have you any outstanding judgments? In the last 7 years, have you been declared bankrupt?	___	___	
Have you had property foreclosed upon or given title or deed in lieu thereof?	___	___	
Are you a co-maker or endorser on a note?	___	___	
Are you a party in a law suit?	___	___	
Are you obligated to pay alimony, child support, or separate maintenance?	___	___	
Is any part of the down payment borrowed?	___	___	

*FHLMC/FNMA require business credit report, signed Federal Income Tax returns for last two years, and, if available, audited Profit and Loss Statements plus balance sheet for same period.

**All Present Monthly Housing Expenses of Borrower and Co-Borrower should be listed on a combined basis.

***Neither FHLMC nor FNMA requires this information.

FHLMC 65 Rev. 8/78   FNMA 1003 Rev. 8/78

FIGURE 10-1a

This Statement and any applicable supporting schedules may be completed jointly by both married and unmarried co-borrowers if their assets and liabilities are sufficiently joined so that the Statement can be meaningfully and fairly presented on a combined basis; otherwise separate Statements and Schedules are required (FHLMC 65A/FNMA 1003A). If the co-borrower section was completed about a spouse, this statement and supporting schedules must be completed about that spouse also. ☐ Completed Jointly   ☐ Not Completed Jointly

ASSETS		LIABILITIES AND PLEDGED ASSETS			
		Indicate by (*) those liabilities or pledged assets which will be satisfied upon sale of real estate owned or upon refinancing of subject property			
Description	Cash or Market Value	Creditors' Name, Address and Account Number	Acct. Name if Not Borrower's	Mo. Pmt. and Mos. left to pay	Unpaid Balance
Cash Deposit Toward Purchase Held By	$	Installment Debts (include "revolving" charge accts)		$ Pmt./Mos.	$
Checking and Savings Accounts (Show Names of Institutions/Acct. Nos.)				/	
Stocks and Bonds (No./Description)				/	
Life Insurance Net Cash Value Face Amount ($)		Other Debts Including Stock Pledges		/	
SUBTOTAL LIQUID ASSETS	$				
Real Estate Owned (Enter Market Value from Schedule of Real Estate Owned)		Real Estate Loans			
Vested Interest in Retirement Fund					
Net Worth of Business Owned (ATTACH FINANCIAL STATEMENT)					
Automobiles (Make and Year)		Automobile Loans			
Furniture and Personal Property		Alimony, Child Support and Separate Maintenance Payments Owed To			
Other Assets (Itemize)					
		TOTAL MONTHLY PAYMENTS		$	
TOTAL ASSETS	A $	NET WORTH (A minus B) $		TOTAL LIABILITIES	B $

SCHEDULE OF REAL ESTATE OWNED (If Additional Properties Owned Attach Separate Schedule)

Address of Property (Indicate S if Sold, PS if Pending Sale or R if Rental being held for income)	Type of Property	Present Market Value	Amount of Mortgages & Liens	Gross Rental Income	Mortgage Payments	Taxes, Ins. Maintenance and Misc.	Net Rental Income
		$	$	$	$	$	$
TOTALS →		$	$	$	$	$	$

LIST PREVIOUS CREDIT REFERENCES

B – Borrower C – Co-Borrower	Creditor's Name and Address	Account Number	Purpose	Highest Balance	Date Paid
				$	

List any additional names under which credit has previously been received _____

AGREEMENT: The undersigned applies for the loan indicated in this application to be secured by a first mortgage or deed of trust on the property described herein, and represents that the property will not be used for any illegal or restricted purpose, and that all statements made in this application are true and are made for the purpose of obtaining the loan. Verification may be obtained from any source named in this application. The original or a copy of this application will be retained by the lender, even if the loan is not granted. The undersigned ☐ intend or ☐ do not intend to occupy the property as their primary residence.

I/we fully understand that it is a federal crime punishable by fine or imprisonment, or both, to knowingly make any false statements concerning any of the above facts as applicable under the provisions of Title 18, United States Code, Section 1014.

_____ Date _____   _____ Date _____
Borrower's Signature   Co-Borrower's Signature

INFORMATION FOR GOVERNMENT MONITORING PURPOSES

The following information is requested by the Federal Government if this loan is related to a dwelling, in order to monitor the lender's compliance with equal credit opportunity and fair housing laws. You are not required to furnish this information, but are encouraged to do so. The law provides that a lender may neither discriminate on the basis of this information, nor on whether you choose to furnish it. However, if you choose not to furnish it, under Federal regulations this lender is required to note race and sex on the basis of visual observation or surname. If you do not wish to furnish the above information, please initial below.

BORROWER: I do not wish to furnish this information (initials)_____
RACE/NATIONAL ORIGIN: ☐ American Indian, Alaskan Native ☐ Asian, Pacific Islander ☐ Black ☐ Hispanic ☐ White ☐ Other (specify) _____
SEX: ☐ Female ☐ Male

CO-BORROWER: I do not wish to furnish this information (initials)_____
RACE/NATIONAL ORIGIN: ☐ American Indian, Alaskan Native ☐ Asian, Pacific Islander ☐ Black ☐ Hispanic ☐ White ☐ Other (specify) _____
SEX: ☐ Female ☐ Male

FOR LENDER'S USE ONLY

(FNMA REQUIREMENT ONLY) This application was taken by ☐ face to face interview ☐ by mail ☐ by telephone

_____
(Interviewer)

San Jacinto Savings Association
Name of Employer of Interviewer

FHLMC 65 Rev. 8/78   REVERSE   FNMA 1003 Rev. 8/78

FIGURE 10-1b

Financial Evaluation of the Borrower

The high loan-to-value ratio (LTVR) of the loan negotiated for house purchases today places a premium on the borrower's repayment ability. The conventional lender or the private mortgage insurance company selected would be hard pressed to make a full recovery of the loan amount in case of an early foreclosure. Proper analysis of the borrower to determine total available income, any claims against that income, as well as the credit record is important for a home loan. A borrower's other assets are helpful as additional security for a loan and can result in a lower rate of interest, but other assets cannot always be counted on for use in repayment. The lender knows that in many cases of actual default in payments the borrower has met with financial problems that were beyond his or her control, such as accidents, job layoffs, or serious illness in the family; and that such problems can deplete most of the family's financial assets, leaving the lender with few means of recourse beyond the house that has been pledged.

No two borrowers ever present the same credit picture. Analysis of a borrower still defies any attempt to impersonalize the procedure to the point of computerization. But there are some guidelines and general rules, mainly based on common sense, that are helpful in determining whether or not a borrower can make a loan repayment. To make a sound prediction, the underwriter of the loan considers two basic questions: (1) What is the applicant's ability to pay? (2) What is the applicant's willingness to pay?

Ability to Pay

More than any other type of loan, the home loan looks to a family's income as the basic resource for repayment. Assets are important but are used in part to determine the spending or saving patterns practiced in the use of that income. Therefore, a careful review of the employment record, present income, and future potential is important. Below are listed some of the income elements considered by a lender, with a commentary on each topic.

Types of Income.   Lenders make a broad distinction between *production-related* income and *assured* income. Production-related income means commissions, bonuses, and in some cases, piecework pay. It does not have the certainty of assured income such as wages or a salary and normally requires a longer record of earnings to qualify. Following are major types of income and comments on their acceptability.

1. *Salary.* The salary is the easiest form of income to determine and generally a more secure type of income.
2. *Bonus.* A bonus should not be counted on unless a regular pattern can be established for several successive years.
3. *Commission.* A straight commission job can be very lucrative, or it can be a complete bust. Only a past record of income culled from several years of tax returns can be accepted as factual.
4. *Hourly wages.* The hourly wage is a solid basis for continuing income and one that can usually be confirmed from an employer.
5. *Overtime wages.* This is an uncertain basis for making a larger loan as most employers try to avoid overtime and use it only as an emergency or temporary practice. Again, a consistent pattern of overtime payments for several years would make this an acceptable addition to the gross effective income.
6. *Second job.* Many persons today hold more than one job on a full- or part-time basis. Teachers, policemen, skilled hourly workers, all can have other capabilities and may spend extra hours augmenting their income. If the second job has been held over a period of several years on a regular basis, it provides a substantial lift to the regular income.
7. *Unreported income.* A few people accept extra work, or even become involved full-time, in jobs that pay in cash and on which income is not reported for tax purposes. Such income, if not reported, is illegal and cannot be used under any condition to justify a loan. This "borrower" could reach an abrupt end to his free income via the prison route.
8. *Coborrower's income.* Prior to the enactment of the Federal Equal Credit Opportunity Act, it was fairly common practice to reduce the effective income that could be accepted from a working wife. The reasoning then was that young married couples who dominate the home buying market were also interested in raising families. And earlier customs generally assigned more of the problems concerned with family emergencies, sickness, pregnancies, and child care to the wife. The new laws recognize changing customs, and a lender is now required to apply the same qualification standards to each borrower without questioning marital status or sex.
9. *Income from children.* While many young men and women living with their parents earn substantial money at full- or part-time jobs, these earnings are not generally a recognized addition to the family income for loan purposes. The obligation on the part of the children to contribute to the family finances for support of the home is not a continuing one, since normally they will leave the homestead and set up their own household within a few years.

Thus, temporary income supplied by grown children lends no real weight to the loan request.

10. *Pensions and trusts.* Few home buyers in the past have enjoyed pensions, retirement funds, or other work benefits at a sufficiently early age to apply them toward a home purchase. However, the pattern is changing. For instance, many veterans of military and other government services have now completed 20 or 30 years of employment before the age of 50. These benefits are, of course, one of the most reliable forms of income.

11. *Child support and alimony.* Some states do not permit alimony but provide child support as a matter of court decree. Other states permit both alimony and child support. Such payments can be considered as regular income for a divorcee or remarried person, depending on the court ruling. However, the record of payment must show dependability over a period of time before it would constitute an acceptable addition to total income in full amount. No information need be given on this source if it is not to be counted as income for repayment of the loan.

12. *Self-employed.* Many persons operate their own businesses or work as individuals in professional capacities. Since there is no employer to verify actual income, the only acceptable method of validating this income is by referral to previous income tax reports. Certified copies of these returns can be obtained from the Internal Revenue Service for a small fee upon application by the taxpayer only. Some small businessmen are able to pay certain living expenses from their business (car expenses and depreciation, entertainment, travel, etc.), but weight can only be given to the actual income reported as taxable.

13. *Interest and dividends.* These funds normally represent a stable income but must be considered from the angle of a possible sale of the asset for another purpose. Again, the past record would indicate the probable future pattern in any given case.

14. *Part-time employment.* Income derived from part-time work has in the past not been accepted at full value towards a person's income applicable to repayment of a mortgage loan. The new ECOA requirements now permit no discounting of this source of income. However, the lender may still require that such income show evidence of stability and reasonable assurance that it will continue.

15. *Welfare assistance.* In the past few years, the concept of welfare as an assist for a disadvantaged person has given way to the idea that this is a right of an individual. Consequently, Congress has determined under the new ECOA requirements that welfare payments must be considered without discount by a lender if the ap-

plicant expects to use welfare assistance as a part of his or her income for repayment of the loan.

Stability of Income.   Along with the size of an applicant's income, the assurance that it will be continued must be investigated. Two factors are involved: (1) time on the job and (2) type of work performed.

1. *Length of time.*   Some lenders hold to a policy of rejecting all applicants with less than three years tenure at their present job. There is a basis for this restriction in that any new job may or may not work out, either due to personality factors or to lack of accomplishment. But with the more rapid changes in jobs today, the job tenure can be more fairly judged from the individual's job history. Has the applicant made a record of "job hopping" without noticeable improvement in his income? Is the present job one of greater responsibility and growth potential than the previous job? Has the applicant maintained a record of employment in a chosen field of work and qualifications, or is the present job an entirely new type of work?

    The question of job tenure does not lend itself to easily defined limits due to the variables mentioned above. But most lenders hold to some minimum term of employment, generally from one to three years.

2. *Type of work.*   While a person with a long record of employment provides the soundest answer to the question of income stability, not everyone seeking loans can provide such a record. The type of work engaged in does give good clues as to future stability.

    Persons with salaried jobs with the larger companies and professional people with tenure are considered the most secure. Hourly workers with the protection of union contracts are far more stable (and often higher paid) than lower level management and clerical staff workers. Government employees carry good security as do teachers, policemen, and other service workers. On the lower side of the scale, new sales representatives enticed by stories of high commissions, entertainers, and seasonal workers give poor evidence of continued stable income. To some lenders, socially unacceptable types of work carry unduly low ratings. Self-employed persons should have a record of successful operations to assure stability as more small businesses fail than ever succeed.

    For women, only recently has the spectrum of jobs available broadened to include almost every type of work. Rated among the highest for stability are teaching, nursing, and the growing executive group. Secretarial work as a class rates rather poorly, mainly from lack of continued interest; but the top legal, professional and executive secretaries not only command good salaries but are virtually assured of continuous work today. A few of the less stable categories are clerical workers, models, actresses, and waitresses. A growing number of young and older women are going into commission sales work with about the same mixed success as men.

Liabilities. All charges or obligations against an applicant's income must be considered in determining the amount available to meet the mortgage obligation. The liability connected with the normal costs of supporting a family and maintaining a house is taken into consideration by limiting the mortgage payment to 20 or 25 percent of the applicant's income.

Both the FHA and VA have developed some standard patterns and ratios to guide the underwriting of their loan commitments insofar as the monthly obligations compare to the applicant's monthly income. With conventional loans there is considerable flexibility in these limitations. Conventional lenders seldom include housing costs such as utilities and maintenance in their monthly charge ratios. Rather, the basic obligation is considered the mortgage payment, which includes principal, interest, taxes and insurance (PITI). A very common ratio used to screen a loan applicant, insofar as liabilities are concerned, is that the mortgage payment cannot exceed 25 percent of the monthly income and the total of all fixed obligations cannot exceed 33 percent. As housing costs have escalated, a greater portion of family income has been required to meet this expense. Over the past few years, lenders have increased the acceptable ratios. A more accurate measure of liability today is that the mortgage payment cannot exceed 33 percent of the borrower's gross income and the mortgage payment plus long-term installment obligations cannot exceed 38 percent of income.

What is meant by *long-term obligations*? The answer is not very specific as lenders differ in what is included. A general definition is any regular payment obligation that extends for longer than 12 months. The obvious payments are for cars, furniture, or other personal goods. Less obvious are such payments as life insurance—some lenders consider this a liability, others class it as a savings and an asset. Revolving charge accounts and credit card obligations are not always easy to classify. Indeed, the growth of consumer credit has resulted in some mortgage loan qualification problems. By 1980, many lenders were reporting that the big problem in borrower qualification was not the mortgage payment itself, but the large amount of other obligations that many families were undertaking.

Assets. Most home buyers are younger couples who have not yet accumulated very many assets. The purchase of a house represents one of the largest investments they will make. But the addition of such values as stocks, bonds, real estate, savings funds, and other assets does indicate an ability to live prudently and conserve a portion of the income. Life insurance is both an asset in its cash value and protection features and a liability in its cost. Cars and boats represent some trade-in value. Furniture and personal property are often overvalued in an applicant's statement of assets because of the owner's personal attachment. Employee trust and pension funds can represent value if the interest is a vested one, that is, if employees can take the funds with them if they leave the job. An interest in one's own business should be determined by an actual financial statement of that business. Accounts and notes receivable should be detailed for proper valuation.

Willingness to Pay

The element of willingness to pay, sometimes called *credit character*, is the most difficult to analyze and judge. Yet this factor alone can be the cause of a loan rejection. The most tangible information concerning an individual's record of handling obligations comes from the credit bureau report. Information may also be derived from public records regarding litigation, judgments, or criminal actions. Conversations with persons involved in the house sale transaction can sometimes bring to light information on the applicant's manner of living, personal attitudes, and activities that might give cause for a more detailed investigation. The initial loan application often is taken at the lending company's offices, but it can be handled at the residence of the applicant. Some lenders expect a personal call to be made on the applicant by their agents, as a person's manner of living can be most helpful in judging the credit character.

Under the category of "willingness to pay," lenders have always tried to assess an applicant's *motivation* for owning a home. Lenders in the past have felt that the strongest incentive for owning a home came from a family unit committed to the rearing of children. But life styles change and many persons today are not interested in having a family but do want houses. Even prior to the enactment of the Equal Credit Opportunity Act, lenders were enlarging the qualification standards and making loans to single persons, both men and women, and nonfamily units where there was a reasonable assurance of continuity of interest in owning a house. ECOA has eliminated sex and marital status as a basis for a loan rejection, but it has not foreclosed the lender's right to exercise judgment as to the continuing need to repay a mortgage loan. This is an area that does not lend itself to clear-cut definitions and presents problems for a responsible loan officer.

Under this category of credit attitude, a formidable barrier must be surmounted: the problem of invasion of privacy. Attitudes are changing among lenders but still range over a broad spectrum. The older, highly personal approach to a loan is still practiced in smaller communities and by many venerable lending institutions. Some savings and loan associations will not approve a loan without personal contact with the applicant by at least one, sometimes two, lending officers.

At the other extreme we find efforts to make the analysis as impersonal as possible. The thought here is to minimize the effects of personalities, of likes and dislikes, or of prejudices that have relatively little bearing on the strength of the applicant. These efforts center around some form of a rating chart with columns such as "good," "fair," and "poor" for judging 10 to 20 basic factors on the applicant's credit record. Each factor carries a different value in points for "good" or "fair" and must total a certain minimum to qualify. More than one rating in the "poor" column can be an automatic rejection.

It is in this area of trying to bridge the gap for the remote lender that the mortgage banker can serve as eyes, ears, and interpreter to bring all the facts into focus. The true picture can be just as advantageous for the borrower as for the lender and is mandatory in making proper judgment on any loan. Individuals asking to borrow someone else's money should be willing to provide complete and accurate information about themselves within the requirements of the Equal Credit Opportunity Act.

Credit Reports

Individual Credit

In most metropolitan areas there are a number of agencies that furnish credit information on individuals and companies. Credit bureaus, by definition, act as impartial gathering points of factual information on consumers. Other reporting firms, known as *investigative* reporting companies collect credit information and also data required by insurance companies on the individual. There are also firms which compile records on businesses, and these are known as *commercial* reporting firms.

The mortgage business, for the most part, has followed the lead of the FHA and VA which make contracts with one of the major agencies for each area. The one selected is usually affiliated with Associated Credit Bureaus, Inc. and has ready access to exchange information from other credit bureaus in other areas of the country.

Credit bureaus are heavily dependent on the cooperation of local banks, merchants, and other financial institutions to relay factual data to them. From the information collected, a credit report is assembled and is available to firms which contract for credit reporting service. Each request for a credit report must be for a permissible purpose as outlined in the Fair Credit Reporting Act.

This law, which was passed by the U.S. Congress in 1970, spells out the obligations of the user of the report as well as the credit bureau. Consumers have the right to know the full contents of their file and may request this information from the credit bureau.

A typical credit report contains four sections. The first two lines contain identifying information. The second section relates to the present employment of the subject of the report. The third section contains data about the individual including former address, former employer, and employment of spouse. The fourth section contains the credit history of the paying habits of the consumers. Each of the 15 columns of the credit history are necessary to provide the reader of the report with a complete picture of the paying habits of the consumer.

In a mortgage credit report it is customary to show a review of the county records for judgments and liens of any kind. Figure 10-2 is a copy of a typical credit report showing how the information is presented by a typical credit bureau. Figure 10-3 gives an explanation of a credit report.

One of the problems of credit reporting is the possibility of misfiling credit information. The confusion of same names, similar names, changes of married names, and just plain errors can cause an unjustified adverse report, or perhaps fail to give a true picture. Social Security numbers provide an obvious answer to minimizing confusion over name similarity. And these numbers are normally requested in credit information reports. However, the Social Security rules themselves make these numbers a private matter. Refusal to disclose a Social Security number cannot be used as a basis for denial of credit.

Another problem besetting credit reporting is the recent successful legal attacks on credit bureaus when an erroneous report causes damage to a person or company. Information detrimental to a person's credit position can be damaging, and many retail companies follow the easiest route to avoid problems by simply not reporting information. This practice of refusing to furnish any information on credit customers in order to avoid possible damage suits diminishes the value of any cooperative report.

The Fair Credit Reporting Act

The Fair Credit Reporting Act is intended to give an individual the right to examine a summary of the information on file with any credit reporting agency making reports on that individual. The individual may re-

☐ SINGLE REFERENCE	☒ IN FILE REPORT	☐ TRADE REPORT
☐ FULL REPORT	☐ EMPLOY & TRADE REPORT	☐ PREVIOUS RESIDENCE REPORT
☐ OTHER _____		

Credit Bureau of Anytown
1311 Main St.
Anytown, Anystate 12345

CONFIDENTIAL
crediscope® REPORT

Date Received	10/9/82
Date Mailed	10/9/82
In File Since	1973
Inquired As	2

FOR

First National Bank
Anytown, Anystate 13440

🔲 Member
Associated Credit Bureaus, Inc.

REPORT ON	LAST NAME	FIRST NAME	INITIAL	SOCIAL SECURITY NUMBER	SPOUSE'S NAME
Consumer		Bob	B.	123-45-6789	Betty

ADDRESS	CITY	STATE	ZIP CODE	SINCE	SPOUSE'S SOCIAL SECURITY NO
812 Elm St.	Anytown	Anystate	12403	1975	987-65-4321

COMPLETE TO HERE FOR TRADE REPORT AND SKIP TO CREDIT REPORT

PRESENT EMPLOYER	POSITION HELD	SINCE	DATE EMPLOY VERIFIED	EST. MONTHLY INCOME
Research Engineers, Inc.	Sr. Vice Pres.	10/76	12/5/81	$ 2500

COMPLETE TO HERE FOR EMPLOYMENT AND TRADE REPORT AND SKIP TO CREDIT HISTORY

DATE OF BIRTH	NUMBER OF DEPENDENTS INCLUDING SELF			
4/38	2	☒ OWNS OR BUYING HOME	☐ RENTS HOME	☐ OTHER (EXPLAIN)

FORMER ADDRESS	CITY	STATE	FROM	TO
123 Oak St.	Thattown	Anystate	1973	1975

FORMER EMPLOYER	POSITION HELD	FROM	TO	EST. MONTHLY INCOME
Sun Research	Engineer	1970	1976	$ - - -

SPOUSE'S EMPLOYER	POSITION HELD	SINCE	DATE EMPLOY VERIFIED	EST. MONTHLY INCOME
Gift World	Owner	1975	12/5/81	$ 1100

CREDIT HISTORY (Complete this section for all reports)

WHOSE	KIND OF BUSINESS AND ID CODE	DATE REPORTED AND METHOD OF REPORTING	DATE OPENED	DATE OF LAST PAYMENT	HIGHEST CREDIT OR LAST CONTRACT	BALANCE OWING	PAST DUE AMOUNT	NO OF PAYMENTS	NO MONTHS HISTORY REVIEWED	30-59 DAYS ONLY	60-89 DAYS AND OVER	90 DAYS AND OVER	TYPE & TERMS (MANNER OF PAYMENT)	REMARKS
3	D608 126438	9/82A	2/78	6/82	172	85	34	2	12	1	1		R $17	
1	B319	9/82M	8/80	8/82	2400	00	0		24				I $100	
2	C526 165020	9/82A	1977	7/82	1264	100	50	1	12	2	1		R $50	
3	N772 161083	9/82A	2/81	7/82	350	160	-	-	12	1			0	DRP
0	D490	5/77M	1977	6/78	700	00	0		-				0-1	

Public Record
County Small Claims Court Case SC-1001, 5/13/81. Plaintiff: Ace Stereo Sales. $325.
Paid 12/1/81.

FORM 2000-5/80

FIGURE 10-2 Copy furnished by courtesy of Associated Credit Bureaus, Inc., Walter R. Kurth, President.

Kind of Business Classification

In most cases, the first letter of the Kind of Business being classified and the code letter itself are the same. For instance, clothing stores are represented by the letter "C". The Kind of Business code letter is combined with the credit bureau member's code number to identify the source of information found in Column 2 of the credit report. Example: C-1234.

Code letters used in the Kind of Business column:

Code	Kind of Business
A	Automotive
B	Banks
C	Clothing
D	Department and Variety
F	Finance
G	Groceries
H	Home Furnishings
I	Insurance
J	Jewelry and Cameras
K	Contractors
L	Lumber, Building Material, Hardware
M	Medical and Related Health

Code	Kind of Business
N	National Credit Card Companies and Air Lines
O	Oil Companies
P	Personal Services Other Than Medical
Q	Mail Order Houses
R	Real Estate and Public Accommodations
S	Sporting Goods
T	Farm and Garden Supplies
U	Utilities and Fuel
V	Government
W	Wholesale
X	Advertising
Y	Collection Services
Z	Miscellaneous

Terms of Sale

The next to last column is headed "Type and Terms (Manner of Payment)." "Type and Terms" will continue to be shown in every instance. This is the space to show whether the account is open, revolving, or installment and, if it is revolving or installment, to show the amount of the monthly payment.

Crediscope groups the information in the "Terms of Sale" column into the following three classifications.

OPEN or "O" accounts include:
An account to be paid after one billing
An account expected to be paid in one payment, such as a 30-day account
An account in which the entire amount is to be paid within certain limits, such as 60 or 90 days, with no interest or service charge

REVOLVING or "R" accounts include:
An account with regular monthly payments based on the amount of the balance due

INSTALLMENT or "I" accounts include:
An account with a fixed number of specified payments — specified as to amounts and time, and including interest charges

NOTE: When the monthly payment is known on Revolving or Installment accounts, it should be written after the identifying letter — I-$78 or R-$20.

Usual Manner of Payment

The Usual Manner of Payment will be used only by the credit bureau to report accounts which were paid out and reported prior to 1977. The new manner of showing historical status replaces any manner of payment listing for accounts which are currently being used.

USUAL MANNER OF PAYMENT	TYPE ACCOUNT		
	O	R	I
Too new to rate; approved but not used	0	0	0
Pays (or paid) within 30 days of billing; pays accounts as agreed	1	1	1
Pays (or paid) in more than 30 days, but not more than 60 days, or not more than one payment past due	2	2	2
Pays (or paid) in more than 60 days, but not more than 90 days, or two payments past due	3	3	3
Pays (or paid) in more than 90 days, but not more than 120 days, or three or more payments past due	4	4	4
Account is at least 120 days overdue but is not yet rated "9"	5	5	5
Paying or Paid Out under Wage Earner Plan or similar arrangements.........	7	7	7
Repossession. (Indicate if it is a voluntary return of merchandise by the customer.)	8	8	8
Bad debt; placed for collection skip	9	9	9

Three-letter abbreviations used in the "Remarks" column:

	ACC	—Account closed by consumer.
	AJP	—Adjustment pending.
(1)	BKL	—Account included in Bankruptcy.
	CCA	—Consumer counseling account. Consumer has retained the services of an organization which is directing payment of his accounts.
	CLA	—Placed for collection.
	DIS	—Dispute following resolution.
	DRP	—Dispute resolution pending.
(2)	JUD	—Judgment obtained for balance shown.
	MOV	—Moved. Left no forwarding address.
	PRL	—Profit and loss write-off.
	RLD	—Repossession. Paid by dealer.
	RLP	—Repossession. Proceeds applied to debt.
	RPO	—Repossession.
	RRE	—Repossession redeemed.
	RVD	—Returned voluntarily. Paid by dealer.
	RVN	—Returned voluntarily.
	RVP	—Returned voluntarily, proceeds applied to debt.
	RVR	—Returned voluntarily, redeemed.
	STL	—Plate stolen or lost.
(1)	WEP	—Wage Earner Plan Account (Chapter XIII of the Bankruptcy Act).

FIGURE 10-3

quire that erroneous information be corrected. The Act does not give the individual the right to inspect the actual credit report covering his or her record, but a summary must be shown free of charge if there has been an adverse record filed. The federal agency responsible for administering this Act is the Federal Trade Commission headquartered in Washington, D.C. with regional offices in major cities.

Corporate Credit Analysis

To analyze adequately the credit-worthiness of a company, it is necessary for the underwriter to become acquainted and fully cognizant of every phase of the business under scrutiny: management, sales, production, purchasing, research and planning, personnel policies, and the physical plant and equipment, as well as to make a careful study of the financial statements. There is wide latitude in the quantity and quality of detail needed to answer the fundamental question of whether or not it would be advisable to make a loan to the corporate applicant.

The underwriter expects to have a current, preferably audited, financial statement presented along with the loan application. An *audited* statement is one in which all the pertinent data is verified by the Certified Public Accountant preparing the report. The figures are presented in a form and according to rules determined by the accountants, and in which the final conclusions are certified as correct and accurate by the accredited accountants. The principal factors a lender will look for are the record of profitable use of existing assets, the accumulation of cash and property versus outstanding obligations, and the very important working ratio of current assets to current liabilities. The latter indicates both the manner of operation and the immediate cushion of assets available to protect the company against a temporary reversal.

Personal interviews with company officers are utilized to fill in more detail of what the company's plans are and how it intends to carry them out. Where larger loans are involved, it is routine procedure to verify the company's market and its ability to sell its product. Comparative balance sheets and profit and loss statements covering the previous ten years of operations give excellent indications of how the company has handled its business and what the general trend will be. Also, a Dun and Bradstreet report (one of the largest national credit reporting services) can give something of the history on the company, which helps to project future capabilities. It is the long-range ability of the company to operate profitably that is the real key to the trouble-free recovery of a loan.

In order to evaluate the results of the loan on the company's finances, it is customary to prepare a *pro forma* statement—both the balance sheet and the profit and loss statement. These statements are a *projection* of what the loan will do, such as increase the investment in productivity, add a new product line, provide an additional service, or broaden a market, as well as the expected effects of that loan on the profitability of the company.

To assure the lender that the proceeds of the loan are used as projected, a loan agreement is drawn up that spells out the purpose of the loan and can provide penalties for nonconformance. In addition, certain restrictive covenants are often added to the loan agreement that will place limits on such things as loans or advances to officers or employees until the loan is paid off, control the payment of salaries and dividends, limit any other borrowing, and require approval of the lender before any major assets, patents, or leasehold interests can be sold. All terms of the loan agreement are negotiable and are designed primarily to assure the lender's interest in the company over a period of time during which the ownership and management can change drastically but the loan obligation continues on.

Questions for Discussion

1. List the essential classes of information that a prospective borrower must provide in a loan application.

2. Discuss ability to repay a loan as may be indicated by type of income and stability of income.

3. List four different types of income that a borrower might report on a loan application and discuss the acceptability of each type.

4. What additional information is necessary to verify the income of self-employed persons?

5. How are liabilities against a family income evaluated?

6. What is meant by *willingness to pay* and how can it be evaluated?

7. What information is normally obtained from a credit report on the loan applicant?

8. In analyzing corporate credit, what further investigation would an underwriter employ beyond a careful study of the company's financial statements?

Residential Loan Analysis

General Analysis of Loans

The process of analyzing and approving a loan is called *underwriting*. The individual who assembles and analyzes the necessary data and usually gives a company's consent to a specific loan is referred to as the *underwriter*. Properly underwriting any loan requires a complete analysis of all pertinent factors, including: (1) the borrower's ability and willingness to pay; (2) the property, its condition, location, and usage; (3) all relevant economic influences; (4) laws controlling foreclosure procedures and assignments of rent; and (5) any unusual conditions that may exist.

An underwriter must examine the future, estimate the continued stability of the borrower, and try to judge the future values in a specific property. The underwriter must look beyond a normal appraisal, which provides an estimate of past or present value, and weigh the forces that affect the future based on his or her experience in this field.

A loan analysis covers a wide assortment of information, and from these diverse elements, an underwriter must determine the degree of risk involved. There is no such thing as a risk-free mortgage loan. It is the underwriter's prime responsibility to determine the magnitude of the risk and to compensate for it in the terms and conditions of the loan. The degree of risk determines the ratio of loan to value, the length of time for repayment, and the interest rate required by the lender.

In this and the succeeding chapters, various types of properties will be analyzed to show the economics involved with each type. The conditions an underwriter looks for vary with the properties, and the most important one is "where will the money come from to repay this loan and how certain is it that the income will continue?" With a residential loan, repayment can be expected from the borrower's personal income, hence the emphasis on a detailed analysis of the borrower's record of employment and earnings. With income property, the underwriter looks for the capability of the property itself to produce sufficient income to repay the loan. A shopping center has medium- to long-term leases that provide solid information on the stability and continuity of income. An apartment project with few leases and month-to-month tenancy depends on the general occupancy records for the area to provide clues to future income capability. Each of the property types presents its variations. The previous chapter studied the questions involved with borrower analysis with emphasis on his or her income. Now the questions involving the property itself will be discussed, starting with residential loans.

Residential Loan Practices

Most people borrow money to purchase a home only once or twice in a lifetime, so it is usually a new experience for the average borrower. How should this uninitiated person proceed? What are the normal practices in the field and to whom should the borrower turn for advice? Fortunately, there are many specialists in the business knowledgeable of local practices who can help the home buyer in making decisions.

The Real Estate Broker

Since the house is normally selected before a loan is considered, one of the first knowledgeable experts to look to is the broker handling the house sale. Most states have licensing and bonding statutes to assure the public of the broker's qualifications. The more competent brokers maintain current information on the various local sources of mortgage money, the types of loans each are negotiating, the interest rate, and the current fees charged for service. Under normal, competitive conditions in large urban areas, it is not at all unusual to have a spread of 1 to 2 percent between the high and low interest rate offered in any one day on the same kind of mortgage loans.

In some areas of the country, particularly in the smaller communities, a knowledgeable real estate broker can and does perform a valuable service for the lender by taking a loan application and handling some of the preliminary steps of asking for verifications. For this work, the broker may earn a portion of the finance fee. Under the rules prescribed by the Real Estate Settlement Procedures Act, whenever actual work is performed and payment is commensurate with the amount of work, a reasonable division of the finance fee is not considered "fee splitting." The splitting of a fee for a referral, or something that does not involve actual work, is now prohibited.

Loan Broker

Independent loan brokers in some areas of the country are very active, maintaining contacts with real estate sales personnel, local savings associations, architects, attorneys, bankers, and any others who would have need for assistance in securing loans for their customers or clients. The independent broker could be called by the real estate broker, for example, in the negotiation of a sales contract to assist the buyer in the proper placement of a loan.

The independent broker has current knowledge of the mortgage market and may be able to contact a willing lender for the type of loan needed to consummate a deal. The brokerage fee is usually 1 to 1½ percent of the loan amount and can run higher for commercial loans. The service provided by a broker includes help in preparing the necessary information for submittal to the lender, following up with any supplemental information needed, and fulfilling the needs of both the borrower and the lender in the collection of information needed to close a loan. Independent brokers are no longer very active in the handling of residential loans. The high volume of relatively small loans does not fit their specialized expertise. It is in the negotiation of small-to-medium-sized commercial loans that most independents find a lucrative market.

Mortgage Companies

Leading the way in the field of merchandizing mortgage loans is the mortgage banking industry. In larger communities, mortgage companies compete heavily with each other through their loan representatives. Because mortgage companies represent a number of lenders from all parts of the country, they may hold money commitments at a time when other local lenders are suffering restraints.

The mortgage company field representative is a specialist trained in the intricacies of loan applications and sensitive to the points that need clarification or verification for proper underwriting evaluation. The mortgage company representative can take an application at the place and time most convenient to the applicant. It has been this type of assistance to the borrower that has enabled the mortgage companies to handle well over half of all home loans in the country.

Savings Associations

As pointed out in Chapter 5, savings and loan associations—the leading source for mortgage money—handle loans both through intermediaries, such as mortgage companies or brokers, and also directly to their customers. Some of the more aggressive savings associations have followed the mortgage companies' practice of sending loan representatives into the field to call on potential loan applicants. But most savings associations rely on their own depositors and the business contacts made by their officers to attract loan applicants into their own building locations to make applications for loans. Qualified lending officers take the loan applications, obtain the necessary substantiating information, and in most cases, personally present the application to the loan committee for approval. In this manner, the committee can interrogate the lending officer for any details they consider pertinent to their judgment of the loan.

Builders

When a new home is purchased directly from a builder, the builder may already hold a commitment for mortgage money that can be used by the home buyer. Some of the ways these commitments are handled are discussed below.

Competitive Method.   The small-to-medium-sized builders may have their construction money secured without any commitment for the permanent loans. For example, a commercial bank carrying the construction financing would have little interest in making a permanent loan. If there is no commitment, the purchaser is free to seek whatever source of mortgage money that may be found.

Commitment Method, Construction.   When a builder, and this would cover all sizes of builders, obtains construction money, the lender may request a first refusal right to all permanent loans on the project. The construction lender thus ties up a good source of loans for the future, which is one of the incentives to make the construction loan in the first place. To enforce this right, the lender can add a penalty provision in the construction loan agreement that provides for an extra ½ or 1 percent of the construction loan to be paid for a release of the construction mortgage if the loan is not handled through the same lender. A purchaser cannot be required to borrow money from a particular lender, but it can be a bit more costly to go elsewhere.

Commitment Method, Purchase.   Some of the larger builders who can qualify for the lowest rates on their construction money, or use their own funds for this purpose, may purchase a future commitment for money direct from a savings association or other major source to protect future customers needing loans. The builder will pay at least 1 percent of the total commitment amount to hold the money or may pay additional fees to assure the future home buyers a lower, more competitive interest rate. This expense, which in effect is a prepayment of interest by the builder for the benefit of the buyer, is charged back into the cost of the house. It is in this manner that some builders can advertise lower than market interest rates and obtain a competitive advantage in the housing market.

Associated Companies. A few of the larger builders who are almost national in scope are organized with their own affiliated mortgage companies or money sources to provide permanent loans. The tie-in is generally competitive with the market rates for money and is intended as a convenience for the buyer. These companies seldom press their full range of services upon a customer, but they carry a competitive edge by being available at the proper time.

Other Sources

Every community has a variety of other potential sources that a borrower may find helpful. These would include local loan offices of insurance companies, employee or labor union credit unions, state or city sponsored pension and trust funds that may be utilized for home loans, or perhaps a fraternal or religious organization that the borrower may be affiliated with which has lendable funds available to its members. Most of these lenders do not aggressively solicit home loans. The potential borrower must seek out these sources to obtain a loan as they do not generally provide the helpful assistance that is a hallmark of mortgage companies and savings associations. But the extra effort on the part of the borrower can be rewarded in the form of slightly lower interest rates.

Conventional Residential Loans

In Chapter 8 on government programs, the requirements for, and methods used by, the FHA and VA in handling residential loans were outlined. In conventional lending, the procedures employed are basically not very different because the goal is the same, namely, to make a sound loan, and this requires adequate information. The variations in conventional lending lie chiefly in the multitude of interpretations and special viewpoints that derive from the vast variety of conventional lenders exercising their individual ideas regarding requirements. Thus, a conventional loan has always been defined in very broad terms as "any loan that is not underwritten by an agency of the government."

Without an FHA or VA commitment, the conventional loan stands more on its own; the credit-worthiness of the borrower and the value of the property held as security become more important to the ultimate lender. Until recently there was nothing else a lender could do in case of default on a conventional loan except turn to the borrower and foreclose the property. Lenders in distant places were reluctant to accept loans that might require the management and disposal of a repossessed house in a remote place. It is in this area of relieving a lender of the post-foreclosure problems that the FHA and the VA gained strength and acceptability.

Beginning in 1971, during a period in which private mortgage insurance became a requirement for home loans in excess of 90 percent, conventional loans grew more acceptable to the large lending institutions in the secondary market. For the borrower, private mortgage insurance made higher loan-to-value ratios more readily available, which permitted lower down payments and broadened the potential market for homes.

As the government-influenced segment of the secondary market has continued to grow in size and influence, a newly defined loan has developed within the framework of a conventional loan. It is called the *conforming* loan; that is, one that conforms to the loan limits as set by the Federal Home Loan Bank Board (or by the Congress). The Federal Home Loan Mortgage Corporation, as an agency reporting to the FHLBB, and the Government National Mortgage Association, as an agency under HUD, both comply with government restrictions on loans. While the Federal National Mortgage Association is a private corporation, its charter requires cooperation with national housing policies. Thus, this major market upholds federal standards by refusing to purchase nonconforming loans.

In the mortgage market, there are residential loans that conform (within maximum limits) and that are written on the prescribed uniform instruments developed by FNMA and FHLMC. There are also loans that can be described as "conforming but with nonuniform documentation." This, of course, means that the standard instruments offered by FNMA and FHLMC have not been used in preparing the loan documents. Examples of the uniform instrument that are referred to appear in this text as follows:

1. Residential Loan Application—Figure 10-1a and b (pages 218 and 219).
2. Residential Appraisal Report—Figure 9-1a and b (pages 203 and 204).

3. Promissory Note—Figures 3-1a and b and 3-2 (pages 41, 42, and 43).
4. Mortgage—Figure 3-3a, b, c, and d (pages 44, 45, 46 and 47).

While there is no requirement that mortgage loans be written on any of the standard forms offered, many conventional loans are so handled to give a lender the flexibility of selling the loans to FNMA or FHLMC should the need arise. Further impetus is added to the use of uniform instruments by the many new laws that now apply to real estate and to credit transactions. Lending officers are anxious to comply with the law and feel that a form prepared and approved by a government agency helps them to follow the requirements. This is particularly true of the Residential Loan Application form.

Except for conforming loans, which follow a "Seller's Guide" (FNMA or FHLMC) similar in detail to the FHA or VA "Underwriting Guide," conventional loan requirements vary considerably and reflect each lender's particular policies. The following discussion outlines a consensus of the market in regard to the basic parameters of conventional loan evaluation—the guidelines most generally used within the industry to determine the acceptability of a loan.

Loan-to-Value Ratio (LTVR)

The loan-to-value ratio denotes the amount of the loan as a percentage of the value of the property. The ratio applies to all types of loans. In line with this formula, the value of the property is the single variable. The most common definition of value favored by lenders is the appraised value of the property, or the selling price, whichever is the least. If a loan is being made where a sale is not involved, then the appraised value is the controlling factor.

Based on the LTVR, most lenders set their "price list" for loans. The higher the ratio of loan, the greater the risk, and thus, the higher the interest rate and discount. A 95 percent loan might require ½ percent more in interest and 1 or 2 points more in discount than a 90 percent loan. The best rate is usually given on an 80 percent loan. Ratios less than 80 percent seldom command any lower interest rates. However, in periods of tight money, many lenders reduce the acceptable LTVR for all loans, and thus increase the required down payment.

Size of Loan

The dollar limit on a conventional residential loan varies. Some state regulatory authorities have set limits which are maximum permissible loan amounts. Lenders under these authorities may always opt for lower loan limits. And some states set no limits. In November, 1980, the Federal Home Loan Bank lifted its dollar limits for federally chartered savings associations. This also removed the maximums that formerly limited FNMA and FHLMC. However, both FNMA and FHLMC have set their own limits, currently at $107,000 for a one-family residential loan.

Both commercial banks and thrift institutions face regulatory restraints on the amount of money they can loan to any one borrower. This is generally expressed as a percentage of the institution's net worth, or possibly a percentage of its gross assets.

There is no real minimum for a loan except pure economics. When a mortgage loan goes under about $10,000, it becomes more expensive to service and the fee received does not justify the time and expense involved. Of course, the efficiency of organizations varies, and the minimums they can handle fluctuate accordingly. Some mortgage companies consider $25,000 the minimum conventional loan that can profitably be accepted. To undertake loans of lesser amounts might mean the company would be forced to sell at greater discounts, which would prove unprofitable.

Loans exceeding a lender's limits can be handled by several banks or associations joining together, with one institution responsible for administering the loan. These are called *participation* loans and are more commonly found in the larger commercial loans. But as home loans continue to increase in size, it is not unusual to find several lenders participating in one home loan. For the largest home loans, roughly those reaching to $250,000 and more, the prudent lender would expect a borrower to show a sustaining annual income of about 60 percent of the loan amount, plus some depth in other personal assets.

Kinds of Mortgages

Much regulatory activity in the past few years has been devoted to residential mortgage designs, mostly variations in permissible mortgage repayment plans. Before a regulated lender can write a particular kind of mortgage, it must have the approval of the proper authority. Approved designs set maximums (or in some cases, minimums) that apply to the different designs. These include such limits as the increases allowed for graduated payment mortgages, caps on changes in interest rates for adjustable rate mortgages, and approval of indexes that can be used to make interest rate adjustments. Within the approved limits, lenders are free to design their own mortgage repayment plans, and many have done so.

Few primary lenders offer a variety of mortgage designs. The normal practice is for a lender to select several different plans and limit their loan offerings to their own approved designs. The borrower may be able to select between a fixed interest rate, constant-level payment plan, one or two variations of adjustable rate plans, or several graduated payment plans, including a GPM, a pledged account mortgage or, perhaps, a buy-down design. The perceived risks of the different designs are reflected in the interest rate and discount required for each plan. With the variety of repayment plans on the market today, the borrower is well advised to shop a bit for the most suitable plan.

Physical Characteristics

There are several considerations concerning the property's physical characteristics that may be used as "go, no-go" determinants in the approval of a mortgage loan.

Dwelling Units. Statistical references class one- to four-family housing as *residential*. However, many lenders in the conventional loan market separate this group into single-family housing, which qualifies for prime loan rates, and commercial property, which is rated for higher risk loans. Both the FHA and VA issue commitments for two-, three-, and four-family housing, but the limits are not as favorable as those for single-family units.

Townhouses and Condos. Townhouses attached to the ground are treated in the same manner as single-family housing. And in most states, condominiums are classed as real estate by enabling legislation that permits first mortgage loans to be made on them.

Number of Bedrooms. Conventional lenders no longer consider the number of bedrooms a major consideration. Years ago it was not unusual to restrict loans to housing that had more than one bedroom. But the market has changed so that a number of buyers prefer limited bedroom space. As long as the lender believes a reasonable market exists for the property should foreclosure become necessary, the collateral is acceptable. (The FHA does base some of its loan limits in certain programs on the number of available bedrooms.)

Square Footage. Minimum house size based on square footage is no longer used as a loan determinant. As builders have endeavored to reduce housing costs, the size of houses has been reduced. The old standard of "not less than 1,000 square feet of living area" is simply not applicable in today's markets. Actually, the importance of square footage is more relevant to the value of the house in an appraisal.

Paved Streets. While most cities have managed to pave their streets, there are some smaller communities that have not. Lenders have used the lack of paving as a "no-go" situation for a loan if it can result in a lessening of the collateral value. For example, the cost of paving is often handled in the form of an additional assessment on the property fronting the new pavement. If the assessment's amount is unknown, it is difficult to make adequate provision for the charge.

Utilities. A loan application may be rejected if the property offered as collateral does not have adequate sewer and water facilities. Top preference is given to a municipally operated or a regulated private operation furnishing both sewer and water services. The use of septic tanks or private water wells may be a cause for rejection. Some lenders will permit a septic tank if the percolation tests of the soil surrounding it meet certain minimum requirements. Also classed as utilities are the services of electricity, natural gas, and telephone. The lack of any of these services, however, is not detrimental for a loan. Also, there are no requirements for electricity or phones to be furnished through underground systems at the present time.

Building Materials. As important as building materials would seem to be, they are not used as a determinant in underwriting a loan. Whether the building is sheathed in aluminum, asbestos, wood, brick, or stone is important to an appraiser in evaluating the building, but not to a lender in determining a "go, no-go" situation. The quality of the building materials is expressed in terms of the value of the building and in its estimated life or apparent age.

Amenities. The extra niceties that exist in some buildings are reflected in the value of the property but are not considered critical for the underwriter. A swimming pool, fine landscaping, exterior lighting, a neighborhood club or recreational area are all added features that increase property value but are never considered a requirement for loan approval.

Location of Property

Lines are drawn by most conventional lenders between urban, suburban, and rural housing. The differences are not always clearly delineated, but they do provide a broad classification that is useful in describing packages of loans.

Due to the sprawl of our great metropolitan areas, the term *suburban* now means almost any location in a recorded subdivision of land in the general area surrounding cities—the region of greatest growth in our country. *Urban* means the downtown and near downtown areas of our cities. *Rural* identifies farm housing and to many lenders, houses existing in the smaller towns. Rural is also occasionally used to identify housing without access to a central water and sewage system.

Neighborhoods. Lenders no longer specify areas or neighborhoods within a city as acceptable or unacceptable for making loans. Obviously, a neighborhood that is allowed to deteriorate does not make an attractive location for a 30-year loan. However, recent federal regulations prohibit lenders from drawing lines on a geographic basis that could constitute discrimination. The practice is known more commonly as "red-lining" from the lines drawn on city maps to guide loan officers. The prohibition is aimed at the elimination of racial discrimination that could result from arbitrary lines drawn around certain neighborhoods. Lenders are asked to qualify houses on their individual merit, rather than on the neighborhood in which they are located. Further, federally regulated lenders are required to disclose the geographic areas in which they have made their loans by census tract or by postal ZIP code number.

Flood-Prone Areas. The federal government has defined certain areas of the country over the past decade as flood plain zones. These are areas that have been flooded in the past 100 years, or that, if records do not exist, are calculated to have a 1 percent chance of being flooded. Houses built in a designated flood plain may not be financed by any lender subject to any federal regulatory body unless minimum elevation requirements are met. The government will assist a homeowner by subsidizing flood insurance in cooperation with selected private insurance companies in approved areas.

Other Disaster-Prone Areas. As new real estate developments increase in areas that are subject to certain kinds of natural disasters, many lenders are refusing to consider taking on loans for such properties. The potential for disasters includes earthquakes, volcanic eruptions, flooding, swelling soils, subsidence of the land, landslides, and geographic faulting. Where adequate hazard insurance is available, however, most lenders will generally make the loans. One problem emerging now is an increasing concern for the continuation of lending in areas where growth has been unintentionally encouraged by government-subsidized hurricane and flood insurance.

Age of Property

The age of a house is a simple, frequently used criterion for determining acceptable and unacceptable loans. The range varies from an insistence by the lender on exclusively new houses, which is unusual, to no fixed limit. Many lenders couple the age of the property with the location of the house. Some neighborhoods maintain their desirability over the years and 30- to 40-year-old homes may qualify for prime loans. Older houses that are not in the prime neighborhoods may still qualify for mortgage loans but at higher interest rates and for shorter terms. The originator of a loan must always keep in mind what the specific requirements of various sources of money are in regard to age.

Conventional loans are handled in two ways regarding the question of age. Standard loans are most often based on the actual age of the property. A "no-go" limit is set at a maximum age, such as not to exceed 15 years, for example. A lender may commit to take loans on new houses only, or perhaps on houses not over 3 years old, or not over 20 years old. It is the responsibility of the appraiser to determine the age of the house, and some flexibility is allowed in his or her professional opinion. It is not necessary, in most cases, to report the date of a building permit or the exact day of commencement of construction. Rather, the appraiser can make a judgment on the *apparent* age of the house. Obviously, a well-kept house and yard would indicate a lower age than one that had been allowed to deteriorate.

The second method used to determine the age of a property for purposes of a conventional loan is the appraiser's judgment of its remaining useful life. In this connection, both FNMA and FHLMC use the same standard as the FHA to qualify loans that they will purchase: the term of the loan cannot exceed 75 percent of the remaining useful life of the property.

Usage of Property

Residential properties can be said to fall into four categories of usage insofar as mortgage loans are concerned. These include:

1. *Owner-occupied.* This property is considered to show prime security usage and accounts for most residential loans. Only owner-occupied units can command the highest ratio loans.
2. *Tenant-occupied.* Such property falls more into the commercial category of loan analysis, though it is still considered a residential loan for savings association tax purposes and so far as banking regulations are concerned. Since a rental house would not command first call on the owner's income, a lender could downgrade the collateral and make a smaller loan of, perhaps, 75 to 80 percent of the value.
3. *Resort housing.* Until recently, resort houses could be described as cottages, sometimes poorly built of nonpermanent materials, and generally not acceptable as security for loans. The locations often lacked proper fire and police protection, were subject to vandalism and excessive storm damage, and were often not connected

to municipal utility systems. In recent years the growth of new, higher class subdivisions in lakefront or mountainous areas has greatly improved the quality and thus the acceptability of these homes as collateral. Lenders do, in fact, make many resort home loans, but they adjust the amount downward from, perhaps, 65 to as high as 90 percent loan-to-value ratio.

In resort-type developments, it is not unusual for a developer to buy a loan commitment, paying the discount fee necessary to provide potential customers with a dependable, economical source of mortgage money.

4. *Second homes.*   Second homes are a close corollary to the resort home, though they differ in several ways. The more affluent society of the 1960s and 1970s has produced a growing number of families financially able to live in two different houses. On occasion, the house in the city might be less lived in and less occupied, on the whole, than the so-called second home in the country. With regard to financing, a lender usually makes a careful determination as to which house might be considered the primary housing entitled to preferential treatment and which one should be downgraded as a second home, receiving an 80 percent or lower loan. A decision such as this would be required where the borrower was interested in making a purchase that is primarily based on a substantial annual income and not enough other assets. The lender must then consider the loan from the viewpoint of a sudden decrease in income due to job loss or working disablement. Which house, then, would most likely have to be forfeited under adverse circumstances?

Condominiums

The outright purchase of a vertical or horizontal apartment unit effectively detached from a piece of land has required state-enabling legislation declaring such a unit to be in the category of "real property." By means of these legal provisions, regulated lending institutions are permitted to accept such property as collateral. Legislation allowing condominium sales was initiated in the eastern states and has spread across the country over a period of years. It has only been in the past few years, however, that a nearly explosive growth has overtaken condominium sales, accompanied by the necessary mortgage loan programs. The groups most interested in this type of property purchase are the young marrieds and senior citizens, together comprising over half the adult population.

The increasing popularity of the condominium concept of home purchase stems from the desire for homeownership, with the tax advantages of deducting interest and property taxes against an individual's income. In addition, there is a measure of inflation protection gained in property ownership plus tax deferment (within code limits) of capital gains from a profitable sale. And, finally, the right to rent the unit as a landlord is possible.

The mortgage loan for a condominium is very similar to that for a single-family residence. Even though the condo may have no attachment to the land itself, state laws grant a condo the status of a parcel of real estate. As such, the unit can be legally described as real property and thus qualifies as collateral for the lender to make a mortgage loan.

Since the lender must always foresee the possibility of foreclosure and subsequent resale of the property, it is necessary to examine some additional problem areas peculiar to a condominium. One of the more important items directly involved in condominium-style living that concerns the lender is that of maintenance costs. To sell the unit, a developer may be able to hold costs down or may even defer some necessary maintenance in order to show a low monthly charge. Subsequent to the project being sold, however, with the builder no longer responsible for its maintenance, the true problems may show up along with added costs for the unwary purchaser. Therefore the maintenance agreement on the property must be acceptable to the lender.

The voting control of the management board for the project can be held by the developer without a time limitation. It is the general practice for developers to assure proper operation and maintenance during the sell-out period of a project, and provided that the individuals involved have high ethical standards, this is a legitimate selling attraction. The problems of management most often arise under circumstances where not all the units are sold, and the developer must reduce prices, or even rent unsold units, leaving the initial unit owners at a disadvantage. It is good practice to place a time limitation on the developer's absolute voting control; a limitation of perhaps two years would minimize potential problems of this nature.

Utilities should be controlled by the unit owners if at all possible. Unfortunate results may occur when a developer continues to exercise control over all utilities such as gas, electricity, sewer, water, and television channels. Such unwarranted control may expose unit owners to excessive rates and poor performance.

An intention to increase the size of a condominium project should be publicly declared in advance and made known to prospective buyers and lenders. If a developer withholds adjacent land for possible additional units, their later construction might overload existing recreational facilities and reduce the value of all units by the sheer size and numbers of the completed project.

The management contract may affect future values and should be examined by the lender. These contracts are normally written prior to the sale of the units, and it is possible to tie down the rights to sell or lease all units for a lengthy period of time. Any restriction on resale rights would be detrimental to the lender's position.

Home Mortgage Documents As Required by FHLMC

As one of the major agencies purchasing home mortgages from savings associations and other approved lenders, the Federal Home Loan Mortgage Corporation (The Mortgage Company) has established a set of requirements for documenting home mortgage loans. Any lender desirous of selling a loan to FHLMC must document that loan in accordance with the rules as listed in the Sellers Guide. The requirements provide a good insight on the kind of information that is needed and the limitations that they have established. The section on mortgages (Part III, Section 5, Delivery of Home Mortgage Documents) is reproduced in Figures 11-1a through 11-1d.

Questions for Discussion

1. List the categories of information required for the proper evaluation of any type of real estate loan.

2. Why do the secondary market requirements influence primary market lending?

3. Discuss the various physical aspects of a house that concern the underwriter in determining acceptability of a property as collateral for a loan.

4. What is the economic climate in your community? Does it have a continuing stability that would attract out-of-state mortgage investment money at the lowest market rates?

5. How would you define the term *suburban* as it is used to classify residential loans?

6. Discuss the advantages and disadvantages for the home buyer in using a loan commitment held by the home builder.

PART III—HOME MORTGAGES
Section 5—Delivery of Home Mortgage Documents

As to each conventional Home Mortgage purchased in whole or in part by FHLMC, Seller represents and warrants that the requirements set forth in this Part III, Section 5 have been met.

3.501 Delivery of Mortgage Documentation.

Seller agrees, at its own expense and within the delivery period required under the purchase programs, to deliver to FHLMC or its designee such documents as are required to be delivered under the Purchase Documents, subject to approval of FHLMC as to proper form and execution.

Each group of mortgages delivered shall be accompanied by a Mortgage Schedule (FHLMC Form 12, Part V, Exhibit G) with each mortgage submitted listed thereon and by a Contract Delivery Summary (FHLMC Form 381, Part V, Exhibit F) that will list purchase control reconciliation totals. Each delivery of mortgages may be for either participation interests or whole loans; however, one delivery may not include both types. The appropriate block of Form 381 should be marked to indicate whether Seller is delivering whole or participation mortgages. In addition to the above specified documents, each delivery of mortgages to be purchased in part must be accompanied by a FHLMC Participation Certificate Conventional Home Mortgage Participation Program, FHLMC Form 58 (Part V, Exhibit D), with the section "For Seller's Use" completed and executed in duplicate, by an authorized officer of Seller.

FHLMC intends to review mortgages submitted to a substantial extent before payment. For this reason, Seller should plan for a reasonable review period prior to the FHLMC Funding Date. (Amount of purchase price is adjusted for interest accrued through the day prior to the FHLMC Funding Date.)

Legible photocopies of the following documents (except for mortgages to be purchased in whole by FHLMC, where the mortgage note must be an original) for each mortgage must be adequately stapled at the top of the right side of a legal size manila folder and arranged in the order listed below with the first item on top, and must be forwarded to the Applicable FHLMC Regional Office or underwriting office (all documents must be delivered simultaneously):

† **a. Mortgage Submission Voucher (FHLMC Form 13SF, Part V, Exhibit H).** FHLMC Form 13SF, as revised 8/78, must be used for all mortgages delivered to FHLMC. This form must be properly completed in detail before a mortgage can be processed by the Applicable FHLMC Regional Office.

The census tract number must be entered in the space provided in the Appraisal Data section of the Form 13 for each mortgage loan submitted. The number will be found on page one in the property identification section of the FHLMC appraisal forms (FHLMC Form 70, FHLMC Form 72 and FHLMC Form 465). This census tract space on Form 13 must be completed before a mortgage can be processed by FHLMC. Either enter the census tract number or check the appropriate block to indicate why there is no census tract number.

NOTE: *In the event of an assumption or other acceptable modification of the mortgage prior to the Delivery Date, all information requested on FHLMC Form 13SF must reflect the terms and parties to the transaction as of the Delivery Date.*

b. The Mortgage Note. For mortgages to be purchased in whole by FHLMC, the mortgage note must be the original and must bear an endorsement by Seller: PAY TO THE ORDER OF FEDERAL HOME LOAN MORTGAGE CORPORATION WITHOUT RECOURSE THIS _____ DAY OF _____, 19____.

(month)

_____
(Name of Seller-Endorser)

_____
(Signature of Duly Authorized Officer)

_____
(Typed Name and Title of Signatory)

Such endorsement "Without Recourse" shall in no way affect Seller's repurchase obligations under the Purchase Documents. The chain of endorsements must be complete from original lender shown on the mortgage note to FHLMC.

FIGURE 11-1a

For mortgages to be purchased in part by FHLMC, a clearly legible copy of the face of the mortgage note must be delivered and, if not closed in Seller's name, a clearly legible copy of the back of the mortgage note as well, in order to show all endorsements from original payee to Seller.

÷ c. **Residential Loan Application.** Seller must use a Residential Loan Application, FHLMC Form 65 (see Section 3.402). The application must be signed and dated by the Borrower(s) as shown on the note and information entered as provided by the Borrower(s).

If the Mortgaged Premises are currently owned by other than the original Borrower(s), Seller must submit a Residential Loan Application (the date the loan was assumed determines which application form is required) and a credit report on the current Borrower(s) and a certification of the terms of sale of the Mortgaged Premises.

÷ d. **Credit Report.** The credit report must be dated within ninety (90) days of the date of the note or assumption agreement, if any.

÷ e. **Verification of Employment and Income.** Written verification(s) of employment and all income reported on the Mortgage Submission Voucher (FHLMC Form 13SF) is required. In the case of self-employed Borrower, the verification must be either acceptable financial statements or Federal income tax returns.

÷ f. **Residential Appraisal Report.** Seller must use the appropriate FHLMC appraisal report:

(1) Residential Appraisal Report, FHLMC Form 70 (see Section 3.302a), or

(2) Appraisal Report-Small Residential Income Property, FHLMC Form 72 (see Section 3.302b), or

(3) Appraisal Report-Individual Condominium or PUD Unit, FHLMC Form 465 (see Section 3.302d and Section 3.501j).

g. **Two Clear Descriptive Photographs.** One photograph should be a front view of the Mortgaged Premises, clearly showing the completed improvements, and the second a street scene showing neighboring improvements. (The two photographs must be originals and are to be attached to a separate sheet of paper.)

h. **Out-of-State Security.** In the event the Mortgaged Premises securing the note is outside the state of Seller's principal office, the first such out-of-state mortgage for each state submitted by Seller must be accompanied by an opinion of counsel, addressed to Seller and FHLMC, provided at Seller's expense, stating that:

(1) Counsel is licensed to practice law in the state where the Mortgaged Premises are located;

(2) Counsel has reviewed the procedure of Seller in originating, selling, servicing and enforcing mortgage loans in such state and all laws and documents relevant thereto;

(3) The mortgage is and will remain a valid first lien whether owned by Seller or by a subsequent purchaser, or by Seller in participation with another party;

(4) The mortgage note and mortgage are enforceable by Seller and transfer of the mortgage or any interest therein to any subsequent purchaser will not detract from its enforceability as a result of such transaction;

(5) No licensing or doing business requirements must be met by the Seller or subsequent purchaser as a result of the purchase and ownership of such mortgage note and mortgage by FHLMC, or, if any such requirements exist, such requirements apply only to Seller and have been fully complied with by Seller;

(6) No fees, taxes, or other charges, or any additional requirements of any nature are required to be paid, or met, by Seller or FHLMC.

i. **Flexible Payment Loan.** In the event that the Home Mortgage purchased in whole or in part by FHLMC is a Flexible Payment Loan, Seller must indicate on the Mortgage Submission Voucher (FHLMC Form 13SF, Part V, Exhibit H) for that particular mortgage, the following information in *Flexible Payment Loan* block of the *Note Data* section—"$_____ Minimum Monthly Pymt. _____ **Months**" to indicate the amount and term of the reduced installments during the initial term.

The amount entered in the *Monthly Installment Principal and Interest Only* block must reflect the amount due each month after the initial period.

j. **Planned Unit Developments and Condominiums.** If the mortgage covers a unit in a PUD or condominium:

(1) FHLMC's Appraisal Report — Individual Condominium or PUD Unit (FHLMC Form 465, Part V, Exhibit KK) must be used for all PUD or condominium mortgages closed after November 1, 1974. It is not necessary to submit Addendum A of the Appraisal form if 70% or more of the units in the project have been sold to bona fide pur-

FIGURE 11-1b

249

chasers; also, Addendum B need not be submitted if the project is one as to which developer control has terminated and whose Homeowners Association has been controlled by unit owners for at least two years. For PUD or condominium mortgages closed before November 1, 1974, the appraisal form used by Seller must be acceptable to FHLMC.

(2) Seller agrees to submit with the delivery of the first mortgage loan in each Class I PUD or Class I condominium project a certification, signed by an authorized officer of Seller, of compliance with the warranties set out in Section 3.207a for Condominium Home Mortgages and Section 3.208a for PUD Home Mortgages. In the event Seller cannot execute such a certification, the Seller shall submit, prior to delivery of the first mortgage, a certification except for those warranties for which Seller specifically requests and recommends a waiver or modification. This certification (and waiver request, if any) must be in the form set out in Part V, Exhibit M and should outline the reasons for recommending either modification or waiver. Seller may also be required to deliver to FHLMC a legal opinion, addressed to Seller and FHLMC, unconditionally confirming the legal conclusions contained in the certification (and waiver request, if any).

(3) If such mortgage is also on a leasehold estate, Seller agrees to submit to FHLMC a Multifamily or Condominium Ground Lease Analysis (FHLMC Form 461, Part V, Exhibit L).

NOTE: In the case of a condominium project on a leasehold see also Sections 3.207a(8) for Class I and 3.207b(8) for Class II and a PUD on a leasehold see also Sections 3.208a(7) for Class I and 3.208b(7) for Class II.

† **k. Mortgage Loans Assumed or Otherwise Modified.** In the event the mortgage delivered to FHLMC is the current obligation of a Borrower(s) other than the original maker(s) or the mortgage and note have been otherwise modified, Seller agrees to submit, in each case, the original modifying instrument if the mortgage is offered for purchase in whole to FHLMC or legible copies of the modifying instruments if the mortgage is offered for purchase in part to FHLMC. Seller need not submit a modifying instrument which, by the terms of such instrument, ceases to be effective upon purchase by FHLMC.

l. Mortgage Loans More Than One Year Old. In the event the mortgage delivered to FHLMC

was closed more than one year prior to the Purchase Contract Date of Acceptance, the Seller agrees to submit the following documentation:

(1) Statement of mortgage loan payment record covering the twelve (12) months preceding the Purchase Contract Date of Acceptance;

(2) Seller/Servicer 1-4 Family Property Inspection Report (FHLMC Form 452, Part V, Exhibit P), properly completed in detail, with current photographs of Mortgaged Premises and street scene attached;

(3) A Residential Loan Application (FHLMC Form 65, Part V, Exhibit I), a credit report on Borrower and a certification of the terms of sale of the Mortgaged Premises whenever the Mortgaged Premises are currently owned by other than the original Borrower.

m. Other Documents. Seller agrees to submit such other documents as FHLMC may request.

3.502   Retention of Conventional Home Mortgage Loan File by Seller/Servicer.

The Seller/Servicer agrees to maintain, during the time that FHLMC owns the mortgage loan or a participation interest therein and thereafter for a minimum of three years from the date the mortgage loan is fully paid or, if the mortgage loan is accelerated, six years from the date the mortgage loan is paid, the entire mortgage loan file, which must contain the original of any documentation submitted to FHLMC (except where the original documents are retained by FHLMC) and the additional documents specified below:

a. The mortgage instruments.

(1) Original mortgage or deed of trust, complete with recordation notation. In those jurisdictions where the applicable law requires the production of the original mortgage or deed of trust to secure a release of the mortgage or deed of trust, or the production of the original mortgage or deed of trust to secure a release is commonly required in the area in which the Mortgaged Premises are located, Seller/Servicer agrees to maintain a certified copy of the original mortgage or deed of trust, complete with recordation notation.

(2) Copy of Note, when original is submitted to FHLMC.

b. For mortgages purchased in whole by FHLMC, assignment of the mortgage to FHLMC in proper form and evidencing recordation, except as provided below:

(1) The assignment of the mortgage is not required to be executed and/or recorded, if such

FIGURE 11-1c

250

recordation is not necessary under applicable law to perfect FHLMC's first lien interest and is not commonly required by private institutional mortgage investors in the area in which the Mortgaged Premises are located. However, Seller agrees to execute and/or record an assignment of the mortgage at Seller's expense upon request by FHLMC.

(2) Where permitted by applicable law, the assignment instrument may cover more than one mortgage, provided all requirements of the Purchase Documents have been met.

c. Title insurance policy or other evidence of title.

d. Plat of survey meeting the requirements of Section 3.204.

✝ **e.** Hazard insurance policies properly endorsed or suitable evidence of insurance as described in Part I, Section 2.108 of the Servicers' Guide and copies of any necessary notices to insurance carriers (as provided in Section 3.203f) unless Seller carries mortgage impairment insurance instead of maintaining possession of hazard insurance policies. (See Section 2.108 of the Servicers' Guide regarding possession by Servicer of hazard insurance policies.)

f. Stock certificate entitling Borrower to an adequate supply of water, duly endorsed to FHLMC, if the Mortgaged Premises are dependent for assurance of an adequate supply of water upon a water or irrigation company that supplies water only to its shareholders.

g. Closing statement, verification of employment and income, and verification or acceptable evidence of source and amount of down payment and prepaid items to substantiate such information as shown on the mortgage application.

h. Mortgage insurance policy or proof of insurance, if the mortgage is required to be insured.

i. Documents affecting leasehold estate, if any, securing the indebtedness.

j. Legal opinion, if any, addressed to Seller and FHLMC, unconditionally confirming the legal conclusions contained in the certification (and waiver request, if any) of compliance with the warranties regarding a Class I condominium project or Class I PUD.

k. All other documents constituting the mortgage file and such other documents as may be requested by FHLMC or as are commonly maintained in mortgage files by private institutional mortgage investors or servicers.

For each mortgage covering an individual Condominium or PUD Unit, Seller agrees to possess (but need not maintain in the individual mortgage file), such other documentation, in addition to the above, with respect to the condominium or PUD project, as required by FHLMC, e.g., the Declaration of Condominium (or Master Deed or similar instrument) and the bylaws and regulations of the condominium project, and Seller agrees to provide such documentation to FHLMC at any time and at Seller's expense.

3.503 Microfilm Copies.

With respect to the documents to be maintained by the Seller/Servicer, except for the documents listed in 3.502(a), such documents may be maintained in the form of microfilm or microfiche provided that:

a. The copy was made in the regular course of business pursuant to an established written policy of the Seller/Servicer applying to all of its loan files;

b. The copy was made by a process that accurately reproduces or forms a durable medium for reproducing the original;

c. The copy is satisfactorily identified;

d. The Seller/Servicer maintains the copies in a manner that will permit ready transfer of legibly printed hard copies of material relating to the loans serviced for FHLMC;

e. Seller/Servicer maintains the copies in the same offices where the loan files are maintained;

f. Reader/copiers are maintained in the offices where copies are kept which can be used by FHLMC representatives.

FIGURE 11-1d

7. What is meant by the *apparent age* of a house as it may be determined by an appraiser?

8. How does a lender adjust the amount of a loan and the interest rate when underwriting a resort property or a second home?

9. How does the topography of a neighborhood influence a lender considering a property loan?

10. Discuss the additional problems associated with a condominium loan that would not pertain to a single-family residence.

11. What dollar limits are placed on residential loans and by whom are they placed?

Seller-Financed Home Mortgages

As the early 1980s brought ever higher mortgage interest rates to historic levels, it became increasingly difficult to sell almost any real estate property without some financing assistance by the seller. In 1982 the National Association of Realtors reported that over 60 percent of the homes sold that year involved some form of seller financing. To give an idea of the size of this market, seller-financed loans were expected to grow from $80 billion in 1982 to $120 billion by 1986. A whole new category of loans developed under the umbrella name of "creative financing." The thrust of creative financing schemes has been to soften the blow of high costs to the buyer while providing a method of taking the seller off the hook as soon as possible. To reach this difficult objective, the creative repayment plans offered a variety of ways to reduce monthly payments in the early years while offering the buyer only short-term financing that would pay off to the seller in a few years. The "few years" was generally accepted as the time span needed for the market to turn around and mortgage money again to be available at reasonable cost. The record is suggesting that creative financing creates about as many downstream problems as it solves at the outset.

First, let's look at some of the methods that have developed to provide seller financing, mostly but not entirely limited to home sales. Later in this chapter, the entry of secondary market purchasers into the field of seller financing will be explained. Sellers are now able to undertake even second mortgage loans, recovering most of their cash by sale of the loan through approved lenders, to a secondary market purchaser. Further, private mortgage insurance companies are extending their coverage to include first and second mortgage seller-financed loans. Still, there are a number of sellers who will not be willing, or the buyers may be unable, to qualify for default insurance or secondary market sale and need to use their own ingenuity to structure a financing package. Following are the basic concepts around which individual sellers have structured their financing assistance in order to sell a house.

Basic Seller-Assist Plans

Reduced Interest Rates

Seller-financed mortgages are generally offered at or below market interest rates. Since one reason for the seller assistance is to encourage the sale of the property, one inducement is to offer a lower-than-market interest rate. If this is accepted, it amounts to a reduction in the price of the property. As the economy falls into a decline in many areas of the country, seller-reduced interest rates have been one method used to lower housing costs. It is possible that a seller will endeavor to recoup some of the lower interest charged by increasing the sales price of the house. It is a matter of negotiation between buyer and seller and a big test for the real estate agent attempting to bring the two parties together.

Sellers are not as apt to ask for an adjustable rate interest clause as would depository institutions because of the greater complexity with calculation of the changing mortgage payment amount. Further, a seller does not have to deal with a cost of funds factor as does a depository institution. Nevertheless, there is no other reason that a seller cannot structure a mortgage take-back loan with an adjustable rate of interest. From a sales standpoint, a seller-held mortgage granting the right to adjust an interest rate, even though tied to a recognized interest rate index, could create serious doubts for the buyer and would be less acceptable than a fixed interest rate.

Monthly Payment Adjustment

There are several popular mortgage repayment plans that offer the buyer a substantially lower monthly payment in the early years. These are mainly graduated payment plans (like the FHA Section 245) and buy-down mortgages. The purpose of such plans is not just to make them more attractive for the buyer but also to permit regulated lenders to grant the buyer loan qualification based on a lower income amount than would otherwise be permissible. The need for formal qualification in this regard is not so important with a seller-financed arrangement. A seller may find it advantageous simply from a sales point of view to arbitrarily lower monthly payments in the early years with annual increases that ultimately provide for a reasonable return on the seller's mortgage loan. (To review how these payments are structured see Chapter 4, "Alternative Mortgages".)

Buyer Qualification.   Certainly one of the major problems in handling a seller-assist transaction is the proper qualification of the buyer as to ability to pay and credit-worthiness. In the eagerness of both the seller and his or her agent to consummate a transaction, there is a tendency to overlook sound lending practices. It is in this area that the new (since 1982) procedures offered by mortgage insurance companies and secondary market purchasers can prove so helpful. For the same reason that a borrower tends to repay a bank loan before a loan by an individual, a buyer-borrower is more likely to accept and comply with the standard procedures and requirements set forth by a professional lender.

First Mortgage Refinancing

It is sometimes advantageous and at other times simply necessary for a seller to undertake refinancing to make a sale. For those properties with no mortgage lien (free and clear), the seller can readily take back a first mortgage as security for a note financing the sale. If there is an existing mortgage paid down to a relatively small amount compared with the property value, it may benefit the parties to the sales transaction to use a down payment to pay off the remaining balance on the existing loan. Thus, the seller-financed amount would hold first lien priority in the event of any later problems with repayment. First mortgage loans represent a high-quality investment for a number of people, and if so, the term for such a loan could be longer, like 20 or 30 years. But if the seller-financing is involuntary (forced upon the seller as the only practical way to sell the property), the loan will be structured for a short term, maybe three to seven years, and will most likely include a due-on-sale clause. Thus, any transfer of interest in the property by the buyer to a new interest owner would require full payment of the loan. This is not unreasonable; after all the seller is not in the business of making mortgage loans. However, short-term loans and positive due-on-sale covenants make reselling the property far more difficult.

There are several ways that interest charges can be assessed with a seller-assist transaction. These are considered as a part of the second mortgage and wrap-around mortgage methods, as explained next, but could apply to first mortgages or a contract for deed.

Second Mortgage, Simple Interest

One of the oldest procedures is to write a second mortgage in favor of the seller for a term as long, or longer, than the remaining term of the existing mortgage. The buyer-borrower under this form assumes the existing mortgage (becomes fully liable for it) and agrees to amortize the second mortgage at a constant-level rate using the same basic payment tables as for the existing mortgage. The interest rate is normally somewhat higher for the second mortgage as there is always an increased risk. But the calculation of payments is based on a simple interest rate, the same as for a normal first mortgage loan, and thus the buyer-borrower benefits from much lower monthly payments than found in some other procedures.

Second Mortgage, Installment Interest Rates

In the past few years, a number of states have authorized their lenders to make second mortgage loans on equity purchases of houses and allow interest to be calculated at add-on rates. The term of the loan might vary with the amount of the loan. Typical of this limit would be a $3,500 loan with a term of 3 years, or up to a $40,000 loan with a term of 20 years. The add-on rates are calculated in the same manner as they would be for a car loan. (Take the annual interest for the initial amount of the loan, times the number of years in the term offered, plus the principal amount of the loan; divide this sum by the number of payments anticipated, and the result is the amount of each monthly payment.) The result allows the lender an effective return substantially higher than the nominal interest rate. For example, an add-on rate calculated at 8 percent produces a yield to the lender of 12 percent to 14 percent depending on the term of the loan. The same procedure may be used by a seller to calculate the payments due on a second mortgage loan offered to sell a house (or any other property). The truth-in-lending laws (Regulation Z of the Federal Reserve Bank) require that a lender disclose the actual cost of money that is loaned by adding all charges associated with the financing and then converting the result to an Annual Percentage Rate (APR). An individual selling his or her own property is not classified as a "provider of credit" under the truth-in-lending rules and therefore is not required to provide a disclosure statement for a seller-financed transaction. However, if an installment-type add-on interest rate is used, the buyer should be informed of the higher effective interest rate that it costs so as to avoid any appearance of deception.

Second Mortgage, Balloon Payment

Since many home buyers today are anticipating only a few years of occupancy, a new payment procedure has developed. This method establishes the payments on the second mortgage at rates used to amortize a 30-year loan but requires full payment of the balance due at the end of 5 years. Of course, the terms can be adjusted in this procedure as may be agreed between lender and borrower; that is, the term might be 7 or 10 years and the amortization rate selected could be 20, 25, or 30 years. Another clause sometimes found in this form of mortgage is that a subsequent sale of the house requires full payment of the balance due to the second mortgage holder.

Wrap-Around Mortgage

The typical wrap procedure described earlier in this text may be used in a house sale with any of the three methods listed above to calculate the interest to be charged. While the normal wrap method does acknowledge an existing mortgage in the terms of "subject to" (the buyer acknowledges but does not accept liability for the existing mortgage), a sale of the property does take place and title is vested in the buyer. The new buyer has accepted liability for payment of the wrap-around mortgage, which includes the full amount of the existing mortgage. Because it is a sale, the wrap-around procedure most probably makes the transaction subject to a due-on-sale clause that may be a part of the existing mortgage. In other words, a wrap-around mortgage should not be considered a means of bypassing the right of a lender to approve a sale of the mortgaged property if the first mortgage terms so require.

Contract for Deed

An owner may sell his or her house under a contract for deed (see Chapter 3). Under this procedure, legal title to the property is *not* passed to the buyer until the payments have been made. The payments may be calculated to pay off the purchase price in 10 or 15 years, or the payments may approximate a rental charge with a balloon requirement for the principal balance due in, say, 5 years. The basic purpose of this procedure is to retain substantial control of the property in the hands of the seller (who still holds legal title) while the buyer awaits a probable transfer to another job, or perhaps a time to come when mortgage money is more reasonably priced. The buyer under a contract for deed should be cautioned that delivery of the title after payments are made is dependent on the seller's solvency and ability to make good on the conveyance of title when it becomes due. Since a contract for deed does not call for an immediate transfer of title, questions have been raised in a number of states as to whether or not this comprises an actual sale of property and is thus subject to the right of a lender to approve the sale (due-on-sale clause) where such covenant is a part of an existing mortgage loan. A seller undertaking this procedure should review the existing mortgage terms and the applicable rulings with competent legal counsel.

Combinations

Imaginative real estate brokers, mortgage loan representatives, and home sellers have developed many unique combinations of the above suggested procedures to accommodate a buyer and seller when normal channels of financing are unavailable. Often, the combination is a financing of the equity interest with part of the money advanced by an institutional lender and part coming from the seller. Thus, a combination could consist of an existing mortgage loan, an add-on second mortgage held by a local savings association, and a wrap-around of both notes with additional financing held by the seller. There is great flexibility in the system—but it does take qualified borrowers who can handle the larger payments.

Other Methods of Reducing Monthly Payments

At best, plans that reduce initial monthly payments offer stop-gap solutions to the basic problem; that of high interest rates and high housing costs. Nevertheless, many creative ideas have been spawned in the sale of houses to enable a buyer to qualify for a loan that might otherwise be out of reach. (The major designs have been described in Chapter 4.) Many of these concepts have been applied to the sale of houses. Following is a review of seller-assist plans that reduce the initial monthly payment amount along with some of the problems involved.

Interest Only

While the average monthly house payment may consist of less than 5 percent to principal and 95 percent to interest, home buyers tend to believe an "interest only" payment means a somewhat better deal than it is. It is an inducement to the buyer and amounts to very little less for the seller. A feature of almost all interest only payment plans is they are short term, maybe one to three years. A loan without some provision for amortization of the principal could prove difficult to sell. Thus, recovery for the home seller is tied to the ability of the buyer to meet the full principal payment when it comes due. Like many of the lower initial payment loans, one reason for undertaking them is that the parties involved anticipate easier financing conditions within the limited time frame of the loan. Experience has shown this is not always realistic.

Buy-Down Mortgages

The concept of the buy-down, as more fully explained in Chapter 4, has its greatest appeal to a home builder seeking better ways to attract qualified buyers. The home builder is not financing the sale; the money is expected to come from a down payment plus a mortgage loan made by a mortgage lending company. In order to buy down the initial monthly payments, the builder accepts a discount from the proceeds of the loan. That is, the $3 to $5 thousand cost of the buy-down is a reduction in the loan funded. This is not so with a home seller who finances all or a portion of the transaction. The home seller does not have an "up-front" cash requirement. He or she simply accepts monthly payments calculated on a lower interest rate. For example, if the seller financing amounts to $50,000 and the agreement is for payments to be amortized on a 30-year basis at an initial 3 percent reduction from a 12 percent interest rate, increasing 1 percent each year to the 12 percent rate, the following payments would be specified in the note (note the change in interest rate):

1st year's payment @ 9% rate $402.32
2nd year's payment @ 10% rate $438.79
3rd year's payment @ 11% rate $476.17
4th year's payment @ 12% rate $514.31 and to maturity.

Keep in mind that the seller considers the interest actually received during the tax year as ordinary income, regardless of the rate shown on the face of the note.

Graduated Payment Mortgage (GPM)

The graduated payment design and the buy-down plans are quite similar in their initial payment procedures and the purposes. The difference comes in how the payment amount is calculated and most likely also in the term of the loan. The reduction required for the initial monthly payment amount for the GPM is not based on a change of interest rate, rather it is an arbitrary amount established so as to permit consistent annual increases (like 7½ percent each year) until the payment amount is sufficient to fully amortize the loan over the remaining term. GPM mortgages are generally long term and fully amortized. Buy-downs can be for short terms with a large principal payment (a balloon payment) due within a few years. There is another disadvantage in a GPM plan for the home seller financing a sale, and that is the initial payment amounts are usually insufficient to pay all of the interest due. The unpaid interest is accrued and added to the principal amount periodically. (See calculations for FHA's Section 245 GPM in Chapter 8.) Note that the unpaid interest is not a tax deduction for the home buyer under such a mortgage, nor is the unpaid interest classified as income to the home seller for cash basis accounting. So far, seller-financed GPM plans have not been accepted by secondary market purchasers, while buy-down plans can be sold (see later discussion in this chapter on sale of seller-financed loans).

Shared Appreciation Mortgage

As explained in Chapter 4, a home seller could accept a lower initial interest rate plus a share of future appreciation. The example used earlier is a situation wherein the lender accepts a 10 percent interest rate, instead of a current market 15 percent, and claims one-third of any property appreciation. Of course, the idea has a much greater appeal for the home-seller/lender when property values show consistent increases. However, it does present another method of reducing the initial cost requirement to buy a home. Should the house be sold within the five- to ten-year term for calculation of appreciation, the determination of the amount (of appreciation) would not be quite so difficult. Should the buyer under a shared appreciation agreement opt to remain in the house, an appraisal would become necessary when the time comes to calculate the shared appreciation. If the home seller has moved to another city, the details involved could present some problems and travel costs.

Land Leases

Historically, land leases have been considered low risk and often command rentals at rates less than the cost of financing. A land lease is most advantageous to the property user if it can be arranged at a lower cost than a purchase. In some areas of the country, homes are being sold with the seller retaining outright ownership of the land and arranging for a long-term lease of the land to the home buyer. The buyer needs to borrow less money if he or she is purchasing only the building.

To exemplify such a lease arrangement let us assume that a buyer wants to purchase a $100,000 property. The land is valued at $40,000, and the building at $60,000. A 30-year loan at 14 percent interest for $40,000 (the cost of the land) amounts to a monthly payment of $474. If the seller will accept, say $250 per month rental on the land, the buyer can reduce his monthly payment by $224. A leasehold mortgage loan can then be arranged to handle the purchase of the building itself. Payment on the land lease would normally be made to the lender as an escrow deposit with the money passed on to the landowner at periodic intervals. Thus the lender has an assurance of proper payment in a manner similar to that used in the handling of property taxes. The lender's security for the loan would be a leasehold mortgage. As described here, the land is not subordinated to the leasehold.

Why would anyone agree to lease, say a $40,000 tract of land, for less than a going market rate of return? There could be several reasons:

1. The lower total monthly payment might qualify a buyer with smaller income and enable the property to be sold.
2. The land value most likely represents an inflated market value figure rather than the original cash cost amount.
3. The land remains within the seller's family as a tangible asset.
4. Appreciation to both land and the improvements thereon ultimately accrue to the benefit of the landowner when the lease expires. Thus, the true rate of return could be much greater, depending on the effect of inflation. (*Note*: There are land leases where the landowner agrees to reimburse the tenant for the appreciated value of improvements when the lease terminates.)

Lease with Option to Buy. A lease may be arranged for the whole property (or the land if it only is leased) which grants the tenant a right to purchase the property at a set price within some specified time period. The purpose could be to allow possession immediately without a long-term, high-cost monthly payment commitment. The hope is that better financing might be arranged at a later date.

Caveat for the Seller. If a personal residence is transferred under a lease with option to buy and the option is not exercised in less than a year, the IRS has ruled that the lease terminates the seller's qualification for a personal residence. The house becomes rental property and no longer is eligible for deferment of the capital gain tax upon sale.

Seller-Assist Financing Aids

While nothing short of lower interest rates or lower housing costs will alleviate the underlying problem, there have been two new developments which offer substantial assistance to a seller who must furnish financing assistance in order to sell a property. These are:

1. Default insurance offered on seller-assist first or second mortgage loans.
2. A plan offered by the Federal National Mortgage Association to buy (convert to cash) first or second mortgage loans taken by sellers.

The importance of these two aids now available to home sellers is that it brings professional lenders with all of their credit knowledge into the handling of this type of loan. Also, it offers to the seller an option to sell the loan on a fair basis for cash. Few home sellers are in the business of making mortgage loans and they no longer need to be placed in the position of an involuntary lender. Following is a discussion of the two kinds of aids available to home sellers.

Default Insurance for Seller-Financed Loans

In the Spring of 1982, private mortgage insurance companies offered to insure seller-assist loans against default by the buyer-borrower. Qualification of the applicant is generally the same as for regular private mortgage insurance. Default insurance is not offered directly to the home seller. It can only be obtained through an approved mortgage lender called a "servicer." The servicer acts as an agent for the *home seller* and handles the necessary qualification procedures for both the property and the buyer to obtain an insurance commitment certificate. Servicers work under a service contract with the insurance company. This contract may vary in different states due to variances in state insurance requirements.

Underwriting Guidelines for Home Seller Coverage. While there is some difference in the coverage offered by insurance companies, the following are fairly standard guidelines for insuring seller-financed loans:

1. Each loan must be secured by a one- to four-family owner-occupied property.
2. The maximum loan-to-value ratio (LTVR) is 90 percent. This means a minimum of 10 percent cash equity by the buyer.

3. Qualification of the buyer-borrower's income is based on the same debt-to-income ratio as that applied to standard lender-financed loans. Generally, these limits are now being used:
   a. The total mortgage payment, including default insurance, cannot exceed 33 percent of the borrower's income.
   b. The total mortgage payment plus long-term installment obligations cannot exceed 38 percent of the borrower's income.
4. The same coverage that applies to standard lender financing also applies to seller-financed first lien mortgages and land contracts in most states.
5. Seller-financed second lien mortgages are also eligible for insurance coverage in most states with coverages ranging from 25 percent to 100 percent.
6. The application form and documentation needed to qualify a seller-financed loan for insurance is the same as that used for standard lender-financed loans. Generally, in the space calling for "type of loan," the applicant indicates "seller-financed."

Claim Procedures. In case of a default on an insured loan, the home seller is offered the same coverage as for standard lender loans for either first or second mortgage coverage. The claim amount includes the unpaid mortgage balance, interest to date of claim, reasonable attorney's fees, and property preservation costs. Following is an example of how a typical claim would be settled on a seller-financed wrap-around mortgage as offered by Mortgage Guaranty Insurance Corporation.

Homeseller: * Insured Seller Financing

Sample Claim: Seller-Financed Wrap-around Lien

The sample claim shown below illustrates the default protection Homeseller offers. This example pertains to a seller-financed wrap-around mortgage or land contract with an underlying lien. The seller is responsible for maintaining the underlying lien.

Facts which apply to Example:

1.	Purchase price	$85,000.00
2.	Down payment	$10,000.00
3.	Seller-financed original wraparound loan amount	$75,000.00
4.	Loan-to-value ratio	88%
5.	Interest rate on wraparound	14%
6.	Wraparound loan term	15 years
7.	Original first mortgage amount	$50,000.00
8.	Interest rate on underlying mortgage	8%
9.	Original underlying mortgage loan term	30 years
10.	12 payments made	
11.	25% MGIC insurance coverage	
12.	Six months (180 days) from initial default by buyer to date of claim, outstanding principal balance of first mortgage at date of claim.	$41,905.50

(continued)

Claim for Loss

1.	Principal balance (from Amortization Table)	$73,414.50
2.	Interest (180 days)	5,139.00
3.	Attorney's fees	750.00
4.	Real estate taxes advanced	600.00
5.	Insurance premiums advanced	150.00
6.	Preservation of property	450.00
7.	Disbursements	300.00
	Total Claim	$80,803.50

MGIC, at its option, would settle this claim through one of the following three methods:

Percentage Payment Option (25% coverage)

Under this option, MGIC would reimburse the servicer on behalf of the seller for $20,200.88. The seller would retain title to the property.

Acquisition Option

Under this option, MGIC would either assume or pay off the first mortgage, taking title to the property. The outstanding balance on the first mortgage would be deducted from the total claim. MGIC would pay the balance of the claim to the servicer on behalf of the seller.

Total claim	$ 80,803.50
Less net of outstanding balance of the first mortgage at date of claim	−41,905.50
Claim payment	$ 38,898.00

Pre-Sold Claim Option

Under this option, the property would be sold and the proceeds deducted from the total claim amount. MGIC would pay the balance of the claim to the servicer on behalf of the seller.

Total claim	$ 80,803.50
Less net proceeds of sale	−68,000.00
Claim payment	$ 12,803.50

Reproduced with the permission of Mortgage Guaranty Insurance Corporation, Milwaukee, Wisconsin
*Registered name for policies offering MGIC protection for seller-financed loans.

How to Secure Insurance Coverage. Insurance coverage against default on a seller-financed loan can only be obtained through an approved mortgage servicing company, that is, one holding a service contract with an insurance carrier. Who are these servicers? They would vary a little in different states but basically comprise those companies normally engaged in making residential mortgage loans. This includes mortgage companies, savings associations, mutual savings banks, and in some states, commercial banks. Not all mortgage lenders handle seller-financed insurance coverage so it is usually necessary to screen the local market. The home seller, or the listing real estate broker, can make the arrangements with the mortgage servicer company. In most cases it is a prudent step to turn buyer-borrower qualification over to a qualified professional. The mortgage servicer has all of the necessary instruments and documentation forms required by the insurance company and can see to it that they are properly completed and meet minimum standards. Credit reports and verifications are routinely handled by mortgage lenders which does relieve the seller of an important burden. The mortgage servicer charges a fee for preparation of the loan package. Further, the mortgage servicer handles monthly collections on behalf of the seller and earns a service fee for this continuing work also.

Secondary Market Purchase of Seller-Financed Loans

In June, 1982, the Federal National Mortgage Association (FNMA) announced plans to purchase seller-financed first and second mortgage loans. This step brings professionalism to the business of seller-financed transactions, opening the door to many home sellers seeking cash for the equity in their homes rather than taking a mortgage note with relatively small monthly payments. As too many home sellers have learned, creative financing ideas that have enabled homes to be sold at inflation-induced prices have also created many problems. Buyers have often overburdened themselves with high monthly payments anticipating increased income or continuing price increases in the property itself. These expectations have not always been realized, resulting in loan defaults. So the advent of a secondary market purchaser willing to pay cash for a seller-financed mortgage note is most important. How does a home seller qualify a loan for sale to FNMA?

How the Program Works. First of all, the home seller must contact an approved FNMA "seller/servicer" lender. These are mortgage companies, savings associations, mutual savings banks, or possibly commercial banks, who have qualified to do business with FNMA. While most mortgage lenders have met this standard, the home seller should screen the local companies and institutions—not all qualified seller/servicers will handle seller-financed transactions. Then the home seller arranges with the FNMA-approved lender to perform all the services associated with originating the loan. This includes necessary documentation such as credit and property appraisal reports. It relieves the home seller's problem of making a decision on the credit-worthiness of a prospective buyer. For this professional help, the seller/servicer will charge an origination fee. Normally, this charge is paid by the buyer-borrower as a cost of obtaining financing.

Eligible Loans. The seller-financed loan can be a first or second mortgage so long as the documentation is orginated by a FNMA-approved lender and meets FNMA's requirements at the time the loan is offered for sale to FNMA.

1. *For first mortgage loans.* For owner-occupied houses, financing can go as high as 95 percent of the current property value, or up to 80 percent if nonowner occupied. The maximum loan amount for a single family conventional mortgage is $107,000. (Two- to four-family homes have higher limits). Private mortgage insurance (see previous section) must be obtained on mortgages with loan-to-value ratios over 80 percent. The mortgage must be fully amortized over the term of the loan which cannot exceed 30 years. Both fixed rate and FNMA standard adjustable rate mortgages are eligible.

2. *For second mortgage loans.* For owner-occupied houses, the total of the first and second mortgage cannot exceed 80 percent of the current property value, 70 percent for nonowner-occupied property. At this writing, the maximum loan permitted by FNMA on any one single family property is $107,000. Thus, if FNMA owns the first mortgage, the combination of the first and second cannot exceed $107,000. But if FNMA does *not* own the first mortgage, then the second mortgage cannot exceed $107,000.

   Private mortgage insurance is required if the combined first and second mortgages exceed 65 percent of the home value. PMI is required on the top 25 percent of the second mortgage.

   There is greater flexibility allowed in repayment for a second mortgage loan than a first mortgage loan. Second mortgages may be fully amortizing (payments sufficient to fully pay the loan within its term) or partially amortizing with the remaining balance due at maturity (a balloon payment). Fully amortized loans may offer repayment terms of 3 to 15 years. Partially amortized loans may offer terms of 5 to 15 years with payment amounts calculated as though the loan amortized in a period up to 30 years. Since partially amortized loans do not pay the full amount of the principal within the monthly payment amount, the full balance due must be paid in a lump sum at the end of the loan term.

How to Sell the Loan to FNMA. Whenever a home seller wishes to sell his or her loan to FNMA (convert it to cash), the seller/servicer who originated the loan must be notified. The seller/servicer can then determine just what the FNMA required yield is at that time. Generally, the FNMA purchase price is based on current mortgage market rates. If the interest rate on the mortgage is the same as, or higher than, prevailing mortgage interest rates at the time of sale to FNMA, the home seller will receive the full remaining principal balance of the loan. If the interest rate on the mortgage is lower than the prevailing mortgage interest rate, the seller will receive a discounted amount.

EXAMPLE

If a first mortgage is being sold:

Outstanding mortgage balance is	$80,000
Interest rate on mortgage is	13%

At the time of sale:

FNMA requires	13%
Home seller receives	$80,000*

Or:

Outstanding mortgage balance is	$80,000
Interest rate on mortgage is	13%

At the time of sale:

FNMA requires	15%
Home seller receives	$71,288*

*Less lender fees to be subtracted.

FNMA reserves the right to review the loan once again at the time it is offered for sale to FNMA to make sure it meets eligibility requirements. FNMA will also require a satisfactory payment record for the loan.

Cost to the Home Seller. FNMA does not set fee requirements for charges made by the seller/servicer who acts as an agent for the home seller. The fees are negotiable and could include:

1. An origination fee for preparing the loan package and obtaining the necessary verifications.
2. A fee for selling the loan to FNMA should the home seller want to convert the loan to cash.
3. A service fee for collecting the monthly payments and handling the tax and insurance escrows. The service fee is usually stated as a percent of the loan amount and, if the home buyer is to pay this cost, the fee is normally included in the interest rate charged on the loan when initially negotiated.

In conclusion then, the home seller would be well advised to shop around among the seller/servicers to obtain the best prices even though the home buyer will most likely end up paying the fees.

Questions for Discussion

1. Discuss the difference between a buy-down mortgage and a graduated payment mortage as to how the initial monthly payments are calculated.

2. What are some of the problems a home seller faces in taking back a mortgage loan as part of the consideration?

3. Does a Contract for Deed bypass the requirements of a due-on-sale clause? Why?

4. Describe a buy-down mortgage and give an example of how the payments can be calculated.

5. List the disadvantages that you see in a shared appreciation mortgage.

6. Why would a home seller want to sell the house and lease the land under it? Is there an advantage for the buyer?

7. How does a home seller obtain private mortgage insurance against default on a seller-financed transaction?

8. On what basis will FNMA buy a seller-financed mortgage; that is, what will they pay for it?

Loan Analysis of Income Properties

General Information

Loans against all types of income properties require the same type of background information as would be needed for analyzing a residential loan. This information package would include a study of the location, the construction and other physical characteristics of the building, the local zoning laws and deed restrictions that may be involved, and the economic potential of the region and local area. In addition, and of greater importance to most investors, is an analysis of the income and expense factors. The lender wants to know how much of the total income is, or will be, available to pay the debt service—those periodic payments of principal and interest on the mortgage loan.

Financial Statements

Income properties are, of course, business operations, and investors must keep adequate financial records to make management decisions as well as to support income tax reports. Two basic statements are prepared for this purpose:

1. *Balance sheet.* A listing of all assets in one column is balanced against all liabilities plus net worth in the other column. The difference between the total assets and the total liabilities is the net worth, or equity.

2. *Profit and loss statement.* The statement first totals all income received for the reporting period (daily, monthly, yearly), then deducts all expenses with the difference being profit or (loss).

A third form of statement, called an *operating statement*, is found in real property investments. This is actually a profit and loss statement without the owner's special tax accounting figures included. Operating statements seldom include property depreciation or any special tax deductions to which the owner may be entitled.

Preparation of Financial Statements

There are no required standards for the preparation of financial statements. How the information is presented, how it is verified, and the conclusions that may be drawn from it are pretty much in the hands of whoever is preparing the statement. However, there are requirements for accountants, who are identified with professional designations. All states offer the designation of *Certified Public Accountant* (CPA), and some states award a *Public Accountant* designation for persons who meet less stringent qualifications than those required for a CPA. For a CPA designation, there are educational and experience requirements plus a comprehensive examination. Only accountants with a CPA designation may prepare *audited* financial statements. An audited statement is one that has been prepared from figures verified by the CPA: thus, it is the most acceptable form of statement for lenders.

Two other forms of financial statements are commonly utilized in the real estate business: (1) stabilized statements and (2) *pro forma* statements. The *stabilized* statement is one that has been adjusted to more accurately reflect the true operations. The adjustments are made for income or expense items that have not been accurately reflected in the time period covered by the statement. The Internal Revenue Service permits taxpayers to keep records on either a cash basis (accounting only for the cash actually received and disbursed during the tax year) or on an accrual basis. The latter basis counts as income when a charge is billed, and an expense when the liability is incurred, rather than when paid. Either method can require adjustment to reflect more accurately the true picture of a specific time period. Any adjustments made in such statements should be fully explained, with proper footnotes to avoid any appearance of deception.

A *pro forma* statement is essentially a projection. A *pro forma* is used to develop the income and expenses that will be generated by a proposed development—figures that enable a lender to evaluate the cash flow potential of a new project. Or, a *pro forma* may be used to assess the impact of refinancing or additional financing on an existing project.

For example, what might be the effect of building space for ten new stores added to an existing shopping center?

Feasibility Report

The analysis of a new project investment often includes an additional study termed a *feasibility report.* By definition the word *feasible* means "capable of being used successfully." Therefore, the purpose of such a study is to ascertain the probable success or failure of the project under consideration.

There is a similarity in the background information needed for both a property appraisal and a feasibility report. The difference lies in the focus of conclusions regarding the timing and the usage of the property. A feasibility report seeks conclusions on the profitability of future operations, whereas the appraisal relates future profitability to present property value. A feasibility report is a preliminary study conducted before plans are drawn or financing is obtained. The information is used to guide the builder-developer and also serves as additional material for a potential lender to analyze.

A feasibility study draws certain conclusions concerning cost estimates and then analyzes the market available for the particular project under consideration, such as an apartment building, office building, or other project. The detailed market analysis is the real meat of the study because it attempts to determine the probability of future income. Almost any income property can be projected into an appearance of profitability by using an arbitrarily high figure that may or may not be substantiated by the actual market available. It is the purpose of the market study portion of the feasibility report to show by actual canvass or survey, by charts of population and business growth, by analysis of present and future traffic and transportation patterns, and by actual comparisons of occupancy and income of comparable existing income properties whether or not a need exists for the proposed project.

Feasibility reports are not guided by any professional group pressing for accuracy and integrity and are therefore subject to a wide variety of interpretations. The best reports are prepared by experts in marketing analysis who have no personal interest in the subject property and are therefore able to make objective judgments. It is not unusual for a report to contain a presentation of information and facts regarding the project and its potential market, leaving the conclusions to be drawn by the reader.

More in the nature of an illustration, rather than as a standard pattern that does not really exist, the following outline could represent the material covered in a comprehensive feasibility study:

1. *Conclusions.* Presented first as these are the answers to the practical questions that the rest of the study has developed.

2. *Property.* A description of the property, location, type of building or buildings, and an estimate of costs showing some detail as to how costs are determined.

3. *Market evaluation.* A study in depth of all factors that affect the marketing of the property, such as traffic patterns, population growth, type of income, other services available in the immediate area, direct and indirect competition, and any laws, regulations, or other restrictions that will affect the project.

4. *Environmental effect.* As local environmental rules expand, the impact of large projects on the area are becoming the subject of intensive and lengthy coverage. The cost of the research and its effect on the cost of the project must be considered in the overall investment.

5. *Expense and income.* An experienced analyst can develop reasonably accurate projections of operating costs. These are best approached as (a) *fixed*, which covers such items as insurance and taxes that do not vary with occupancy, and (b) *operating* expenses, such as water, electricity, and maintenance, that do fluctuate with occupancy. From these figures, a breakeven ratio can be determined. The income projection must be based on some factual data of comparable rents and occupancy figures, but does remain essentially an estimate drawn from knowledge and experience.

A feasibility report does not attempt to recommend financing methods or detail the expenses involved with interest costs. The conclusions stop with an estimate of total cash that would be available for debt service. The timing of the financing, how it is arranged, and under what type of commitments—these are problems for the developer to resolve.

Analysis Techniques

There are a variety of statistical tables available to the real estate underwriter that are often used to calculate and compare the return from income properties.* Tables are offered that give factors to compute the interest portion of a monthly payment, capitalization of income, re-

---

*Amortization tables and loan-constant tables are available from Financial Publishing Co., 82 Brookline Ave., Boston, MA 02215, or Professional Publishing Corp., 122 Paul Dr., San Rafael, CA 94903.

maining principal balances, present worth of $1.00 (if delivered in a future year), constants for computing principal and interest payments, and many others. Unfortunately, the use of various tables for analysis work generally depends on fixed interest rate financing. This is no longer an assured thing. Nevertheless, a basis is needed for any projection, and the cost of money becomes another variable to be considered. Only two of the more widely used tables are discussed in this text.

Payment To Amortize a $1,000 Loan. Amortization tables for residential loans (including the separate tables needed to compute an FHA payment that includes the mortgage insurance premium) are widely circulated and give the actual payments for a sequence of normal residential loan amounts and interest rates. The tables used to amortize a $1,000 loan provide a payment figure that can be multiplied by the number of $1,000 units in the loan amount to give the actual payment. Thus, they are more adaptable to the larger loans found in commercial real estate. Also, the $1,000 tables come in monthly, quarterly, semi-annual, and annual payment figures that cover almost all possible payment intervals.

Loan Constant. A loan constant is the annual (or monthly) debt service expressed as a percentage of the loan amount. The constant figure is often used in the negotiation and comparison of commercial loans because it gives the required debt service rather than the interest rate and term, which make comparison difficult. For example, if a loan applicant is offered loans from two different sources—one at 11 percent for a 20-year term and the other at 10 percent for a 15-year term—a quick comparison as to which has the lesser debt service is difficult. But if the first offer mentioned is quoted as a "constant of 12.39" and the second as "12.90," the comparison is simple. The constant times the amount of the loan is the debt service (in this example, principal and interest expressed as the sum of 12 equal monthly payments).

Apartments

Apartments, or multifamily housing, as the FHA broadly classifies them, can range from a four-family building to upward of 2,500 units or more. Since apartments are residential housing, qualifications similar to single-family housing are necessary. This would include location, type and stability of the neighborhood and the region, laws governing foreclosure procedures, and the architectural style of the building itself.

Because an apartment is an investment property as well as a residence, there are many variables involved in determining the risks. Experienced apartment operators judge three factors to be of almost equal importance in a successful operation. These are: (1) location, (2) physical facilities, and (3) management. Obviously, a careful underwriting analysis must consider all three factors in determining the risk involved.

Location is usually the first limiting requirement of an apartment seeker along with size of the unit and its price. A major consideration of location is easy access to jobs; freeways affect and broaden accessibility. Also important in judging location is proximity to schools and churches. The availability of recreational facilities, such as parks and golf courses, along with restaurants and other entertainment, are all to be considered. Apartment dwellers, as a group, are not as burdened with housework and yard maintenance as single-family residents would be.

Since location is a major determinant of the available market, it is necessary to evaluate the market in that area. For instance, does the proposed rental structure fit the requirements and will it be competitive? Do the size and type of units meet these demands?

The physical plant must meet the market requirements, not only in size of units, but also in architectural style and amenities available. Amenities would include such factors as playground areas, tennis courts, swimming pool, club room, and entertainment facilities. If the market is primarily a family type, the two- or three-bedroom units would be the most popular choice; if intended for young singles, the one-bedroom and studio design would be in greatest demand. The elderly, on the other hand, might prefer one or two bedrooms with a minimum of stairs to climb. Sometimes an assortment of units is used with the hope of covering all phases of the market. This "shotgun" approach is a poor substitute for careful analysis of the market as it may result in one type or style of unit easily rented and maintaining good occupancy while others go begging for tenants. Before building begins on an apartment complex, knowledgeable operators (developers) study the market for particular requirements and then use their merchandising power to attract suitable occupants.

Management is a major factor known well to experienced operators and too often underestimated by newcomers to the field. Together with the location and the physical plant, management, too, can be a "make or break" factor. Large cities throughout the country have companies that specialize in apartment management, offering a complete management service for a fee of 3 to 5 percent of the gross revenues. Maintaining routine cleanliness of the public areas, prompt repairs of equipment or damaged sections of the building, and fair enforcement of rules for the mutual well-being of the tenants are all necessary to achieve and maintain a high occupancy rate. Experienced operators learn how to cope with the special requirements of rental properties such as initial screening of tenants, the most effective methods of collecting rents and keeping them current, the special problems created by domestic pets, the handling of skip-outs and of tenants who create disturbances for other occupants. Consequently, an underwriter will look much more favorably, riskwise, on a property under the management of competent individuals or companies.

As apartment-style living proliferates in the cities, an underwriter must recognize that the better planned, better maintained facilities are those that will sustain occupancy in soft or competitive markets. And a continuous high occupancy rate is the key to survival in this business.

Analysis of Income and Expenses

On proposed apartment construction, a projected statement can be prepared to show anticipated gross revenues from each unit and all miscellaneous revenues (for example, from laundry rooms), less a vacancy factor and credit losses. This will produce an effective income from which deductions can be made for all expenses. Fixed expenses include such items as taxes and insurance which do not fluctuate with the occupancy rates. Operating expenses are the costs of utilities, maintenance, supplies, labor, and management. A special expense that is frequently overlooked or underestimated is the replacement cost—items such as drapes and carpeting, equipment such as ranges or dishwashers, all in continuous use, have a tendency to wear out, and allowances must be set aside for replacements. The cash remaining after these deductions then becomes available for debt service. Any remaining cash, after all expenses and debt service have been covered, serves as a cushion against a loss or a slow period.

It is apparent then that there are many variables among these figures that are subject to interpretation. For example, what occupancy rate may be reliably projected? FHA uses a percentage figure of 93. Conventional lenders generally tend to select an occupancy rate substantiated by actual rates prevailing in a particular area. Most lenders require proof of an occupancy rate near 90 percent before they will entertain a loan application. Rental rates also must be in line with the going market. Expenses can be projected with reasonable accuracy. In general, they range from 36 percent of the gross operating income to 45 percent, depending on the size of the operation and the efficiency of the management.

As previously defined, debt service is the monthly or annual cost of interest and principal payment and should be tailored to insure the timely retirement of the full loan. By careful analysis of the cash available for debt service, the underwriter can determine the most effective loan for the proposed apartment. Adjustable and negotiable factors are the *term*, which under conventional loans ranges from 15 upward to 30 years, and the *loan-to-value* ratio, which determines the equity cash required. The interest rate is generally pegged at current market rates and is less subject to negotiation.

The tax rules governing depreciation allow a property owner to compute depreciation on the total value of a building rather than solely on the equity investment. The 1981 Tax Act substantially altered the methods used to calculate the depreciation, or cost recovery deduction, on an investment. Accelerated methods are still available for real property investments, but if taken, such deductions are subject to *recapture* (that is, they must be reported as ordinary income) when the property is disposed of. Straight line methods could be a better choice as the new law allows for a recovery period of 15 years for real property used for business purposes. While depreciation is a deductible expense, whether derived from the building or from personal property consumed in the operation, the loan underwriter distinguishes between the two. Depreciation attributable to expendable personal property represents a reduction in the cash available for repayment of a loan, while depreciation attributable to the building is a noncash deduction and tends to increase the cash available. Inflation has brought increases in the value of most buildings—a gain that is not taxed until the property is disposed of.

Cooperative Apartments

Cooperative apartments are a variety of apartments in which the ownership of an individual unit is vested in the tenant-owner, and the ownership of the land and public facilities is vested jointly with all the other tenant-owners of the complex. The most practical method of operating this type of facility is to set up a corporation with shares of stock representing the jointly owned interests. Another method would be to place the joint interests in trust with a trust company, which then issues certificates of beneficial interest.

Cooperative apartments can offer the purchaser of a unit tax advantages similar to those offered the owner of a condominium or single-family home. However, the ownership of the land through stock held in a corporation or trust can place some restrictions on the owner's freedom to sell the unit. As a result, condominiums have become the more popular property.

Financing the construction of a cooperative apartment (or a condominium project) has the disadvantage of requiring a number of units to be built with the initial commitment of money. Unlike a single-family housing development, which allows houses to be built at about the same rate as they are sold, the cooperative apartment must be built as a complete project. One method that is sometimes used to assure a construction lender of loan repayment is to presell a certain number of the units. Release of the construction funding can be made contingent on the sale of a specified number of units.

Rule-of-Thumb Analysis

In order to properly analyze an apartment income property, a detailed study of all information regarding operating costs, fixed expenses, and gross income, with allowances for credit loss and vacancies, must be considered in relation to the total investment required. However, investors have developed certain guidelines that are useful in providing a quick evaluation on an apartment loan application to determine if it is worthy of further analysis. The use of these methods varies among investors and according to practices in the area of the country in which they do business, but some of the more commonly employed ratios and evaluations can be listed as follows:

Mortgage Multiplier. The factor that converts effective gross rent to an estimated mortgage amount ranges from four to six. For example, if a project grosses $4,800 per unit annually, it could attract a mortgage loan of $24,000 per unit if a multiplier of five is used.

Loan per Room. The required size of a "room" in an apartment is not standardized. One company might consider a minimum livingroom size for a two-bedroom apartment to be 160 square feet with the smallest dimension being 11 feet, or a living-dining alcove combination for a two-bedroom apartment with 200 square feet would be counted as one and one-half rooms. The average loan per room will vary from $4,500 to $9,500.

Gross Rent Multiplier. This is a rule-of-thumb method for converting gross project rental income into an estimate of value or sales price. The measure varies from 5½ (or 66 months' income) to 8 times annual income.

Site Value Ratio. The site value ratio is the ratio of the value of the site to the total value of land and improvements. The percentage varies from 6 to 25 percent.

Shopping Centers

Shopping in urban areas has relocated substantially from the downtown section to outlying districts and suburbs. The movement dates from approximately World War II and was brought about largely by the automobile which, along with freeway systems, produced a major change in our living patterns and altered our population centers.

Merchants in the downtown areas recognized these changing patterns and, for the most part, were in the vanguard of the development of regional shopping centers. Specialized development companies grew up in this period, and their purpose was to organize the merchants, locate proper land sites, arrange for financing, and then handle construction and even management of the completed center.

Size Categories

The variety of shopping centers found in the United States ranges from a small strip of stores along a frontage road to huge regional complexes. Many show considerable imagination and innovation in their design. The larger complexes often offer free entertainment in a patio or mall to attract more potential customers. However, there are no clear lines separating shopping centers by size categories.

A widely accepted distinction is drawn as to the services offered. In this sense, a *neighborhood center* provides daily essentials such as food, drugs, hardware, and other everyday services. A *community center* offers all the services found in a neighborhood center plus apparel stores, furniture outlets, professional services, and some recreational facilities. The largest category, a *regional shopping center*, offers all types of services usually with several major stores, scores of lesser shops, a variety of restaurants, and substantial other recreational facilities. Often the center is surrounded with office buildings and apartment complexes.

Classification for Financing

Shopping center facilities fall into three major categories when considered for financing: (1) owner occupied, (2) preleased space built by a developer, and (3) space built for speculative leasing. These categories are not always clearly differentiated in that many centers carry a combination of all three types, but they are used here to distinguish differences important to an underwriter's analysis.

Owner Occupied. While this type of store building is not as common as it once was, there are still many being built. The largest of all retail merchants, Sears, Roebuck and Co., generally leases its small stores but buys the land and builds its own facilities for the large centers. A free-standing discount store is usually owner occupied as are many of the newer warehouse-type furniture stores. Some of the largest local merchants undertake development of their own outlying stores. In all cases of owner-occupied facilities, the financial strength and credit record of the owner are the key to good financing. The type of merchandiser capable of building a substantial new facility for sales expansion generally has the experience to know the extent of the market. Regardless of the merchandiser's experience or reputation, however, comprehensive independent market studies are undertaken and made available to the underwriter.

The largest merchants may resort to the sale of bonds for financing expansion rather than a mortgage loan, depending on the cost of the money. In either case, it is the credit reputation of the borrower, rather than the real estate pledged, that determines the interest rate as well as the terms and the amount of the loan.

Preleased. Many merchants prefer to utilize their cash and borrowing capacity for growth in inventory and accounts receivable, rather than for real estate investments. Consequently, they work with investors or builder-developers who are knowledgeable in construction and property management. In order to obtain the physical facility desired, the merchant is often willing to sign a long-term lease ranging from 15 to 25 years, thus assuring the builder-investor of a continuing income. The lease payments must be calculated to cover such maintenance as the owner is held responsible for, plus the debt service. Taxes and insurance increases can be passed on to the tenant with an escalation clause in the lease. The inflationary spiral that began to accelerate in late 1973 has brought about considerable adjustments in the terms contained in all long-term leases. Landlords can no longer give any reasonable assurance that any costs will adhere to a predictable escalation pattern. Consequently, the newer long-term leases contain protective clauses for the landlord which allow any increases in operating costs to be passed on to the tenant in addition to the fixed cost increases which have been normal for taxes and insurance.

The actual lease, the strength of the lessee, and the terms of the lease itself are the keys to financing the building. For a strong lease, a lender will fund a major percentage of the total amount of the lease payments without substantial reference to the building itself. This may run as high as 75 percent of the total amount of the lease payments and can provide for an assignment of the lease payments directly to the lender.

If the lessees are less credit-worthy or of smaller size, the lender will still take an assignment of rentals but also looks more to the strength of the lessor. In this case, too, the size of the loan may be reduced to a percentage, say 70 percent, of the actual investment in land and buildings. The rental from smaller shops such as barber shops, boutiques, and fashion stores, with little established credit would not be considered as a measure for the loan except that such leases in hand would provide an addition to the overall occupancy of a multistore center.

One of the problems that becomes particularly important regarding preleased space is the ability of the developer to complete the building within the projected cost figures. Leases do not provide for rental increases to cover a builder's mistakes. Consequently, the prudent lender must not only determine the accuracy of projected costs of building with the income and expenses that will be generated, but must also be reasonably certain that the builder is sufficiently experienced and capable of completing the project within the specified budget.

Speculative. The substantial growth of all business, and particularly the service-oriented businesses requiring limited store space, has provided a lucrative field for the speculative builder. This is space built in bare-wall form, from the small corner shopping strip to portions of the large regional centers, without a lease or even a prospective tenant. When a tenant is found, the store space is completed to the particular tenant's requirements, either at the tenant's initial expense or added onto lease payments.

From the lender's standpoint, loans to build speculative store space rate rather low in desirability because of the risk. An empty store, after all, is only an expense. A lender who entertains such a loan must rely on the ability and financial strength of the builder-owner. If the builder is strong or has an excellent record of finding qualified tenants for previous projects, a lender is more likely to approve the loan.

The building of space for speculative leasing is accepted by lenders when it is a relatively small portion of a large regional center, most of which is already preleased. It has been well established that major stores generate traffic beneficial to many smaller merchants and service-type facilities.

Considerations in the Underwriting Analysis

There are some problems common to the development and continued successful operation of all types of shopping facilities, from the very largest down to the single-store operation. Problems that must be examined include: (1) location, (2) the physical facilities to be constructed, (3) the management and general plan of operation, (4) tenants and sales volumes, (5) types of leases, and (6) lease terms. Discussion of these problems with possible answers to questions that arise follows.

Location. As in other types of real estate, location of a shopping center dictates the market. The population of the surrounding area should be studied for density, potential growth, family purchasing income, market habits, and other competition to determine if there is a real need for the proposed store or shopping center. From this study it should be possible to project the total retail volume in the general area and to reduce this to an estimate of sales per store. With regard to a large-scale center, it would be advisable to employ a market analyst for such a study, as it becomes intricately involved with such facets of the problems as the nature of the center, accessibility, and shopping habits of the prospective customers in or near this location.

The location should also be selected for ease of entry and exit. Long-range plans should also recognize the fact that the flow of traffic at any given center might be substantially altered by future developments.

Physical Plan. There are many ways to build a shopping center, and no single plan insures success. The huge regional centers show great imagination in design, layout, decor, and various attractions offered to the shopper. Many have become recreational centers as well as shopping centers. Entertainment is often provided in the public malls in the form of musicians, demonstrations, art shows, and other types of exhibits. Modern centers exude something of a carnival atmosphere at times in their all-out efforts to attract shoppers and overshadow the competition from small centers. Inevitably, middle-level centers are finding it more difficult to compete with the many extra attractions offered by the large centers. However, the small convenience centers in good locations hold onto a local trade and are generally sound investments.

Since parking is one of the big advantages of a shopping center, these facilities should be adequate. As a general rule, three square feet of parking area should be provided for every one square foot of rentable shop space. An alternative rule would be to allow five or six parking spaces for each 1,000 square feet of shop. Employee parking is best designated and kept apart from the prime locations. Supermarkets require the most parking space of any type of store.

The physical plan should be carefully examined to make certain that floor plans are of proper size with access readily available, that there is adequate heating and air conditioning, and that sufficient space has been provided for the handling of incoming merchandise and outgoing waste materials. These are mainly architectural and engineering concerns, but if costly mistakes can be prevented, the lender's money will be better secured. Considering the complexities involved, it is always a safer investment to employ experienced builders.

Management and Operations. Management plays a very important role in all types of income properties, and shopping centers are no exception. Large centers rely heavily on competent management, not only to handle the tenants and maintain the facility, but to provide attractive decorations, timely promotional advertising, control of traffic, policing of crowds, and even some entertainment. The management usually works with an organized merchants' association in providing some of these services. Good promotional organization provides assurance to the lender that there will be a continuity of the entire project as all shopping center store units have a degree of interdependence.

In the area of operations, management can either place much of the responsibility for interior maintenance and daily upkeep on the tenant or provide the service as a separate charge that can be adjusted as costs change. In the smaller operations and in the single-building facility, the owner usually takes responsibility only for exterior maintenance and the parking areas.

The experience of the operators is very soon evidenced by the manner in which they detail the responsibility for costs: both in how the costs for finishing out a store for a particular lessee are allocated between the owner and the tenant, and in how the operating costs are detailed. Such seemingly minor items as an electric eye-controlled doorway can cause continual maintenance problems. Is this an interior or exterior feature? The knowledgeable operator does not leave such items to later negotiation but spells them out in the written agreement. The lender should have an interest in any potential problem that might be inherited.

In the analysis of a proposed shopping center, the underwriter should definitely determine that adequate allowance has been made for initial planning and start-up costs. The new emphasis on environmental impact adds another cost for the investor who must now prepare studies and submit the necessary reports to authorized officials. Lease-up costs and initial advertising must all be provided for in the financing proposal as well as allowances for probable tax increases on any undeveloped land that is held for future growth.

Tenants. Another area of management responsibility to be examined by the underwriter is the policy used in selecting tenants and locating them within the center. The granting of exclusive franchises is not beneficial to the owner but may be necessary for a large store such as a supermarket. Any franchise granted in broad or general terminology, such as allowing a restaurant an exclusive franchise for "food handling," can be very restrictive to future growth of the center. Tenants should have the financial strength to undertake the lease obligations plus the ability to serve the public in a successful manner. Customer problems involving any single store can cast a poor reflection on the entire shopping center. Also a good diversity of stores is helpful in luring shoppers back again.

As previously indicated in this section, the quality of the tenants in a preleased center is a major factor in securing a mortgage loan. Sometimes there is an overemphasis on the desirability of the national chain-type stores as lucrative tenants. Recent statistical data indicate that localized chains and independent stores are very effective sales producers and that more often than not they turn over a larger volume of sales per square foot of floor space than do national operations. Sales volume is the key to larger rental income on percentage leases. The continued security of the mortgage payments rests to a considerable extent on the ability of the merchants to achieve profitable sales volumes.

Types of Leases.   The type of lease used and the detail it contains are vital to the loan analysis. Three main types are:

1. Term leases.   Term leases are used by most of the smaller shops and by some of the larger stores. This means paying flat monthly rentals figured on a basis of store size or square footage. These leases can allow for automatic increases every year or two and can provide renewal options.

2. Percentage lease.   The larger merchants (such as drug stores, supermarkets, and department stores) operate on minimum or base rentals plus a percentage of the gross sales. Percentages can vary from 1 to 6 percent of gross sales depending on type of store and sales volume. A no-minimum lease sets up a risky situation for a lender as the store may be able to operate profitably at a sales volume that does not pay the cost of the space occupied.

3. Net leases.   Another form of lease arrangement consists of operating the bare property strictly as an investment for the owner with the tenant paying all maintenance, taxes, and insurance. This type of operation is known as a net lease to the owner, covering only a reasonable return on the property investment. Management and operational problems would all be minimized by passing the entire burden on to the tenant. The net lease procedure is frequently used by individuals or by development companies who have decided to build a facility in a distant location for a major tenant, a supermarket for instance, but simply do not have the personnel available and are not interested in accepting management responsibilities.

Lease Terms.   The investment required to furnish a large store requires a long-term lease, which has advantages and disadvantages for the owner. The long term gives the lender good assurance of repayment and makes for better loan terms. The disadvantage lies in the fixed return on an investment over a number of years when costs of all kinds continue to increase over a period of time. Insurance costs also tend to increase and are related to risks that tenants may introduce. Consequently, long-term leases will normally carry escalation clauses that provide for any increase in taxes and insurance to be passed on to the tenant. It is becoming more common to allow increases in maintenance and operating costs to be added to the rental charges.

The smaller stores or shops, such as beauty parlors, florists, and boutiques, generally contract a three- to five-year lease, which is subject to rental increases periodically in anticipation of rising costs. The smaller shops seldom agree to percentage leases as they lack the necessary sales volume and the more complicated bookkeeping procedures required.

There are some lease provisions of special concern to a lender, particularly those that could bring about a premature cancellation of the lease. For example, leases that tie the occupancy of one store to the continued occupancy of another store present an obvious problem. Any type of exclusive clause restricting other shops from carrying competing lines or type of service can be detrimental. Stores can and do change their sales patterns over the years.

Occasionally special leases are permitted a major tenant based on a below-cost figure as a means of capitalizing on the inherent attraction of well-known merchants. The traffic generated by one big store is expected to provide sales for the lesser merchants. From a lender's standpoint, however, this type of subsidized rent structure suggests an undesirable pattern since it places a heavier burden on the remaining tenants to compensate for the loss sustained on the single below-cost lease.

Costs that continually escalate without positive controls can be set out in a lease agreement as separate expenses or in clauses allowing an equitable rental adjustment. Such services as heating and air conditioning, participating advertising, waste disposal, janitorial services, and security services may be covered under a separate service contract that can be adjusted for escalation, as may be necessary. Such a contract should contain protective clauses for the tenant to prevent the unscrupulous use of terms as a device for increasing costs unfairly, which might bring about default on the lease itself.

Example of a Shopping Center Lease

An example of a *percentage lease* for a supermarket of 20,000 square feet would be as follows:

> Assume the rental is set at a minimum of $3 per square foot, per year, based on 1½ percent of the gross sales. The $3 for 20,000 square feet would amount to a rent of $60,000 per year. So, calculating a gross sales volume of $4,000,000 or less per year, the supermarket would pay the $60,000 per year minimum. If the total volume goes over $4,000,000, the 1½ percent of the gross would apply above that amount.

A typical shopping center deal would vary considerably across the country, depending upon land values and construction costs in a particular area. However, the proportions are similar, and the figures confirm this similarity. Assuming land cost at $3 per square foot and using the three-to-one ratio on parking space, the rentable shop space would then cost $12 per foot in land contributed. For a reasonably simple structure, the building costs would come to about $35 per square foot, which includes paving and lighting the parking lot. The total investment, using these figures, would add up to $47 per square foot. At this investment level, base operating costs would be limited to $2.25 per square foot per year. Rentals for space such as this would average $8 per square foot per year. Table 13-1 shows how the investment works out using a highly simplified procedure for greater clarity.

Based on the figures in Table 13-1, the investment would show a 9.87 percent cash return on the equity investment. However, many unforeseen contingencies could upset this return, such as lower occupancy than expected, failure to collect all rentals due, and runaway operating costs. In the example cited, the cash return cannot be considered the only profit since principal payments on the loan are also a part of the profit. However, the depreciation allowed offers a tax de-

TABLE 13-1

Projection for Shopping Center Investment (Figures are hypothetical using a 50,000 square foot building located on 200,000 square feet of land. Total cost: $2,350,000.)

Capital Investment		
Equity Investment (20%)	$ 470,000	
80% mortgage loan	1,880,000	
Total Investment		$2,350,000

Annual Operating Calculations		
Gross Scheduled Income ($8.00 per sq ft)	400,000	
Less 5% vacancy and credit loss	20,000	
Gross Operating Income		$380,000
Less Expenses—		
All operating costs @ 2.25 per sq ft		112,500
Net Operating Income		$267,500
Less Debt Service—		
11% for 25-year term		
Constant—.1176 × 1,880,000		221,088
Cash flow before taxes		$ 46,412

duction. The lender must look to the margin of cash over and above the operating costs and the debt service, in order to estimate the margin of financial safety that can be counted on in any given investment.

Office Buildings

The owners of all types and sizes of office buildings, ranging from the largest to the smallest, acquire or construct them for one of two purposes: (1) their own occupancy or (2) for lease to others.

Owner-Occupied Buildings

Many owner-occupied office buildings are held by companies or persons with a financial history that makes the decisions on underwriting such a property somewhat easier for the lender. This is due to the fact that the credit reputation of the owner is the major qualifying factor under consideration, whereas the real estate that is to be pledged is of secondary importance. Ultimately, the source of loan repayment is closely tied to the owner-occupant's record of profitability and the manner in which previous financial obligations have been met.

In financing large owner-occupied buildings an alternative choice to straight mortgage financing would be the sale of first-mortgage bonds through an investment banker or a mortgage banker. Acquisition of large office buildings by investing institutions, such as banks or insurance companies, is a common practice. In this way, the owners simply finance large buildings from their own investment funds.

Various local, state, and federal governments and their agencies build office buildings for their own use with legislative appropriations. But some government buildings, such as post offices, are built by private investors under long-term lease contracts and are financed through private sources.

Office Buildings for Lease to Others

The underwriting of buildings intended for lease to others calls for some specialized techniques of real estate mortgage financing and requires extensive analysis of the property involved. In this category there are three main groups: (1) a builder-investor with preleased office space to build, (2) the speculative builder hoping to attract tenants before the building is completed or soon thereafter, and (3) the owner-occupied building with extra space for lease.

Preleased Office Space. The preleased building is the more conservative method and provides the underwriter with a lease to analyze, a tenant to examine for credit-worthiness, and a building and location to study. If the building is specialized to meet the tenant's unusual requirements (such as heavy electrical gear, raised or lowered floors, or special wall patterns), the term of the lease should be sufficient to recover the extra investment. Most underwriters will limit a loan to a percentage of the total lease payments as this is the main source of the loan recovery. Similar to a shopping center, a preleased office building faces an inflexible situation in regard to an overrun on construction costs. The building must be designed and located in such manner that it meets the projected costs, and the contractor must have the ability to complete the project within the contract terms. Bonding of the contractor is a normal requirement. Escalation clauses should be provided in any long-term lease agreement to cover rising taxes, insurance costs, and more recently, maintenance and operating costs. As mentioned previously, preleased office buildings for single tenants are usually "bare-wall" leases; that is, the tenant finishes and furnishes the interior and provides the maintenance.

Speculative Office Buildings. The speculative builder presents a greater risk to an underwriter and only the more experienced and credit-worthy builders can command this type of loan. In addition to the usual analysis of the building and its location, consideration must be given to the market and the regional economic pattern. What are the chances of the speculative building becoming fully leased? The underwriter, however, is not in the business of chance by choice, so a protective restriction can be established that would require the building to have a 75, 80, or perhaps 85 percent occupancy with bona fide tenants before the permanent loan will be released. Of course, this throws a real burden on the construction financing and usually means that the builder of a speculative building must have the credit strength or cash reserves to build and lease the building without an assured permanent commitment. It is not unusual for a knowledgeable builder-contractor to build and lease an office building with his own funds, then mortgage-out for more than his costs. In such a case the loan security rests as much on an assignment of the lease income as on the mortgage pledge. With regard to speculative office buildings, lenders often set rental minimums to protect their repayments. Buildings with multitenant occupancy usually provide for janitorial service, which can be a separate agreement subject to escalation if costs increase.

Owner-Occupied Building with Space to Lease. The third type of building loan in this building category is the owner-occupied with space to lease. In this situation there can be a mixture of several types of income including the owner's normal rental payment, plus rent anticipated from space for speculative lease, as well as rent from space already preleased. But no one source may provide sufficient revenue to assure recovery of a normal ratio loan. The underwriter must analyze the property as a whole and make certain that the full loan has a reasonable chance of recovery before any portion of that loan is permitted to be released.

General Guidelines

In today's business world, office buildings are under construction in many locations with one major aspect in common—business growth. Even though downtown areas are somewhat congested and offer only limited parking, they are still highly desirable locations for businesses requiring convenient access to banks, accounting firms, attorneys, or other service-oriented facilities, plus easy contact and association with customers, suppliers, other allied businesses, hotel accommodations, and transportation.

As freeway patterns have developed in urban areas, many businesses have opted for outlying locations that provide ease of parking and close proximity to potential office workers. The decline of mass transportation systems, hastened by the increasing use of cars, has made freeway locations in some cases more accessible than downtown. It should be noted in passing, however, that the next generation may very possibly witness a reversal of this trend, especially in view of the costs of driving a car.

Even though it is a generally accepted idea that the true value of an income property is what it will earn, the physical aspects of the office building should be fully covered in an underwriting analysis. Factors such as the flexibility of interior partitions will affect future ability to rent space. It has been demonstrated that excessive public space may become a heavy burden as the building grows older. Also mechanical equipment can cause problems, and in the case of older buildings may need replacement.

The ability to maintain high occupancy in office buildings is less dependent on economic inducements than on such intangible qualities as prestige and status. For example, ground floor space rented to a dignified, prestigious merchant can enhance the value of upper-floor space. The class of tenants can add to a particular building's value; that is, a building known for top-rate law firms or a medical office building of high-caliber tenancy will attract other professional people. Companies and business concerns seeking a high-class clientele are often willing to pay a few dollars more each month in rentals for the advertising value of a prestige address.

The expenses of operating an office building must be considered in the total loan picture. Unlike other types of real estate properties, office buildings usually furnish a janitorial service for the tenant as well as for the public areas. There are many companies specializing in contract cleaning services and competition will allow some control to be exercised over these costs. If a building is new, projected operating costs must be utilized, but actual operating costs should be available in the records kept on existing buildings. Care must be taken in analyzing any cost figures to minimize distortions that might lead to misleading conclusions. For example, expense items may be omitted, maintenance work can be neglected, incidental repairs may sometimes be capitalized to reduce expense figures, and tenant services can be held to a dangerously low level in order to distort earnings figures in an upward direction. All of these factors should become apparent to the experienced underwriter and properly weighed in the final loan analysis.

Like other properties, the operating management is a key ingredient in continuing success. Poor management can discourage occupancy and drive good tenants away.

Example of an Office Building Loan

The impact of high interest costs and the concern of long-term lenders for inflation is most strongly reflected in the loan example illustrated in Table 13-2. The loan itself is a high-ratio (90 percent) commitment for

TABLE 13-2

Projected Statement for Office Building (Based on 100,000 sq ft net rentable space costing $54.00 per sq ft. Total—$5,400,000.)

Capital Investment		
Equity Investment (10%)	$ 540,000	
90% mortgage loan	4,860,000	
Total Investment		$5,400,000
Annual Operating Calculations		
Gross Scheduled Income ($11.00 per sq ft)	$1,100,000	
Less 5% vacancy and credit loss	55,000	
Gross Operating Income		$1,045,000
Less Expenses—		
All operating costs @ 34.5% of gross operating income		360,525
Net Operating Income		$ 684,475
Less Debt Service—		
12% interest for 30-year term		
Constant .1234 × 4,860,000		599,724
Cash flow before taxes		$ 84,751

a commercial loan. And the lender felt that a participation in the property income was justified. The terms outlined in the three features of the loan agreement are called *income participation* and are usually limited to the duration of the loan. Another form of participation by lenders is called *equity participation* and is an ownership interest extending beyond the term of the loan.

Following are the three income participation requirements:

1. The land amounting to 100,000 square feet was purchased by the lender for $5 per square foot and then leased back to the owner of the building for a ground rental of $70,000 per year.
2. As additional ground rental, the lender took 3 percent of the gross annual income, which amounted to approximately $30,000 more.
3. With the repayment of the loan calculated on an $11 per square foot rental, the lender demanded 15 percent of any rentals earned in excess of $11 per foot as a hedge against inflation.

With the substantial participation protection available to the lender in this loan agreement, there was no requirement for personal endorsement on the part of the borrower.

Warehouse Buildings

Another type of income property that is preferred by many investors because of its relatively low maintenance and management requirements is the warehouse building. The demand for warehouse space has grown substantially in the past decade for several reasons. Many types of companies use general warehouse space to store merchandise in peak seasons, to keep a product closer to its ultimate market, or to house an unusually large stock of a particular raw material.

Somewhat like office buildings, this type of facility can be built for use by an owner, such as a grocery chain operator; or it can be built for use in part by an owner, such as a light manufacturer, with portions available for lease to others; or it can be built for speculative leasing as commercial warehouse space. It is the speculative warehouse that requires the most careful loan evaluation of the property. Owner-occupied or partially occupied buildings provide an established business with a source of income to substantiate and undergird the loan analysis. Warehouses are built fully preleased and partially preleased in much the same way as office buildings and shopping centers, so that the analysis of the different types are similar.

There are several basic requirements for effective warehouse space that would make it more easily rentable during the life of a loan. Like all other income properties, location is of paramount importance. The location of a warehouse should include accessibility by roads running in several directions and capable of handling large trucks. The warehouse should also be accessible to rail spurs, if possible. The land need not be in high-density traffic zones as required by shopping centers and some office buildings, but neither should it be locked into small street patterns that limit the size of the truck that can be accommodated. Availability of a rail siding is not essential to every user, but lack of this facility may limit future marketability. Another requirement that must be checked out is the availability of adequate water lines and pressures to support proper fire extinguisher installations. Without adequate fire protection, insurance rates skyrocket and greatly increase storage costs for the prospective tenant.

In the construction design of the building itself, provision should be made for loading docks capable of handling truck and freight-car loadings at the proper heights. The ceilings must be high, generally over 15 feet for more efficient stack storage of merchandise.

The costs of construction of a warehouse building are similar to those for a shopping center building inasmuch as both are fairly high ceiling buildings with little or no interior finishing provided by the builder. Warehouses require heavier floors to support more weight, but use much less parking space than a shopping center building. Further, the cost of land suitable for a warehouse is much lower than that required for freeway-accessible shopping sites.

Warehouse leases often provide for a net/net return to the owner, which means the *tenant* pays all maintenance and operating costs, plus all insurance and taxes on the building. In such a lease, management expenses would be held to a bare minimum. The cash available for debt service is thus very easy to calculate. On general warehouses with multitenant occupancy, the owner may provide some services and, most likely, will be responsible for taxes and insurance costs.

Miniwarehouses

In recent years a relatively new form of investment has grown up in the building of one-story structures partitioned into small rental spaces. The market for such space comes from the more affluent and mobile citizens who accumulate material goods but are unable to accommodate them in small apartments and houses. The structures usually contain from 100 to 300 rental spaces each ranging in size from 5 × 5 to 20 × 20 feet.

The management requirement, depending somewhat on size, ranges from almost nil to full-time administrative personnel and security guards. The returns on an investment have been good. Owners have reported that a completed warehouse averages about one-half the cost per square foot of that for an apartment building, and the rental rates *per square foot* are about the same.

Questions for Discussion

1. What is the purpose of a feasibility report?

2. How is a loan constant used to facilitate a real estate loan transaction?

3. List and explain the importance of the three essential elements for the successful operation of an apartment project.

4. What is meant by the term *debt service*?

5. What is a *mortgage multiplier* as used for a rule-of-thumb guide?

6. Why are the type and quality of leases important to a lender considering a shopping center loan?

7. How does an owner protect himself against construction cost overruns in building a preleased office building? How does the lender protect himself?

8. What procedure is being used to handle the continued increase in both fixed and operating costs when making a long-term lease for building space?

9. Discuss the advantages and disadvantages of owning an office building; a shopping center; a warehouse.

Loan Analysis of Industrial, Rural, and Development Properties

Special-Purpose Buildings

Buildings erected for specific purposes have more limited market ability or access to income than those categorized in the preceding chapter as income properties. Under this limited usage category falls industrial plants with specially designed floors to support heavy machinery or technical equipment, and/or with overhead structures carrying large cranes and conveyor systems. Also, processing plants such as refineries and chemical-or mineral-handling facilities have singular usage. Other specialized buildings, with a somewhat broader usage because of the large retail markets they serve, are service stations, food franchise outlets, and automobile dealerships.

Large companies, who are the principal builders and owners of specialized properties, have the capability of generating investment money through the sale of bonds or through an increase in their issues/shares of stock. The discussion here focuses only on those circumstances in which an individual or company is seeking a mortgage loan to finance the construction or purchase of a special-purpose plant or building.

In evaluating a building of limited usage for a mortgage loan, the lender will obviously look to something in addition to the real estate value represented in the property itself. There are three methods that can be used to justify such a loan.

Money Good. To establish the amount of a loan that might be made, the money good approach would determine at what price the property could be liquidated under a forced sale. This is the amount of money that could be realized through foreclosure.

A loan made for such an amount would be reasonably well secured by the property. But the loan amount would probably be too small, relative to the total investment required, to be of practical value to the borrower. This method is not very common in today's financial markets, but it has been used.

Earnings Record of Borrower.   Since the recovery of the loan in an orderly manner depends on the borrower's ability to produce income, the past record of profitable production is of paramount importance in the underwriting of a special-purpose property loan. A large company with established credit presents little problem. A small company, seeking to expand with a major investment, would require closer scrutiny. This would not only involve the credit record but also a review of the management personnel with their experience and capabilities.

Any new venture into a specialized area of business or production is generally not suitable for the mortgage lender's portfolio. Such enterprises can find suitable capital in the equity funding provided by the sale of stock. The security required by a mortgage lender limits the loans to reasonably well-proven and experienced people and companies.

Endorsement.   The endorsement of a loan either by a customer or by a supplier is a fairly common practice when it proves advantageous to both parties.

An example of a customer giving loan support to a supplier might be a major grocery chain furnishing credit support to a truck gardener or a cattle feeder. Or a large equipment distributor could be giving financial assistance to one of its smaller manufacturing sources. The purpose, of course, is to assure the customer of a continued or enlarged source of product to sell. The method can be in the form of an outright endorsement of the mortgage note for a new facility; or it can be given in the form of a letter-agreement guaranteeing certain amounts of purchases and providing for an assignment of the payments to a lender if required.

There are many instances in business today of a manufacturer or other supplier of materials assisting its customers by endorsement of their mortgage loans. The reason is to provide the supplier with better marketing facilities through which to sell more products. Examples of this type of assistance abound in the manufacturer-automobile dealer relationship and also in the pairing of major oil companies and their dealer-owned service stations. Some fast-food franchise operations, motel chains, and equipment rental and distributorships commonly use the endorsement power of the licensing company to facilitate expansion. The endorsement need not be in the full amount of the loan to be helpful, but may entail underwriting a certain portion or specific amount.

By spreading the risk of the mortgage loan over several borrowers or endorsers, the lender may offer a lower interest rate and a longer term for repayment, if that is desirable.

Farm and Ranch Loans

At the turn of this century, 90 percent of our country's population lived on farms. Today, farmers make up less than 4 percent of the total population. And the farm loan business has changed, also. Two general categories of farm loans are: (1) the family-resident loan and (2) the agri-corporate loan.

Family-Resident Farm Loans

The family-resident farm loan has not changed a great deal in the past 30 years. It is still based on the three legs of any good mortgage loan: (1) a credit-worthy borrower, (2) a piece of real estate of sufficient value to provide good collateral, and (3) the ability of the property and the borrower to produce an income assuring repayment of the loan. Judgments on farm land value require good knowledge and experience in given geographical area. A single-crop farm is the most vulnerable to failure and subsequent loan default. A diversified crop operation, plus some livestock, gives the best security. So the ability of the farm to produce a continued income, regardless of an occasional crop failure or a fluctuating market, is a prime consideration in making a sound farm loan. The land value itself may be distorted by outside pressures such as a city growing nearby, a large neighboring farm desiring to expand, or possibly a new freeway providing much frontage acreage. But the farm underwriter should confine the analysis to the producing factors: soil conditions, weather, available irrigation, type of crops, nearness to markets, and condition of the markets, for it is these factors that will produce the income from which the loan can be recovered. To give any substantial weight to the rising land values takes the loan into the category of land development.

Agri-Corporate Farm Loans

Our agri-corporate loans show some similarity to special-purpose property loans. Large commercial farm companies control much of the nation's agriculture today and usually provide good business records to assist an underwriter in making an evaluation. Studies of land productivity with various crops and fertilizers, of the most effective methods of breeding and feeding livestock, and of the management techniques of cost control are all helpful in evaluating the operating procedures of commercial farms. These large farms have proved economical in their operations, and they are willing to test new technologies. Equipment can be more fully utilized and better maintained than on smaller holdings. But, along with the advantages, a word of caution: the dependency on hired labor and the management costs of a large commercial farm make them less flexible and more difficult to retrench in periods of lowering prices. The lender should hold the loan-to-value ratio at a conservative level in this type of operation.

The term of a farm loan varies as to need and may run from 10 to 40 years with 33 years a popular term, partly because the Federal Land Bank formerly used 33 years. More leniency is given in the repayment of farm loans than other real estate loans. A farmer's income is subject to greater variation, and a rigid payment schedule can be self-defeating. But any long-term farm loan should have full amortization as a goal.

Ranch Loans

A ranch presents only slight variations to a farm loan in that it produces livestock as the principal source of revenue. Because ranches are predominately in the water-short southwestern regions, an underwriter must take care to analyze the water situation. Often water rights can be of greater value than the land since without water the land may be worthless. A common practice in ranching is to lease public lands for grazing. The acreage so leased becomes of value to the ranch only in the productivity the land can add to the ranch, and this can be limited by the term of the lease. But leased land or grazing rights do add value and should be included in the appraisal for loan purposes. Sometimes ranches produce additional revenues from the sale of timber rights, from mineral leasing, and even from hunting leases and dude ranching. All income has its value but must be considered according to its tenure and stability.

Land Purchase Loans

With the increasing interest in urban and suburban growth, the purchase of land for the purpose of speculative resale has grown substantially in the past ten years. A limited number of lending institutions do make loans for raw land purchases, notably some commercial banks and a very few savings associations. The loan-to-value limits are generally lower, perhaps 50 to 60 percent of value, and the term is seldom over three years.

Lenders do not like to look at the actual sale of the collateral as the normal means of recovering on a mortgage loan (exceptions: house construction and land development loans). And lenders are particularly wary of a tract of raw land that may or may not have a market. Hence, such loans are made primarily to persons or companies that have substantial assets, and secondarily in those cases where there is a future intended use or sale that can be confirmed.

With respect to a future intended use or sale, the land may be purchased for a housing development, or perhaps a shopping center, and so more time is needed to complete plans and permanent financing. The lender assisting in the immediate purchase of the land is thus in a prime position to make the construction and permanent loans if the conditions meet his requirements.

Sometimes a land broker or a developer will locate a tract of land highly suitable for a particular purchaser. It could be a small tract for a service station or a larger parcel on which to erect a retail store outlet. But at the time the property becomes available, the ultimate user may not be in a position to consummate the land purchase. In such a circumstance, a binding letter of intent issued to a real estate broker or developer of some substance would greatly facilitate a raw land loan to acquire the chosen site. The land broker would be presenting the lender a reasonably sure sale for the land within a specified time period, with the land itself as collateral.

A loan for the purchase of raw land, regardless of its intended use, classifies as a commercial loan for a savings association and therefore falls into the limited, nonresidential end of the loan portfolio.

Land Development

The next step after the purchase of raw land is its development. *Land development* for loan purposes means the building of streets and utilities to prepare lots for resale as home sites. The development work associated with the construction of an apartment or office building project is in the category of *site development*, or land preparation, and is an integral part of the project construction costs.

Since the work called for in the land development plans can easily identify the project for residential purposes, such a loan is much more acceptable to a savings association than the land purchase itself.

A development loan can be made for as much as 75 or 80 percent of the appraised value of the finished lots, but is seldom permitted to exceed the costs incurred in the land acquisition and construction costs. This is one of several types of loans that generate what might be called a certain distortion in values, due to the fact that the very development being financed greatly enhances the value of the raw land. Federal regulations for savings associations permit a loan at 75 percent of the appraised value for residential land development. Conceivably, the appraised value of the completed lots based on an existing market would be substantially greater than the development costs. A 75 percent loan would permit the developer to borrow an amount in excess of the actual investment. In lending terminology, the amount of a loan that exceeds a borrower's actual costs is called *walking money*—money the borrower can walk away with upon completion. The prudent lender is reluctant to permit a borrower to obtain a cash "profit" from a development or construction loan since this has a tendency to lessen the incentive to sell the property as intended.

An integral part of a land development loan agreement is the *release* mechanism. This is the clause that spells out when, how, and at what price any lot or lots may be released. The release terms may call for an order of priorities by which the land can be developed and will state in what manner the lot will be released, and most important, they will specify the amount of money from each lot sale that must be paid to the lender for the release.

The release itself is a specific release of the mortgage lien on the lot or lots being sold and is intended to permit the delivery of a clear title to the lot purchaser by the developer. The amount of money required to release a lot may be a percentage of the sales price of the lot, stating a minimum sales price. In this procedure any increase in sales price over the minimum would increase the payment to the lender and amortize the loan more rapidly. Another method is to set a flat sum on each lot for release and let the developer sell at whatever price he or she can. The flat sum per lot is usually calculated so as to repay the development loan with interest in full when somewhere between 50 and 75 percent of the lots have been sold.

Since 1968, the Department of Housing and Urban Development (HUD) has had an Office of Interstate Land Sales charged by Congress with the responsiblility of establishing guidelines and procedures for land developers in an effort to minimize deceptive practices and outright frauds. Sale of lots, developed and undeveloped, has grown substantially in this country and has brought out some unscrupulous operators. Basically, the rules require nothing more than a full disclosure of the essential facts for the land buyer and can serve as a protection for both buyer and seller. As one explanation goes, a developer can still sell a lot that is completely under water, but he must state in writing that it is under water! The rules apply to any development with over 50 lots for sale, of less than five acres each, and on which no construction is required. Failure to comply with the HUD regulations can involve a fine and imprisonment for the *lender* as well as the developer and his agents.

Construction Loans

The construction industry employs over 6 million people in this country and depends heavily on the availability of lendable funds. However, several large segments of the construction business are not so dependent on the capital market. These are government projects such as streets, highways, dams, and public buildings, which can be paid for from tax revenues. Various types of bonds, which are usually based on a pledge of tax revenues, might be sold to finance the construction. Another major factor in the construction market is the large corporation which builds industrial plants and utilities. These corporations often finance expansion out of their own revenues or, perhaps, through the sale of bonds.

The type of construction lending discussed in this text concerns a building loan—the money needed to construct a house, an office building, or a shopping center. While these loans vary substantially in size, there is a similarity in the risks involved. All are secured by a first mortgage on the property to be constructed; all are funded only after each stage of construction has been completed; almost all require a permanent loan commitment or take-out of some kind to assure repayment of the construction loan immediately upon completion of the project. So where is the big risk?

The risk to the construction lender is whether or not the building can be completed with the available money and whether it meets all required specifications. Many factors that are difficult to foresee enter into the successful completion of a building. Some are the weather, labor difficulties and strikes, delays in the delivery of materials, changes in the plans or specifications, and the latest requirement, environmental considerations, which have encouraged delaying lawsuits.

Definition

The definition of a construction loan focuses on the special requirements for this type of financing. A construction loan is initially a loan commitment which provides for the money to be disbursed at intervals during construction in a manner that insures payment of all construction costs and finance charges and requires completion of the building in accordance with the plans and specifications so as to deliver a valid first mortgage upon completion.

Further explanation of each part of the definition follows:

Disbursement during Construction. Unlike other types of loans, a construction loan is not funded when the borrower signs the note. All the borrower has at the beginning is a commitment that funds will be released as construction progresses. There are two basic ways that progress payments are released. One is at regular time intervals, usually monthly. With this method the building progress is inspected each month and the amount of work completed is duly noted. The lender then releases that portion of the loan that has been allocated to the work accomplished. The second method of handling progress payments is by stages of work completed. Under this plan, the lender and borrower agree at the outset on about five stages of progress, which when reached, will release that amount of the loan proceeds. An example of a first stage might be the completion of all underground work and the pouring of the foundation.

Assurance of Payment of Costs. While it is the borrower's prime responsibility to use the loan proceeds for the payment of charges on the construction, the lender has an important stake in making sure that all labor and materials are paid as the money is released. Every so often, a builder, by design or in error, may mix the records and use the proceeds from one construction loan to pay charges accruing from another project. The result can be labor liens and materialmen's liens filed on the property while still under construction. There are many ways that lenders can use to minimize the risk of improper disbursement. One is for the lender to handle the payments to contractors and subcontractors. Another is to require proof of payment for costs incurred by the borrower before any funds are released from the loan. Another is to require a waiver of lien form signed by each contractor involved with every progress payment. Perhaps the most important protection for the lender on this problem is to know the borrower's reputation for handling building projects. Then make close inspection a standard procedure.

Completion in Accordance with Plans. Again it is the borrower who is primarily concerned that the building is constructed according to the plans and specifications. But the lender also has a real interest in this question as the failure to meet the plans can be a cause for refusal by the permanent lender to release the loan. The problems are mostly technical ones such as the size of pipes and wiring, the grade and thickness of concrete, the amount of reinforcing used, the compaction of foundation and parking areas, and many others. A construction lender should employ a knowledgeable construction person on its staff who can check the work as it progresses. On small projects, the lender may rely on its own staff for inspection approvals. On large projects it is more common to employ an independent firm or professional to serve as the inspector. Both architects and engineers are used for this purpose, and the decision of the professional is usually accepted by both the borrower and the lender as final determination of the acceptability of the project as it is built.

Delivering a Valid First Mortgage. Insofar as the lender is concerned, the goal of the successful construction loan is to complete the project within the money allocated, all bills paid, and no liens filed. The construction loan can then be repaid through funding of a permanent loan or the sale of the property if it is a house or a condominium.

Additional Comments. It is customary in a construction loan for the lender to withold 10 percent from each progress payment until final completion. The purpose is to provide a reserve against unexpected liens. Some lenders will hold this reserve until the statutory lien period has expired after completion before releasing it to the borrower. If an unexpected cost is encountered that was not allowed for in the loan committed, the lender will ask, or demand, that the borrower make such payment. The same procedure is used if the borrower decides to make some changes in the plans after the loan has been committed. Such changes must be approved by the lender, and if it should cause an increase in the anticipated cost, the borrower will be expected to use his or her own funds for payment. The lender does not want to have a building only partially completed with all loan funds exhausted.

The personal endorsement of the borrower-owner is almost always required on a construction loan. The same lender may agree to make a long-term permanent loan with no personal endorsement required but will refuse to do so on the construction loan for the same project. The reason is not just the added security given by another endorsement, but in addition, it is the borrower-owner who is in a controlling position during construction to insist on changes in the plans or create costly problems that can upset orderly construction work. The lender just wants to make certain that the borrower-owner carries his full share of responsibility.

The principal sources for construction money are commercial banks with specialized construction loan departments, savings associations, and mortgage companies. The commercial banks' interest is in the higher yields and short terms represented in construction lending; savings associations and mortgage companies prefer the higher yields, but also are usually in a position to pick up the permanent loans at a minimum of expense to themselves.

There are many variations in the handling of construction loans. Some procedures used in major categories of buildings are outlined below in the following discussion.

Construction Loans for Residential Properties

Single-family detached houses and some townhouse projects are financed by builders on both a contract basis and a speculative basis.

Contract Basis. A house built for an owner under contract represents a reduced risk to the construction lender. The normal sales contract is a firm commitment by the purchaser and includes a permanent loan commitment for closing. Often the permanent commitment is made by the same lender handling the construction financing as a sort of packaged deal, which minimizes paper work. On such a loan the risk to the construction lender is primarily in the builder's ability to complete the house within the contract terms. The builder's record must be known to the lender.

In smaller communities and rural areas, houses are often constructed under contract by a local builder, who also operates a lumber yard, with the builder providing the construction financing from personal resources. A nearby savings association will have already agreed to make the permanent loan when the house is completed.

Speculative Basis. Many builders, mostly in the growing suburban areas, build houses with the expectation of selling them by the time they are completed. To the risk of being able to complete the house within the projected cost figure is added the risk of selling the house at a profitable price upon completion. A lender must look at the strength and capability of a speculative builder before accepting such a loan. As a builder proves himself to the lender, his construction line of credit can be expanded.

When the housing market fluctuates downward, the speculative builder is the first to be hurt. He can be caught with many unsold houses on which the high interest of the construction loan continues to eat at any profits. More and more, construction lenders are seeking to protect themselves against a soft market by demanding a *take-out commitment* before they will agree to the construction loan. As described in Chapter 7, a take-out commitment for a house loan would be an agreement to make the permanent house loan directly to the builder if the house is not sold within one year from the commitment date. The cost of the commitment is usually one point payable at issuance. The loan so committed to the builder would be at the same ratio as the construction loan, usually 80 percent of the sales value of the house, but the rate of interest would be one to three percentage points over the going rate and the term much shorter, probably ten years, than if the loan had been made to the intended occupant-buyer. The builder still has the problem of selling the house but has a little breather in facing a monthly amortization payment rather than full repayment of the construction loan, while the construction lender is clear with all his money back.

Construction Loans for Income Properties

Apartments, office buildings, shopping centers, and warehouses all use construction financing, sometimes termed *interim financing*, to accomplish the building of the project. As pointed out earlier, only the very strongest builder-developers are capable of commanding construction financing of any income property without a permanent loan commitment to pay off the construction loan at completion. The terms of the permanent loan influence the manner in which the construction money can be handled. Special requirements for funding the permanent loan, such as an 80 percent lease-up before release of the loan proceeds, place the construction lender in a far more risky position. If a permanent lender is currently unavailable, the developer may resort to a standby commitment in the same genre, or identical to, a take out commitment that calls for much higher payments. The construction lender must have a closing date for the takeout within a reasonable period (one to three years) for proper recovery of the construction loan.

Construction lending calls for highly experienced personnel who can work with builders and who understand construction progress and procedures so as to make timely releases of the loan proceeds. Most lenders will not release a progress draw without physically inspecting the project or having an independent architect inspector submit an estimate of work accomplished. The trick is to be able to complete the project within the money available and still have 10 percent of the loan amount retained at completion to protect the lender against any unforeseen contingencies. When the lender is satisfied that all bills are paid and that no valid liens can be filed, this 10 percent retainage can be released.

Mobile Home Parks

A fairly recent addition to the national scene as a property investment is the mobile home park. This type of project has long been developed in such resort areas as California, Arizona, and Florida, but only since the late sixties has the mobile home park concept spread to most of the country as a way of life.

Mobile home parks considered in this text are those projects that are built for the leasing of land space to the owners of mobile homes. Some mobile home parks are handled much like ordinary subdivisions in that the land is sold to the mobile home owner. As a subdivision development for the sale of lots, the financing would be much the same as discussed earlier in this chapter under the heading of Land Development. The use of the completed park facility for the *rental* of lots presents the problem of permanent financing for the entire development. This can be done either with a conventional loan similar to an apartment loan or with an FHA-insured commitment.

The original impetus for mobile home parks, outside of resort areas, was to provide a lower cost type of housing. The mobile home, no longer just a trailer that could be pulled behind the family car, became a completely furnished living unit 40 to 60 feet in length. The smaller units can be purchased, including furniture, for $8,000 to $15,000, can be parked in a space that provides little more than a parking lot, and can provide adequate living accommodations at considerably less cost than a normal house. The larger units with "double width" sections can exceed average housing costs.

So again there is considerable variation in the size of investment involved in a mobile home park. The more Spartan projects provide ten or twenty spaces, often built personally by the owner of the land, and can be very lucrative if kept occupied. One of the major attractions to this form of land use is the low maintenance costs.

The middle-size mobile home park has shown the greatest growth and was spurred by a broadening of the Federal Housing Administration insuring requirements in 1969. In an effort to provide more housing for middle and lower income families, the FHA increased their insurable limits to 90 percent of the finished park's value and to terms of 30 years. The insurance provided by the FHA brought in many private investors who would otherwise not have been able to finance such an undertaking. And the FHA set some sound standards of quality for their parks to avoid the "parking lot syndrome." Paved streets were required, minimal landscaping was specified, and some storage space for each housing unit was included. The density of units per acre was limited to a maximum of eight, and recreational facilities such as a clubhouse, swimming pool, or tennis courts were encouraged.

Because the FHA procedures called for a final closing of the permanent loan that would include the entire project, it was necessary to complete all spaces, or pads, in one stage. Lease-up of the large parks thus developed was often slow and caused financial drains to the investors. Foreclosure rates have been unfortunately high.

Conventional lenders for mobile home parks permit the development in stages to allow for lease-up and growth of income before proceeding with the next stage.

In 1970, the Veterans Administration added a new benefit for veterans to permit a mobile home to be financed and a lot to be purchased under its guarantee programs. The interest rate and term allowed initially were not sufficient to provide much enthusiasm among lenders, but further modification has helped promote some growth in mobile homes as a living accommodation.

Analysis of a Park

Like other forms of income property, a mobile home park must be well located and serve a market demand. The "building" consists of site preparation, underground utilities, connecting streets, and concrete or all-weather pads for placement of the housing units. The only structures involved are usually a clubhouse-office building, a laundry building, and such recreational facilities as the developer elects to provide.

Maintenance requirements are minimal as the tenant is primarily leasing a piece of land. Mobile home parks operate on a cost as low as 20 to 25 percent of their gross rental income.

Mobile home living has been most popular where at least one of the following five situations exists: (1) a military base, (2) a construction project, (3) a college or university, (4) a resort area, or (5) a retirement-oriented community.

One of the problems in the profitable development has been the longer lease-up period. Unlike apartments, which can be leased to good occupancy over fairly short periods in a strong market, the mobile home park tends to lease-up at a slower rate. Sources within the industry have reported an average rate of rent-up at ten to twelve spaces per month for a new park. However, it has also been observed that once a mobile home is moved into location, it seldom moves out of the park. One reason, of course, is that mobile homes are not built for travel, but are actually semipermanent dwellings. Also, where moving is contemplated, the cost of moving at $2 or more per mile serves as a deterrent since the moving costs could easily exceed the value of the equity in the mobile home. Hence, it is far more common for an owner who may be transferred to a new location to simply offer the mobile home for sale on its present location and purchase another at the future destination. The result for the owner of a mobile home park is that a more stable income than in an apartment investment can be counted on. Once the pad is leased, there is a security provided by the mobile home itself that provides good assurance of continuous rental payments.

The lending industry does not respond quickly to anything new, preferring instead the comfortable security of a proven good thing. So, in many areas of the country, conventional loans have been slow to surface for the development of mobile home parks. As more experience has demonstrated the values of this type of investment, financing is more easily obtained. A park loan can now be insured against default by private mortgage insurance companies, thus facilitating the trading of these loans in the secondary market.

Financing Mobile Homes

Unless permanently attached to the ground as may be defined by a state's property laws, a mobile home is considered personal property, not realty. As such, its use as collateral for loans follows different procedures. Financing of these homes will be considered briefly here, since they represent some 20 to 25 percent of the housing units built for sale or rental in this country each year.

Partly because they are an outgrowth of the much smaller house trailer, the mobile home is often financed in a similiar manner to an automobile. Many states license and tax them as a highway vehicle, causing some dissension and controversy within communities where mobile homes locate and utilize local schools and police and fire protection facilities.

Underwriting programs by both the FHA and VA have provided some impetus to the growth of mobile home sales. And conventional procedures have kept pace. All these loans follow the pattern of a consumer loan, not a mortgage loan, and are secured by an assignment or a lien on the title registered with the state agency for vehicles.

The term for mobile home loans is longer than for a car, generally running for ten to twelve years. But the interest is the same add-on type used in car loans. According to this method, for example, a 7.5 percent add-on interest produces a 12.41 percent annual rate for a ten-year loan and a 12.10 percent annual rate for a twelve-year loan.

The majority of conventional lenders handling mobile home loans employ the services of one of several companies specializing in the insuring and processing of vehicle loans. For a small fee, usually a percentage of the monthly payment, the service company sells a default insurance policy similar to that handled by private mortgage insurance for homes. In case of a default on the payments, the service company itself pays off the lender and undertakes the repossession of the mobile home. Some lenders prefer to make their loans through the service company. In this procedure, the service company handles the collections and accounting for the outstanding loans and performs in a similar capacity as that of a mortgage banker for home loans.

Questions for Discussion

1. For loan purposes, what is meant by a *special-purpose building*? *Name three types.*

2. What is accomplished by the endorsement of a loan by a third party and why is the procedure sometimes used?

3. What do you consider the most important factors for the sound underwriting of a farm loan?

4. Why are raw land loans among the most difficult to obtain? What are the risks involved?

5. In a land development loan, how does a release clause function?

6. What is the importance of the Office of Interstate Land Sales Registration (under HUD) to the lender who is involved with land development projects?

7. Define a *construction loan* and list the various risks that can be involved.

8. What special problems are associated with a mobile home park development from a lender's viewpoint?

9. What is the best source of funds for use in funding a new business venture?

Other Financing Techniques

Sale of Mortgage Bonds

At several points in the text, reference has been made to the sale of bonds as a method of financing a real estate project. In finance, a *bond* is a certificate evidencing indebtedness that is issued by governments and business corporations in return for loans. Money is borrowed by selling the bond certificates. Bonds can be secured, such as mortgage bonds and equipment bonds, or they can be unsecured. Prior to 1929, the sale of mortgage bonds was a principal means of raising real estate investment money. The record of repayment was excellent and the bonds were a popular security for investors. But the collapse of the security markets in 1929, partially due to the unregulated nature of the securities being sold, brought a halt to this source of mortgage money. The rebirth of the mortgage companies after the Great Depression of the 1930s came about through the utilization of existing pools of investment funds such as those held by insurance companies and savings associations, rather than through the sale of bonds to the general public. Gradually the sale of bonds has returned as a method of financing real estate investments. In fact, a new source of mortgage funds has been tapped through the sale of a debt certificate called a *mortgage-*

backed security. As a form of security offered to the general public, these, too, fall under government regulation.

The creation of the Securities and Exchange Commission (SEC) in 1934 introduced some measure of control to the securities industry, and the enforcement of these regulations was helpful in preventing fraud, deception, and abusive practices in connection with the sale of stocks and bonds. In today's market, only a few of the very largest companies, such as American Telephone, attempt to sell large issues of bonds directly to the general public. The majority of companies work in tandem with investment bankers who are knowledgeable in securities regulations, and whose organizations are staffed with sales personnel capable of handling the distribution.

Because the sale of any kind of security, whether stocks or bonds, requires some established record and credibility, developers and home builders taking this step are usually limited to better known companies and individuals of strong financial worth. Considerable initial time and expense are required for the proper registration of a bond issue, involving extensive legal work and accounting data to be submitted to the SEC, which must then approve the issue, clearing it for sale to the public. The cost of registration alone, for instance, can run as high as several hundred thousand dollars.

A bond issue secured by a pledge of real property would be termed a *mortgage* bond. There are also *equipment* bonds secured by such things as freight cars or airplanes. A bond that is not secured is called a *debenture* bond and is similar to a promissory note. What the SEC requires is that the issuer fully disclose all information relative to the company and its key personnel, the security behind the bond issue, and how the proceeds of the sale will be used. Failure to comply with SEC requirements is a felony offense, subject to fine and imprisonment.

Once a bond issue has been registered and approved, the investment banker can handle the sale in two different ways. First, an outright purchase of the entire issue can be made at a discount off the full value. The issue is then resold to investor clients at a higher price, usually with the help of a network of associated investment banking firms across the country. With very large issues, several of the major investment houses may join together to underwrite the issue. It takes an intimate knowledge of the market conditions to handle a block purchase with the expectation of making a profit from the markup of its discount price.

The second method can be termed the "best efforts" plan. This actually means just what the name implies—the investment banker will sell the issue at whatever the market will bring, retaining a fixed commission.

Private Placement of Securities

The growth of major investors, such as the insurance companies, the mutual funds, and pension funds, has recently dominated the activity on the national security exchanges. However, there is a growing trend to bypass these public markets and place both stock and bond issues directly with an investor. From the point of view of the issuer, the procedure has some advantages, including: (1) no SEC registration required; (2) no publicity—no public pronouncements of proprietary information regarding company products or processes; (3) financial conditions of closely held companies remain confidential information; (4) more flexibility in terms with a negotiated private placement, thereby benefiting both the borrower and the lender; and (5) lower sales costs for the issue.

It is within this field of the private placement of securities that mortgage bankers have become increasingly active and directly competitive with the investment banker. Mortgage companies have good contacts with many sources of money and are familiar with the special needs of each for investments. The sale of a block of securities to their regular investors is a natural expansion of their business relationship.

SEC Regulations for Real Estate Sales

The growth in sales of various types of "certificates" to finance real estate developments has brought increased scrutiny by the SEC as to any violations of the securities laws. In general, the SEC considers the sale of any form of an *intended* interest in land to the general public as a type of security and subject to its regulations. For example, the sale might be of a future right to choose a lot in a resort development rather than a down payment on a designated tract of land. The many forms in which real estate developers present their various "deals" has brought a number of new rulings, all with the purpose of protecting the general public against fraud and misrepresentation. In various new rulings, the SEC has considered a predevelopment sale of certificates for lots as a form of securities; the sale of condominium units that may be available for rental purposes has come under registration guidelines; and if the sale of partnership interests is solicited publicly, as opposed to a contact *from* an interested purchaser, then a clearance is needed from the SEC.

In any real estate project involving ownership by a group of persons or companies, the prudent lender will obtain a legal opinion to determine if proper compliance is being made with both federal and state security regulations.

Sale and Lease-Back

The purpose of a sale and lease-back is to allow a property owner to convert the equity value of an owned building into cash, while retaining the possession and use of the property. For the purchaser of the property, the arrangement provides a sound income-producing investment in a proven, existing property. For example, a wholesale supply firm owns an existing warehouse building and is in need of more capital to expand inventory. The building is sold to an insurance company in need of a long-term investment for its money. Simultaneously, a lease is executed with the wholesale supply firm granting continued occupancy of the premises. The supply firm now has the cash to expand and the lease payments are tax-deductible expenses.

A variation of the sale and lease-back procedure is a *build-to-lease* agreement. Instead of purchasing an existing building, the investor contracts with a tenant to build a suitable building and lease it upon completion. In this manner, the investor has an assured income from future rentals (which can be used to assist further financing), and the tenant obtains the use of a specially designed building that best suits his purposes.

The build-to-lease procedure is used by major companies, such as oil companies seeking to expand their marketing operations, who will build and lease a service station for a particular tenant. Another variation of this procedure is the municipally owned industrial park. A city that wants to increase business and the number of jobs for the community will acquire a suitable tract of land, develop it, and build buildings for lease to acceptable tenants, all for the purpose of attracting more industry. The money for such land purchase and construction is generated by the sale of municipal bonds, not always guaranteed by the issuing community, but always in the tax-exempt municipal category.

Land Leases

Businessmen have always felt a strong need for owning something tangible, and with some individuals there has been an almost fanatical pursuit of landownership and the consequent feelings of security such ownership provides. The urge to own land simply as land, however, is gradually giving way to a more realistic approach that values land for the uses that can be made of it. Most of the material things we consider essential to sustain and maintain our lifestyle, such as houses, cars, appliances, and furniture, can now be rented. Business enterprises have long been accustomed to renting buildings as well as owning them, but they usually insisted on owning their own equipment. Now, through specialized leasing companies, even the most intricate machinery and equipment can be leased. The advantage to the lessee is that his capital is not tied up, the lease payments are all tax-deductible expenses, and the equipment may be more easily exchanged for newer models, thereby reducing the problem of obsolescence.

As land increases in value, sometimes to the point that it is removed from the market altogether except for lease, there has been increasing interest in the use of leasehold financing as a means of development. A leasehold on land possesses value, and under certain conditions can be offered as collateral for a first mortgage leasehold loan. The procedure is widely used in Hawaii, in Orange County, California, and in many urban centers. Whenever a lease on land is consummated between a landowner and a builder, the contract is generally known and referred to as a *ground lease*. The landowner's interest is termed the *underlying fee*, and the lessee's (builder's) interest is known as the *leasehold*.

Under the stipulations of a gound lease, the leasehold interest may be pledged to secure a mortgage loan, but not the underlying fee. Since this situation creates problems for a potential lender, two procedures have been developed to overcome some of the lender's objections to financing a long-term loan.

Unsubordinated Leasehold Mortgage

In this procedure, the leased land is not subject to the mortgage, and thus a default in payment of the ground rent can bring about, or lead to, foreclosure and a termination of all leasehold rights. An acceptable method of overcoming this obstacle in a leasehold loan is a provision that allows the lender to step into the lessee's position upon notification of default and continue the payments on ground rent. As a precaution in such a loan, a lender would normally require the borrower to make payments of the ground rent as a part of the mortgage payment, similiar to the payment of taxes required in a first mortgage residential loan. Ground rents thus held by the lender in escrow would be passed on to the landowner when due.

Subordinated Ground Lease

Under a subordinated ground lease, the landowner agrees to make his ownership interest inferior, or of secondary priority, to that of the lender's mortgage rights. The result is that the leasehold interest becomes the risk equivalent of a fee interest insofar as the designated mortgage is concerned. For the lender, the security is the same as a first mortgage on the land. A default in the mortgage payments could result in a foreclosure and loss of the land by the landowner. Protection for the landowner against such a development would be a specified right to step into the position of the borrower and continue the mortgage payments. The subordinated form of ground lease is sometimes used by motel developers and fast-food franchise operations.

Use of Other Collateral

Mortgage loans can be made on the basis of the real property plus some other form of collateral that may be pledged. If the borrower needs more money than the property alone will permit, the lender can ask for more security: additional property, stocks or bonds, an assignment of equipment, or such other assets mutually agreed to by the lender and borrower. With additional collateral, the lender has recourse to other assets for recovery of the loan if it becomes necessary.

Personal Endorsement

The personal endorsement by an individual for the benefit of a company, relative, or associate is a form of additional collateral to the lender. Large corporate borrowers do not use personal endorsements, but with smaller companies and those under majority control by one stockholder, it is not uncommon to request the personal endorsement of the principals—one or all of them. A personal guarantee on a mortgage loan can be limited. For example, if five men are endorsing a $100,000 loan, each might ask to limit individual liability to $20,000. Approval would be a matter of decision by the lender. Without a specific limitation, each endorser of a note is exposed, or is said to carry a contingent liability, to the full amount of the debt.

Compensating Balances

Cash balances carried in an account with the lending institution, when it is a commercial bank or savings association, can be deemed additional collateral when a minimum balance is required as a condition of the loan agreement. This procedure is also called a *compensating balance*. The requirement to maintain a certain minimum cash balance is not unusual since it gives the lender some assurance that cash is on hand, and this does add some strength to the borrower's financial statement. Many lenders do not acknowledge a compensating balance as any inducement to grant a loan because of the abuses and pressures that can occur. For a one- or two-point fee, a cash deposit could be transferred to the lender's institution solely to support a loan, but the deposit would not be under the control of the borrower. This does not add strength to the borrower and can encourage lending to an unworthy borrower. But it is hard to deny the importance for a borrower to maintain a sound cash position—and why not on deposit with the lending institution?

Assignment of Life Insurance

Life insurance companies are probably more interested than other lenders in adding the assignment of life insurance policies on the principal borrowers' lives to the list of additional collateral. This practice is a reasonable requirement for any lender when the successful payout of a loan is heavily based on the ability of one or two principals to operate a business. Some homeowners also carry mortgage payout life insurance, a declining balance form that covers the amortized balance due on a loan in case of the premature death of the borrower. However, lenders do not require this particular type of insurance in conjunction with the granting of a home loan.

Sale of Equity Interests

Two types of equity investment have become popular as methods for financing real estate—syndications and realty funds.

Syndication

The *syndication of land* is a term that describes land or property acquisition and ownership by a group of participants. The participants may be individuals, partnerships, or corporations. A syndicate is not a form of business organization, rather it is a name applied to any form set up to pursue a limited objective in business. While there are a number of forms that may be used in the organization of a syndicate, the most popular is the *limited partnership*. As a business form, the limited partnership is recognized in all states. Essentially, it provides for one or more general partners who are responsible for the management and who are personally liable for the partnership's obligations. Another class of partners is also recognized—the limited partners, who are not permitted to participate in management decisions, and whose liability is limited to the amount of their invested capital. A limited partnership must file its chartering agreement with the state in accordance with the applicable laws.

Two basic types of syndicates include:

1. *Sale of interests in existing properties.* Under this method, the property is identified for the participants. For example, a builder or developer (usually called the *syndicator*) owns or controls (by option or contract of sale) a suitable investment property. The syndicator then sells participating interests to raise the money to develop the land, or possibly to complete the acquisition of an existing building.

2. *Sale of interests in property to be acquired.* The syndicator sells interests to raise money for the acquisition of property as determined later by the syndicator. This procedure is also referred to, quite accurately, as a *blind pool*. Because it allows so much freedom to the syndicator in the use of other people's money, many states forbid its use.

Since a participating interest in a syndicate can be classed as a form of security investment, most states place limits on the number of participations that can be *offered* without a complete registration under the state's security law. If the sales are made across state lines, or the number to whom participations are offered exceeds 35, then a registration must be made with the federal Securities and Exchange Commission. Failure to comply with the law can result in felony action against the syndicator for the sale of unregistered securities.

Realty Funds

Whenever a larger group is formed to participate in a real estate venture, and registration with federal and state regulatory agencies is necessary, the participation can be in the form of "units" purchased in a realty fund, usually formed as a limited partnership.

Realty funds are organized by persons or companies wishing to raise equity money for real estate projects, such as the purchase of raw land, a construction development, or the purchase of existing income properties. The interests are sold in the form of participating certificates at a fixed price per unit. A unit generally costs anywhere from $100 to $5,000, depending on the plan of organization, and represents a certain percent of interest in the total fund. Federal and most state laws classify the sale of such participating interests as a sale of securities that must be registered and approved before any sale can be made.

The participant is actually a limited partner and may share in the tax losses and depreciation as well as the profits generated through the fund's investments. The organizer of the fund is usually the general partner, or a company he controls is so designated, and he also serves as the managing agent for the fund's properties.

Special Types of Financing

While most mortgage financing follows a fairly standard pattern of a first mortgage as security based on a reasonable loan to value ratio and fully amortized over the term of the loan, there are some interesting variations that can be used in special circumstances. When the situation calls for a more flexible approach to a loan, the following basic methods might be considered, either separately or in combination, as need or imagination may inspire.

Although some proposals become more imaginative than realistic, proper use of specialized financing techniques can rescue a faltering real estate sale or breathe new life into an otherwise stalled project. In the hands of a skilled promoter, some of these procedures reflect the so-called wheeler-dealer concept of development financing. But there is a telling story in an old cartoon depicting a rather seedy looking tramp relaxed on a park bench and picking his teeth with a piece of straw. The caption reads, "I never quite got the hang of it. I was always dealing when I should have been wheeling, and wheeling when I should have been dealing."

Wrap-Around Mortgage

A wrap-around mortgage is a junior lien–type of financing that includes an existing mortgage claim, or claims, in the amount of the note. Liability for the existing mortgage is not assumed by the buyer granting a wrap-around mortgage; the property is taken "subject to" the existing mortgage. Thus, the obligation on a wrap-around mortgage agreement is to the holder of the wrap, who in turn is obligated to the holder of the prior existing mortgage claim, or claims. If the buyer granting a wrap mortgage also assumes existing mortgage claims, the buyer could be liable for a duplication in the amount of the debt; that is, liable for both the existing and the wrap claims. Even though liability on the existing obligation is not assumed in this kind of transaction, title to the property must pass to the buyer granting the wrap, otherwise there could be no wrap mortgage.

The purpose of the wrap procedure is to utilize the advantages in an existing mortgage. There could be several. The most obvious is to hold on to an older, lower interest rate. Some mortgages, such as FHA and VA types, still permit a passing on of the old note to a new buyer without an increase in the interest rate. Some mortgages allow for a negotiated rate in case of a transfer of ownership rights. However, the wrap-around mortgage should not be considered a device to circumvent the right of an existing mortgage lender under the due-on-sale clause. Failure to advise an existing lender when a transfer of property rights occurs could create serious problems, particularly if the new buyer causes a default and court action becomes necessary.

Another advantage that is gained in the wrap-around mortgage procedure is the holding of the earlier mortgage priority. This can be of importance when an existing lender undertakes additional financing. Instead of rewriting a new mortgage, the lender may prefer to wrap the existing loan. A further advantage that is more important for a home seller undertaking a wrap mortgage is the additional control over the continued payments on the existing mortgage. With payments passed through the holder of the wrap or a designated escrow agent, there is better assurance of timely payments to the existing lender. If problems in payment should develop, protective action might be taken before it is too late.

While the wrap-around method has found some popularity with home sellers wanting to take advantage of an existing lower interest rate loan, the concept is used in commercial transactions, and such financing can be undertaken by any lender, not just a seller. When used for seller financing, there is considerable room for negotiation as to the interest rate, the down payment required, and the term of the loan.

To illustrate with a hypothetical example, let us say a building is offered for sale at a price of $100,000, which is acceptable to the buyer. The first mortgage loan, now 10 years old with an interest rate of 8 percent, is paid down to a balance due of $55,000. On a straight assumption basis, the buyer would need $45,000 cash. Or with a new first mortgage loan on the older building, the maximum loan-to-value ratio being offered would be 75 percent, which would require $25,000 cash. But the buyer does not want to use even that much initial cash in the purchase. Under such conditions a wrap-around mortgage might well resolve the problem and make the sale possible. The proposal is for the buyer to pay just $10,000 cash and grant to the seller a wrap-around mortgage on the property for $90,000 at 11 percent interest, which is subject to the existing first mortgage. Under this arrangement the seller is actually undertaking a second mortgage loan in the amount of $35,000, at a fair interest rate, plus earning an additional 3 percent of interest on the first mortgage. Normally, the seller would continue to make the regular payments on the first mortgage obligation, using the proceeds from the wrap mortgage payments to do so. The buyer, paying on a $90,000 obligation each month, would of course require some protective clause granting the right to make the first mortgage payments direct to the first mortgagee if a potential default should arise.

Balloon Note

A balloon note is one that calls for a substantial payment on principal at maturity. Technically, the payment would be more than two monthly installments. And it could be the full amount of the loan wherein interest only is paid until maturity. Its purpose is to permit smaller monthly installments for the first few years and to retain the loan in a short-term classification for the lending institution. The smaller monthly payments (less than the amount to fully amortize the loan) are made for, say, three years, at which time the full unpaid balance becomes due.

If, for example, the borrower needed $25,000 and offered adequate collateral, the lender under this type of loan would accept principal payments of $200 per month, plus accrued interest, for up to three years. At the end of the third year, the final payment due in full would be $18,000, plus interest. (Payments of $200 each for 35 months amount to a principal reduction of $7,000.)

It is often assumed that if the payments are promptly made, the lender will renew and extend the final balloon payment for another limited term of small principal payments. But the lender is by no means legally obligated to do so, and circumstances can force the lender to require a full payoff on the note when due.

Interest Only

The expression *interest only* covers a variation of the balloon note procedure in that for the first year or so nothing is paid on the principal, and only the interest is due. This method is most commonly used today in the sale of raw land but is applicable to any kind of loan.

If sellers are commanding a good market price for their land and do not need immediate cash, they have a better chance of selling the property by handling their own financing and making it attractive to the speculative buyer, such as a syndicated group. In such a case, the purchaser, buying the land for resale rather than development, wants as small a cash investment as possible, hoping to resell within several years at a profit.

To use an example: if a person owns 40 acres of land and sells it for $5,000 per acre, or $200,000 total, the sales amount may be carried as a loan to the buyer and 8 percent interest collected for the first two years. Thus, the buyer takes title to the property, subject to the seller's mortgage in the amount of $200,000, and each year pays $16,000 to the seller as tax-deductible interest. Before the two years have elapsed, the buyer finds another company who will pay $8,000 an acre for the land in cash. Now, the second sale at a later date for $320,000 clears the $200,000 first mortgage and any accrued interest, leaving a substantial profit on a relatively small cash investment. The trick is being able to make that second sale.

Extended Terms

Most companies selling a service or product need their accounts receivable paid promptly and often offer cash discounts for such payments. A few companies utilize credit terms as an incentive to do business with them and, in so doing, provide additional financing for the customer.

In building an apartment, an office building, or even a house, a major supplier such as a lumber dealer, a cement company, or an electrical or plumbing contractor may agree to extend payment terms for 60 or 90 days, or in some cases, until the project is finished and sold. This method does conserve cash for the builder-developer, but usually comes at a higher price—an increase in the product or service price plus interest. And the supplier may be exposed to a payment delay that usually means a forfeiture of lien rights if it exceeds 120 days.

This *extended terms* method of auxiliary finance is not to be confused with slow payment or nonpayment of materialmen's bills; both are very poor procedures. Building supply companies are fully aware of the 90- to 120-day time limits within which to file liens for nonpayment and normally make sure that their interests are protected.

Supplier Loans

In recent years some of the major appliance companies and, in a few cases, utility companies, have given larger builder-developers financial assistance with outright loans secured by second mortgages. The ulterior motive in such cases is always to insure the use of the lender's products. This could be heating and air conditioning equipment, or a full range of kitchen equipment, or it could be a utility company seeking a competitive advantage.

Subordination

Subordination is a procedure used to grant priority to a specific lien so as to permit better financing of a project. In this method, landowners or mortgage holders, for a consideration, might subordinate their position in favor of a specific lending institution in order to meet a loan requirement.

A possible situation wherein this procedure could be used would be a landowner who, not wishing to sell the land, but desiring development and income, agrees to a long-term land lease to, say, a motel chain. In order to help finance the construction of the motel building, the landowner would agree to subordinate (to make inferior) his or her ownership rights to the mortgage lien, as arranged by the motel chain. Normally, the motel chain would have to be sufficiently strong financially to give the landowner reasonable assurance of performance under the lease terms. And the landowner would expect to retain the right to step in and assume the mortgage payments, with rights to the motel's income, in case of an act in default by the motel chain.

Questions for Discussion

1. Describe how the sale of bonds is used to finance a real estate investment.

2. What is meant by the private placement of securities and how does this method compare with public offerings?

3. Discuss the position of the Securities and Exchange Commission in regard to the sale of participating interests in real estate deals.

4. Describe a typical sale lease-back agreement.

5. How can a mortgage loan be made for a property where the land is leased to the loan applicant?

6. What is a syndication and how would it be set up to acquire real property?

7. Describe how a realty fund is organized and operated.

8. What is a *wrap-around mortgage* and how does it work?

9. Describe a *balloon note* and an *interest only* agreement.

10. What is meant by the term *subordination*?

11. Describe at least two different ways that a homeowner can assist in the selling of his house.

Settlement Procedures

Settlement Practices

Since property laws are essentially determined by each state, their diversity is reflected in the methods used to close, or settle, real estate transactions. Customs and practices have developed in every region of the country that best suit its unique business and legal requirements. The person or company selected to bring together the instruments of conveyance, mortgages, promissory notes, and, of course, the monetary considerations to be exchanged between the buyer and seller of real estate is most generally known as the *settlement agent*. The agent can be a lender, a real estate broker, a title company, an attorney, or a company specializing in these procedures called an escrow company. In most parts of the country, the settlement agent arranges for the principals involved in the transaction to meet together at a location where all the documents needed to transfer title and to secure and fund a loan can be reviewed and executed. At the conclusion of this process, if all documents are in order, the documents and the money are then distributed to the various parties entitled to receive them.

Another procedure, called *escrow closing*, is commonly used in some states. In this procedure, however, the parties involved do not meet around a table to sign instruments or exchange any cash or documents. Rather, at the time of entering a contract of sale, the parties sign an escrow agreement. The agreement requires the deposit of certain documents and funds with the escrow agent within an agreed time. The agent is responsible for meeting the requirements of the escrow agreement, which usually include the adjustment of taxes, insurance, and rentals, if any, between the buyer and seller, the payoff of any existing loan, arrangements for hazard insurance coverage, the computing of interest, and any other requirements for a new loan. If all papers and monies are deposited within the agreed time limit, the escrow is considered closed. The appropriate documents are then recorded and delivered to the proper parties along with the money that each is entitled to receive.

It was this area of diverse procedures that Congress focused on in 1974 and began to regulate. The purpose of the proposed legislation, by its own findings, was to protect consumers from "unnecessarily high settlement charges caused by certain abusive practices that have developed in some areas of the country." The result of congressional efforts was the enactment of the Real Estate Settlement Procedures Act (RESPA). Unfortunately, this Act in its initial form was vaguely worded and contained a number of ill-defined requirements. Its effect on the real estate industry was one of substantial confusion as it was difficult to determine exactly what activities were considered legal or illegal. A temporary moratorium on the provisions of the Act helped restore normal business, and in 1976 an amendment to the Act effectively modified it, resulting in more practical legislation. The amended Act adds several new requirements to the closing procedures of a residential real estate transaction. It does not change any local practices and sets no prices for settlement services. Mostly, it is directed towards providing better information on the settlement process so that a home buyer can make informed decisions.

Preliminary Procedures

There are two pieces of information closely associated with the settlement of a real estate transaction that are noted separately here because of their special usefulness in any property disposition. These are an existing *loan status report* and a *preliminary title report*. Many good real estate brokers arrange for both pieces of information at the time a property is listed for sale. In this way, if there are problems with either an existing loan or legal title to the property, it is discovered early on, allowing more time for resolution before the seller is faced with an impending closing date. Also, it is very important that the seller or agent have accurate information on these two subjects since they are of intense interest to any prospective buyer.

Loan Status Report

Several different names are used within the industry to describe the information contained in the status report on an existing mortgage loan. Some call it a Mortgagor's Information Letter, some a Mortgagee's Report. Further confusion is added to the nomenclature because in some areas of the country a Mortgagee's Information Letter means a preliminary title report on the land. What is referred to here is a report on the current status of an existing loan prepared by the mortgagee for the mortgagor. It is a statement, usually in letter form, giving the remaining balance due on the loan, the monthly payments required, the reserve held in the escrow account, and the requirements and cost of a loan payoff.

A request for this information must come from the mortgagor, although brokers often use form letters for the request that require only the mortgagor's signature. While this information is very helpful in providing accurate sales information, it is not normally used by the settlement agent in closing a real estate transaction. The agent calls for a current report that reflects the loan status as of the date a settlement actually takes place.

Preliminary Title Report

When an earnest money contract has been signed, it is a good idea to "open title" with whatever title insurance company has been selected to handle the closing. Under the new RESPA procedures, the seller may not require that title insurance be purchased from a particular title company as a condition of the sale. But the mortgage lender still has a right to accept or reject a proposed title company. So it is a good suggestion for buyers to make certain that they are selecting an acceptable title company when they decide. Lending institutions are now required to submit a statement to the borrower listing acceptable title companies and attorneys, along with the anticipated charges the borrower might expect. Also, any business relationship between the lender and *any* settlement service provider must be disclosed. In order to simplify handling, the title company selected is normally one located in the same county as the property being sold.

The preliminary title report is furnished by the title company to both the real estate agent and the mortgage company. The information contained is a confirmation of the correct legal description, and it also includes the names of the owners of the property according to the county records, any restrictions or liens on the property, any judgments against the owners of record, and a listing of any requirements the title company may have to perfect title and to issue a title insurance policy. The report is for information only; it is not to be confused with a title *binder*, which legally obligates the title company for specific insurance. The title companies normally make no charge for the preliminary report; it is part of their service in anticipation of writing the title insurance policy at closing.

RESPA Requirements

The Real Estate Settlement Procedures Act, as amended in 1976, applies to *residential* mortgage loans. Commercial loans are not included in the provisions of the Act. Residential mortgage loans are those used to finance the purchase of one- to four-family housing, a condominium, a cooperative apartment unit, a lot with a mobile home, or a lot on which a house is to be built or a mobile home located. RESPA requirements can be divided into two general categories: (1) information requirements and (2) prohibited practices.

Information Requirements

Lenders are now required to furnish certain specific information to each loan *applicant* and additional information to the borrower prior to closing a loan.

Information Booklet.   At the time of a loan application, or not later than three business days after, the lender must give the applicant a copy of the HUD-prepared booklet entitled "A Homebuyer's Guide to Settlement Costs." The booklet is prepared by the Office of Consumer Affairs and Regulatory Functions of the U.S. Department of Housing and Urban Development. The information provided is discussed in two parts.

1. *Part One* describes the settlement process and the nature of the charges that are incurred. Questions are suggested for the home buyer to ask that might help clarify charges and procedures. It also lists unfair and illegal practices and gives information on the rights and remedies available to home buyers should they encounter a wrongful practice.
2. *Part Two* is an item-by-item explanation of settlement services and costs. Sample forms and worksheets are included to help guide the home buyer in making cost comparisons.

Good Faith Estimate.   Within three business days of accepting a loan application, a lender is required to submit a *good faith estimate* of settlement costs to the loan applicant. The settlement charges are estimated for each item anticipated, except for prepaid hazard insurance and cash reserves deposited with the lender. (Reserves are subject to RESPA restrictions, which are detailed later.) The estimate may be stated in either a dollar amount or as a range for each charge, and the information must be furnished in a clear and concise manner (no special form is required). A typical Good Faith Estimate is illustrated in Figure 16-1, which uses the terminology and account numbers from Section L of the mandatory Settlement Statement (Figures 16-3a and 16-3b).

Designated Service Providers.   If a lender designates settlement service providers, who perform such tasks as legal services, title examination, title insurance, or the conduct of the settlement, the normal charges for these specific providers must be used in the good faith estimate. Fur-

GOOD FAITH ESTIMATE

Name: _____   Re: _____
                                 Property: _____

This list gives an estimate of most of the charges you will have to pay at the settlement of your loan. The figures shown, as *estimates*, are subject to change. The figures shown are computed based on sales price and proposed mortgage amount as stated on your loan application.

ESTIMATED SETTLEMENT CHARGES

801	Loan Origination Fee 1%	_____
803	Appraisal Fee	_____
804	Credit Report	_____
901*	Interest	_____
902	Mortgage Insurance Premium	_____
1107	Attorney's Fees	_____
1108	Title Insurance	_____
1201	Recording Fees	_____
____	_____	_____
____	_____	_____
1301	Survey	_____

Your contractual agreement with the Seller may limit your payment of the above charges.

* This interest calculation represents the greatest amount of interest you could be required to pay at settlement. The actual amount will be determined by which day of the month your settlement is conducted. To determine the amount you will have to pay, multiply the number of days remaining in the month in which you settle times _____, which is the daily interest charge for your loan.

THIS FORM DOES NOT COVER ALL ITEMS YOU WILL BE REQUIRED TO PAY IN CASH AT SETTLEMENT. YOU MAY BE REQUIRED TO PAY OTHER ADDITIONAL AMOUNTS AT TIME OF LOAN SETTLEMENT.

FIGURE 16-1   Good Faith Estimate.

ther, when this designation occurs, the lender must provide as a part of the good faith estimate, additional information giving the name, address, and telephone number of each designated provider. Any business relationship between the lender and the service provider must be fully disclosed.

Disclosure of Settlement Costs.   As a part of the RESPA requirements, the use of a uniform Settlement Statement has been made mandatory for residential loan closings. Account numbers and terminology are standardized on the form, and it is expected that settlement charges, however designated in various parts of the country, be fitted into this form (Figures 16-3a and 16-3b). A copy of the completed form must be delivered by the settlement agent to both the buyer and the seller at or before the closing. Since some of the information needed to complete the form may not be available until the time of actual closing, the borrower may waive the right of delivery at closing. However, in such a case, the completed settlement statement must be mailed at the earliest practical date.

Borrower's Right to Disclosure of Costs Prior to Closing.   A borrower has the right under RESPA to request an inspection of the Settlement Statement one business day prior to closing. The form is completed by the person who will conduct the settlement procedures. The Act does recognize that all costs may not be available one day prior to closing, but there is an obligation to show the borrower what is available, if requested.

Prohibited Practices

The vast majority of settlement procedures have always been conducted in an ethical manner by qualified professionals. However, abuses do occur occasionally, and it is one of the purposes RESPA to expose unfair practices and make them illegal. Two such practices are described below.

Kickbacks.   The law specifically prohibits any arrangement by means of which a fee is charged, or accepted, where no services have actually been performed. The requirement does not prevent agents for the lender, attorneys, or others from actually performing a service in connection with the mortgage loan or settlement procedure. Nor does it prohibit cooperative brokerage arrangements such as are normally found in multiple listing services or referral arrangements between real estate agents and brokers. The target for the prohibition is the arrangement wherein one party returns a part of his fee (such as a loan origination fee) to obtain business from the referring party. The abuse involved here, of course, is that such an arrangement can result in a higher settlement fee for the borrower with no increase in the services rendered.

Title Companies. A *seller* is not permitted to require the use of a specified title insurance company as a condition of sale. The buyer has the right to compare the services and charges of competing title companies. In many states the rates for title insurance come under the regulatory authority of the state and are thus uniform. Also, lenders retain the right to reject title companies that do not meet their minimum requirements of financial strength.

Truth-In-Lending Act

The Truth-In-Lending Act is a federal law that became effective in July 1969, as a part of the Consumer Credit Protection Act and is implemented by the Federal Reserve Board's Regulation Z. The purpose of the law is to require lenders to give meaningful information to borrowers on the cost of consumer credit, which includes credit extended in real estate transactions. The credit covered must involve a finance charge or be payable in more than four installments. Credit extended for business purposes, which includes dwelling units containing more than four family units, is not covered by the law. No maximum or minimum interest rates or charges for credit are set by the law, for its purpose is primarily one of disclosure.

While the Act contains a limited right allowing the borrower to rescind or cancel the credit transaction and covers *all* types of advertising to promote the extension of consumer credit, the principal features are the disclosure of the *Finance Charge* and the *Annual Percentage Rate* (APR).

Finance Charge

The finance charge is the total amount of all costs that the consumer must pay for obtaining credit. These costs include interest, the loan fee, a loan finder's fee, time-price differentials, discount points, and the cost of credit life insurance if it is a condition for granting credit. In a real estate transaction, purchase costs that would be paid regardless of whether or not credit is extended are *not* included in the finance charge, provided these charges are reasonable and bona fide and not included to circumvent the law. Among these excluded purchase costs are legal fees, taxes not included in the cash price, recording fees, title insurance premiums, and credit report charges. However, such charges must be itemized and disclosed to the customer. In the case of first mortgages intended to purchase residential dwellings, the total dollar finance charge need not be stated, although the annual percentage rate must be disclosed.

Annual Percentage Rate

The annual percentage rate as determined under Regulation Z is not an "interest rate." Interest is one of the costs included in the finance charge. The APR is the relationship of the total finance charge to the total amount to be financed and must be computed to the nearest 1/4 percent. Figure 16-2 illustrates a typical form used in a real estate transaction prepared in compliance with Regulation Z.

Settlement Practices and Costs

As noted earlier in this chapter, settlement practices vary considerably in different sections of the country. There is no federal requirement to change any basic practices for residential loans except where it is necessary to add some disclosure procedures and to eliminate any prohibited practices. There are limitations set by RESPA on the amount of reserve, or escrow, accounts that may be held by lenders, and there is one mandatory form to be used in the settlement of residential loans.

The mandatory uniform Settlement Statement form is illustrated in Figures 16-3a and 16-3b and will be used as the basis for the following discussion of the various services involved with a loan closing. While the emphasis is on residential loan practices, the procedures used in closing commercial loans involve most of the same services.

Settlement Statement

The design of the Settlement Statement places all of the costs chargeable to the buyer or the seller on the first page and a detail of these costs on the second page. A cursory examination of the statement shows that the first section, A through I, contains information concerning the loan and the parties involved. Section J lists the amounts due from, or paid by, the borrower, and Section K details the same for the seller. The bottom line in each column indicates the cash due by the borrower-buyer on the left-hand side, and that due by the seller on the right-hand side. Whatever money must change hands is clearly the result of the two figures. Section L on the second page of the form lists the various settlement services that can be involved in a closing with some blank lines for any separate entries not otherwise clearly identified.

This particular form must be completed for the settlement meeting by the person conducting the settlement procedures. A copy of the completed form is either given to both the buyer and seller at the meeting, or mailed as soon as practical after the meeting. If there is no actual

STATEMENT OF COST OF LOAN
Federal Truth-in-Lending Statement

FORM G

Processor:_____ Loan Type: FHA__VA__Conv___   Re: Loan No._____
Lender:_____   Date:_____
Name(s) of Borrower_____

1. A. The FINANCE CHARGE begins to accrue on the date lender disburses funds, estimated to
      be_____, 19___. Borrower will obligate himself to pay the principal
      of the loan, "the loan amount" of $_____, plus simple interest
      of _____% per annum in _____ monthly installments of $_____
      beginning _____, 19____ which will be increased by the estimated 1/12th
      of the annual charges for the following: 1.) Hazard Insurance; 2.) Ad valorem taxes;
      3.) Maintenance assessments, if any; 4.) FHA mortgage insurance (if this is an FHA loan)
      ranging from $_____per month in the first installment to $_____
      per month in the final installment; or 5.) If a conventional loan partially covered by
      private mortgage insurance an additional amount ranging over the _____months
      beginning with the 1st monthly payment due _____, 19____ in the amount of
      $_____and ending with the last monthly payment of $_____ due on
      _____,
      The total of payments will be $_____.
   B. The amount of the loan is ....$_____
   C. Less any prepaid finance charges:
      Origination fee or points paid by borrower $_____
      Loan discount or points paid by seller $_____
      Interest from_____to_____ $_____
      Initial Mortgage Insurance Premium
        (FHA Loans only) $_____
      Private Mortgage Insurance
        (1st. year or single premium) $_____
      Commitment fee $_____
      Application fee, final inspection fee $_____
      _____ $_____
      _____ $_____
         Total Prepaid FINANCE CHARGE ....$_____
   D. Equal amount financed ....$_____
2. The FINANCE CHARGE consists of:
   A. Total of interest (simple annual rate of
      _____%) $_____
   B. Total prepaid finance charge
        (from 1.C. above) $_____
   C. FHA Insurance (compute total) $_____
   D. PMI Insurance (compute total) $_____
   E. Total FINANCE CHARGE ....$_____
3. The ANNUAL PERCENTAGE RATE on the amount financed is ....%
4. In the event of late payments received more than 15 days after the due date, charges may be
   assessed as follows on the total monthly payment:_____%.
5. Prepayment Penalty: ( )FHA Loan: May be prepaid in full or in part without penalty with
   30-days written notice. ( )VA Loan: Payment in full or partial payments not less than the
   amount of one installment, or one hundred dollars, whichever is less, may be made at any
   time without penalty. (X)Conventional Loan: Borrower may prepay without penalty, during
   any one year, up to 20% of the original principal amount of the loan. Penalties are
   required for all other prepayments: 5% of the excess during first five years, 3% during
   next 5 years, and 1% thereafter.

6. Assigned life insurance, accident, health or loss of income Insurance is not required as a
   condition to extending of the loan provided for herein, nor is there required any insurance
   to protect Lender against the borrower's default or other credit loss.
7. Fire and hazard insurance with extended coverage and physical loss form with loss payable
   clause to Lender is required as a condition of this loan. This insurance may be purchased
   from any insurance company of Borrower's choice which is acceptable to Lender, and Lender
   estimates that the cost of such insurance will be approximately $_____ for a
   _____year period and $_____for a one year Flood Insurance premium.
8. The funds which I (we) will borrow from Lender are for the purpose of _____
   _____.
9. I (we) acknowledge receipt of this statement on _____, 19___, prior to the
   execution of any other loan documents, and that I (we) approve same and request that this
   transaction be closed.

_____   _____
(Signature of Borrower)   (Signature of Witness)

_____   _____
(Signature of Borrower)   (Signature of Witness)

FIGURE 16-2 Truth-in-Lending Disclosure Statement.

Form Approved
OMB No. 63-R1501

A.		B. TYPE OF LOAN:
	U.S. DEPARTMENT OF HOUSING AND URBAN DEVELOPMENT	1. ☐ FHA 2. ☐ FMHA 3. ☐ CONV. UNINS. 4. ☐ VA 5. ☐ CONV. INS.

CAPITAL TITLE COMPANY, INC.

6. FILE NUMBER	7. LOAN NUMBER

SETTLEMENT STATEMENT

8. MORTG. INS. CASE NO.

C. NOTE: This form is furnished to give you a statement of actual settlement costs. Amounts paid to and by the settlement agent are shown. Items marked "(p.o.c.)" were paid outside the closing; they are shown here for informational purposes and are not included in the totals.

D. NAME OF BORROWER	E. NAME OF SELLER	F. NAME OF LENDER

G. PROPERTY LOCATION	H. SETTLEMENT AGENT	I. SETTLEMENT DATE:
	PLACE OF SETTLEMENT	

J. SUMMARY OF BORROWER'S TRANSACTION		K. SUMMARY OF SELLER'S TRANSACTION	
100. GROSS AMOUNT DUE FROM BORROWER:		**400. GROSS AMOUNT DUE TO SELLER:**	
101. Contract sales price		401. Contract sales price	
102. Personal property		402. Personal property	
103. Settlement charges to borrower *(line 1400)*		403.	
104.		404.	
105.		405.	
		Adjustments for items paid by seller in advance:	
Adjustments for items paid by seller in advance:		406. City/town taxes to	
		407. County taxes to	
106. City/town taxes to		408. Assessments to	
107. County taxes to		409. Maintenance to	
108. Assessments to		410. Commitment Fee to	
109. Maintenance to		411. to	
110. School/Taxes to		412. to	
111. to		**420. GROSS AMOUNT DUE TO SELLER:**	
112. to			
120. GROSS AMOUNT DUE FROM BORROWER:		**500. REDUCTIONS IN AMOUNT DUE TO SELLER:**	
200. AMOUNTS PAID BY OR IN BEHALF OF BORROWER:		501. Excess deposit (see instructions)	
201. Deposit or earnest money		502. Settlement charges to seller *(line 1400)*	
202. Principal amount of new loan(s)		503. Existing loan(s) taken subject to	
203. Existing loan(s) taken subject to		504. Payoff of first mortgage loan	
204. Commitment Fee		505. Payoff of second mortgage loan	
205.		506.	
206.		507.	
207.		508.	
208.		509.	
209.			
Adjustments for items unpaid by seller:		Adjustments for items unpaid by seller:	
210. City/town taxes to		510. City/town taxes to	
211. County taxes to		511. County Taxes to	
212. Assessments to		512. Assessments to	
213. School/Taxes to		513. Maintenance to	
214. to		514. School/Taxes to	
215. to		515. to	
216. to		516. to	
217. to		517. to	
218. to		518. to	
219. to		519. to	
220. TOTAL PAID BY/FOR BORROWER:		**520. TOTAL REDUCTION AMOUNT DUE SELLER:**	
300. CASH AT SETTLEMENT FROM/TO BORROWER:		**600. CASH AT SETTLEMENT TO/FROM SELLER:**	
301. Gross amount due from borrower *(line 120)*		601. Gross amount due to seller *(line 420)*	
302. Less amounts paid by/for borrower *(line 220)* ( )		602. Less total reductions in amount due seller *(line 520)* ( )	
303. CASH (☐ FROM) (☐ TO) BORROWER:		603. CASH (☐ TO) (☐ FROM) SELLER	

(Rev. 5-76)

FIGURE 16-3a   HUD Settlement Statement for Residential Loans.

L. SETTLEMENT CHARGES		PAID FROM BORROWER'S FUNDS AT SETTLEMENT	PAID FROM SELLER'S FUNDS AT SETTLEMENT
700. **TOTAL SALES/BROKER'S COMMISSION Based on price** $ @ % =			
Division of commission (line 700) as follows:			
701. $ to			
702. $ to			
703. Commission paid at settlement			
704.			
800. **ITEMS PAYABLE IN CONNECTION WITH LOAN.**			
801. Loan Origination fee %			
802. Loan Discount %			
803. Appraisal Fee to			
804. Credit Report to			
805. Lender's inspection fee			
806. Mortgage Insurance application fee to			
807. Assumption Fee			
808. Commitment Fee			
809. FNMA Processing Fee			
810. Pictures			
811.			
900. **ITEMS REQUIRED BY LENDER TO BE PAID IN ADVANCE.**			
901. Interest from to @ $ /day			
902. Mortgage insurance premium for mo. to			
903. Hazard insurance premium for yrs. to			
904. Flood Insurance yrs. to			
905.			
1000. **RESERVES DEPOSITED WITH LENDER**			
1001. Hazard insurance mo. @ $ per mo.			
1002. Mortgage insurance mo. @ $ per mo.			
1003. City property taxes mo. @ $ per mo.			
1004. County property taxes mo. @ $ per mo.			
1005. Annual assessments (Maint.) mo. @ $ per mo.			
1006. School Property Taxes mo. @ $ per mo.			
1007. Water Dist. Prop. Tax mo. @ $ per mo.			
1008. Flood Insurance mo. @ $ per mo.			
1100. **TITLE CHARGES:**			
1101. Settlement or closing fee to			
1102. Abstract or title search to			
1103. Title examination to			
1104. Title insurance binder to			
1105. Document preparation to			
1106. Notary fees to			
1107. Attorney's fees to to			
(includes above items No.:			
1108. Title insurance to			
(includes above items No.:			
1109. Lender's coverage $			
1110. Owner's coverage $			
1111. Escrow Fee			
1112. Restrictions			
1113. Messenger Service			
1200. **GOVERNMENT RECORDING AND TRANSFER CHARGES**			
1201. Recording fees: Deed $ Mortgage $ Releases $			
1202. City/county tax/stamps: Deed $ Mortgage $			
1203. State tax/stamps: Deed $ Mortgage $			
1204. Tax Certificates			
1205.			
1300. **ADDITIONAL SETTLEMENT CHARGES**			
1301. Survey to			
1302. Pest inspection to			
1303.			
1304.			
1305.			
1400. **TOTAL SETTLEMENT CHARGES** (entered on lines 103, Section J and 502, Section K)			

SELLER'S AND/OR PURCHASER'S STATEMENT

Seller's and Purchaser's signature hereon acknowledges his/their approval of tax prorations, and signifies their understanding that prorations were based on figures for preceding year, or estimates for current year, and in event of any change for current year, all necessary adjustments must be made between Seller and Purchaser direct; likewise any DEFICIT in delinquent taxes will be reimbursed to Title Company by the Seller.

We approve the foregoing settlement statement, in its entirety, authorize payments in accordance therewith and acknowledge receipt of a copy thereof.

Signature_____   _____

_____   _____
Seller   Purchaser

_____
Escrow Officer   HUD-1 (Rev. 5-76)

FIGURE 16-3b HUD Settlement Statement for Residential Loans.

meeting of the parties involved for settlement, the agent must still mail the completed forms after the closing has been finalized. This is the same form that a borrower has the right to inspect one business day prior to closing. It is not required that all information be filled in one day prior to closing, but the settlement agent must disclose whatever is available if requested to do so by the borrower.

A Settlement Costs Worksheet is also available and is intended for use by the prospective borrower as a handy guide for making comparisons of the charges quoted by the various service providers.

Sales/Broker's Commission (Item 700)

The sales commission is usually paid by the seller and is listed on the settlement in the total dollar amount, then divided between participating brokers as the sales agreement may provide. The amount is negotiable and may be a flat fee for the sale or a percentage of the sales amount.

Items Payable in Connection with Loan (Item 800)

As identified by RESPA, the costs of the loan are the fees charged by the lenders to process, approve, and make the mortgage loan.

Loan Origination (801). This is the fee charged by the primary lender to assemble information necessary to evaluate a loan application, to determine its acceptability and to prepare the completed loan package. The charge is negotiable and varies from 1 percent to 1 1/2 percent of the loan amount.

Loan Discount (802). The loan discount is not truly a fee in that it is not considered payment for services rendered. Rather, the discount, expressed in points or as a percent of the loan amount, is the procedure used in all financial markets to adjust the yield on a fixed interest rate certificate to a level of return that is commensurate with the current market rate for money loaned. In a practical sense, the discount is interest, or a cost of borrowed money, paid in advance—sometimes explained as a down payment on the cost of borrowed money. As a cost of borrowed money paid at the time of loan settlement, a loan discount must properly be charged as one of the items payable in connection with the loan.

Appraisal Fee (803). An appraisal of the property is necessary to establish the value basis for a mortgage loan. All regulated lenders must have an appraisal prepared by an independent professional appraiser, or by a qualified member of the lender's staff, to provide factual data on the value of the property offered as loan collateral. Since an appraisal is of value to both the buyer and seller of property, it may be paid for by either one. In some cases the cost of an appraisal may be included as a part of the initial application fee (either for the loan, or for the mortgage insurance).

Credit Report Fee (804).   All applicants for mortgage loans are required to submit credit reports that are obtained by the lender from local credit bureaus. This report is a necessary verification of information submitted in the loan application plus statistical information on the bill-paying record of the applicant. The credit report is one source of information that a lender uses to determine if the applicant is an acceptable credit risk. Payment for the report is most often made by the borrower.

Lender's Inspection Fee (805).   The lender is permitted to assess a charge for an inspection of the property offered as collateral. The inspection can be made by the lender's personnel or by an independent inspector. Such an inspection is most often made when the house is newly constructed. This inspection is not to be confused with pest inspections, which are discussed later.

Mortgage Insurance Application Fee (806).   Private mortgage insurance companies charge fees for the processing of a loan application. This fee sometimes covers both an appraisal fee and an application fee.

Assumption Fee (807).   An assumption fee is essentially a paper-processing fee charged in transactions in which the buyer takes over and assumes liability for payments on a prior loan of the seller.

Items Required by Lender To Be Paid in Advance (Item 900)

There are certain items that must be paid in advance at the closing of a loan.

Interest (901).   Since mortgage loans extend for long terms, it is a common practice to adjust the monthly payment to a convenient date each month, most often the first of each month. The normal monthly payment on a mortgage loan includes a charge for interest at the end of the month; that is *after* the borrower has had the use of the money loaned. So in order to adjust the monthly payment to a date other than that of loan closing, the interest charge is computed for the time period from the date of closing to the beginning of the period covered by the first monthly payment. For example, if the settlement takes place on

June 16, a prepayment of charges is needed through June 30. The period covered by the regular monthly payment begins on July 1, and the first payment is due on August 1.

To compute the interest charges for 15 days (June 16 through June 30) on a $45,000 loan at 10 percent interest:

$45,000 × .10	= $4,500	Annual interest cost
$4,500 ÷ 360	= $12.50	Daily interest cost
$12.50 × 15 days	= $187.50	*Prepaid interest due*

Mortgage Insurance Premium (902). Almost all lenders now require private mortgage insurance on loans in excess of 80 percent of the property value. The protection is against a borrower default in the payment of the loan. It enables a lender to make higher ratio (up to 95 percent) loans than would otherwise be possible and thus allows lower down payments for the borrower. The first premium charged is always higher than the continuing annual payments, as it includes an issuing fee and is payable in full at the loan closing. This type of mortgage insurance should not be confused with mortgage life, credit life, or disability insurance, which are designed to pay off a mortgage in the event of physical disability or death of the borrower.

Hazard Insurance Premium (903). Hazard insurance protects both the lender and the borrower against loss to the building by fire, windstorm, or other natural hazard. Such coverage is a requirement for mortgage loans and includes the naming of the lender as a loss payee (in addition to the homeowner) should a loss be incurred. The normal lender requirement is for insurance coverage in an amount not less than the loan amount. With escalation of home value, coverage in the amount of a loan may quickly prove inadequate. Coinsurance clauses found in most insurance policies require a minimum coverage (usually 80 percent of the building value at the time of loss) to protect the homeowner on full recovery of partial losses. So while the lender may set a minimum requirement, the buyer may elect to take increased coverage with an escalation protection policy. It should be noted that hazard insurance coverage does not necessarily include flood insurance. In certain areas of the country, federally subsidized flood insurance is available under the National Flood Insurance Act. Most lenders require a full first year's premium of hazard insurance paid at the time of closing. Often, the paid-up policy is delivered at the closing table. In addition to the first year's premium, lenders may require a reserve of up to two months of annual premiums deposited with them at closing.

Reserves Deposited with Lenders (Item 1000)

Almost all residential loans require cash deposited with the lender at the time of loan closing to be used for future payment of recurring annual charges such as taxes, insurance, and maintenance assessments. The identification of these accounts differs as they may be referred to as reserves, escrow accounts, impound accounts, or reserve accruals. The purpose of the initial deposits is to give the lender enough cash to make the first annual payment that comes due after the closing date. Because real estate practices differ throughout the country, RESPA leaves the actual calculation of the initial deposit up to the lender. In some areas, taxes are paid for a year in advance; in others, they are paid for at the end of the tax year. The same is true of maintenance assessments. But RESPA does place a limit on the deposits that may be required to meet the first year's payments: the amount to be deposited cannot exceed a sum sufficient to pay taxes, insurance premiums, or other charges that would have been paid under normal lending practices *up to the due date* of the first full monthly installment payment.

There is a second restriction in the amount of reserves that may be held by a lender on a *continuing* basis. At the time of closing, a lender can require that the deposit of up to two months of annual charges for taxes, insurance, and other recurring assessments be held by the lender. This is in addition to the deposits that may be needed to handle the first year's charges. Then, each monthly installment payment can include one-twelfth of the annual charges on a continuing basis. RESPA rules restrict the lender to collecting no more than one-twelfth of the annual taxes and other charges, unless a larger payment is necessary to make up a deficit in the reserve account. Further, RESPA restricts the cushion that a lender may hold against a possible deficit in the account to one-sixth of the annual charges. A deficit in the account may be caused, for example, by raises in the taxes and insurance premiums during the loan payment year. These monthly mortgage payment reserve limitations apply to *all* RESPA-covered mortgage loans, whether originated before or after the implementation of RESPA.

Example of Initial Reserve Calculation:

For a settlement date of June 30, 1980
First mortgage payment due on August 1, 1980
Annual taxes $900 (Monthly = $75.00)
Due date for taxes—December 1 for calendar year
Initial reserve requirement: From December 1 to July 30
      8 months × $75   = $600.00
Plus two months cushion
      2 months × $75   = $150.00
Deposit required at closing for taxes   = $750.00

In considering this example, keep in mind that the taxes due for the months prior to the actual sale of the house are the financial responsibility of the seller. So the settlement statement would reflect the proration of the tax liability, and thus most of the reserve deposit for this purpose (taxes) would be from the seller, not the buyer. If the house is newly constructed, the tax assessment during the construction period would most likely be a lesser amount than that for the finished house. In areas where taxes are paid at the beginning of each tax year, the deposit requirement to meet the coming year's taxes would fall to the buyer. Insurance premiums (if an existing policy is continued) and other recurring charges are handled in the same manner.

Hazard Insurance (1001). Since most home buyers elect to purchase new insurance policies to fit their own needs, no adjustment for an initial reserve requirement is needed. The normal lender requirement, approved as being in compliance with RESPA restrictions, is for a one-year premium paid in advance plus a deposit to a reserve account in the amount of two months of the annual premium. A buyer may purchase hazard insurance from whatever company he or she chooses so long as the company meets the lender's minimum standards for insurance carriers.

Mortgage Insurance (1002). The premium reserve requirement for mortgage insurance is negotiable with the lender. It may be required that a part of the total annual premium be placed in a reserve account, but no more than one-sixth of the annual premium could be held as a cushion by the lender.

City/County Property Taxes (1003-1004). Initial reserve requirements have been detailed in the earlier example of this section. Lenders do require monthly payments of one-twelfth the annual taxes to be paid into the reserve account.

Annual Assessments (1005). The reserve that may be required for assessments is for such charges as a homeowner's association fee, a condominium maintenance charge, or a municipal improvement assessment. The same previously described RESPA reserve limitations apply to all forms of reserves.

Title Charges (Item 1100)

In the uniform Settlement Statement, *title charges* designates a variety of services performed to properly conclude a real estate transaction. These include searching records, preparing documents, and acquiring insurance against title failure. While practices and terminology differ in some areas, the services needed are basically similar.

Settlement or Closing Fee (1101). The charges made by the person or company for the service of handling the settlement procedures. The payment of the fee is negotiable between buyer and seller and is often divided equally between them.

Abstract or Title Search, Title Examination, Title Insurance Binder (1102–1104). In a real estate transaction it is reasonable to expect that a seller offer some solid proof of his or her right to convey the property to be purchased. This can be accomplished through a search of all the recorded documents affecting the land title (an abstract of title) culminating in an attorney's opinion as to the quality of the title, or, more commonly, through a title insurance company, which continuously searches the records and insures their title opinions. Title to real property is a matter of public record and that record can also contain other instruments or claims that affect the ownership rights of a potential seller. Thus the cost of assuring good title most often is paid by the seller.

Document Preparation (1105). The charge for preparing the legal documents may be listed separately or may be included with other service fees, most likely as a part of the attorney's fee.

Notary Fee (1106). Instruments that are to be recorded in the public records usually require that all signatures be witnessed by a Notary Public. Settlement agents are often licensed for this purpose and may ask a separate charge for their official services in this capacity.

Attorney's Fees (1107). Few lenders will permit a loan to be closed without the assurance of a qualified attorney that all instruments have been properly prepared and executed. In any real estate transaction, the buyer and the seller may each be represented by their own attorney, and, in such case, each may pay the attorney outside the closing procedure. In the handling of residential loans, the title company or settlement agent involved may employ an attorney to handle the legal requirements, and, if both parties agree, allocate the charges equally between buyer and seller.

Title Insurance (1108). Title insurance offers protection to the policyholder against adverse claims to the ownership rights of a landholder. It is issued in two separate policy forms: one to protect the landowner, the other to protect the lender whose mortgage claim is dependent on the landholder's right to dispose of the land.

Lender's Title Policy (1109). The lender's title policy is paid for as a single premium at closing. It is also called a *mortgagee's policy*, and in many areas it is issued simultaneously with an owner's policy, since the same basic risk is covered. Local practice varies as to whether the lender's or the owner's policy must pay the major share of premium cost. If the lender's policy carries the major cost, the owner's policy is usually issued for a nominal amount. Payment for a lender's policy is most likely to be made by a buyer as it is clearly part of the cost of obtaining a loan. There are some differences in a lender's policy as compared with an owner's policy. The lender's policy runs with the loan; that is, the amount of insurance is reduced as the mortgage balance is reduced, and it covers the designated holder of the mortgage note (an owner's policy cannot be assigned). Furthermore, a payoff of the loan automatically cancels the lender's insurance coverage.

Owner's Title Insurance (1110). The owner's policy is purchased at closing with a one-time premium charge and continues to protect the holder up to the face value of the policy for as long as responsibility exists for an adverse claim. The time period for responsibility is determined by each state's limitation statutes on adverse claims. Even though an owner may hold actual title to property for a short period, say a year or so, at the time the property is sold, the warranty deed normally used to convey title leaves the seller with a responsibility. The wording of the conveyance reads that seller "will warrant and defend generally the title to the property against all claims and demands." So the owner's title policy protects the owner not only while he or she is in possession of the insured premises, but also for the time period after it may be sold during which the seller remains liable for possible adverse claims. Customs vary locally as to whether or not the buyer or seller pays for owner's title insurance. Since the issuance of such a policy represents a good proof of the validity of the seller's own title to the land to be conveyed, in some areas the cost is paid by the seller. In other areas, if the seller can prove good title to the property through an attorney's opinion based on the abstract of title, or by the issuance of a title binder by a title company, then payment for the owner's policy falls to the buyer—he or she is the one being protected.

Government Recording and Transfer Charges (Item 1200)

Recording and transfer fees are those charged by city, county, or state governments for recording services, or as a tax on the transaction. The fees may be based on the amount of the mortgage loan or on the value of the property being transferred. Payment of these charges is negotiable between buyer and seller but are usually paid by the buyer.

Additional Settlement Charges (Item 1300)

Charges that are not easily classified within the previous categories of costs can be listed under this section of additional charges. Mostly, they include the costs of a survey and any inspections of the property that may be required to determine adequacy of the structure.

Survey (1301). Almost all lenders require that a survey of the property offered as collateral be included in the loan package. A survey, which can only be prepared by a registered surveyor, gives a picture description of the land with an outline of its perimeter boundaries. It should show the precise location of buildings as well as any easements or rights-of-way that may cross the land. The survey can disclose any encroachments on the land that may create a cloud on the ownership rights. It is not unusual for an attorney to require a survey before preparing a deed or mortgage instrument to make sure of the land and the rights being conveyed. Payment for the survey is negotiable—the seller has an obligation to prove exactly what land is to be conveyed while the buyer has a need for the survey in order to complete the loan requirements.

Pest and Other Inspections (1302). In certain areas of the country where termites or other insects infest buildings and can create damage, it is normal to require a separate pest inspection. In such areas, sales agreements may call for the property to be delivered free of infestation. The pest inspection, with a certified letter of proof, is the seller's method of fulfilling this requirement. Regardless of a sales agreement, lenders may require a pest inspection to assure them that the property offered as collateral is free of pest-caused structural damage. In such a case, the cost may be paid by the buyer as a part of the requirements for obtaining a mortgage loan.

Total Settlement Charges (Item 1400)

At the bottom of the page listing the various settlement charges, the totals for borrower's charges and for the seller's charges are listed and transferred to the summary section of the first page.

Final Closing Instructions

Mortgagee's Closing Instructions

Once a loan has been approved, the mortgage company prepares a sheet of instructions for delivery to the settlement agent handling closing procedures. The instructions detail such items as the correct legal name of the mortgagee, the name of the trustee for the deed of trust, the terms of the mortgage note, and special requirements to be included in the mortgage or deed of trust (that is, if the mortgage company is not submitting its own forms for a note and mortgage), specific instructions on monthly payments to be given to the borrowers, details of the escrow requirements, and details of disbursement procedures. Along with the instructions, the mortgage company will send the buyer-seller affidavits as may be required, which certify to the actual down payment (cash and/or property exchanged) and to the use of the loan proceeds, which must be acknowledged by the notarized signatures of all buyers and sellers. Also, a truth-in-lending statement is prepared for the purchaser-borrower signature at closing. Some mortgage companies require certifications of occupancy (for homestead information). The forms vary between companies according to how their legal counselors interpret the state laws.

The instructions of the mortgage company invariably call for a certain amount of work on the part of the settlement agent closing the loan, if only as a means of clarifying the loan requirements. This is in addition to the other details of closing that a settlement agent must handle, such as assembling the title information, preparing or reviewing the note and deed of trust, verifying tax requirements, and determining the insurance payments needed.

It is advisable to allow the settlement agent a reasonable time for its work in preparing for a closing. A forced deadline can induce errors and omissions. Figures 16-4a and 16-4b give an example of typical mortgagee's closing instructions.

Setting the Closing

When the mortgage company has approved the loan and prepared its closing instructions, it is the responsibility of the real estate agent, or agents, involved to arrange a mutually agreeable closing time. Practices vary in different parts of the country—in some areas all parties meet around a table for the settlement procedures; in other parts, no actual meeting is required and escrow agents are authorized to request that the necessary instruments be delivered to them for release after all escrow requirements have been met.

Whenever the local practices require a meeting of the parties involved, it is usually held in the offices of the company or person designated to handle the settlement procedures. This may be a title company, an attorney, a real estate agent, an escrow agent, or the lender itself. Whoever handles the loan closing must have the approval of the lender as it is its money that is generally most involved. Closings can be accomplished with separate meetings, the buyer at one time and the seller at another, leaving the settlement agent to escrow the instruments and consideration until the procedure is completed and distribution can be made.

It is easier for the agents involved, as well as providing greater clarity for both buyer and seller, to arrange for a single meeting. Although

Mortgagee's Closing Instructions

DATE:_____
CLOSING DATE:_____TIME:_____
FIRST PAYMENT:_____
FINAL PAYMENT:_____

TO: _____

      _____

      _____

CLOSER:_____PHONE:_____

SECURITY GENERAL INVESTMENT COMPANY   FHA
6401 Southwest Freeway
Houston, Texas 77074   771-4681

GF #_____
Seller:_____
_____
FHA Case #_____
Mortgagor(s)_____
Property Address_____
_____Zip_____
Mailing Address_____
_____Zip_____

We have approved an FHA loan for the above borrower(s). The loan papers are to be prepared by
CARL, LEE AND FISHER, 1500 Austin @ Bell, Houston, Texas 77001, 659-6494.

LOAN INFORMATION: Loan Amount $_____Rate_____Term_____Yrs._____Mos.

P&I $_____Sales Price $_____Valuation $_____

Warrantor if New Construction:_____

(1) The Note is to be made payable to SECURITY GENERAL INVESTMENT COMPANY.
(2) The Trustee is Ethel Alzofon of Harris County, Texas.
(3) The following items are to be included as fixtures and a part of the realty on the
    Deed of Trust:
    1.   4.
    2.   5.
    3.   6.

LEGAL DESCRIPTION:

INSURANCE: The ORIGINAL hazard insurance policy is to be furnished to you by _____
_____. Fire & Extended Coverage insurance with Physical Loss Form is
required in an amount not less than $_____with loss payable in favor of
SECURITY GENERAL INVESTMENT COMPANY, 6401 Southwest Freeway, Houston, Texas 77074.
A paid receipt is required for the first year's premium on all policies and a copy
of the premium finance note is required on 3-year policies. Policy must be acceptable
to lender having an A:Class XI rating or better. Guaranty bonds and reinsurance
agreements are unacceptable unless preapproved by lender. Names, address and legal
must be the same as that on legal documents or endorsements must be attached to policy
prior to funding. If there is a 224 exclusion clause, an ORIGINAL windstorm policy
will be required. LENDER WILL APPROVE ALL POLICIES PRIOR TO FUNDING BASED ON
INVESTOR REQUIREMENTS. We suggest all closers have policies approved by lender prior
to closing to avoid possible funding delays. Insurance escrow deposits noted below
are based on policy being effective date of closing. If effective date is a month
other than that of the closing, escrows must be adjusted accordingly.

EXPENSES AND DEPOSITS FOR SECURITY GENERAL INVESTMENT COMPANY:
(1) Interest from the date of our disbursement check to the first of the month immediately
    preceding the month of the first payment. Calculate interest on a 30-day month
    @_____per day from_____to_____.................$_____
(2) *Monthly Tax Escrow Deposit (_____mos)......................$_____
(3) **Monthly Maintenance Escrow Deposit (_____mos).............$_____
(4) Two months Hazard Insurance Escrow Deposit @_____/mo........$_____
(5) Two months Flood Insurance Escrow Deposit @_____/mo.........$_____
(6) One months FHA Insurance Premium..............................$_____
(7) 1% Origination Fee..$_____
(8) _____% Discount from Seller (Subject to change prior to funding).$_____
(9) Credit Report...$_____
(10) Photographs..$_____
(11) Recording Fee from Seller....................................$_____
(12) Appraisal Fee..$_____

POC ITEMS: The following items have been paid outside closing and must be reflected on the RESPA
           settlement statement as such:_____
           _____
           (Type of charge, dollar amount and who paid it)

DO NOT CHANGE THE TERMINOLOGY OF ANY OF THE ABOVE CHARGES WHEN PREPARING THE RESPA SETTLEMENT
STATEMENT. ALSO KEEP IN MIND THAT THE LENDER IS SECURITY GENERAL INVESTMENT COMPANY! THE RESPA
SETTLEMENT STATEMENT MUST BE COMPLETED IN ITS ENTIRETY WITH ALL APPROPRIATE BLANKS BEING PROPERLY
COMPLETED.   IMPORTANT NOTE: PURCHASER MUST PAY ALL HIS PREPAIDS!

FIGURE 16-4a Mortgagee's Closing Instructions.

FURNISH IN THE SAME ORDER DOCUMENTS LISTED BELOW AS INDICATED BY AN "X" OR THE WORD "NEED". ALL
ITEMS SO INDICATED WILL BE REQUIRED PRIOR TO FUNDING:

NEED   1. Tax Information Sheet completed in its entirety.
NEED   2. Original and two certified copies of Note.
NEED   3. Original and two certified copies of Deed of Trust.
NEED   4. Two certified copies of Mortgagee's Title Policy issued thru_____
    _____. We will exchange disbursement check for original policy.
_____   5. Three blueline surveys properly certified by registered surveyor. See notes below.
_____   6. Original effective Hazard Insurance Policy, paid receipt for 1st year's premium and
     a copy of premium finance note if applicable.
_____   7. Original effective Flood Insurance Policy and paid receipt. OR copy of flood
     insurance application, paid receipt and copy of agent's check to flood pool. (If
     copy of agent's check is not available, a statement from agent certifying policy has
     been ordered will suffice - memo must reference all pertinent information).
_____   8. Original effective Windstorm Policy and paid receipt.
NEED   9. RESPA Settlement Statement - 2 certified copies properly completed with signatures.
NEED   10. Truth-in-Lending - 2 certified copies with original signatures.
NEED   11. Mortgagor's Affidavit properly executed.
NEED   12. Firm Commitment (2 carbons).
NEED   13. Photocopy of Warranty Deed with signatures.
_____   14. Final Inspection by FHA / Lender's certification of completed repairs.
_____   15. Wood Infestation Report / Soil Poisoning Certificate.
_____   16. Owner-Seller Certification / Roofing Certification / Flood Letter / Housing Code.
_____   17. Certifications issued by licensed specialists: Plumbing / Water Heater /
     Heating & Air / Electrical.
_____   18. 2 sets of all restrictions and any other instruments mentioned in the exceptions on
     Schedule B of Mortgagee's Title Policy. Also need Map Records locating our property
     by street, lot and block; as well as any instruments reflected in the legal
     description.
_____   19. _____

MORTGAGEE'S TITLE POLICY: The Mortgagee's Title Policy must insure that at the date of the filing
     of the Deed of Trust for record the title to the premises described therein was as shown in
     Schedule A thereof and that said Deed of Trust was a valid first lien thereon.

SCHEDULE A: Name of Insured should read - SECURITY GENERAL INVESTMENT COMPANY and/or THE SECRETARY
     OF HOUSING AND URBAN DEVELOPMENT OF WASHINGTON, D.C., HIS RESPECTIVE SUCCESSORS AND ASSIGNS
     AS THEIR INTEREST MAY APPEAR.

Schedule B: If there are no restrictive covenants affecting the premises the policy must state
     NONE OF RECORD. If there are restrictive covenants, each instrument must be cited by volume
     and page and must tell what records each was filed under. The policy must clearly state the
     nature of each exception, citing volume and page of each instrument creating each exception.
     This loan is not to be closed without our prior written approval if the restrictions contain
     a RIGHT OF REVERSION.
     EASEMENT EXCEPTIONS must be defined as to location on property, length and/or width and
     purpose for said easement. Any ground easement under Schedule B must appear on the survey or
     be deleted from the policy. Unlocated pipeline easements as well as unlocated right of ways
     are unacceptable on the Mortgagee's Title Policy.
     WATER DISTRICT information cannot appear on the Mortgagee's Title Policy.
     ITEM B-2 - The preprinted exception regarding any discrepancies, conflicts and shortages in
     area and boundaries or encroachments or overlap of improvements must be deleted and initialed.
     If B-2 cannot be deleted in its entirety, then delete and initial all pretyped wording except
     "Shortages in area" or "Any shortages in area". Do not add any additional wording.
     *TAXES are paid beginning October 1st of each year. If the MTP is dated on or after October 1st
     collect taxes due for the year and pay all taxing authorities. If the MTP is dated prior to
     October 1st, collect and remit tax deposits in accordance with instructions from lender. The
     words "not yet due and payable" must follow the exception to taxes contained in the MTP.
     **MAINTENANCE must be subordinated or a 60-day letter furnished to lender. Maintenance must be
     paid through current year. (After October 1st, maintenance for the following year must be
     paid in full and guaranteed on the MTP). Escrows on page 1 are based on a January to January
     maintenance year. We require that maintenance be remitted annually in advance by lender.
     Please notify if any problems arise in regards to the maintenance fund before closing.

     ALL DELETIONS FROM THE MTP MUST BE INITIALED BY AN AUTHORIZED SIGNATORY. IF A XEROX COPY OF
     ANY PAGE OF THE MTP IS TO BE USED AS PART OF THE ORIGINAL POLICY, IT MUST BE ORIGINALLY
     INITIALED.

SURVEY: Survey must be checked for the following: (a) Must show access to our property - driveway,
     etc.; (b) Must reflect recorded reference of subd plat; (c) Must have buyer's name spelled
     correctly; (d) Must have legal description identical to legal documents; (e) Must be no older
     than 2 mos; (f) Must be signed and have surveyor's seal; (g) Must state northerly direction;
     (h) Must show dimensions of property; (i) Must show nearest cross street; (j) Must reflect
     ground easements noted in MTP by type of easement, length and/or width and location; (k) Must
     show lot number on each lot; (l) Must have metes and bounds attached if applicable, and metes
     and bounds must correspond to notations on actual survey; (m) Must reflect entire lot if our
     property consists of just a portion of a lot; (n) Must have correct address.

BEFORE RETURNING PAPERS TO US PLEASE REVIEW. WE REQUIRE THAT ALL THE FORMS BE SIGNED THE WAY THE
LEGAL DOCUMENTS ARE DRAWN UNLESS OTHERWISE NOTED. DO NOT CHANGE ANY PAPERS WITHOUT APPROVAL FROM
KAREN DELAFOSSE.

PREPARED BY:_____. RETURN ORIGINAL PAPERS TO:_____
         (Loan Processor)   (Disbursement Officer)

FIGURE 16-4b   Mortgagee's Closing Instructions.

a closing is no place for negotiations, if any misunderstanding should crop up, it can be more readily resolved if all parties are immediately available for decisions.

Disbursement of Funds

In many parts of the country, a closing is just that; instruments are signed and funds are disbursed before anyone leaves the closing table. In some areas, it is more common to execute and acknowledge the instruments at the closing but delay the disbursement of funds until later.

The purpose for any delay in releasing funds is twofold: first, to give the lender an opportunity to make a second review of all instruments and to verify proper signatures and acknowledgements; and second, to allow the settlement agent time to clear any checks that may have been submitted by the parties involved before releasing its own disbursement checks. One interpretation of state regulations governing title insurance companies calls *any* check paid to a title company an "escrow receivable," rather than a cash item, until the check has actually cleared the bank. However, there is growing pressure to handle a closing in its proper sequence and not call for the parties to meet until all the loose ends have been accomplished and the money is available for distribution.

The actual disbursement of funds at or following the settlement procedures is usually made to several different individuals and companies as well as the cash due to the seller. One of the reasons an escrow agent is employed in the settlement is to make sure that all parties with claims in the settlement are paid. The mortgage lender wants to be certain that taxes are paid, that the insurance coverage has been paid for, and that no subsequent claims can be filed that might cloud their right to a first mortgage lien securing their loan. Sales agents, inspectors, attorneys, and the service agents all expect to receive their fees from the closing agent. After all required payments have been made, the required instruments are filed of record, the balance due the seller is then disbursed, and the transaction is considered closed.

Questions for Discussion

1. Discuss the purpose of the Real Estate Settlement Procedures Act and how it is accomplished.

2. Does RESPA prescribe any limitations on fees that may be charged in closing a loan?

3. Discuss the importance of a survey in the settlement procedure.

4. How does RESPA define its prohibition against a "kickback"?

5. What is the reason for a prepayment of interest at the time of settlement procedures?

6. Where are loan closings normally held in your community? Who is the agent usually selected to represent the mortgage company at the closing procedure?

7. What information is furnished to the settlement agent (closer) by the mortgage lender just prior to closing?

8. Describe at least three RESPA requirements that call for disclosure of information to the borrower.

9. Discuss the requirements of the Truth-in-Lending Act as it relates to mortgage loans.

10. What are the limitations on reserve deposits that may be held by a lender for a residential mortgage loan?

Glossary

The following terms are those most frequently used in real estate financing, which are considered essential in understanding the material presented in this text.

Abstract. The recorded history of a land title. A compilation of all instruments affecting the title to a tract of land.

Acceleration. A clause in a mortgage instrument that permits the lender to declare the entire balance due and payable in the event of a default on the mortgage terms.

Acknowledgment. For real estate purposes, a signature witnessed or notarized in a manner that can be recorded.

Adjustable Rate Mortgage (ARM). A mortgage design that permits the lender to adjust the interest rate at periodic intervals with the amount of change generally tied to an independent published index of interest rates or yields.

Alienation. The act of transferring ownership in real property from one person to another. Sometimes used to identify the clause in a mortgage that allows the lender to declare the balance due and payable if the mortgaged property is sold.

Alternative Mortgage. Any mortgage repayment plan other than a fixed interest constant level plan that allows either, or both, a periodic change in the monthly payment amount, or an adjustment in the rate of interest.

Amortization. The systematic and continuous payment of an obligation through installments until such time as that debt has been paid off in full.

Appraisal. An estimate of property value by a qualified person.

Appreciation. An increase in value. In real estate appreciation is considered the passive increase in property value resulting from population growth and/or the changing value of money.

Assessed Value. Property value as determined by a taxing authority.

Assessment. A charge against a property owner for purposes of taxation; i.e., the property owner pays his share of community improvements and maintenance according to the valuation of his property.

Assets. Real and personal property that may be chargeable with the debts of the owner.

Assignment of Mortgage. Transfer by the lender (mortgagee) of the mortgage obligation.

Assumption Agreement. A contract, by deed or other form, through which a buyer undertakes the obligations of an existing mortgage.

Balloon Payment. A debt repayment plan wherein the installments are less than required for a full amortization, with the balance due in a lump sum at maturity. Technically, a final payment greater than two monthly payments.

Basis Points. The movement of interest rates or yields expressed in hundredths of a percent; i.e., a change in yield from 7.45% to 7.55% would be termed an increase of 10 basis points.

Basket Provision. Regulations applicable to financial institutions that permit a small percentage of total assets to be held in otherwise unauthorized investments.

Blanket Mortgage. A type of mortgage that pledges more than one parcel of real estate as collateral.

Bond. A form of security that guarantees payment of the face value with interest to the purchaser (lender), and usually secured with a pledge of property or a commitment of income such as a tax revenue bond. A debt instrument.

Borrower. A person or company using another's money or property, who has both a legal and moral obligation to repay the loan.

Broker. An intermediary between buyer and seller, or between lender and borrower, usually acting as agent for one or more parties, who arranges loans or sells property in return for a fee or commission.

Capitalization. The conversion of an income stream into a property valuation for purposes of appraisal.

Cash Flow. The amount of cash received over a period of time from an income property.

Certificate of Reasonable Value (CRV). An estimate of property value prepared in accordance with requirements of the Veterans Administration. A VA appraisal.

Chain of Title. The sequence of ownership interests in a tract of land.

Chattel.   An article of property that can be moved; personal property.

Chattel Mortgage.   A type of lien (legal claim) that applies to personal property as distinguished from real property.

Closer.   The individual responsible for making final settlement of the property transaction and disbursement of the loan proceeds.

Closing.   The consummation of a real estate transaction wherein certain rights of ownership are transferred in exchange for the monetary and other considerations agreed upon. Also called *loan closing*.

Collateral.   Property acceptable as security for a loan.

Commitment.   A promise of loanable funds.

Commitment Fee.   Money paid in return for the pledge of a future loan.

Community Property.   Property owned in common by a husband and wife.

Compensating Balance.   A minimum balance held on deposit in accordance with a loan agreement.

Conditional Sale.   An agreement granting title to property after all payments have been made.

Condominium.   A unit in a multifamily structure or office building wherein the owner holds a fee simple title to the unit he or she occupies and a tenancy in common with the other owners of the common elements.

Consideration.   The cash, services, or token given in exchange for property or services.

Constant Payment.   A fixed payment amount, covering the interest due and a partial reduction of principal. Usually calculated in a manner that repays the loan within its term.

Constant Rate.   Also called *constant*, is that percentage of the initial loan amount which must be paid periodically to repay the loan within the specified term.

Construction Loan.   A type of mortgage loan to finance construction, which is funded by the lender to the builder at periodic intervals as the work progresses.

Contingent Interest.   The amount that a lender expects to earn from his share of appreciation as calculated in a shared appreciation mortgage.

Contingent Liability.   The responsibility assumed by a third party who accepts liability for an obligation upon the failure of an initial obligor to perform as agreed.

Contract for Deed.   An agreement to sell property wherein title to the property is delivered to the buyer after payment has been made.

Contract of Sale.   An agreement between a buyer and a seller of real property to deliver good title in return for a consideration.

Conventional Loan.   A loan that is not underwritten by a federal agency.

Conveyance.   The written instrument by which an interest in real property is transferred from one party to another.

Covenant.   An agreement between two or more parties.

Creative Financing. A generalized term applied to many kinds of unconventional mortgage repayment plans. More specifically, refers to reduction of initial payment amounts with the principal balance coming due in a short term of 3 to 5 years.

Debenture Bond. An unsecured pledge to repay a debt.

Debt. An obligation to be repaid by a borrower to a lender.

Debt Service. The periodic payment due on a loan, which includes principal, interest, mortgage insurance, and any other periodic fees required by the loan agreement.

Deed. A written instrument by which real estate is transferred to another owner. The deed is signed, sealed, and delivered by the seller.

Deed of Trust. A type of mortgage that conditionally conveys real property to a third party for holding in trust as security for payment of a loan.

Deed Restriction. A clause in a deed that restricts the use of the land being conveyed.

Default. The failure to perform on an obligation as agreed in a contract.

Delinquency. A loan payment that is overdue but within the grace period allowed before actual default is declared.

Depreciation. The loss in value to property due to wear and tear, obsolescence, or economic factors. To offset depreciation, tax laws permit recovery of the cost of an investment through annual deductions from taxable income.

Development Loan. Money loaned for the purpose of improving land by the building of streets and utilities so as to make lots suitable for sale or use in construction.

Discount. The difference between the amount paid for a note and the nominal, or face value, of that note. The reduction in the amount paid is normally expressed in ''points'' as a percentage of the note amount.

Due on Sale. A clause found in some mortgage agreements that gives a lender the right to declare the balance due in full if the property is sold.

Earnest Money. A portion of the down payment delivered to the seller or an escrow agent as evidence of good faith to bind the purchase.

Encroachment. Any physical intrusion upon the property rights of another.

Equity. The ownership interest—that portion of a property's value beyond any liability therein.

Escalation. The right of a lender to increase the rate of interest in a loan agreement.

Escrow. Property, money, or something of value held in custody by a third party in accordance with an agreement.

Execute. The act of signing a legal instrument by the involved parties, usually witnessed or notarized, so that it may be recorded.

Fee Simple. A legal term designating the highest interest in land that includes all the rights of ownership.

FHA Loan. A loan insured by the Insuring Office of the Department of Housing and Urban Development; the Federal Housing Administration.

Fixture. Personal property so affixed to the land as to become a part of the realty.

Foreclosure. Legal action to bar a mortgagor's claims to property after default has occurred.

Graduated Payment Adjustable Rate Mortgage. (GPARM, also called GPAM) A mortgage repayment plan that provides for lower initial monthly payments, increasing annually for 3 to 5 years, then changing to a fully amortized payment amount with interest rate periodically adjusted by the lender.

Graduated Payment Mortgage. A repayment plan popularized by the FHA, but also approved as a conventional loan, that offers first year monthly payments substantially lower than a constant-level plan permitting easier qualification for a borrower. Payment amounts increase annually at a predetermined rate until reaching a level that fully amortizes the loan within its term.

Gross Income. The total money received from an operating property over a given period of time.

Guarantee (verb). The act of pledging by a third party to assure payment.

Guaranty (noun). A pledge by a third party to assume the obligation of another.

Hazard Insurance. The insurance covering physical damage to property.

Homestead. A legal life estate in land created in differing ways by state laws devised to protect the possession and enjoyment of the owner against the claims of certain creditors.

HUD. The Department of Housing and Urban Development.

Income Property. Real estate capable of producing net revenue.

Instrument. A legal document in writing.

Interest. The payment for the use of money.

Interim Loan. Or *interim financing*. A loan made with the expectation of repayment from the proceeds of another loan. Most often used in reference to a construction loan.

Junior Mortgage. A mortgage claim of lesser than first lien priority.

Land Contract. Another term used to indicate a Contract for Deed.

Land Loan. Money loaned for the purchase of raw land.

Late Charge. A fee added to an installment as a penalty for failure to make a timely payment.

Leverage. The capacity to borrow an amount greater than the equity in property. The larger the loan in relation to the equity, the greater the leverage.

Lien. A legal claim or attachment, filed on record, against property as security for payment of an obligation.

Limitation. A time limit as determined by statute within which period litigation may be undertaken.

Liquidity. The extent to which assets held in other forms can be easily and quickly converted into cash.

Loan. A granting of the use of money in return for the payment of interest.

Loan-to-Value-Ratio (LTVR). The relationship between the amount of a loan and the value of the property pledged.

Marginal Property. Capable of making only a very low economic return.

Maturity. The date that final payment is due on a loan.

Mechanic's Lien. Also known as *Mechanic's* and *Materialmen's Lien*, or *M & M Lien*. A claim for payment for services rendered or materials furnished to a landowner and filed of record in the county where the property is located.

Mortgage. A conditional conveyance of property as security for a debt.

Mortgagee. The lender of money and the receiver of the security in the form of a mortgage. (*Memory note*: Lender and mortgagee both have two "ee"s.)

Mortgage Note. A description of the debt and a promise to pay—the instrument that is secured by the mortgage.

Mortgage Release. A disclaimer of further liability on the mortgage note granted by the lender.

Mortgaging Out. Securing a loan upon completion of a project that is sufficient to cover all costs: a 100% loan.

Mortgagor. The borrower of money and the giver of a mortgage as security.

Multifamily Mortgage. An FHA term designating an apartment or any housing with more than four family units.

Negative Amortization. An increase in the principal balance due on a mortgage loan, usually resulting from unpaid interest added to the principal periodically.

Net Income. That portion of gross income remaining after payment of all expenses.

Note. A unilateral instrument containing a promise to pay a sum of money at a specified time.

Open-end Mortgage. A mortgage with a clause permitting additional money to be advanced by the lender secured by the same collateral pledge.

Option. The right to purchase or lease a piece of property at a certain price for a designated period.

Origination Fee. The amount charged for services performed by the company handling the initial application and processing of a loan.

Package Mortgage. A mortgage pledge that includes both real and personal property.

Partial Release. The removal of a general mortgage lien from a specific portion of the land that has been pledged.

Participation Loan. A loan funded by more than one lender and serviced by one of them.

Permanent Loan. A mortgage loan granted for a long term based on the economic life of a property.

Personal Property. A possession: any item of value that is not real estate.

PITI. An alphabetical abbreviation used to identify the components of a mortgage payment: Principal, Interest, Taxes, Insurance.

Planned Unit Development (PUD). A comprehensive land development plan employed primarily in the planning and construction of residential areas.

Pledged Account Mortgage (PAM). A mortgage repayment plan that features lower initial monthly payment amounts. The borrower deposits a portion of the down-payment in an escrow account with the lender. Each month the lender withdraws enough money from the escrow account to supplement the borrower's payments so that a constant level, fully amortized payment amount is applied to the loan each month.

Points. A unit of measure for charges that amounts to one percent of a loan. One point is one percent of the subject loan.

Possession. Occupancy: the highest form of "notice."

Principal. The amount of the mortgage debt.

Private Mortgage Insurance (PMI). Insurance against payment default on a mortgage loan as offered by private insurance carriers.

Purchase Money Mortgage. A mortgage taken by the seller as all or part of the purchase consideration. Also identifies a mortgage wherein the proceeds of the loan are used to purchase the property.

Real Estate. Land and that attached thereto, including minerals and resources inherent to the land, and any man-made improvements so affixed as to become a part of the land. Also known as *realty* or *real property*.

Realtor. A registered word designating a member in good standing of the National Association of Realtors.

Recording. To file a legal instrument in the public records of a county.

Refinancing. To obtain a loan for the purpose of repaying an existing loan.

Reverse Annuity Mortgage. A mortgage form designed to use the equity value of a home as collateral for installment payments made by the lender to the borrower to supplement living costs.

Secondary Financing. Negotiation of a second mortgage, or a junior mortgage.

Secondary Market. Large investors who buy and sell mortgage loans that they do not originate.

Seller/Servicer. Loan originators who service loans as approved by FNMA or FHLMC.

Servicing. (Loan Servicing). The work of an agent, usually a mortgage company, comprising the collection of mortgage payments, securing of escrow funds, payment of property taxes and insurance from the escrowed funds, followup on delinquencies, accounting for and remitting principal, and interest payments to the lender.

Settlement Procedure. The steps taken to finalize the funding of a loan agreement and a property transfer. Also called a loan closing.

Shared Appreciation Mortgage (SAM). A mortgage repayment plan whereby the lender accepts a reduced interest rate on condition that a share of any property appreciation is given to the lender. For example, a reduction in the interest rate from 15% to 10% with the requirement that one third of any appreciation belongs to the lender.

Single-Family Mortgage. A mortgage loan on property occupied by one family.

Spot Loan. Money loaned on individual houses in various neighborhoods, as contrasted to new houses in a single development.

Statutory Redemption. A state law that permits a mortgagor a limited time after foreclosure to pay off the debt and reclaim the mortgaged property.

Subordination. To make a claim to real property inferior to that of another by specific agreement.

Survey. The measurement and description of land by a registered surveyor.

Sweat Equity. An ownership interest in property earned by the performance of manual labor on that property.

Syndication. A group of individuals or companies joined together in pursuit of a limited investment purpose.

Takeout Loan. A type of loan commitment—a promise to make a loan at a future specified time. It is most commonly used to designate a higher cost, shorter term, backup commitment as a support for construction financing until a suitable permanent loan can be secured.

Term. The time limit within which a loan must be repaid in full.

Time Deposits. Money held in savings accounts not subject to demand withdrawal.

Title. The right to ownership in land.

Tract Loan. Individual mortgage loan negotiated for houses of similar character located in a new development.

Trade Fixture. Personal property, peculiar to a trade, which remains personal even though affixed to real property.

Trustee. In a deed of trust, the person vested with contingent title to the collateral property, with the power to act in behalf of the lender in the event of a default.

Underwriter. The person or company taking responsibility for approving a mortgage loan.

Unsecured Loan. A loan made without the benefit of a pledge of collateral.

Usury. Interest in excess of that permitted by state law.

Variable Rate Mortgage. A type of mortgage agreement that allows for periodic adjustment of the interest rate in keeping with a fluctuating market.

VA Loan. A loan made by private lenders that is partially guaranteed by the Veterans Administration.

Vendor's Lien. A lien securing the loan by a seller which is used to purchase the property.

Warehousing. The practice, mostly by mortgage bankers, of pledging mortgage notes to a commercial bank for cash used to fund the mortgage loans. A line of credit.

Whole Loan. A term used in the secondary market to indicate the full amount of a loan is available for sale with no portion, or participation, retained by the seller.

Wrap-around Mortgage. A junior mortgage that acknowledges and includes an existing mortgage loan in its principal amount due and in its payment conditions. Payment is made to the holder of the wrap, or his agent, who in turn makes payment on the existing mortgage. The purpose is to gain some advantage in the lower interest cost on an existing loan; to hold the mortgage priority of the existing loan, and to retain an element of control over the loan payments.

Yield. The total money earned on a loan for the term of the loan computed on an annual percentage basis.

Index